Surviving as *Indians*
The Challenge of Self-Government

This book is about a just future for Indians in Canada. It defines justice in terms of the survival and well-being of Indians as *Indians*, that is, defined by their traditional principles and philosophies, not by the Indian Act or by their experience of colonialism. Menno Boldt calls for social action, not theory, holding that unless Indians revitalize, adapt, and develop their traditional philosophies and principles for living and surviving in the context of Canadian society, polity, and economy, they will become extinct as *Indians*; they will survive only as a legal-racial category created by the Indian Act. Moreover, Boldt argues, so long as the mass of Indians continue to live in conditions of degrading dependence, destitution, and powerlessness, Indian government will be a travesty.

Surviving as Indians examines the roots of injustice to Indians, and then analyses Canadian Indian policies, Indian leadership, culture, and economy. Boldt stresses five imperatives: moral justice for Indians; Canadian policies that treat Indian rights, interests, aspirations, and needs as equal to those of Canadians; Indian leadership that is committed to eliminating the colonial political and bureaucratic structures on their reserves, and to returning Indian government into the hands of their people; revitalizing Indian cultures, languages, and social systems that are adapted and developed within the framework of traditional philosophies and principles; and economic self-sufficiency and independence to be achieved through employment in the Canadian mainstream.

The Indians' future must inevitably be worked out with Canadians. *Surviving as Indians* intends to open a dialogue between the two groups.

MENNO BOLDT, a professor with the Department of Sociology, University of Lethbridge, has researched and worked with Indians for more than twenty years in a variety of personal and professional capacities.

Surviving as *Indians*

The Challenge
of Self-Government

MENNO BOLDT

UNIVERSITY OF TORONTO PRESS
Toronto Buffalo London

© University of Toronto Press Incorporated 1993
Toronto Buffalo London
Printed in Canada

Paperback reprinted 1993, 1994, 1998

ISBN 0-8020-2939-6 (cloth)
ISBN 0-8020-7767-6 (paper)

Printed on acid-free paper

Canadian Cataloguing in Publication Data
Boldt, Menno, 1930–
    Surviving as Indians

    Includes bibliographical references and index.
    ISBN 0-8020-2939-6 (bound) ISBN 0-8020-7767-6 (pbk.)

    1. Indians of North America – Canada. I. Title.

E78.C2B76 1993   971'.00497   C92-095696-3

This book has been published with assistance from the Canada Council
and the Ontario Arts Council under their block grant programs.

To Anne and our children, Elaine, Debbie, and Karen,
with love for your understanding and encouragement over the years

Contents

Appendices:
Selected Documents, Tables, Charts, and Summaries

Acknowledgments

The ideas expressed in this book are solely my responsibility; however, in composing this volume I have become indebted to many people. While I can mention only a few, my gratitude goes out to all who have played a helpful role in this accomplishment. I want to express special appreciation to Professor Wendell Bell, Yale University. He has been teacher, adviser, motivator, and friend to me. My debt to him is enormous, as are my appreciation and respect for him. It was also my good fortune to have colleagues and friends who took an interest in the writing of this volume. I offer heartfelt thanks to my colleagues at the University of Lethbridge – Leroy Little Bear, David Brown, Tony Long, and Tony Hall – and to my friends Gary Teichrob, Paul Bryant, and Michael Thiesen, for many stimulating conversations on the ideas expressed in this book. The editorial assistance and suggestions of Virgil Duff, Suzanne Rancourt, and Beverley Beetham Endersby at the University of Toronto Press, as well as the comments of two anonymous reviewers, have been extremely valuable to the production of this book. I am also indebted to the Department of Sociology, University of Lethbridge, chaired by Pat Chuchryk. Despite tight budgets, all needed resources were readily made available to me. Lacking typing skills, I was completely dependent upon Carol Tomomitsu, secretary of the department, for typing many drafts of the manuscript. Her unfailing courtesy, cooperation, and commitment to high quality made the task easier and pleasant. I am very grateful to her.

Prologue

This book is about the future of Indians in Canada. Indians represent one of the three distinct legal categories (i.e., Indian, Inuit, and Metis) subsumed under the term 'aboriginal people' in section 35 (1) of the Constitution Act, 1982. In the constitution, the term 'Indian' is used to refer to those peoples in Canada who are legally defined as being Indian under the provisions of the Indian Act. The term 'Indian' as used in the Indian Act was adopted by the colonial powers for purposes of political control and administrative convenience. For these reasons, indigenous peoples, generally, find the term 'Indian' objectionable. As a legal category, it denies their nationhood, their tribal cultures, and their histories as Squamish, Blackfoot, Mohawk, Dakota, Micmac, and so on. But, despite its offensive origins and obvious deficiencies, the term 'Indian' has a constitutional, legal reality, and after more than a century of Indian Act application, it has also acquired a socio-political reality. In this book, I use the term in two different ways: I use 'Indian' to signify the Indian Act definition, and I use '*Indian*' to signify the traditional nations. That is, 'Indian' is a legal concept; '*Indian*' is a cultural concept. Both categories comprise a large number of bands/tribes that are diverse in cultural, political, economic, and social history and development. This fact should be kept in mind whenever the term 'Indian' or '*Indian*' is used to frame the issues introduced in this book.

At present, two prominent discourses are ongoing with respect to the future of Indians in Canada. One is conducted from an Indian perspective; the other from a Canadian perspective. Each is conducted in isolation and is insulated from the other, and the participants in each seem to be imprisoned in the concepts and logic of their particular discourse. In this book, I adopt an evaluative and critical perspective (although not one that is deliberately oppositional) towards both discourses. My intention is to open up a new discourse that transcends the present ones in ways that will provoke the reader to envision alternative and better worlds for Indians.

My motivation for writing this book originates from an ongoing internal discussion that has been nurtured by what I have seen of conditions on Indian reserves and in urban Indian ghettos; by statistics on the Indian condition; by what I have heard from frustrated, angry, and despairing victims of the present system; by what has been revealed to me in many interviews and discussions with Indian leaders and others involved in the conduct of Indian affairs; and by what I have read. Written in a rhetorical style, this book presents an expression of my ideas and thoughts on selected issues and actions that are important to the future of Indians in Canada.

At the time of this writing, Canada has just completed a process of constitutional renewal that included an 'aboriginal constitutional process.' Also at this time, a royal commission on aboriginal matters, appointed by the Government of Canada, is traversing the country, examining problems in all aspects of aboriginal life. Thus, it is a time when much can be gained from a fresh discourse on the future of Indians in Canada – what is best and how best to get there. Much of my attention falls on the governments, courts, and citizens of Canada, and on Indian leadership; all will play a decisive role in shaping the future of Indians. Throughout this book I seek to develop my ideas within the framework of Indian cultural, political, and social aspirations.

Every writer has biases. A strongly held bias that pervades this book is that the dichotomy between Indians and non-Indians should not be characterized in racial terms, that is, as being between 'Indians' and 'Whites.' My aversion to the 'Indian–White' dichotomy does not imply a denial of racism in Canada; the fact of massive injury to Indians by persistent racism in Canadian society is undeniable. Rather, my aversion to the use of the 'Indian–White' dichotomy comes from a conviction that to define the Indian–non-Indian relationship in racial terms, even for benevolent purposes, causes us to 'see' race and lays the psychological foundation for race-based Canadian policies, stereotyping, and other invidious designs. Arguably, because racism is repugnant to all enlightened people, a racial designation can afford a serviceable mantle of protection to a minority group where there are laws against racism. It is precisely to gain this protection that some minority groups will don the racial mantle. But doing so carries an ominous contingency: being classed as a 'race' is always a threat to a minority group.

In its favour, the 'Indian–White' dichotomy is convenient and communicates effectively the racist reality in which Indians in Canada live. For example, it provides an explanation for the shameful miscarriage of justice in the wrongful conviction and nineteen-year imprisonment of a Micmac in Nova Scotia for a murder he didn't commit, and for the fatal shooting by a Winnipeg police officer of a Cree leader whose only 'crime' seemingly was being an Indian in a public place, and for the fifteen-year-long silence of many non-Indian citizens of The Pas, Manitoba, who knew enough to indict four non-Indian youths who raped and brutally murdered a young Indian girl. But scholars who legitimate a 'racism' analysis of injustice to Indians, by juxtaposing 'Indian' and 'White,' are not serving the interests of Indian peoples. A 'racism' paradigm robs Indians of the most significant elements of Indian identity – their history, nationhood, cultures, and languages – and thereby undermines their historical and moral claims to self-determination. In an enlightened world, peoples who are defined primarily in racial terms are not regarded as having a legitimate claim to nationhood.

A 'racism' paradigm inspired the 1969 White Paper on Indian policy. Erstwhile prime minister Pierre Elliott Trudeau analysed the 'Indian problem' as one of Canadian racism. He assumed Canadian racism towards Indians would halt if Indians became 'Canadians as all other Canadians.' From this assumption, he proceeded logically to his 'solution': deracializing Indians by eliminating their aboriginal and treaty rights – in effect, denying their historical claim to inherent nationhood. Confounded by his 'racial analysis,' Trudeau was unable to see that his proposed 'solution' would have compounded, not ameliorated, the injustice with which Indians have been treated in Canada.

Canadian injustice to Indians goes beyond racism, and to define it as racism serves to trivialize Canadian iniquity towards Indians. A 'racism' paradigm 'individualizes' injustice to Indians and creates a false perception that such injustice is primarily a social problem that can be rectified by the Charter of Rights and Freedoms. Thereby, it diverts attention from political, cultural, and economic imperialism, which are mainly responsible for Canadian policies that have historically denied justice to Indians. It is my view that scholars should use the 'Indian–White' dichotomy only when an analysis of injustice to Indians, or of a particular issue, necessitates a racial characterization.

However, the dichotomy between Indians and non-Indians is real and must be articulated. What construction do we place on this dichotomy? What categories do we use? I considered calling the dichotomy 'Indian–non-Indian,' but decided that those who are referred to as 'non-Indians' also have a positive identity – they are Canadians. So, throughout this book I dichotomize the two peoples as 'Indians and Canadians.' This dichotomy allows us to interpret 'Indian' as representing a diversity of cultural nations rather than a single racial group. The 'Indian–Canadian' dichotomy is appropriate in another important sense. It draws attention to the fact that Indians collectively have never formally or attitudinally accepted Canadian citizenship or Canadian sovereignty, which citizenship implies. Historically, both Indians and the Canadian government have drawn sharp distinctions between Canadian citizenship and Indian status. For almost a century after Confederation a strong constitutional line between Indians and Canadians denied Indians the right of citizenship. The right to vote in federal elections was not granted until 1960. Prior to 1960, Indians who wanted to vote were required to forfeit aboriginal and treaty rights, thus ceasing to be Indian Act Indians. On the other side, Indians have always rejected Canadian sovereignty and have consistently held that being granted the vote does not create Canadian citizenship for them. They insist they are not part of the Canadian social contract and demand recognition for their historical aboriginal nationhood and citizenship.

My book embodies a 'platform' and is cast in the framework of social action, not research and theory. The 'platform' is a moral commitment to justice for Indians, which I define as the survival and well-being of Indians as *Indians*. Both a cultural and a social concern are implicit. The cultural concern is implied in the term *'Indians,'* which has reference to their traditional cultural identity and heritage – more particularly, to the fundamental philosophies and principles inherent in their ancestral customs and traditions. Unless Indians can revitalize their traditional philosophies and principles they will become extinct as *Indians*; they will survive only as Indians, that is, as a legal-racial category defined in the Indian Act.

The social concern in my 'platform' has reference to the condition of massive destitution, misery, and hopelessness that prevails in virtually all Indian communities. To state my social platform in one long sentence: I am for whatever will make life better (and against what doesn't) for the mass of Indians who live in conditions of degrading dependence, destitution, and powerlessness; who are psychologically defeated; and who feel spurned and abandoned, even by their own leadership. It is this segment of the Indian population that experiences extraordinary and unconscionable levels of alcoholism, infant mortality, foetal alcohol syndrome, incarceration, homicide, and the highest ongoing rate of suicide reported for any identifiable population in the world. This is a growing tragedy and not, as the Canadian government would have us believe, a 'passing crisis.'

No doubt there are some heroes in this tragedy, but this book is not about heroes. It is an uncompromising critique of the regime and the policies that have created this tragedy. The premise of this book is that there is no redeeming value in the existing regime or policies – a premise that is amply corroborated by the Indian tragedy. The message of my social platform is: we must act now to end this tragedy. In this book I develop some models designed to actualize that message.

Acton's aphorism states that 'absolute power corrupts absolutely.' But, the apathy and the dulled emotions – the feeling of not caring about self, others, or even life itself – which are pervasive in most Indian communities stand as evidence that absolute powerlessness destroys absolutely. Indian powerlessness has its roots in Canada's Indian policies. The story of Canadian government oppression and exploitation of Indians has been well documented. However, another story is emerging today. As political and economic authority are devolved to band/tribal councils, responsibility for the continuing sense of powerlessness by Indian peoples increasingly falls on the shoulders of Indian leaders. In this regard, my discussion takes note of some disturbing trends associated with Indian 'advancement,' specifically, the bifurcation of the Indian community into a ruling élite class and a powerless lower class. The telling of this story is important for an understanding of the Indian future.

An important purpose of this book is to engage not only the 'experts' in the field of Indian affairs but all Indians and Canadians, on the basis of a shared sense of humanity. There is much to be gained from members of these two communities entering into a shared discourse for the purpose of learning from each other, about each other, and about themselves as part of the human community. Such a discourse can be achieved only in a climate of open and free communication, in which any facts, issues, and ideas aimed at the survival and well-being of Indians as *Indians* can be creatively explored. In this regard, I made a decision at the outset that I would not narrow my discussion or shape it to accommodate vague notions of 'political correctness,' whether of the right, left, or centre. Consequently, in my commitment to confront the injustice and intolerable reality in which most Indians live today, I may stray from some popular norms in the academic discipline of minority-group studies about what should and should not be discussed. Doing so involves taking some risks, saying some things to which some readers may take strong exception. But the survival and well-being of Indians as *Indians* is a vital human concern, much is at stake, and some risk taking is warranted.

For the same reason, I have not allowed my discussion to be constrained by the idea of 'intellectual segregation,' that is, the notion that the right to offer critical analysis of a minority issue must be reserved for members of the affected minority group and that those who break this norm are guilty of paternalism, if not worse. It is my view that because the survival and well-being of Indians as *Indians* is a matter of great human concern, scholars cannot allow themselves to be locked into silence on this issue because of their identity. In matters of great human concern, the principle of a common humanity requires scholars to transcend the boundaries of their identity to find common human ground. Paternalism lies not in offering one's views or advice – we do this to our friends and equals all the time – but in insisting or coercing people to pattern their lives according to one's views and advice. It is condescending to hold that Indians are unable to resist, reject, or defend themselves against views and advice they don't like.

Moreover, the Indian future will inevitably be worked out with Canadians. Thus, there may be merit in hearing the views of a Canadian, which I am. Obviously, an 'outsider' cannot claim to apprehend the Indian experience of their culture or the injustice they have suffered, but an 'outsider' may be able to see things and interpret events to which an 'insider' may be blind. I hasten to add that discourses are necessarily based on subjective *interpretations* of facts, events, history, motives, and so on, and there is no intended pretension here of presenting any definitive 'solution,' nor claiming to put forward the 'best design' for the future of Indians in Canada. Readers obviously are free to accept or reject or improve upon the ideas expressed in this book.

Indian–Canadian relations are complex and encompass profound issues. Moreover, everything is connected to something else. But, books have limits, and cannot be comprehensive or exhaustive. So I have been forced to make choices about what to include and what to leave out. However, these decisions have not been arbitrary. I have resorted to deliberate selection and exclusion to move the discourse in a particular direction, one that I consider to be especially relevant to Indians' struggle for well-being and survival as *Indians*. Inevitably, there are many gaps and loose ends, but a book may be better with such, for they provoke criticism, discussion, rebuttal, and refinement.

The production of a book necessitates organization. This book is organized into five chapters. Although presented here as conceptually distinct, in real life the issues addressed in the five chapters form a virtually seamless whole within which the future of Indians as *Indians* will evolve in Canada.

To avoid the trap of discussing Indian–Canadian relations against a backdrop of 'clear blue sky,' I have placed the chapter on 'justice' first. It is the backdrop against which the rest of the book must be interpreted. In this first chapter I review the roots and nature of Canadian injustice towards Indians, and I propose a paradigm for affording justice to Indians, based on the spirit and intent of the treaties and on the United Nations charters.

In the second chapter, I provide an analysis and critique of Canada's Indian policy. Here, I develop the conception that Canada's injustice to Indians flows primarily from the 'sidestream' effect of Canadian mainstream policies that are designed to serve the 'national interest' at the expense of Indian interests. I also expand on the idea that the Canadian government is moving constitutionally, legislatively, and administratively to bring an end to Indian status and Indian policy through a process of institutional assimilation.

In the third chapter I make an assessment of Indian leadership and politics. In this chapter the focus changes from relations between Indians and Canadians to relations *within* Indian communities. Here I consider the effects of the colonial political and bureaucratic leadership structures that have been imposed on Indian peoples. I also consider the social class structure that is emerging in Indian communities as privatization supersedes communalism as the dominant value base in Indian communities. I emphasize the important role Indian leaders must play to empower their people if Indians are to be decolonized. I put forth a proposal for indigenous constitutional development as a means for achieving this objective.

The fourth chapter provides a discussion on the future of *Indian* cultures. Here, I take the perspective that contemporary Indian distinctness is defined significantly by a 'culture of dependence,' and that *Indian* cultures are in a state of crisis. I propose that if Indians are to survive as *Indians* they must engage in an urgent initiative to identify their fundamental traditional philosophies and principles.

And, guided by these philosophies and principles, they must revitalize, adapt and develop their cultures for living and surviving in the modern world.

The last chapter deals with Indian economic issues. I evaluate present designs for Indian economic development. This part of the book emphasizes the essential importance of economic self-sufficiency and independence for Indian political autonomy and social health. I introduce a design for achieving these objectives through participation in the mainstream Canadian economy.

A number of appendices are included. They contain definitions, information, and/or comments on concepts that may be unfamiliar to some readers. By providing this information in the appendices, I attempt to open the discourse on the future of Indian–Canadian relations to the broadest readership possible, without unduly burdening informed readers with needless specifics. A list of the appendices appears in the table of contents. I heartily encourage readers who are not knowledgeable about any of the concepts, issues, or events contained in the appendices to read them first.

Finally, this book is conceived as a contribution to an ordinary social discourse, not as a discipline-based contribution to an evolving edifice of academic research and theory; thus I have not followed the conventional academic model of ritual citations. Citations in this book are limited to direct quotes, the ideas of others that are basic to the discourse, and facts that are not yet well known. However, this book is a product of twenty-five years of study, and I could not have written it without standing on the shoulders of many who have influenced my perceptions in one way or another. It is impossible to properly acknowledge every influence, but I gratefully acknowledge the most germane of them in the bibliography. For the benefit of readers who wish to study some matters in greater depth, I include a reference section in which relevant sources from the bibliography are grouped by chapter, according to key issues discussed in the text.

Surviving as *Indians*

1 Justice

A quest for justice always springs from the presence of injustice. The Indian quest for justice began shortly after first contact with the forces of European imperialism. European imperialists in the seventeenth century promulgated a self-serving, villainous doctrine that held that, by right of 'first discovery,' a Christian nation was divinely mandated to exercise dominion over non-Christian 'primitives' and to assert proprietary title to any 'unoccupied' lands. Under this doctrine, every European 'Christian' nation with a navy and an army sent its agents prowling to the remote corners of the world in search of potentially lucrative 'unoccupied' territories under the aegis of vulnerable non-Christian 'primitives.'

The Royal Proclamation of 1763 grew out of this villainous doctrine of 'first discovery,' 'divine right,' and 'might makes right.' Under the Royal Proclamation, the British Crown unilaterally asserted its sovereignty over self-governing indigenous nations in North America, and claimed proprietary title to lands on which Indians had lived and survived from time immemorial – lands they believed to be their 'sacred trust' from the Creator. The Royal Proclamation was uniquely framed to dispossess Indians of their sovereignty and lands. Even by the then prevailing principles that governed European domestic and international relations, the British Crown's assertion of sovereignty over indigenous peoples and proprietary title to their lands represented a corruption of justice. Under then-existing internation law, 'first discovery' entitled a state to declare sovereignty over and to claim title to only *unoccupied* territory. The British Crown knew North America was not unoccupied. Thus, the Crown knowingly violated two of the prevailing European principles of internation justice: it declared sovereignty over Indians and claimed title to their lands.

In 1763 Indian nations had the potential to form military alliances with each other or with other European nations, alliances that were capable of devastating British settlements. To avoid provoking a conflict with Indians the Crown cunningly resorted to a 'stealth' tactic in its Royal Proclamation. Crown *sovereignty* was made invisible by negotiating treaties with Indians; in effect, the Crown pretended to recognize Indian nationhood. But, if the Crown's true intent had been to recognize Indian nationhood it would not have made Indians wards of the Crown. Crown *title* to Indian lands was rendered invisible to Indians by introducing the device of 'aboriginal title.' Under 'aboriginal title' the Crown averted confrontation with Indians by allowing them to continue to live unmolested on their traditional lands at the Crown's pleasure. Because Indians had no notion or understanding of the abstract concepts 'sovereignty' and 'proprietary title,' it appeared to them that nothing had been taken from them. Invisible to them was the reality that the Royal Proclamation had created a legal foundation and framework for the Crown to claim, at its pleasure, all of their ancestral lands and to place them under colonial authority. While these intentions were invisible to Indians, they were well understood by France and any other European nation with a yen for Indian lands.

The Royal Proclamation created the concept of aboriginal title by making a distinction between 'proprietary title' and 'use and possession' of the land. It set forth five important principles: (1) legal proprietary title to all lands was vested in the Crown; (2) the Crown recognized a usufructuary/possessory (aboriginal) right of Indians in their ancestral lands (that is, use and benefit, not ownership); (3) Indian usufructuary/possessory (aboriginal) right in the lands could be surrendered (or sold) only to the Crown; (4) the Crown could, at its pleasure, extinguish the Indians' usufructuary/possessory (aboriginal) right, subject to reasonable compensation; and (5) selected lands (Indian reserves) were to be set aside for the exclusive use and possession of Indians.

Significantly, the framers of the Royal Proclamation did not entrench aboriginal rights as a principle of justice for Indians. The framers' concern (beyond asserting Crown sovereignty and title) was (1) to establish a legal framework for engaging Indians in a treaty-making process for the legal surrender of their aboriginal title to the Crown; and (2) to achieve political order in the colony by eliminating private-person purchase of Indian lands. In effect, the Crown was establishing itself as the exclusive real-estate agent for vast tracts of Indian land that were destined to be surrendered under treaties. Then, on the basis of purchase and grants, the Crown transferred proprietary title to land surrendered by Indians, from itself to the provinces, to settlers, and to corporations (e.g., the Hudson's Bay Company). But it consistently denied Indians proprietary title to any of their ancestral lands, even to their reserves.

To better appreciate the villainous nature of the Royal Proclamation, we should place it in a contemporary context. An analogous situation would occur if the president of the United States, in the name of 'Americanism,' were to issue unilaterally a presidential proclamation of U.S. sovereignty over Canadians, including an assertion of U.S. proprietary title to all real estate and resources within our borders. He would justify his action on the ground that we have failed to develop the economic potential of our territories fully. In order to mitigate Canadian hostility to his proclamation, the president would acknowledge a 'Canadian usufructuary interest' in the land, that is, a right to use and possess the property we at present hold. But this right could be extinguished subject to reasonable compensation at any time, at 'the pleasure of the president.' In order to avoid conflicts over claims to Canadian property and resources by U.S. corporations and citizens, and to facilitate an orderly accommodation of an expected influx of enterprising Americans into Canada, the president would declare his office to be the exclusive real-estate agent for all Canadian property and resources; that is, all 'unoccupied' and 'surrendered' property and resources would be appropriated by the office of the president for orderly resale to Americans. As we became progressively dispossessed of our property under this regime, we would be assigned to designated backwater territories 'reserved' for us. Except for a few token Canadians we would be denied the opportunity to participate in the mainstream U.S. society. The U.S. Congress would then pass a 'Canada Act' and other laws to legalize U.S. sovereignty and title over Canadians. After four generations of social, psychological, and spiritual devastation we would still be required to respect and be loyal to the government and the laws that dispossessed us.

Current Canadian policy regarding Indians and their lands is based on premises that conform closely to the villainous doctrine of the Royal Proclamation. As 'offspring' of the Crown, successive Canadian governments have proceeded on the premise that Canada is sovereign over Indians and the legal heir of proprietary title to all Indian lands usurped under the Royal Proclamation. Canada has consistently denied Indian claims to inherent 'pre-Crown' sovereignty and proprietary title to their ancestral territories, or even to the lands reserved for them by the treaties. The Indian Act describes 'reserve lands' as those for which legal title is vested in the Crown. The band merely holds rights to 'the use and benefit of the land' (i.e., aboriginal title). The band has the 'power to surrender' its right to the use and benefit of reserve land, but only to the Canadian government.

All contemporary Indian land claims are being negotiated by the Canadian government on the principles contained in the Royal Proclamation. That is, there is no recognition of Indian proprietary title to their ancestral lands. Land-claims settlements allow Indians to retain only usufructuary/possessory rights to small areas of selected lands, and they provide Indians with 'reasonable' compensation (i.e., cash and some other entitlements) for loss of usufructuary/possessory benefits on surrendered lands. Invariably, the Canadian government requires Indians to forfeit all claims to aboriginal rights in all surrendered lands. Indians, have unsuccessfully sought to maintain that they hold a proprietary title to their ancestral lands, and they insist that the 'compensation' they accept represents only an initial instalment for giving Canadians a usufructuary/possessory right in the 'surrendered' lands.

A review of Canadian policy towards Indians since 1867 reveals a disturbing pattern of continuing erosion of the impaired standard of justice and morality that was first objectified by the Royal Proclamation. Canada has placed its policies firmly on a path to neutralize and invalidate Indian aboriginal rights that were acknowledged in the Royal Proclamation and the treaties. Successive Canadian governments have empowered themselves and their appointed judiciary to undermine these aboriginal rights. In so doing, the Canadian government – like its progenitor, the British Crown – is breaching international standards of law and moral justice. Under international standards, treaties between nations and the rights of 'a people' are extinguishable only by negotiated agreement between equals, and the conditions must be acceptable to both sides.

The list of historical injustices to Indians is not limited to the dispossession of their lands and their autonomy, and the abrogation of their aboriginal and treaty rights. The list also includes: colonial oppression and exploitation; destruction of their traditional means of subsistence; subversion of their social systems, cultures, languages, and spiritual heritages; abduction and alienation of their children; breaches of the federal government's trust obligations; and prejudice and discrimination in every sphere of contact with the dominant society (e.g., health, education, employment, living accommodations, and law enforcement). To this list can be added innumerable examples of government fraud, betrayal, negligence, mismanagement, malfeasance, arbitrary actions, and incompetence.

Contemporary injustice

Injustice to Indians in Canada rests on three pillars: the Canadian government, the Canadian courts, and the Canadian people. I will deal briefly with each.

The government

In the world community of nations, Canada likes to pretend it is living in an upper-class, moral neighbourhood. This pretension has been particularly evident in Canada's posture towards South Africa. The Canadian government has condemned, in its shrillest, most self-righteous voice, South African racism and injustice towards its indigenous peoples. Not unlike the televangelist who damns carnality in others while privately cavorting with prostitutes, the Canadian government self-righteously damns oppression, racism, and injustice in South Africa while practising such sins at home. But, if the Canadian government wants to claim the moral high ground in the world community of nations, it must be prepared to have its treatment of Indians judged by the same standards it applies to South Africa.

The Canadian government has censured the South African government for five heinous sins: for legally classifying people by race; for segregating indigenous peoples into 'homelands' and urban ghettos; for dispossessing indigenous peoples from most of their lands; for administering indigenous peoples as a separate 'department' of government; and for denying indigenous peoples the right to vote. But, how different are these sins from the treatment the indigenous peoples have experienced in Canada? The Indian Act has defined Indian status in essentially racial terms; with few exceptions, Indians are de facto segregated on reserves and in urban ghettos; Indians have been dispossessed of almost all of their lands; Indians are administered under a separate department (the Department of Indian Affairs and Northern Development [DIAND]); and, although Indians were given the federal franchise in 1960, 'one person, one vote' has left them powerless; it has not liberated them from political oppression, nor has it eliminated racism and injustice.

Because Indians in Canada are allowed to exercise some 'democratic' rights denied to Blacks in South Africa, the Canadian government pretends that its treatment of Indians is more enlightened. But, what evidence is there that Canadian oppression, racism, and injustice to Indians are more benign than the treatment received by Blacks in South Africa? Indians in Canada and Blacks in South Africa share a debilitating malaise. Both peoples live in conditions of destitution. Both experience unconscionable rates of morbidity, infant mortality, and violent deaths. Both have been forced into a state of dependence by being denied the opportunity to provide for themselves. In short, the parallels between the two nations in respect of the consequences of oppression, racism, and injustice are equally real and substantial and virtually identical. Archbishop Desmond Tutu, during his visit to Canadian Indian reserves in 1990, drew public attention to these parallels when comparing the plight of Indians in Canada with that of South African Blacks. From the victims' perspective, the effects of oppression, injustice, and racism are equally pernicious whether they result from tyranny by the minority, as in South Africa, or from tyranny of the majority, as in Canada.

Indians in Canada and Blacks in South Africa have the same goals: both pursue self-determination for the purpose of liberating themselves from oppression, racism, and injustice. However, self-determination calls for different approaches in different circumstances. Blacks in South Africa, who constitute a numerical majority in their state, could best achieve self-determination through the 'democratic' concept of 'one person, one vote,' so they pursue this goal. But South African Whites, the dominant group, rejected this notion and, instead, offered to Blacks 'homelands' where they could exercise self-government. Indians in Canada constitute approximately 2 per cent of the population, and they cannot possibly achieve self-determination through 'one person, one vote,' so they press for adequate 'homelands' (reserves) with *Indian* self-government. But, the Canadian government, representing the dominant group, insists on giving them 'one person, one vote' instead. The tactics are opposite, but the motives of the two governments are identical: both are protecting existing constitutional power arrangements and both are determined to use their powers to forestall any significant shift in those arrangements. Indians in Canada were given the vote contrary to their wishes; Blacks in South Africa were offered self-government in their homelands contrary to their wishes. In both cases, the proposed 'concessions' posed the least threat to the interests of the respective Canadian and South African power establishments. Put another way, in both states the only pathway to self-determination has been effectively blocked. If we were to move the Black majority from South Africa to Canada, and the Indian minority from Canada to South Africa, predictably both governments would reverse their legal positions and tactics.

The Canadian government (like the South African government) has used its political might to institute a political-judicial *system* that allows it to create and implement any legal position it wants in respect of its Indian wards. It is able to do so because the supremacy of Parliament gives it the sovereign powers to enact laws that supersede Indian rights and claims; its appointed judges are mandated to interpret the laws regarding Indian rights and claims so as to serve the Canadian interest; its bureaucrats, whose career progress depends upon how effectively they protect Canadian interests, have administrative authority to decide the merits of Indian rights and claims. In effect, the government and its appointed officials act as lawmaker, judge, jury, and executor in regard to Indian rights and claims.

How are these practices different from those of South Africa? And why is such a standard of justice deemed to be acceptable for Canada, but a matter for international censure for South Africa? The answer is simple: whereas tyranny of the minority renders South African injustice and racism offensively naked, tyranny of the majority allows Canada to dress its injustice and racism in a carefully tailored 'democratic' suit. Canada commits its injustice under the guise of a venerated democratic principle – 'one person, one vote,' 'rule by majority.' This 'principle' makes it possible for the Canadian government to disregard the rights and will of a colonized people (Indians) for self-determination. Moreover, in a remarkable perversion of democratic principle, the Canadian government, in briefs to the United Nations, has characterized Indian aspirations to self-determination as undermining Canada's democratic government. The best principle of democracy for a multinational state such as Canada is one that devolves as much power as is legitimately required to permit the 'distinct societies' within state boundaries to protect and enhance their cultural identities.

Indians are not deceived by the hypocrisy of the Canadian government's 'democratic' stance. To emphasize this fact, in 1987 Chief Louis Stevenson of the Peguis Indian Reserve invited the South African ambassador to Canada to inspect the run-down and overcrowded houses, the decrepit schools, and the horrendous social conditions on Manitoba's largest Indian reserve. In a speech to an overflow crowd of Peguis Reserve residents, the ambassador drew parallels between the circumstances of Indians in Canada and those of Blacks in South Africa. He pointed out that his government has acknowledged the shortcomings of their system and is committed to correcting them. The ambassador's speech was interrupted at several points by enthusiastic applause and, at the end, his Indian audience gave him a standing ovation. If the South African government proceeds to put its house in order, then, perhaps, world attention will begin to shift to a people it has largely neglected – the aboriginal peoples of the world, most particularly those who dwell in one of the citadels of 'democracy,' Canada.

There is nothing in Canadian law or the Constitution that prohibits the Canadian government from acting justly and fairly towards Indians. Nor are the concepts lacking in the Canadian political lexicon that would enable politicians to conceptualize and articulate a just and fair response to Indian rights and claims. Only the political *will* is lacking to conceptualize and articulate a just and fair response. Instead, the Canadian government's will is driven by political and economic calculations to use all of its available administrative, legislative, and judicial powers to twist and turn out of honouring Canada's historical and moral obligations to Indians and thus to deprive them of their aboriginal rights. Not once during the entire process leading up to patriation of the Canadian constitution, nor in the deliberations over amendments to the constitution, nor in the four subsequent First Ministers' Conferences (FMCs) called to deal with Indian constitutional issues, did the representatives of Canada's ten governments engage in a meaningful or serious soul-searching discussion as to what the prevailing principles of enlightened justice might require Canadians to do in respect of Indian rights. Always the focus was on defending the existing constitutional power arrangements by mystifying, minimizing, discounting or denying aboriginal rights. Rather than seeking out ways to deal fairly and justly with Indians, the Canadian government resorted to tactics of political stonewalling, reducing Indian expectations through drawn-out and pointless negotiations, and by defining issues so as to factionalize the Indian community. Although the Canadian governments' public posture during the Canada Round of constitutional negotiations was one of fairness, generosity, goodwill, and justice for Indians, their words may turn out to be as empty as the constitutional promise of 'existing aboriginal rights' and the promise of justice contained in the treaties have proved to be. I will say more about this in the next chapter.

The prime minister of Canada, the Right Honourable Brian Mulroney, without any apparent moral qualms, regularly offers empty promises of justice for Indians *in exchange* for their compliant behaviour. For example, he offered Indians justice if they would withdraw their opposition to the Meech Lake Accord. Yet, passage of the Accord would have given each provincial government veto power over Indian self-determination. More recently, he offered them justice if they would lay down their arms at Oka. Indians are entitled to justice not as a bribe for compliant behaviour, but because, as human beings, they have an inherent and inalienable right to receive justice. That is a fundamental principle of human rights. When Mulroney denies this principle, he perverts the meaning of justice.

The courts

In regard to land title and to sovereignty the Supreme Court of Canada has consistently upheld the villainous colonial doctrines of 'first discovery,' 'divine right,' and 'might makes right' that were enshrined in the Royal Proclamation of 1763. Today's Canadian judiciary are fully aware that the lands claimed by King George III were occupied by the aboriginal people in accordance with their customs, and that the Crown's denial of aboriginal rights and interests in their ancestral lands on grounds that they were 'uncivilized' was based on racism, yet the Canadian court continues to flatly reject Indian claims to proprietary title to their ancestral lands and it denies Indian claims to sovereignty. This line of judicial logic has been confirmed by the courts again and again, most recently in the 1990 *Sparrow* decision. It has allowed so much land to be taken from Indians that today the implications for Indians of this judicial practice have been staggering. They must live in a state of dependence and destitution. Even a minimal standard of enlightened justice would hold that the original occupants of this land should have at least enough land to enable them to feed themselves.

Ideally, the principles of enlightened justice should prevail over the interests of the dominant group, but the history of Canadian court decisions on significant Indian rights and claims shows that, consistently, the dominant group's interests, not principles of enlightened justice, are the currency of Canadian courts. In cases involving low stakes and having clearly limited implications, Canadian judges have on occasion mustered the moral courage to render carefully circumscribed and nuanced decisions that appear to treat Indian rights as valid even when they may be contrary to the dominant group's interests (e.g., upholding the right of Indians to hunt game for food out of season on vacant Crown lands). But, in any significant decision with open-ended consequences (such as sovereignty and land title), when an Indian right is deemed to be in conflict with vital Canadian interests, judges, who are appointed to guard the Canadian interests, assiduously explore voids in the law, vagueness of wording, omission, mandate of the legislators, judicial principle, hierarchy of principles, etc., etc., that will support an analysis and interpretation that prefers Canadian interests over Indian rights. Since no law is exempt from one or another type of void, vagueness, or omission, the cumulative effect of judicial interpretations, which has consistently given Canadian interests priority over Indian rights, has been to create a legal structure that renders Indian aboriginal and treaty rights virtually meaningless.

A recent example of such an interpretation is the August 1989 Ontario Court of Appeal ruling that regulations passed under the federal Fisheries Act take precedence over aboriginal, treaty, or other rights or freedoms. The treaty in question, the Robinson Huron Treaty of 1850, gave bands 'the full and free privilege to hunt over the territory now ceded to them, and to fish in the waters thereof, as they have heretofore been in the habit of doing.' Speaking for the court, Judge Gordon Blair observed that, in 1850, fish and game might have been limitless resources, but that today conservation and management of fish and game are required to preserve them for the benefit of *Canadians*. Thus, Indian rights explicitly set out under the treaties must be subordinated to the interests of Canadians. Different judges take different routes, but all arrive at the same goal – to serve the interests of the dominant group.

It is true that Canadian judges don't make the law. But, this does not absolve them of accountability for giving the *imprimatur* of the court to many unenlightened and unjust legislative actions against Indians. Oliver Wendell Holmes said, 'law is whatever the greatest force in the community can make it at any given time.'[1] The courts affirm and compound the legislative tyranny of the majority when they serve as handmaidens to the 'greatest force in the community.' Such was the case in *The Attorney-General of Canada* v *Lavell* (1974),[2] where the Supreme Court concurred with the 'greatest force in the community' by ruling in favour of the Canadian government in upholding section 12 (1)(b) of the Indian Act. Section 12 (1)(b) denied Indian status to Indian women who married non-Indians. It fell to the U.N. Human Rights Commission to correct this moral injustice. The Human Rights Commission condemned this section of the Indian Act as blatant gender discrimination, impelling the Canadian government in 1985 to amend the act (Bill C-31), repealing section 12 (1)(b).

The Canadian judicial system has also failed Indians at the level of *individuals* seeking justice before the courts. Confirmation of this fact was provided recently by the Nova Scotia royal commission (1987–8)[3] investigating the wrongful conviction and imprisonment of Donald Marshall Jr, a Micmac Indian, who spent eleven years in prison for a murder he did not commit. The report of the royal commission, published in 1990 (eighteen years after Marshall's wrongful conviction), implicates police, defence lawyers, prosecutors, trial judges at lower- and appeal-court levels, and senior government officials as having participated in a charade of justice characterized by malice, negligence, malfeasance, incompetence, and improper actions emanating from racial stereotyping.

Canadians can take no comfort in thoughts that the *Marshall* case represents an isolated, unusual, or rare event. Other recent provincial inquiries in Ontario (1987), Manitoba (1991), and Alberta (1991)[4] corroborate the Nova Scotia royal commission's findings that Indians encounter shocking abuses in their dealings with police and the criminal courts. Indians appearing before these inquiries have repeatedly testified about the 'colour of justice' in Canada. They have pointed out that the justice system effectively excludes Indians from positions as judges and prosecutors, and even from serving on juries. They have argued that the so-called objective standards used by judges for sentencing decisions (e.g., employment history, family stability, and permanence of residence) serve as proxies for racial discrimination. Some, who had been jailed, felt that their only crime was 'being Indian in a public place.'

Official statistics, which show Indians to be grossly overrepresented among those arrested, convicted, and imprisoned, lend support to Indian grievances that racism in the Canadian justice system is pervasive and runs deep. Indians have experienced it and proclaimed it for years, but, except for the recent provincial inquiries, the justice system has denied the validity of such grievances. The findings of the various provincial inquiries that uniformly confirm that Canadian judicial standards and practices are such that Indians cannot be assured of receiving a fair trial in Canadian courts ought to dismay all Canadians. If the very institution that exists to provide justice and fair play defaults, then what can Indians expect from Canada's other institutions – political, economic, and social?

Felix Cohen, an American legal scholar, compared Indians in U.S. society to a 'miners' canary.'[5] Cohen drew his metaphor from an ancient miners' practice of taking canaries into mineshafts to test for the presence of poisonous gas. A perishing canary served as an early warning to miners that the shaft contained lethal gas. The point of Cohen's metaphor is that how Indians fare in the U.S. justice system is a reliable indicator of the moral health of that system. The metaphor is apt for the Canadian justice system as well. When Indians fare badly in the Canadian justice system, when the fundamental guarantee of justice is denied to Indians, it should serve as an ominous early warning that all Canadians are threatened in their claim to justice. By creating a guarantee of justice for Indians, Canadians ensure justice for themselves. Conversely, if they allow justice for Indians to be corrupted, then all will be served by corrupted justice. If Donald Marshall is taken for the 'miners' canary,' then Canadians have reason to be alarmed about the health of their justice system.

The people

How do Canadians feel about the denial of justice and rights to Indians by their government and courts? Some national surveys purport to show that the Canadian public supports just dealings with Indians in their rights and claims. But such 'findings' should be viewed with a healthy scepticism. Most Canadians want to see themselves as 'enlightened'; being supportive of Indian rights and claims when interviewed for a national survey is consistent with that desired self-image. Being supportive of Indian constitutional objectives is also consistent with that self-image. This is not to deny that many Canadians have a vague and abstract sense of goodwill towards Indians, but very few understand the political implications and the monetary cost of rendering justice in regard to Indian rights and claims. Few Canadians know the meaning of basic concepts such as 'aboriginal title,' 'treaty rights,' 'Indian self-government.' Most do not even understand the legal distinction between status and non-status Indians or between Indian and Metis. They have no idea what sacrifice is required or what inconvenience it would mean for them if justice were rendered to Indians.

Clearly, Canadian politicians are not persuaded by national surveys of uninformed public opinion that show support for justice to Indians.

Quite to the contrary, politicians are convinced that Canadians are unwilling to make sacrifices to honour Indian rights and claims. The ''Nielsen Report' explicitly states that 'most Canadians are not entirely persuaded by arguments for special rights. This reticence can be expected to increase as knowledge of the costs associated with new definitions of rights is brought into focus.'[6] Politicians have an 'educated' intuition that, when Canadians are confronted with the bottom political and fiscal line, their support for Indian rights and claims will vanish into thin air. In part, this 'educated' intuition about Canadian values and priorities constrains Canadian governments from responding to churches, labour unions, and other concerned public voices when they urge respect for Indian rights and claims.

Much more disquieting than the dubious dependability of uninformed Canadian support for Indian rights and claims is the valuation that Canadians place upon Indians. Canadians seem unable to recognize Indians as people with whom they share a common humanity. They seem not to place the same worth on an Indian life that they place on the life of a Canadian. Such a conclusion is indicated by the sheer indifference Canadians display towards the ongoing tragedies in Indian communities that they regularly see, hear, and read about. Indian suicide rates are unmatched in any other population in the world; their life expectancy is ten years less than for all Canadians; they experience epidemics of tuberculosis that do not occur in any other part of Canadian society; their rate of infant mortality is 2.5 times the Canadian rate; the number of children 'in care' is 6 times the Canadian rate; their incidence of alcoholism is 13 times the Canadian rate; their rate of foetal alcohol syndrome is between 15 and 20 times the Canadian rate; their rate of incarceration is 5 times the Canadian rate; the death rate for Indians under age thirty-five is 3 times the Canadian rate; their rate of unemployment stands around 70 per cent on most reserves; 80 per cent live under the 'poverty line.' Data from the 1981 Canadian census show Indians to be the most poorly housed people in Canada. Living conditions in some isolated communities are so poor that some youths commit crimes as a means of access to the healthier conditions offered in jail.

Although Canadian government officials talk much less about this massive human tragedy than about the high cost of welfare support to Indians, these facts are not hidden from public view. Canadians have often heard these statistics, but they shrug them off. They react to these statistics as an accountant reacts to unfavourable numbers in a clients' ledger. These horrendous statistics do not penetrate the

Canadian conscience because, seemingly, they do not translate into a *human* tragedy. As the Indians' condition worsens, Canadians respond by ratcheting up their tolerance for the unconscionable. Canadians appear not to identify with the pain Indians feel. But, like their governments, they increasingly complain about the high cost of welfare support to Indians.

What is it about Indians that numbs Canadians to the deplorable condition of Indians? The reason goes beyond ethnocentrism, or even racism. It derives from an incapacity rather than an unwillingness to accept Indians as fully human. Humans derive their identity and humanity from their past. But Canadians repress or deny the Indians' past: that their nations were destroyed by colonization; that our forefathers arbitrarily moved in on them and dispossessed them of their means of subsistence; that their children were forcibly taken from them and alienated from their customs and values; that their cultures were devastated and their religious ceremonies outlawed; that their right to self-determination has been denied; and so on. When Canadians repress or deny so much about the Indians' past they deny the humanity of an entire people, so that when they hear about the devastating conditions of Indian life, or when they pass Indians on the street, they can't relate to them as fully human persons whose homelands have been taken, whose identity has been destroyed and who must live in destitution.

It is troubling that Canadians have such an incapacity to feel the pain of Indians. Most Canadians are fugitives or descendants of fugitives who came to Canada to escape political oppression, religious persecution, or economic deprivation. In many instances they or their forebears have fled injustice to find this haven. Yet, these very Canadians continue to subject Indians to the same (or worse) persecution, oppression, and deprivation from which they or their forebears escaped. Seemingly without a meaningful twinge of conscience, Canadians are destroying the very peoples whose lands have given them a chance for freedom and well-being. It must be taken as an adverse measure of the spiritual and moral state of Canadians that they choose to enrich themselves beyond measure rather than act justly and morally towards Indians.

Recently many Canadian citizens bristled with resentment against wealthy Chinese immigrants from Hong Kong for buying up prime real estate in Canadian cities. They viewed it as a form of wrongful dispossession, even though these new immigrants paid premium prices for the properties they acquired. Yet, Canadians seem incapable of

understanding the sense of injustice that Indians feel over the dispossession of most of their ancestral lands with only token or no
compensation.

During the 1960s, the spillover of idealism from worldwide liberation movements briefly animated Canadians' concern over the
Indian condition of destitution, discrimination, and government paternalism, but this quickly faded into apathy during the 1970s. During
the 1980s, patriation of the Canadian constitution and the follow-up
First Ministers' Conferences, dealing with unresolved aboriginal constitutional issues, again, briefly, raised Canadian consciousness and
concern for Indians. But this constitutional process, which ended in
disappointment for Indians, left many Canadians with a false sense
that Indians had had their 'day in court,' diminishing public empathy
and concern for Indians.

The last half of the 1980s has witnessed a profound shift in Canadians' social and political priorities, to the detriment of Indian rights
and claims. A runaway national debt and the chronic menace of economic recession have turned public concerns from a humanistic emphasis to economic priorities. Canadians gave expression to their
economic priorities in 1988 by electing a Conservative government
that ran on a platform of curtailing government spending. Consistent
with their economic priorities, Canadians appear quite willing to accept limitations on funds for Indian programs, even though such limits
infringe on Indian rights and incur debilitating social consequences
for Indians. In effect, social justice has fallen victim to economic expedience. This attitude was evident when the Canadian government
introduced restrictions on funding for Indian post-secondary education. The Canadian public paid scant attention to Indian protests. Even
a hunger strike by Indian students was treated as Indian 'discontent-
as-usual.'

As we begin the final decade of the twentieth century, the evidence
indicates there remains only a small residue of Canadian public concern that justice be secured for Indians. Even many enlightened Canadians are content to ritually vilify Columbus, or their forebears,
or the government for what has been done to Indians and leave it at
that. It would seem the Canadian people, their governments, and the
judiciary have reached an ideological concord to deny the historical
rights and claims of Indians because it would cost too much to honour
them. This concord is fully supported by powerful corporate interest
groups who are placing intense pressure on Canadian governments
to 'disencumber' lands in Canada from any residue of Indian rights

and claims. Only the 'external' constraints of international opinion still prevail on Canadians, their governments, and the courts to move slowly in eliminating those rights and claims entirely.

Guilt management

Although there is little tangible evidence of genuine remorse, Canadians have been plagued by guilt over their treatment of Indians. L.F.S. Upton[8] has noted that, from the beginning of Canadian nationhood, an expression of guilt prefaced almost every government account of the plight of Indians: 'guilt for destroying his independence, his manliness, for killing him through war and disease, and demoralizing him with liquor.' Similar evidence of guilt can be detected in recent parliamentary advisements such as the Report of the Task Force on Canadian Unity and the Report of the Parliamentary Task Force on Indian Self-Government (the Penner Report).[9] Both admit to Canadian government culpability (but not duplicity) in respect to the intolerable circumstances in which Indians live.

But, this sense of guilt has never moved Canadians to render justice to Indians. In lieu of rendering justice, Canadians have adopted a paradigm of 'guilt management.' Canada's Indian policies can be seen to have been shaped by three strategies of guilt management, which I call civilization, charity, and myth. I will deal briefly with each.

Civilization

Guilt management under a paradigm of 'civilization' has taken a variety of ethnocentric and paternalistic forms. From the beginning of nationhood to the 1960s, Canada's 'civilization policy' emphasized forced cultural assimilation, and 'saving' Indians by treating them as wards of the state. Beginning in the 1960s, the Canadian government began to redefine its 'civilization policy' into one of upgrading the Indians' self-reliance within Canadian society, polity, and economy. The 1969 White Paper on Indian Policy exemplified this changed design. Under this new design of self-reliance, 'civilization policy' has emphasized the removal of Indian special status and the remaking of Indians into 'Canadians as all other Canadians.'

Incompatibility between the Canadian government's guilt-management initiatives, on the one hand, and its continuing agenda of colonialism, on the other hand, has turned Canada's 'civilization' policy into a paradigm of contradictory goals. For example, out of guilt management, Indians were provided with schooling, but, out of colonialism, they were viewed as aliens, and so they were deliberately isolated on reserves, and barriers were raised to keep them out of Canadian society; out of guilt management, the Canadian government allocated money for funding Indian associations, but out of colonialism it attempted to co-opt the leaders of these associations; out of guilt management, the Canadian government provided resources for band/tribal research into the legal foundations of their aboriginal rights and land claims, but out of colonialism the Canadian government ignores or denies most of the evidence Indians have marshalled for their aboriginal rights and land claims; out of guilt management, the Canadian government, in the name of 'Indian self-government,' devolves administration of selected programs and services to band/tribal councils, but out of colonialism it imposes a stifling set of federal government rules, regulations, and controls to govern Indian administration of these programs and services.

In all of its forms the Canadian government's policy of 'civilization' has served primarily to spin a 'just cause' around Canadian colonialism. Because Canada's 'civilization' policy has been motivated by guilt management, not principles of justice, most initiatives taken under this policy have proved destructive for the survival and well-being of Indians as *Indians*.

Charity

Another approach to guilt management is through 'charity' or 'humanitarian aid.' Moved by a need to reduce their guilt, Canadians have made Indians into a charitable cause. In lieu of justice for Indians, Canada has developed a massive and encompassing system of social assistance for them. Currently, more than half of the Indian population survives on social assistance. On many reserves up to 70 per cent of the residents are dependent upon direct social assistance, while most of the remaining 30 per cent depend on jobs directly funded or subsidized by Canadian governments. In addition, the government pays program-specific assistance for housing, health services, education, economic development, and so on. Virtually every facet of reserve life is dependent upon direct or indirect government funding. Since the Second World War, the Department of Indian Affairs and Northern Development has functioned primarily as an agency to administer various types of Canadian social assistance – that is, 'charity' or 'humanitarian aid' – to Indians.

Charity has served Canadians quite well as a strategy of guilt management. It has a positive connotation in the Canadian lexicon, and it has a surface plausibility as a surrogate for justice. But, because charity is done to gain relief from guilt, not as an act of justice towards Indians, the consequences for Indians have been massively destructive. Canadian charity can be seen to have driven Indians into a condition of destitution and total dependence.

In the past, the Canadian government has tolerated the burden of charity to Indians as an unwanted but obligatory costs of guilt management. Recently, however, the federal Conservative government, driven by economic priorities rather than by humanitarian concern, has concluded that this form of guilt management has become too costly to continue. This attitude was given voice by the Nielson Report, which recommended that the federal government should fulfil only its 'legal' fiscal obligations to Indians and that the bulk of the cost of humanitarian aid to Indians should be assumed by the provinces. By implementing some of the recommendations contained in this report (e.g., capping budgets for Indian programs) the Canadian government has signalled that it is prepared to endure higher levels of guilt towards Indians in order to achieve its fiscal priorities.

Most Indians have a powerful vested interest in seeing the Canadian government's policy of charity continue undiminished – their day-to-day survival depends upon it. But they would prefer to redefine the government's social assistance from 'charity' to 'rent' for lands and resources taken from them. Such a redefinition, however, would require the Canadian government to place its Indian policies in the framework of 'justice' rather than 'guilt management', and the Canadian government is unwilling to confront the vast implications of such a paradigmatic policy shift.

Myths

Repression or denial of guilt through myths is another prominent and enduring strategy in Canadian 'guilt management.' Canada lacks myths to inspire its citizens to dream of greatness for their nation, but its history books are filled with myths to abate Canadians guilt over unconscionable actions towards Indians. One deeply rooted historic myth is that the British Crown possessed a moral and legal right to assert its sovereignty over Indians and to claim proprietary title to their lands. According to this myth, the Crown was morally and legally entitled to Indian lands: as a right of 'divine' source; as a right of 'first discovery'; because Indians were 'barbarians'; because the lands were 'unoccupied'; because Indians' 'voluntarily submitted' to the sovereignty of the Crown; and because aboriginal title was extinguished through 'voluntary cession.'

When Canada achieved nationhood, these myths metamorphosed into the fiction that, as heir to the Crown, the government of Canada legitimately inherited the moral and legal right to sovereignty over Indians and title to their lands. This myth was given legal force by the British North America Act, 1867, which proclaimed Canadian sovereignty over Indians and lands reserved for Indians, and by the Indian Act, which describes a reserve as 'a tract of land, the legal title to which is vested in Her Majesty for the use and benefit of a band.' This myth has been given added legal force by a series of court decisions, which were backed up by another myth: that Canadian courts render justice to Indians.

But trying to hide our injustice to Indians by mythologizing our past isn't working. It is almost impossible to hide the fact that a mere 150 years ago this was "Indian country,' and that Canada exists as a product of colonial greed and fraud. Moreover, there is simply too much continuing evidence of injustice to Indians around us today for us to trust the myths that allege moral and just dealings with Indians. We are imprisoned by the evidence of our injustice to Indians.

'The Just Society'

The Right Honourable Pierre Elliott Trudeau, erstwhile prime minister of Canada, played a major role in shaping the landscape of contemporary Canadian Indian policy. His initiatives firmly placed Indians on the Canadian political agenda and ultimately led to the constitutional entrenchment of aboriginal rights. It started in the 1968 federal election when Trudeau led the Liberal party to power under the slogan 'The Just Society.' The true meaning of this catchy phrase was brought home to Indians in 1969, when Trudeau's Liberal government introduced its White Paper on Indian Policy. Although the 1969 White Paper represented an 'enlightened' attempt to shift Canadian Indian policy from the framework of 'guilt management' to the framework of 'justice,' it quickly became clear that Trudeau's vision of justice for Indians was referenced into Western-liberal ideology.

Trudeau's Western-liberal concept of justice contained two consequential premises. One was that Canadian injustice to Indians derived from their collective special status. He characterized the 'Indian problem' as one of race-based non-acceptance of Indians by other Canadians for reasons rooted in their special status, and he proposed that the first step towards eradicating the Canadian racial psychology was to accept that every *individual* in Canadian society has equal rights.[10] Trudeau firmly believed that Indian special status was a fundamental obstacle to Indian participation and to Indians' acceptance as equals in the Canadian mainstream. He reasoned that by removing special status for Indians the racial psychology of Canadians would begin to change, and the 'Indian problem' would be transformed from one of racism to one of individual inequality of opportunity. He asked Indians to forfeit their special status, their land claims, and their aboriginal rights in exchange for a chance to share equally as *individuals* in Canada's future. In brief, Trudeau's design for justice was to 'decolonize' Indians by making them, in his words, into 'Canadians as all other Canadians.' The 1969 White paper sketched Trudeau's mission to bring Indians into the Canadian social contract as individuals, as equals, as Canadians. It should be noted that Trudeau was not consciously advocating the cultural assimilation of Indians. On the contrary, he emphasized that he felt the same great respect for Indian cultures as he had for French-Canadian culture. What he did not understand is that, while French-Canadian culture could survive in his Just Society, *Indian* communal cultures would inevitably be destroyed by his Western-liberal vision of their place in Canada.

The other critical premise contained in Trudeau's Western-liberal vision of justice was that the historical dimension of Canadian injustice to Indians was best denied. He proposed to remove the fact of Canadian injustice to Indians from Canadian history and memory. In response to Indians who articulated their sense of historical injustice over loss of lands, of means of subsistence, of nationhood, and of culture, Trudeau advocated 'amnesia' as the cure for their grievances. He espoused the philosophy that Canadians ought not to devote their future to redressing past injustices to Indians. In his words: 'No nation can continue to live if it doesn't want to forgive a lot of the past. The best we can do is to try to be fair in our time ... If we try to undo the things we have done wrong we would be enemies among ourselves.'[11] In effect, Trudeau was advocating the cancellation of all entries on the 'debit' side of Canada's account with Indians, while retaining all of the assets that Canadians had purloined from Indians. Not only did Trudeau refuse to enter into an accounting of historical fraud and injustice, he gave no indication of willingness to analyse the past in order to gain knowledge and awareness for more just future policies and actions in regard to aboriginal rights and land claims.

Indians reacted very negatively to Trudeau's vision of 'The Just Society.' Although they did not argue with his assertion that justice requires a social order founded on equality and human rights, Indians could not accept Trudeau's individualistic conception of their social order. Nor could they accept his premise that prospective individual equality and rights constituted an appropriate settlement for their loss of ancestral lands, subsistence, culture, and sovereignty. Indians could not forget the past, nor could they accept Trudeau's racial conception of their 'special status.' They asserted that their identity had been, since time immemorial, that of distinct cultural nations, not of a racial group, and their struggle for special status was for cultural integrity and nationhood, not for racial segregation. In short, Indians felt that Trudeau's vision of 'The Just Society' trampled on thousands of years of their history, identity, and collective rights.

Arguably, Trudeau's 'ahistorical' vision has some surface validity. Forgetting nothing can be psychologically and socially debilitating; a chronic sense of injustice can produce endless frustration, apathy, malaise, hopelessness, and hostility. It can paralyse societies and turn them into anachronisms whose primary identity derives from their victimization. One could reason that if Indians were able to relinquish some of their bitterest memories it would free them to concentrate on creating a better future for their children. But, such logic is misleading. It implies that Indians' sense of injustice is a function of their memories, instead of a function of Canadian political, judicial, economic, and social processes, attitudes, and actions. It disregards the fact that Canadian injustice to Indians is *real* and ongoing and it cannot be treated as a figment of Indian memory. It pervades all of Canada's social, political, economic, and legal systems, and it covers the entire time spectrum: past, present, and future. Amnesia will not guarantee Indians a just future. How can Indians have confidence in future justice before past injustices have been corrected? Retroactive atonement is the only trustworthy indicator that a sense of justice towards Indians has entered the Canadian conscience.

Moreover, in *Indian* cultures it is not possible to separate past from present from future. In their myths past, present, and future are unified. Traditions, customs, elders – all draw their significance from their linkage to the founding design of the Creator. *Indian* cultures place a heavy responsibility upon each generation to honour the design of the Creator, which is the essence of their *Indian-ness* and their

identity. The present generation of Indians would betray their ancestors and they would be negligent of their responsibility for the survival
of future generations if they did not insist on a redress of past injustices, because past injustices are also present and future injustices.

To his credit, Trudeau conceded to Indian leaders that the White
Paper 'may have been naive, maybe shortsighted or misguided,' and
he promised his government would not 'ram it down their throats.'[12]
Moreover, at the March 1983 First Ministers' Conference on Aboriginal Constitutional Matters, a politically resurrected Trudeau observed
in his opening statement, 'Clearly, our aboriginal peoples each occupied a special place in history. To my way of thinking this entitles
them to special recognition in the constitution and to their own place
in Canadian society, distinct from each other and distinct from other
groups.' At the 1984 First Ministers' Conference Trudeau's acceptance
of aboriginal rights was even more emphatic: 'A hundred and some
years have not changed the minds of aboriginal peoples ... They have
not assimilated ... They must be given a chance to run their own
affairs and self-governing institutions.' Trudeau had made a pilgrim-
age from 'denial' (amnesia) to a recognition of Indian history and
Canada's duty to Indians. But, at the same time that he orchestrated
the entrenchment of aboriginal rights in the constitution, Trudeau
also managed the entrenchment of 'The Charter of Rights and Freedoms.' As we will see later, Trudeau's Western-liberal legacy continues to beleaguer Indians in their quest for collective justice.

Parameters and instrumentalities of justice

The reality of Canadian injustice to Indians is undeniable, and the
tragic consequences of this injustice are indisputable. For each generation of Indians 'justice delayed is justice denied.' Assuming Canadians want justice for Indians, what is required? This is a complex
and important question for Indians as well as Canadians. In the absence of a coherent consensual Canadian–Indian conception of justice,
the Indians' quest for justice has necessarily taken the form of an ad
hoc, fragmented, and unfocused wrangle with the Canadian government on an array of fronts. The issues under contention (aboriginal
rights, land claims, treaty rights, the Indian Act, self-government,
economic development, trust obligations, funding arrangements, and
so on) are diffuse. In this fragmented approach to justice, the negotiation process is driven by immediate expedience on both sides, and
it is decided by power, with Indians coming off as losers.

One virtue in Trudeau's misguided and failed 1969 White Paper is that it attempted to formulate a coherent Canadian ideology of justice for Indians. It sought to delineate coherent principles and parameters of justice based on individual equality and human rights. To date it stands as the only attempt by a Canadian government to develop a coherent ideology of justice for Indians. Indian leaders, in contrast, do not lack an ideology of justice. They hold 'aboriginal rights' as their ideology of justice, and they have focused on entrenchment of aboriginal rights in the constitution as their primary instrument for achieving justice.

In this section I argue that, as an ideology for justice, 'aboriginal rights' contains cultural, historical, and moral inconsistencies, and that it does not provide functional principles and parameters of justice. I also argue that the Canadian constitution, because it is subordinate to the supremacy of federal and provincial legislatures, and subject to the interpretations of Canadian courts, represents an ineffectual instrument for achieving justice for Indians. I propose, instead, that functional principles and parameters of justice for Indians in Canada are best sought in the treaties, and that the most promising instrument for achieving justice is to be found in the guarantee of 'peoples' rights' contained in the great charters of the United Nations.

Such assertions require elaboration. I deal, first, with the problematic cultural, historical, moral, and political-legal aspects of the concept of aboriginal rights as a source and basis of functional principles and parameters of justice. Then, I take up the dubious effectiveness of the Constitution Act as a political and legal tool for achieving justice for Indians. I conclude the discussion with a proposal for an alternative ideology and instrument for achieving justice for Indians.

Aboriginal rights

Aboriginal rights provide the paramount ideology defining Indian leaders' political and judicial initiatives to achieve justice for their people. 'Aboriginal rights' refer to rights deemed to be held by the indigenous peoples of Canada by virtue of their ancestors' original and long-standing nationhood and their use and occupancy of the land. As popularly used by Indian leaders, the term 'aboriginal rights' means band/tribal sovereignty, proprietary title to their ancestral lands, and the practice of their traditional cultures.

The definitions and reasonings put forward by contemporary Indian leaders in support of their concept of aboriginal rights derive from pre-contact, pre–Royal Proclamation reality. The Royal Proclamation, although it may be interpreted as confirming aboriginal rights, explicitly asserts that sovereignty and land title are vested in the Crown. In other words, claims by Indian leaders that sovereignty and land title represent an aboriginal right are inconsistent with the acknowledgment of aboriginal rights as set out in the provisions of the Royal Proclamation. Thus, Indians must reach 'behind' the Royal Proclamation to make their case for Indian sovereignty and land title. While this can be readily justified as a principle of justice, it slights important cultural, historical, and moral realities.

The notion of aboriginal rights is not inherent in traditional *Indian* cultures; it emerged in response to colonial oppression of *Indian* cultural, political, social, and economic communities. In fact, the philosophy underlying aboriginal rights is a British invention that stands in sharp contradiction to traditional *Indian* cultures on several key points. For example, the claim to land title, which Indians assert as an aboriginal right, would have been alien to the Indian ancients and to the chiefs who marked the treaties. 'Title' implies ownership: if the Indian ancients held any concept of land title, they would have deemed such a title to be vested in the Creator, not the tribe or band. They acknowledged and claimed only a usufructuary right to the land to meet subsistence needs. It was the only concept of 'right in land' that they understood. That is why the doctrine of Crown sovereignty and proprietary title that is asserted in the Royal Proclamation was "invisible" to them. They believed the Creator put the land there for the benefit of all, so all living things might share in its fruits. They could not imagine that any group or person could claim exclusive ownership of the land. Thus, from a traditional *Indian* perspective, the injustice of the Royal Proclamation did not derive from the Crown's denial of proprietary land title to Indians but, rather, from the Crown's assertion of proprietary title in its own name. It was beyond their comprehension how the Crown could extinguish the Creator's title to the land. When the chiefs marked the treaties, they believed they were agreeing to share, in peace, and for the mutual benefit of all, a usufructuary right in land that belonged to the Creator.

Contemporary Indian leaders sometimes argue that they use the Euro-Western term 'land title' reluctantly, out of necessity, because the English language lacks the words needed to convey what they have in mind – that what they have in mind is the right to maintain a way of life in harmony with nature and with other people. But, wherever they operationalize the concept of title it is always in terms of demands for ownership of land or compensation for loss of ownership of land. That is, Indian leaders impose meanings on their concept of land title that are derived from the Euro-Western lexicon, not from traditional *Indian* philosophies and principles.

From a historical perspective, it seems, aboriginal rights exist to be lost. That is, they appear to have a transitional or 'time-limited' political, legal, and social legitimacy. In the world today, only a handful of small colonized societies still lay claim to aboriginal rights. Wherever else such rights have existed in the past their political and social legitimacy seem to have expired as the distinction between 'aboriginals' (that is, the original peoples) and 'indigenals' (that is, native by birth) has faded. Aboriginality is somewhat akin to the status of 'first born' in a family. Traditionally, in some cultures the first born, especially if male, was entitled to special status and pre-eminent claim to the family heritage. But, in the context of enlightened values, a special privilege such as primogeniture is no longer deemed a just, equitable, or acceptable practice. Except in the archaic world of royalty, 'first born' no longer retains legal status or special claims in modern enlightened societies. It holds only a symbolic and sentimental valence. The concept of aboriginality similarly has suffered diminished political, legal, and social relevance and legitimacy as a basis for special status and claims.

Do aboriginal rights have moral legitimacy? The answer depends upon how Indians define aboriginal rights. If they define aboriginal rights to mean that Indians are entitled, by virtue of biological ancestry and first habitation, to a pre-eminent claim to all of the land in Canada, while the immigrants and their descendants become tenants, indentured to pay perpetual rent to the descendants of the original 'landowners,' such a definition merely inverts all the elements of injustice to be found in the present treatment of Indians by Canadians. Moreover, it is inconsistent with the universal principle of justice that *no* group should arrogate to itself a pre-eminent claim to another group's only means of survival. Thus, it is doubtful that a moral justification exists for a definition of aboriginal rights such as is implied in the concept of 'non-extinguishment' at present championed by Indian leaders.[13] Nor is such a definition required for the survival and well-being of Indians as *Indians*.

Aboriginal rights are also a problematical concept in international politics and law. Indians root their claims to aboriginal rights in spiritual ground. They claim these rights are derived from the Creator. International law (like Canadian domestic law) is based on Euro-

Western standards which are biased in such a way as to deny rights derived from the Creator. Moreover, the concept of aboriginal rights is parochial and has little authenticity in the domestic laws of most nations of the world. Consequently, there is little in the way of international political consensus or accumulated legal structure and precedents in international law that Indians can refer to when they seek to defend aboriginal rights in international tribunals. Thus, Indians have virtually no protection in international politics and law against erosion of their aboriginal rights when Canadian governments use the instrumentalities of Canadian laws and jurisprudence to negate such rights.

To sum up, as an ideology of justice for Indians the concept of aboriginal rights manifests some important cultural, historical, moral, and political-legal flaws. It does not provide functional principles and parameters for defining justice for Indians.

The constitution

The instrument that Indian leaders believe offers the best hope for realizing their version of justice is the Constitution of Canada. Indian leaders believe that constitutional entrenchment of their version of aboriginal rights will create a warrant that each Indian band/tribe could exercise against the Canadian government in claiming their particular inherent right to sovereignty, land title, monetary reparations, and the preservation of their culture. They also believe that it would make these rights secure. Thus, when the Canadian government decided to patriate the constitution, Indian leaders saw an opportunity to rectify the historical omission of their aboriginal rights from Canada's founding charter. Consistent with this perspective, the entrenchment of aboriginal rights in the constitution was accorded the highest priority on the political agenda of Indians in Canada. Sparing no resources or effort, Indian leaders successfully mobilized a pan-Indian movement and Canadian public support for constitutional entrenchment of aboriginal rights. But, as the political and legal dust begins to settle, it is becoming evident that constitutional entrenchment of aboriginal rights is not translating into justice for Indians.

While entrenchment may have given a small measure of legal and political legitimacy to aboriginal rights, a strong case can be made that entrenchment has placed aboriginal rights in legal and political quicksand. As a consequence of entrenchment, Indians have essentially forfeited their prerogative to define these rights. Because entrenched aboriginal rights can be constitutionally defined only by amendment, if and when there is a constitutional amendment that defines aboriginal rights it will say what the eleven governments of Canada want it to say. If there is no constitutional amendment, then the Canadian courts will define aboriginal rights. Either way, whether the definition is made by a political process or by a judicial process, Indians will be spectators (euphemistically termed 'consultants'), not decision makers or arbitrators.

At present, aboriginal rights are twisting impotently in the political/ constitutional winds, meanwhile they are being incrementally defined by the courts. Ironically, from the Indians' perspective, the present impotent political/constitutional state may be the best fate for aboriginal rights. It is far preferable that they sit in the constitution as an ''empty promise' than that the ten provincial governments impose their definition on those rights. This truth was well illustrated by the 'compromise solution' proposed by the Canadian government at the 1985 and 1987 First Ministers' conferences on aboriginal issues. In a desperate and bizarre effort to break the unbridgeable impasse between Indian demands that aboriginal rights to self-government be entrenched as an *inherent* right, and the adamant refusal by a number of provinces to entrench any reference at all to self-government as an aboriginal right, the prime minister proposed the simultaneous entrenchment of the Indians' right to self-government and the provincial governments' right (or paramountcy) to define what authority would be delegated to Indian self-governments.

Until Indians have a firm guarantee that Canada's eleven governments are ready to adopt a constitutional amendment that would give the Indians' meaning to aboriginal rights, they are well advised to declare a moratorium on any constitutional amendments to define their rights. A guarantee for the Indians' version of aboriginal rights is unlikely to materialize in the near or distant future. For Indians to achieve their definition of aboriginal rights through the constitutional approach, seven of the ten provincial governments representing more than 50 per cent of the Canadian population would have to set aside more than a century of political and legal precedents and practices that deny Indian sovereignty and land title. Canada's eleven governments have given no indication that they are prepared to remodel Canada's 'constitutional house' to make jurisdictional room for a 'third order' of sovereign government in the Canadian federation. At four FMCs dealing with constitutional Indian matters, the message was clear and consistent: the constitutional process will not lead to amendments that guarantee the Indians' version of aboriginal rights.

Already the preponderance of evidence suggests that entrenchment of aboriginal rights has enfeebled Indian claims to true self-government. Entrenchment implies that future Indian governments must conform to all constitutional jurisdictions, mandates, assumptions, and structures, and that they are limited to the exercise of only such powers as are jointly delegated by the federal and provincial governments. As we will see in the next chapter, the 'Canada Round' of constitutional reform defines Indian self-government in terms of 'contingent,' not 'sovereign,' rights. Moreover, by achieving entrenchment, Indians forfeited their historic exclusive relationship with the federal government. Negotiations for Indian self-government have moved out of a bilateral forum (i.e., Indians vis-à-vis the Canadian government) into a multilateral forum which includes ten provincial governments.

The constitution, while it influences the political process, is, in fact, written for litigation. At the end of the day, when the political process cannot resolve constitutional disputes, the courts take over. Considering past judicial interpretations of the Royal Proclamation, the British North America Act, and the treaties, all of which Indian leaders cite as already recognizing and affirming their aboriginal rights, it is perplexing why Indian leaders believe that constitutional entrenchment of their rights will improve Indian chances for justice. Even if Indians and the Canadian government could achieve agreement on the wording of a constitutional amendment defining aboriginal rights, past experience with Canadian judicial interpretations of their rights should teach Indians that such an amendment will not guarantee their version of these rights. Judicial interpretations have consistently used any vague wording in political and legal documents to serve the interests of the dominant group, not Indians. The wording, meaning, and intent can never by so precisely and clearly stated that future political and judicial interpretations will not be loaded in favour of Canadian interests over Indian interests. Sometimes vague wording is deliberately inserted in constitutional texts to create a politically and judicially exploitable ambiguity. The term 'existing,' which appears before 'aboriginal rights' in section 35 (1), is an example of such 'forked tongue' artistry. It was inserted at the sometimes petulant and sometimes strident insistence of the Honourable Peter Lougheed, then premier of Alberta. It is a politically and judicially exploitable ambiguity, a 'weasel word,' which places the onus on Indians to prove to the court that any aboriginal right they may claim continues to exist – that it hasn't already been extinguished by the Crown.

Indians would have greatly preferred a constitutional guarantee of their *inherent* aboriginal rights instead of their *existing* aboriginal rights, just as, now, they seek constitutional entrenchment of their *inherent* right to self-government, not their existing right. But, one must wonder, does it really matter how an empty promise is worded? Ultimately, the Canadian politicians and courts, like the Queen of Hearts in *Alice in Wonderland*, will decide what all of the words mean.

Anyone who imagines that Canadian politicians and courts will legitimate the Indians' version of aboriginal rights is guilty of 'vulgar optimism.' All of the laws ever passed by Parliament were designed to serve Canadian interest, not Indian interests. This accumulated legal structure serves as an edifice of judicial bias contrary to Indian interests, and stands as a bastion to protect Canadian interests, not Indian interests. When all the laws are set up to advance Canadian interests, then the decisions of judges, who unquestioningly follow these laws, will be biased against Indians interests whenever these come into conflict with Canadian interests, even when judges are not racially prejudiced.

Some Indian leaders, swayed by fantasy (not by past judicial precedents), are inclined to take a chance in the courts on obtaining legitimation for their version of aboriginal rights. They are beguiled by rare instances where a judge has decided a case on the basis of a unique point of law that seems adverse to the accumulated legal structure and precedents. Naïvely, they imagine they have found such a 'point of law,' which will discredit the legal structure and precedents and persuade a judge to legitimate the Indians' version of aboriginal rights. But, the prospects are better for finding the Holy Grail in one's lunch pail than that Indians will obtain such a judicial decision from the Supreme Court of Canada. While there may be an occasional aberrant judge at the lower-court level who might allow his or her personal sense of moral justice to override precedent, when the case comes to the higher-court level, seasoned and career-minded judges will never allow unique points of law or any personal sense of moral justice to supersede accumulated legal structures and precedents unless there is a compelling 'national interest' to do so. Legitimation of the Indians' conception of aboriginal rights does not now, and is unlikely in the future, to meet this judicial standard.

Given this reality, the constitution can never serve as an effective instrument for achieving justice through litigation for Indians. Proof for this assertion can be found in the Supreme Court's recent judgment in the case of *The Queen* v *Sparrow* (3 May 1990).[14] The *Sparrow* case involved a Musqueem band member (Ronald Edward Sparrow) who was charged in 1984 for fishing in Canoe Passage with a drift net longer than permitted under the Fisheries Act. At issue in *Sparrow* was the authority of the government to regulate the maximum length of drift nets used by Musqueem band members. Sparrow asserted that such a regulation infringed upon his aboriginal rights pursuant to section 35 (1) of the Constitution Act, 1982, which recognized and affirmed his existing aboriginal rights. Because Sparrow's appeal was based on the Constitution Act, 1982, it presented the Supreme Court (in its interpretation of aboriginal rights) with a unique side door to escape centuries-old, unenlightened legal structures and precedents established by an unenlightened colonial judiciary, based on the villainous, imperialistic, and archaic assumptions of 'divine right,' 'first discovery,' and 'might makes right' on which the Royal Proclamation of 1763 is premised.

When the *Sparrow* decision was published, it was immediately hailed by Indian leaders and their legal advisers as a progressive and landmark decision. George Erasmus, then national chief of the Assembly of First Nations, described it as 'an extremely major victory.'[15] Why Indian leaders and their legal advisers saw reason to celebrate *Sparrow* as a victory is puzzling to say the least. In *Sparrow*, the Supreme Court of Canada explicitly affirmed all of the most villainous, imperialistic, and archaic assumptions of the Royal Proclamation, that is, the assumptions of Crown sovereignty over Indian peoples and Crown title to Indian lands. The High Court also affirmed that aboriginal title is merely a usufructuary and possessory interest in their ancestral lands, which the Crown has the prerogative to extinguish 'at its pleasure.' Instead of using the opening that was provided by section 35 (1) to start building a new legal structure and precedent based on contemporary enlightenment values, Canada's Chief Justices chose to affirm past judicial interpretations and archaic assumptions from the colonial era. They reached, not *behind* the Royal Proclamation, but *into* the Royal Proclamation and its regressive colonial standards for their principles of justice.

In short, there is absolutely no evidence in *Sparrow* of the beginning of an evolutionary process of judicial restructuring of the corrupt colonial code regarding aboriginal rights. Instead, the Chief Justices used the *Sparrow* case to firmly shut and lock all doors and windows of hope that section 35 (1) will ever be used by the Canadian judiciary to start to lay the foundation for a new legal structure that would begin to correct centuries of colonial injustice. And, in so doing, the *Sparrow* decision undermines any meaningful political leverage that Indians may have hoped to derive from constitutional entrenchment of aboriginal rights. At best it provides Indians with some legal devices to inconvenience government designs. This may translate into some modest political leverage.

In *Sparrow*, the Supreme Court made a crucial differentiation between the *existence* of aboriginal rights and the *exercise* of those rights. It confirmed the *existence* of aboriginal rights by holding that, pursuant to section 35 (1), such rights have an abstract, permanent quality, and that *unextinguished* aboriginal rights continue to exist in their 'pristine state,' that is, as they existed prior to the Royal Proclamation, the Indian Act, or any other executive order or legislative provision. At first glance, it appears as if the Court had reached behind the Royal Proclamation for a principle of justice in defining aboriginal rights. Perhaps this perception excited Indian leaders and their legal advisers and occasioned the unwarranted celebrations. But, unfortunately for Indians, the Court, in the same breath, utterly trivialized the existence of these abstract, permanent, pristine 'unextinguished rights' by subordinating the *exercise* of these rights to government legislation and by defining them in the narrowest of terms.

Specifically, the Court characterized existing or unextinguished aboriginal rights in terms of *tribe-specific* hunting, fishing, and gathering rights, as these were exercised by their ancestors in 1763, for food, ceremony, and social purposes (but, even for these restricted purposes, their rights are subject to conservation measures and do not include commercial purposes). In other words, the Court did not construct a universal, abstract, permanent, and pristine aboriginal right that could be cited by Indians as a legal basis for asserting their rights and claims. Rather, it established a tribe-by-tribe, case-by-case approach for the determination of the existence of such rights. By so doing, the Chief Justices, consistent with past judicial practice, circumscribed any open-ended implications that their lower-court colleagues might infer from their analysis. Considering that tribal hunting, fishing, and gathering pursuits have already diminished in practical importance to a very small scale, and will inevitably continue to diminish as they are supplanted by social welfare, by government-subsidized programs, and by employment, *Sparrow* represents an extremely guarded judicial rendering of aboriginal rights.

Sparrow yields a small judicial point to Indians by protecting aboriginal rights against extinguishment by *regulations* enacted to limit the *exercise* of aboriginal rights such as hunting, fishing, and gathering. Stated in positive terms, the Court held that an existing aboriginal right can be extinguished only if the government does so with a 'clear and plainly stated intent.' In other words, an aboriginal right continues to exist in its abstract, permanent, and pristine state until the government explicitly extinguishes it. But, again without stopping to take a breath, the Honourable Justices go on to trivialize this constitutional protection by affirming that the government has the absolute power to enact regulations that restrict and even completely deny the *exercise* of an existing aboriginal right. On a practical level, if offers small comfort to Indians that the Supreme Court has protected the *existence* of their abstract, permanent, and pristine aboriginal rights from extinguishment by government regulation when, concurrently, it asserts that the government has the absolute legislative power to restrict or deny the *exercise* of those rights by regulation.

Sparrow offers another small concession by requiring the government to *justify* any regulation that infringes or denies the exercise of aboriginal rights. But the test for justification is not referenced to any violation of the existing (i.e., unextinguished) abstract, permanent, pristine, aboriginal rights the Court has acknowledged. Rather, it is referenced to the *consequences* that such infringement or denial of the exercise of an aboriginal right by regulation imposes on Indians: that is, does it constitute an unreasonable intrusion or impose an undue hardship on the affected Indians? This line of reasoning is analogous to saying that if a thief steals an heirloom from you, the test of a violation will not be referenced to the law against theft, but will be based on whether the theft was an unreasonable intrusion upon you, or imposed an undue hardship on you. Adding insult to injury, the Court has placed the legal onus on Indians to prove the existence of the particular aboriginal right being claimed. In order to establish an aboriginal right, the Court requires proof of traditional occupancy and use of the lands prior to colonization. The standard of proof demanded by the Court may be impossible to satisfy because there are no living witnesses to the events.

The formidable judicial bias and legal impediments that confront Indians who seek to establish aboriginal title and rights to ancestral lands was revealed in the case of *Delgamuuleu* v *The Queen* (1991),[16] heard by Chief Justice Allan McEachern of the BC Supreme Court. In this case the Gitskan and Wet'suwet'en Indian nations were laying claim to some 57,000 square kilometres of ancestral living, hunting, and fishing territories. Justice McEachern dismissed the Indians' oral history and masses of other evidence of tribal occupation, use, and jurisdiction on grounds that, while these met the standards of 'aboriginal laws,' they did not meet the standards of the 'white man's law.' But, even if Indians are successful in establishing aboriginal title and rights to their ancestral lands, they must still prove that the aboriginal rights they claim have, in fact, been infringed upon or denied. And, finally, they must prove that the regulation of that right constitutes an unreasonable intrusion or undue hardship on them.

Continuing the analogy of the 'thief,' the Court's decision is comparable to requiring you to prove (at your expense): first, that the stolen heirloom belongs to you; second, that the thief stole it from you; and, third, that the theft was unreasonable or imposed an undue hardship on you. Only after the Indians concerned have established the existence of their aboriginal rights and have proven that these rights have been infringed upon or denied, and that the intrusion was unreasonable or caused them undue hardship, does the onus shift to the government (or the thief) to justify the infringement/denial (or the theft). And, if the government (or the thief) fails to justify the infringement/denial (or the theft), there is no punitive action or black mark against the perpetrator.

The test of justification of infringement/denial involves two steps. First, the government must establish a 'valid legislative objective' for interfering with the aboriginal right. Second, it must show the objective is being attained with minimum interference and in such a way as to uphold the 'honour of the Queen and the fiduciary duty of the Crown.' The standard also requires that Indians must be 'consulted' with respect to the legislative measures taken and, in a case of expropriation, fair compensation must be offered. The vagueness and ambiguity in the Supreme Court's standards of justification (e.g., 'valid objective,' 'minimum interference,' 'honour of the Queen,' 'fiduciary duty of the Crown') may not have been deliberate, but it leaves their meaning wide open to political and judicial interpretations that will subordinate Indian interests to those of the dominant group.

Sparrow provides another small gain to Indians by emphasizing the Canadian government's obligation to reconcile its sovereign legislative powers over Indians with its historic constitutional fiduciary (i.e., trust) responsibility for Indians. But, it immediately qualifies this requirement by suggesting that when Indian interests come into conflict with Canadian interests the government can resolve the conflict in favour of Canadian interests. In other words, when the Canadian government, acting as trustee for Indians, finds Indian interests to be in conflict with Canadian interests, it is legally justified to sacrifice or subordinate Indian interests to the Canadian interest. Also, it is worth noting that the fiduciary relationship emphasized in *Sparrow* reinforces the historical relationship of Canadian paternalism over Indians, a relationship that is totally inconsistent with the Indian conception of their nationhood.

Arguably, by affirming that the Canadian government cannot legitimately extinguish aboriginal rights by regulation but only if it does so with a 'clear and plainly-stated intent,' the Court has introduced a procedure to discourage perfidy by the Canadian government in its dealings with Indian aboriginal rights. And, by requiring the government to have a 'valid legislative objective' before it can compromise existing aboriginal rights, the Court has tempered the Crown's supreme power to infringe upon or extinguish such rights on a whim. However, any other variances from previous Court rulings regarding Indian aboriginal rights are mainly cosmetic. For example, the Court has created the illusion of a progressive judgment by numerous platitudinous references to 'honour of the Queen'; by reiteration of clichés about 'trust relationship'; and by exhortations to lower-court colleagues to render 'generous, liberal interpretations,' to 'hold the Crown to a high standard of honourable dealing,' and to 'be sensitive to the aboriginal perspective.' But, these words have a remarkably gloomy ring to them when, in the same breath, the Chief Justices assert that only 'unextinguished' aboriginal rights at the time of the Constitution Act, 1982, are 'protected' by section 35 (1), and that 'extinguished' aboriginal rights cannot be revived, even if they were extinguished illegally. Apparently, the Court's concern for the 'honour of the Queen,' and for justice to Indians, were not retroactive: lower-court colleagues are not bidden to *rehabilitate* the 'honour of the Queen' by restoring aboriginal rights that had been wrongfully extinguished. They are asked only not to sully her honour in future. In this respect, the Court seems to have adopted Trudeau's infamous counsel to remedy past dishonour and injustice by amnesia.

In *Sparrow*, the Supreme Court unambiguously and mechanically subordinated aboriginal rights to the standards of Crown sovereignty, Crown title, parliamentary supremacy, the national interest, and even to considerations of cost to the federal treasury. In effect, the Chief Justices seem to have taken upon themselves to rescue Canadian politicians from the horns of a dilemma by proceeding to define the constitutional meaning of 'existing aboriginal rights.' In a series of decisions, the Court is incrementally defining the constitution's 'empty promise' of aboriginal rights, thus accomplishing what the politicians lacked the honesty and fortitude to do during four First Ministers' Conferences. Moreover, the Court has defined aboriginal rights in terms the First Ministers can applaud. In so doing, the Court cannot plead that 'precedent required us to do it'; the Court had other options, but if purposively interpreted the constitution so as to deny utterly the Indian version of aboriginal rights. Obviously, and unfortunately for Indians, the Chief Justices chose not to take the path of progressive jurisprudence; there is no new found sense of social justice in their interpretation of section 35 (1). They delivered a ruling that sanctimoniously calls for a kinder, gentler judiciary, but provides only a tiny glimmer of light to show lower-court colleagues the way.

The *Sparrow* decision was rooted in the Royal Proclamation of 1763, and it is worth reiterating at this point that the concept of aboriginal rights as it appears in the Royal Proclamation was not regarded by the framers of the proclamation as a legal-moral principle of justice. Aboriginal rights in the Royal Proclamation were framed by the Crown to avoid war with Indians, to discourage claims by other European nations, to facilitate colonization, and to avoid conflict over land on the frontier. But, today, aboriginal rights have become a legal, political, and economic liability without any redeeming value for Canada. The Supreme Court's ruling in the *Sparrow* case leaves no doubt that, under these circumstances, the Canadian judiciary are unwilling to use the Constitution Act, 1982, as an opportunity to transmute an eighteenth-century act of colonization into an enlightened twentieth-century judicial principle of moral justice and decolonization – especially not when 'political expedience' also describes the motive of the eleven Canadian governments when they entrenched aboriginal rights in the Constitution Act, 1982.

Canada is a stranger to principle. At every significant 'nation-building' event in its history it has opted for political expedience over principle. Aboriginal rights were not entrenched as a moral-legal principle of justice for Indians. Aboriginal rights were expediently entrenched in the Constitution Act, 1982, to facilitate patriation of the constitution, not to decolonize Indians. Because aboriginal rights were entrenched as a political expedient, the courts feel no obligation to treat those rights as more than a political expedient. In the spirit of 'what expedience can create, expedience can negate,' Parliament, its appointed judges, and the provincial legislatures have been acting consistently and concertedly to limit the moral-legal efficacy of the ideology of aboriginal rights as an instrument for achieving moral-legal justice for Indians. Canadian legislatures and the courts have, over the years, been moving expeditiously and systematically to establish legal structures and precedents that ultimately will negate these rights. The Supreme Court, in *Sparrow*, was unlikely to undo all of that past effort by validating the Indian version of their aboriginal rights.

The primacy of political expedience over principles of moral-legal justice when it comes to the interpretation of aboriginal rights was plain, also, when Sir Anthony Kershaw explained Great Britain's position on the occasion of the patriation of the constitution (November and December 1980). Sir Anthony opined that the Indians' aboriginal rights had fallen 'between the cracks' of the Royal Proclamation and the BNA Act. He argued that Britain's obligations to Indians under the Royal Proclamation ended with Canada's independence by Statute of Westminster, 1931. And, that Canada no longer has an obligation to honour the terms of the Royal Proclamation because it was never entrenched in the BNA acts of 1867–1930. Political expedients regularly fall between cracks, and Indians today can only stand by and observe as their constitutionally entrenched aboriginal rights disappear between the cracks of federal and provincial jurisdiction, and in the fog of judicial interpretation.

Contrary to constitutional mirages (e.g., the entrenchment of aboriginal rights and aboriginal self-government), or judicial feints (e.g., the Supreme Court stalemate on the Nishga claim), or occasional judicial tilts (e.g., recent court decisions protecting fishing and hunting rights of selected tribes) – mere 'teasers' that mislead Indians into thinking they may be getting closer to achieving their version of aboriginal rights – it is now abundantly clear that the governments and courts of Canada have no intention of rescinding constitutional, legislative, and judicial doctrines, precedents and practices that have been built up since 1763, which deny the inherent aboriginal rights to land title and to sovereignty claimed by Indian peoples.

To sum up, Indians believe they have strong cultural, historical, and moral arguments for their version of aboriginal rights, but, given contemporary political and legal realities, these rights are unlikely to achieve more than symbolic meaning. Aboriginal rights can be likened to a 'security blanket' from which the Canadian government and courts have historically been weaning Indians by gradually cutting down its dimensions. During a century of political and judicial trimming, the concept of aboriginal rights has been reduced to a small tattered remnant that Indians clutch tightly in their hands because it still yields psychological and emotional security and gratification. But, within the Canadian legislative, constitutional, and jurisprudential framework, parliamentary and judicial collaboration have already effectively trivialized aboriginal rights to the point where they are virtually meaningless. And, as documented in Chapter 2, the new round of constitutional reform promises no change in this historical trend. In the face of this hard reality, Indians need to re-evaluate the wisdom of clinging to a concept that carries so little legitimacy in domestic and international politics and law, and offers so little prospect for achieving their goal of justice – that is, their survival and well-being as *Indians*.

The treaties

Ideally, the search for reference points for a paradigm of justice for Indians ought to begin by looking behind the Royal Proclamation and its villainous doctrine of Crown sovereignty and Crown title. But, for the sake of survival, sometimes reality requires a compromise of important ideals. If we were to uncompromisingly deny the legitimacy of the Royal Proclamation, we would place Indian rights in a political and constitutional void. Such a void may be conducive to some great fantasies about what might be, but it is not a promising base for achieving the survival and well-being of Indians as *Indians*. Given the 'real politic' of the nation in which they live, a constitutional void poses a significant threat to the survival and well-being of Indians as *Indians*, because it is the eleven Canadian governments, not the Indians, that will decide how such a void will be filled. The Royal Proclamation and the treaties were framed at a time when Indians still had consequential power, and they contain some accommodations of Indian rights, interests, needs, and aspirations. In the following discussion, therefore, I take the treaties as the most promising startingpoint for establishing parameters of justice for Indians, even though the treaties have their roots in the villainous doctrine of the Royal Proclamation.

Although Indians participated in the treaty-making process under severe constraints and duress (e.g., the Crown had already asserted its sovereignty and title in the lands that were subject to treaty negotiation and the Crown had the military might to back up its claim), none the less, the treaties represent a negotiated agreement. And the chiefs who marked the treaties were not naïve, they did not mark the treaties on the spur of the moment; they were not participating in a quick swap of ancestral lands for baubles. They had given the implications of treaty making much careful thought and discussion. They had options other than to mark the treaties. They knew the newcomers needed to eat. They considered uniting their forces and denying the colonizers access to the food supply. But, they also understood that this would lead to a war they probably could not win. It would merely delay the inevitable at a great cost of lives and, in the end, their descendants would have been a vanquished and landless people.

Moreover, living, as they did, at the level of subsistence, and threatened periodically by scarcity and starvation, they could see some benefit in sharing access to their ancestral lands with people who knew how to produce a more dependable supply of food than they could. In exchange for consenting to let the newcomers share their traditional hunting, fishing, and gathering territories, the chiefs sought firm guarantees from the Crown for their survival and well-being as *Indians* 'for as long as the sun shines, the grass grows, the rivers flow.' This purpose – the survival and well-being of *Indians* for all time – defines the chiefs' spirit and intent when they negotiated and marked the treaties.

The chiefs who negotiated the treaties were not oblivious to potential negative impacts of European settlement upon their traditional means of subsistence. Therefore, they strained to peer over the horizon of their time to see what their future needs for survival and well-being as *Indians* would be in the emerging world. They foresaw that the loss of an essential part of their traditional food supply would necessitate supplementary means of subsistence, and that they would need aid in making this transition. Accordingly, they negotiated treaty articles for the provision of livestock, agricultural tools and skills, health care, education, and economic assistance that would enable them to supplement their declining traditional means of subsistence with new means. They were encouraged in this line of thought by the representatives of the Crown during treaty negotiations. For instance, when David Laird was negotiating Treaty 7 with the Blackfoot Nation, he told the participating chiefs: 'In a very few years, the buffalo will probably be all destroyed, and for this reason the Queen wishes to help you to live in the future in some other way. She wishes you to allow her white children to come and live on your land and raise cattle, and should you agree to this, she will assist you to raise cattle and grain, and thus give you the means of living when the buffalo are no more.'[17]

But, to apprehend the treaties in terms of the sum of the specific provisions is to miss entirely the chiefs' spirit and intent when they negotiated the treaties. The chiefs who marked the treaties profoundly believed themselves to be entrusted by the Creator with the protection of their tribal cultures – the Creator's blueprint for their survival and well-being. When they participated in the treaty-making process they did so from a conviction that they were honouring this sacred trust. In their minds, the treaty was an instrument for fulfilling this sacred obligation to the Creator, to their ancestors, and to generations yet to come. Another implicit understanding of the chiefs who marked the treaties was that they were autonomous peoples, and that the treaties affirmed the continuity of their autonomy. They marked the treaties in the spirit of coexistence, mutual obligation, sharing, and benefit, and as an agreement between themselves and the newcomers not to interfere with each other's way of life. They assumed the treaties would enshrine this intent and spirit as a permanent and living legacy. Thus, as a frame of reference for justice, the treaties provide a paradigm of high idealism.

For a proper appreciation of the treaty-making process, it is essential to understand that each side drew on their own universe of meanings and values, but they knew little about the other side's 'universe.' Subsequently, as a result, deep and enduring misunderstandings arose between the two sides, most particularly in regard to land tenure and political autonomy. Indians had a spiritual attachment to the land, which grew out of their total and immediate dependence upon it for survival. They considered the land and its fruits to be a sacred trust from the Creator for the welfare of all living things, present and future. Thus, in their universe of meanings and values, no individual or group could have more than a usufructuary interest in the land. This interest coexisted with the interest of all other life forms. That is, all had the right to take from the land what was needed for survival. Because all tribes claimed this right, and sometimes with reference to harvesting the same territories, it occasioned conflicts between tribes, particularly in times of food scarcity. But, these conflicts were not over *ownership* of land. In the Indian universe of meanings and values, if land had an 'owner,' it could be only the Creator.

Consistent with the meanings and values of European culture, the representatives of the Crown viewed the land as transferable and alienable *property* – in effect, as real estate. They considered the treaties to be devices for acquiring real estate from the Indians without going to war. They entered the treaty-making process with the spirit and intent of achieving an atmosphere of peace and stability that would facilitate settlement, real-estate speculation, and commerce with the objective of making huge fortunes in the new land. Consistent with this view, the Crown's representatives were negotiating lucrative 'real-estate deals' with Indians for huge tracts of land which it then opened up for settlement and commercial exploitation. In short, each side entered the treaty-making process with a different 'spirit and intent.'

How well have the respective 'spirits and intents' been fulfilled? In retrospect, it is very clear that the Crown's side has realized not only everything they bargained for, but much more then they could have imagined in their greediest fantasies. The Indians' side, however, has lost everything they bargained for. They have lost the usufruct of their ancestral lands, their traditional self-sufficiency, their culture, and their autonomy. In effect, the treaties have functioned as instruments for Indian political subordination, economic dependence, social and cultural disintegration, and spiritual demoralization – the antithesis of the chiefs' spirit and intent.

Why did this happen? Did the chiefs who marked the treaties simply make a bad deal? This is a reasonable conclusion if we view the treaties as an exchange of land for 'so many blankets, balls of twine and rounds of ammunition.' If the treaties are interpreted as real-estate deals, then the Indians were fleeced by sharp traders. But, such an assessment unfairly ignores the chiefs' universe of meaning and the 'spirit and intent' with which they marked the treaties. They were not making a real-estate transaction. They were negotiating a relationship of coexistence, mutual obligation, sharing, and benefit. With their backs against the wall, they were negotiating terms for the future survival and well-being of their people as *Indians* for all time to come. They considered the treaties as sacred and living covenants that would evolve so as to continue to fulfil this basic spirit and intent.

Indians have fared badly not because the chiefs who marked the treaties were less perspicacious or far-sighted than the Crown's representatives, but because the Crown and successive Canadian governments have held the power, through legislation, judicial interpretation, and administrative action, to shape, reshape, interpret and reinterpret the treaties to serve the Canadian interest. Canadian governments have dealt with the treaties as flexible legal documents to serve Canadian interest at the expense of Indian interests. They have used their powers to reduce Indians to the status of dependents and to extinguish aboriginal title to most Indian lands. The signatory chiefs did not make a bad deal; rather, their version of the 'spirit and intent' of the treaties – the survival and well-being of Indians as *Indians* – has been totally betrayed by the Crown and successive Canadian governments. Indians, from the beginning, were troubled about whether the Crown could be trusted to fulfil its treaty promises, but they could only hope for the best.

What parameters of justice for Indians can be teased out of the treaties? After all, the treaties are founded on the Royal Proclamation's assertion of Crown sovereignty, Crown title, and the Crown's prerogative to extinguish aboriginal title at its own pleasure. Moreover, as was the case with the Royal Proclamation, Indians had no say in establishing the basic premises of the treaties. In this discussion I develop the thesis that the parameters of justice for Indians must be derived from the spirit and intent held by the chiefs as they negotiated and marked the treaties. To reiterate, the paramount spirit and intent that animated the chiefs who marked the treaties was the survival and well-being of Indians as *Indians* for all time to come. It is this spirit and intent that must define the parameters of justice for Indians in Canada. If any generation of Indian leaders betrays this spirit and intent, they betray not only their ancestors but all future generations as well. If contemporary Indian leaders do not frame their demands for justice holding true to this spirit and intent, then the 'solutions' they achieve will compound the betrayals that have already occurred. In their quest for justice, Indian leaders must always keep this thought in the forefront of their minds.

Indians, understandably and appropriately, express a strong conviction that Canada 'owes' them a great deal. But, contemporary Indian leaders who seek justice through reparations for the taking of their ancestors' lands must take great care how they define what is owed to their people. Increasingly, Indian leaders, proceeding from an acculturated perspective, are subscribing to the Crown's 'spirit and intent.' That is, they define and calculate their treaty heritage in terms of property values for land taken from their ancestors. In effect, they are conducting their negotiations for land claims within the framework of retroactive, belated or updated settlements for the fleecing of their ancestors in large real-estate transactions.

Negotiations of land-claims settlements based on some concept of market values constitute not only a betrayal of the spirit and intent of the chiefs who marked the treaties, but also a sell-out of the birth-right of future generations of Indians. Today's land claim settlements based on real estate plus cash are arguably not in the best interest of future generations of Indians. However unwelcome it is from the Indian point of view, Canadians have made and continue to make a tremendous investment of labour and capital in the development of the land. This investment has already greatly enhanced the 'market value' of the land. As the Canadian economy grows, the 'value added' component of Indian ancestral lands will undoubtedly continue to appreciate. Consequently, future generations of Indians may well judge today's real estate plus cash claims settlements to be a 'give-away' of their ancestral inheritance on the scale of the apocryphal 'Manhattan Island deal.' It also raises a moral question: Why should *this* generation of Indians receive special consideration in the redress of past wrongs at the expense of future generations? Settlements that diminish the heritage of future generations and thereby diminish their prospects of surviving as *Indians* are not in harmony with the spirit and intent of the chiefs who negotiated the treaties. If contemporary Indian leaders want to honour the spirit and intent of the chiefs who marked the treaties, they must negotiate their land claims settlements with the purpose of securing the survival and well-being of future generations of *Indians*.

Some Indian leaders, in recognition of the fact that past wrongs also affect future generations of Indians, are advocating that part of the reparation settlement must include provision for payment of a perpetual annuity. They propose that the annuity can be justified as an annual rent payable by Canadians for the use of what was, historically, Indian land. However, this solution also betrays the spirit and intent of their forefathers. Traditionally, self-sufficiency in Indian communities came from a fully employed work force. Custom required that every able-bodied member work and contribute to the survival and welfare of the community. Consistent with their universe of values and meanings, their forefathers, who negotiated the treaties, intended that their people should have the opportunity to survive as *Indians* by providing for their own needs, not by depending on a perpetual annuity.

Moreover, experience teaches that unearned income encourages habits of sloth and dependence rather than self-sufficiency. Unearned income encourages idleness, and the idleness of unemployment is corrosive to the self-concept, the morale, and the soul. In almost all societies the concept of justice holds that everyone should have the opportunity to work, has a responsibility to work, and is entitled to a decent standard of living for his or her work. The concept of an 'annuity in perpetuity' is contrary to Indian traditions, and it is alien to the prevailing standards of justice in most of the world's societies.

Another peril to the original *Indian* spirit and intent of the treaties lies in the growing tendency by Indian leaders, at the behest of the Canadian government, to regard the treaties as domestic legal documents. In the past decade, Indians have placed a heavy emphasis on establishing a domestic legal basis for their treaty rights, through constitutional entrenchment and court rulings. In their approach to the federal government for programs, services, and grants, Indian leaders frequently emphasize the government's 'legal' obligation to provide these benefits under the treaties. In part, this 'legal' emphasis derives from their heavy and increasing reliance upon the advice of legal consultants in asserting their treaty-related rights and claims. But, Indian leaders should consider carefully where this course will take them. Why is the federal government encouraging them to take this path by underwriting the costs of preparing their legal claims? The federal government is well aware that, as domestic legal documents, the treaties are fragile and extremely vulnerable to a variety of political and judicial tactics.

As domestic legal documents the treaties are vulnerable to constant legislative paring, as the government passes statutes to restrict treaty rights related to traditional hunting, fishing, and gathering modes of subsistence (e.g., the Migratory Birds Convention Act, the Fisheries Act). As domestic legal documents, the treaties are also vulnerable to minimalist interpretations that trivialize government obligations to Indians. For example, the government insists that its legal obligations are limited to a literal reading of the specific provisions (i.e., a certain number of blankets, balls of twine, and rounds of ammunition). Moreover, the federal government has repeatedly declared that most of the benefits it currently provides to Indians are not provided as a legal treaty obligation, but as part of its normal constitutional mandate to meet the basic needs of all citizens of Canada – in other words, the benefits are provided under the rubric of 'humanitarian aid.'

The 1969 White Paper, in the section on Indian treaties and claims, stressed the minimal nature of the Canadian government's 'legal' obligations to Indians. And, when the government officially repudiated the White Paper in 1971, the minister of Indian Affairs (Jean Chrétien) was careful to emphasize the government's intent to fulfil its 'lawful' obligations to Indians. More recently this phrase resurfaced in the Nielsen task force report. The task force recommended that the government reduce its fiscal obligations to Indians to 'strictly legal' requirements. These should sound as foreboding echoes in the ears of Indians leaders.

When Indians assent to regard their treaty rights as domestic legal matters, and to pursue them in the Canadian courts, it is tantamount to engaging in a war where the enemy establishes the rules of battle, determines which weapons and strategies are permissible, occupies all of the high ground and every position of ambush, acts as 'score-keeper,' and, when the skirmish ends, declares who won and who lost. For example, in Canadian courts, it is irrelevant that Indians have never acceded to the Crown's claim of title to their ancestral lands. What is relevant to Canadian judges is that the Royal Procla-mation declared Crown title in the land; that the BNA Act confirms that title; that the Canadian government in its policies and practices has always upheld it; and that judicial precedents affirm it.

The chiefs who marked the treaties had no conception of the treaties as domestic legal documents. Their understanding of the treaties grew out of their culture, experience, and circumstances. They could not anticipate all of the future needs of their people any more than we, today, are able to anticipate the future needs of our descendants. To the extent that the future needs of their people were apparent to them, the chiefs insisted on some specific provisions in the treaties to meet these needs. But, for the chiefs, the treaties represented much more than any legal rendering of the listed provisions. Even if the courts were to accept the Indians' interpretation of the specific treaty articles (e.g., if the Court were to rule that a 'medicine chest' means com-prehensive health care, and so on) it would represent a distortion of the chiefs' spirit and intent. In the chiefs' ordering of values the par-amount concern was not expressed in the listed benefits; the para-mount concern was the survival and well-being of their people and their descendants as *Indians*. For them, the treaties represented a 'living' covenant that guaranteed the survival and well-being of their people as *Indians*, for all time. For them the articles, which require the Crown to provide a certain number of blankets, balls of twine, rounds of ammunition, and so on, merely symbolized the spirit and intent of a 'living' covenant of coexistence, mutual obligation, sharing, and benefit. Legalizing the specific provisions of the treaties betrays the chiefs' spirit and intent because it denies the paramount principle of justice contained in the treaties – the survival and well-being of

Indians as *Indians* – that the chiefs in their wisdom insisted upon when they negotiated the treaties.

Peoples' rights

Colonized aboriginal peoples such as Indians in Canada were by-passed by the 'wave' of third-world liberation from colonialism following the Second World War. Now, there is a new wave of liberation building worldwide. This time the energy is coming from ethnically defined 'peoples' who, not unlike Indians in Canada, are trapped against their will within the borders of larger nation-states. The world is seething with such 'peoples,' who are determined to achieve liberation. The USSR and Yugoslavia already have been torn apart by this wave of liberation. And, the states – Canada among them – being confronted by 'peoples' within their borders who are seeking political self-determination are many, and increasing.

The momentum of this 'wave' of liberation already represents a powerful and ominous threat to world peace that demands a high priority on the agenda of the United Nations. Indians in Canada have an opportunity to take advantage of this mounting wave of liberation. But they must position themselves to catch the emerging wave; otherwise, it will wash over them and they will be left floundering in its wake. My premise here is that, if Indians want to catch the emerging wave of liberation, they must adopt as their instrument the article on 'peoples' rights' inscribed in the U.N. Charter of Rights. Not only does the concept of 'peoples' rights' inscribed in the U.N. charters hold a recognized status in international law but, as we will see, it also has empirical authenticity in the historical, political, and legal relationship of Indians and Canadians.

The concept of 'peoples' rights' that is affirmed in the U.N. charter Article 55 has the force of a treaty. Both of the covenants that partially comprise the International Bill of Rights – the International Covenant on Civil and Political Rights and the International Covenant on Economic, Social and Cultural Rights – provide for the right of all 'peoples' to self-determination. The latter covenant states in article 1, part 1:

1 All peoples have the right of self-determination. By virtue of that right they freely determine their political status and freely pursue their economic, social and cultural development.
2 All peoples may, for their own ends, freely dispose of their natural

wealth and resources without prejudice to any obligations arising out of international economic co-operation, based upon the principle of mutual benefit, and international law. In no case may a people be deprived of its own means of subsistence.

3 The States Parties to the present Covenant, including those having responsibility for the administration of Non–Self-Governing and Trust Territories, shall promote the realization of the right of self-determination, and shall respect that right, in conformity with the provision of the Charter of the United Nations.

In the same vein, the Helsinki Accord[18] stipulates that participating states must respect the rights of 'peoples' to self-determination. It declares, in part: 'All people always have rights, in full freedom, to determine when and as they wish, their internal political status, without external interference, and to pursue as they wish, their political, economic, social and cultural development.' Moreover, the United Nations has evidenced a particular concern about *indigenous* peoples. Acknowledgment of indigenous peoples' rights appears repeatedly and in various contexts in U.N.-sponsored resolutions, declarations, and proceedings.[19] In 1981, the U.N. Working Group on Indigenous Populations was established, and it is currently drafting a universal declaration of indigenous rights.

As a member of the United Nations and a signatory nation of the International Covenant on Human Rights, Canada is obliged to 'fulfil in good faith' all of its terms, including the principle in article 1 of the covenant that 'all peoples have the right of self-determination [and to] freely determine their political status.' These are rights not of *individuals*, but of *peoples*, whether or not such peoples are recognized as states.

Already, the Canadian government has been called to account in regard to its position on Indian 'peoples' rights.' The secretary general of the United Nations requested Canada's comments on a communication to the Human Rights Committee submitted by the Grand Council of the Micmac tribal society, seeking the right to self-determination. In its response, dated 30 January 1986, the Canadian government submitted that the Micmacs' right to self-determination was inapplicable on four substantive grounds: First, it would harm the national unity and territorial integrity of Canada. Second, under article 1 of the U.N. covenant, the right of self-determination applies to 'peoples.' The Canadian government holds that the Micmacs, as citizens of Canada, living in the midst of other citizens in a democratic state, do not qualify as 'peoples' within the meaning of article 1. Third, it asserted that the Micmacs have never been recognized as an independent state and, because the treaties with the Micmacs remain in force under domestic law, it is incorrect to infer that existence of the treaties confirms the Micmacs' existence as a national entity. Finally, the Canadian government points out that because the Canadian constitution refers to the 'aboriginal peoples of Canada,' Indians are a *domestic* circumstance and not participants in an *international* relationship.

The implications in the first point of the Canadian government's submission – that Indian demands for self-determination threaten the integrity of the Canadian nation – is, of course, patently perverse. Indian leaders have, on a number of occasions, expressed a willingness to forfeit all rights to separation and secession from the Canadian state and to evolve their self-determination within the framework of Canadian federalism. Indian leaders have said repeatedly that they seek self-determination as a 'third order' of government, akin to provincial status, within the framework of the Canadian federation.[20] The Canadian government has never petitioned the U.N. to deny the rights of the provinces on the grounds that their constitutional powers threaten the integrity of the Canadian nation. If the Canadian government genuinely fears that a 'third order' Indian government would threaten its integrity, then, surely, such a fear is what an elephant feels towards a mouse. None the less, the Canadian government's guileful or phobic allusion to an imperilled national integrity has a considerable impact on how other U.N. member nations view Indian demands, because many of them likewise are confronted with separatist nationalist demands by ethnic/racial minorities within their own borders, and are thus averse to establishing precedents that could come back to haunt them. Moreover, the right to self-determination, while it is described in the U.N. covenant as subsuming a people's right to cultural preservation, apparently does not include the right to political independence if it has negative implications for the integrity of the state.

In points 2 through 4 of its submission, the Canadian government cunningly seeks to exploit the debilitating vagueness that plagues the phrase 'all peoples have the right to self-determination.' Although it is arguable that the idea of 'peoples' rights' has achieved the status of an international political, legal, and moral principle, unfortunately some key and fundamental concepts that define 'peoples' and their 'rights' lack the legal precision that would make them readily claimable. This vagueness has been used by a number of U.N. members states, besides Canada, as a pretext for denying 'peoples' rights' to peoples within their borders. Do Indians in Canada qualify as 'peoples' within the intent of the framers of the U.N. covenant? Clearly, the intent of those who framed the phrase 'all people have the right to self-determination,' was to terminate the practice of colonialism, and to affirm human dignity, by freeing all colonized people. It was not the intent of the framers that this principle be limited by self-serving interpretation of the colonizing state.

Although there is no precise definition of 'peoples' set forth in the U.N. charters, none the less, by the standards implicit in the charters, and by accepted social-scientific criteria, Indians in Canada must be judged to have one of the strongest historical, cultural, legal, and political claims for being defined as 'peoples.' *Historically*, Indians in Canada have an indisputable continuing claim to 'peoplehood' based on the principles of political community, and possession of their ancestral lands, both of which existed from time immemorial. Moreover, the treaties lend themselves to a claim of 'peoples' rights' by confirming the historic peoplehood of Indians. *Culturally*, their claim to peoplehood is affirmed by the fact that members of the various bands/tribes continue to express their traditional cultural identities (language, spiritually, ethnicity, ancestry, etc.) through their collectivity. *Legally*, the Royal Proclamation, which predates the formation of the Canadian state, recognized their peoplehood through special status, which was subsequently acknowledged by the Canadian government in the Indian Act; the BNA Act; the Constitution Act, 1982; the Citizenship Act; the Canadian Immigration Act; and the Fisheries Act; and in the ongoing treaty relationship with Indians. *Politically*, they are a 'people' who were robbed of their independence and nationhood by colonization. This point is evidenced in various British and Canadian edicts and declarations, beginning with the Royal Proclamation, and it continues today as their affairs are being administered under a special law (the Indian Act) and under a separate department of government (DIAND) that originated as the colonial arm of the government. Moreover, Indians continue to retain a collective aspiration for liberation from colonial rule. Canadian citizenship was unilaterally imposed on Indians by the Canadian government against the will of most Indians.

Indians in Canada also have a strong humanitarian argument for their claim to 'peoplehood.' Unlike the English, the French, and other Canadian immigrant communities whose mother countries serve as a 'cultural preserve,' Indians in Canada are the only repository of their cultures, and if they are not empowered to save their cultures they will disappear completely. The U.N. Human Rights Commission has accepted as a rationale for a claim to collective rights, the goal of cultural survival. The U.N. Sixth Subcommittee, in its 1982 report, stated that there is a consensus under modern international law that the goal of survival of aboriginal cultures not only is legitimate but should be promoted.

However, Indian claims to 'peoples' rights' before the United Nations are hampered not only by vagueness and by the reluctance of U.N. members to establish potentially troublesome precedents, they are also hampered by the overriding ideological thrust of the Universal Declaration of Human Rights in the direction of Western-liberal individualism, not collectivism. This was evident in the U.N. Human Rights Committee deliberations on the *Lovelace* case. Sandra Lovelace, a Maliseit Indian whose Indian status had been revoked under section 12 (1)(b) of the Indian Act for marrying a non-Indian, brought her grievance before the U.N. Human Rights Committee. The committee declared that Canada was in violation of the International Covenant on Civil and Political Rights for denying Indian status to Indian women who married non-Indians. But, the committee, in its deliberations on *Lovelace*, based its determination on article 27 of the International Covenant on Civil and Political Rights. This had the effect of defining Indians as a *minority group* in Canada, not as a *nation of peoples*. Moreover, under the provisions of this article, only *individuals*, not *collectives*, are permitted to approach the United Nations with a claim of violation of rights. The committee ruled in favour of Lovelace but, because of its Western-liberal-individualistic bias, it failed to apprehend the Indian position that their cultural rights are not the sum of individual rights, that their right as a 'people' to self-determination is not addressed by implementation of individual rights, and that their survival and well-being as *Indians* in Canada cannot be achieved through individual rights. These issues can be adequately addressed only if Indians are recognized as 'peoples' under the U.N. Charter.

The Canadian government, having decided that 'peoplehood' status for Indians is not in the 'national interest,' has committed itself to the duplicitous course of using its influence within the United Nations to frustrate Indian claims to 'peoplehood.' As a case in point, while the U.N. public record shows Canada voted in favour of the 1957 U.N. Convention 107, which set out standards of indigenous rights, confidential documents reveal this support came only after the Canadian delegation failed in surreptitious lobbying against the convention. The Canadian government did not want to draw adverse attention to and criticism of its policy towards its indigenous population, so the Canadian delegation had been secretly instructed by the government to lobby and vote against the convention, but not in the face of majority support for the covention by other national delegations. In the event of majority support for the convention, the Canadian delegation was instructed to vote affirmatively, and then use all of its influence to limit any possibility of U.N. meddling in Canada's handling of its indigenous affairs.

More recently, Canada's delegation at a meeting of the fifty-nation International Labour Organization (an affiliate of the United Nations) in Geneva, in June 1988, lobbied other members and moved an amendment to revise Convention 107 to refer to indigenous peoples as 'populations' rather than 'peoples.' The Canadian government spokesperson said it was taking this position because the use of the word 'peoples' in international law recognizes a right to self-determination that could include secession. At the same meeting, Canada sought an amendment opposing the principle of Native territorial or land *rights*, promoting, instead, an optional approach by allowing for land *claims*. In another context, Canada, as one of five 'expert' countries working on a draft declaration of indigenous human rights for the United Nations, declared its support for a principle of collective rights that would protect Indians against *physical* genocide, but it opposed collective rights that would protect Indians against *cultural* genocide. In general, the Canadian government favoured the concept of collective 'objectives' over collective 'rights.'[21]

In its domestic policy, Canada's position on collective claims – the basis for 'peoples' rights' – has been confusing. On the one hand, it has been firmly committed to the goal of institutional assimilation for all of its citizens as individuals. On the other hand, in response to political imperatives, successive Canadian governments have implicitly or explicitly acknowledged and sought to accommodate certain collective claims on an *ad hoc* basis. Examples can be found in constitutional, legislative, administrative, and institutional provisions that recognize certain minority collective rights and entitlements. For instance, section 93 of the British North America Act, 1867, is aimed at protecting the rights of the Catholic minority in Ontario and the Protestant minority in Quebec in education on matters of religion and morals; section 29 of the Charter of the Constitution Act, 1982, states that 'nothing in this Charter abrogates or derogates from any rights or privileges guaranteed by or under the Constitution of Canada in respect of denominational, separate or dissentient schools.' Section 35 of the Constitution Act, 1982, recognizes the principle of collectively held aboriginal rights, and Canada's policy of linguistic duality implies recognition of special collective rights of anglophone and francophone minorities inside and outside Quebec.

A recent ruling by the Supreme Court of Canada has the effect of undergirding collective rights. The Court held that certain collective rights are protected from individual rights: 'Collective or group rights, such as those concerning languages and those concerning certain denominations of separate schools, are asserted by individuals or groups of individuals because of their membership in the protected group. Individual rights are asserted equally by everyone despite membership in certain ascertainable groups. To that extent, they are an exception from the equality rights provided equally to everyone.'[22] In the same reference, Estey J reasoned that section 91 (24) of the Constitution Act, 1867, authorizes the Parliament of Canada to legislate for the *benefit* of the Indian population in a preferential, discriminatory, or distinctive fashion vis-à-vis others and if it does not impair Indian-ness or aboriginality.

Coexisting uneasily with this acquiescence to collective rights is a paramount 'liberal' concern for the rights of the individual. This 'liberal' concern was given initial legislative expression in the Canadian Bill of Rights, which was enacted in 1960. A number of provincial legislatures followed suit with provincial charters to protect and enhance individual rights. However, the major Canadian initiative to protect and enhance individual rights occurred with the constitutionalization of the Charter of Rights and Freedoms in 1982. The charter is conceived in terms of a liberal-democratic vision of Canada. The pre-eminent force behind this initiative was the prime minister of the day, Pierre Elliott Trudeau, who viewed 'collective rights' and 'equality' as contradictory concepts. From this perspective, individuals act for themselves in relation to the state, not as members of collectivities. And social justice is understood in terms of individual rights and equality.

Trudeau sought to elevate the charter and its emphasis on individual equality to a paramount constitutional principle. However, at the time the charter was entrenched, some provincial premiers insisted upon maintaining the paramountcy of their legislatures over its provisions. In order to break the political stalemate, Trudeau expediently, albeit reluctantly, agreed to the inclusion of a 'notwith-standing' clause in the constitution. This clause essentially empowers provincial governments to pass legislation 'notwithstanding' the fact such legislation may contravene the provisions of the charter.

This compromise of principle was exploited recently by the government of Quebec to enhance the collective cultural and linguistic rights of the Québécois. In 1977, the government of Quebec had enacted a language law (Bill 101) restricting the use of languages other than French. A Supreme Court of Canada decision (1989) struck down parts of Bill 101 on grounds this legislation was an infringement of the Charter of Rights and Freedom's protection of individual rights and, therefore, was unconstitutional. In order to override the court's ruling, the government of Quebec invoked the 'notwithstanding' clause and passed a new law (Bill 178, 1988) that outlawed English on commercial signs.

When the premier of Quebec, Robert Bourassa, was asked publicly to justify his government's decision to invoke the 'notwithstanding' clause to enforce Quebec's language law, he characterized it as an arbitration between 'two fundamental values' – individual rights and collective rights. His government, he said, had arbitrated in favour of collective rights because they deemed it 'vital to the survival of the community.' It was, in his words, 'a moral decision,' and he asserted that Canadians must accept that Quebec is a distinct society within Canada – one in which the collective rights of francophones in Quebec have predominance over individual rights guaranteed in the Canadian Charter of Rights and Freedoms.

This action by the Quebec government breached a long-standing Western-liberal constitutional tradition in Canada establishing the paramountcy of individual rights over collective rights. By invoking the 'notwithstanding' clause to preserve their 'distinct society,' the Québécois established a significant Canadian precedent for preferring collective rights over individual rights. Arguably, in the Canadian domestic context, Indians can make a stronger moral and historical case for collective rights than can the Québécois – but, unfortunately for them, they do not have the resources to make a persuasive political case.

Canada's recent constitutional initiatives have been plagued by issues of collective rights: the four FMCs on aboriginal constitutional matters, the Meech Lake Accord, and the Canada Round of constitutional renewal were afflicted with claims of collective rights by francophone and/or aboriginal peoples. The woes derived significantly from a constitution that is not designed to effectively accommodate or guarantee collective rights within a framework of federal responsibility. In the absence of an effective constitutional guarantee of collective rights within a framework of federal responsibility, an informal practice has grown up of 'trading-off' the collective cultural-linguistic rights of minority francophones outside Quebec and minority anglophones inside Quebec, to achieve a measure of comparability. In effect, the collective rights of each is held hostage against the collective rights of the other. This practice is contrary to the U.N. charter which holds the cultural and linguistic rights of 'a people' to be unconditional and inalienable.

The lack of an effective constitutional provision to protect the collective cultural-linguistic rights of francophones within a federal framework has given the Québécois both a political pretext and a moral warrant for demanding 'distinct society' status in order to guarantee collective francophone cultural-linguistic rights within the geographic-political borders of their province. Arguably, fitting a guarantee of francophone collective rights into a provincial (Quebec) framework has a measure of validity, because of the concentration of francophones in Quebec. However, this geographical-political approach to the guarantee of francophone collective rights carries two consequential deficits: it disregards the collective rights of non-Québécois 'peoples' and it imperils the territorial-political integrity of the Canadian state.

In respect to the first of these two defects, 'distinct society' status, as Quebec would have it, offers no protection for the collective cultural-linguistic rights of francophones living outside Quebec. Moreover, inside Quebec borders minority anglophone and Indian collective rights can be subordinated to Québécois collective rights and powers, on grounds that equal rights for these minorities threatens Quebec's territorial and political integrity. It is evident from this that Québécois aspirations to 'distinct society' status are driven more by ambitions for enhanced political sovereignty than by universal principles or values of collective cultural-linguistic rights. If principles or values of collective cultural-linguistic rights were the paramount concern of the Québécois, then their definition of 'distinct society' status would surely follow cultural boundaries, not geographical-political borders; that is, they would include francophones outside Quebec in the constitutional definition of 'distinct society.' Moreover, if universal principles and values of collective cultural-linguistic rights were the dominant concern of Québécois, then minority anglophones and Indians inside

Quebec borders would have no reason to fear that their collective cultural-linguistic rights might be denied them. In its present config-uration, 'distinct society' status is primarily a design for translating Québécois nationalism into greater provincial political autonomy and power.

The second defect in the geographical-political 'distinct society' ap-proach to the guarantee of collective francophone rights (i.e., the peril to the integrity of the Canadian state) derives from Quebec's insistence on a significant transfer of constitutional authority from Ottawa to Quebec. The response of the other Canadian provinces to Quebec's demands is quite revealing as to their own political ambitions. On the one hand, they sanctioned Quebec's provincial 'distinct society' approach to the guarantee of francophone collective cultural-linguistic rights because it was preferable to a federal constitutional guarantee of these rights that would require them to offer a full range of fran-cophone cultural and language programs and services within their own borders. Moreover, they saw in Quebec's aptitude to translate ethnic nationalism, and the threat of a 'sovereignty' referendum, into an effective weapon for extorting federal powers, a 'coat tail' oppor-tunity to enhance their own provincial constitutional mandates. On the other hand, they did not accept Quebec's design of 'distinct so-ciety' status as a 'political duality' based on 'two founding nations' (i.e., an equal partnership between Quebec and the rest of Canada) because it implies a transfer of power from the other provinces to Quebec. They insisted, instead, that 'distinct society' must be based on the principle, and exist within a framework, of provincial political equality. They also recognized that the centrifugal pressures gener-ated by Quebec's demands for more and more federal powers, on the pretext of safeguarding francophone collective cultural-linguistic rights in that province, could ultimately bring about the worst outcome of all: the dissolution of the Canadian federation.

Although the proposed Canada Clause contained the phrase 'Ca-nadians and their governments are committed to the vitality and de-velopment of official language minority communities throughout Canada,' this provision is vague and probably would have been unen-forceable. It is noteworthy that Quebec insisted the French-language version of this provision should be changed to read 'attached to' instead of 'commitment to,' thus diminishing Quebec's constitutional legal obligation to nurture the 'vitality and development' of the Eng-lish-language minority within its borders. Significantly, Indians were not included in this commitment. They were guaranteed only 'the right to promote their language, cultures and traditions.' To the extent that the Canada Round of constitutional reforms contained enforceable guarantees of collective linguistic and cultural rights, these were formulated in such a way as to vest the responsibility in geographically defined governments. But governments with geographically defined jurisdiction cannot effectively guarantee and protect the collective cultural-linguistic rights of those of their people who live outside the designated geographical-political borders. Speaking to the case of Indians, it is very doubtful that the Canada Round of constitutional reforms constitute a design for their survival as *Indians*. This assertion will be more fully developed in chapter 4.

It should be obvious from the foregoing that the concept of 'peoples' rights' does not offer an unproblematic approach to justice for Indians. The Canadian government has demonstrated that it will challenge all claims by Indians to 'peoples' rights' and it will stoop to chicanery to close off avenues of appeal to the United Nations. It will require a great effort on the part of Indian leaders, and they will need to focus much of their resources on the concept of 'peoples' rights' if they are to succeed in translating this concept into an effective instrument for achieving justice. But, all things considered, the concept of 'peoples' rights' arguably holds greater promise for Indian aspirations to justice than does the concept of aboriginal rights. In the final analysis, achieving justice (defined as the survival and well-being of *Indians*) will be a matter of power politics, not a matter of principle or 'inherent rights.' Cast in these terms, Indians have a better probability of achieving justice if they pursue this objective in alliance with other 'peoples' in the international arena rather than pursuing aboriginal rights in isolation in the Canadian domestic arena.

The efficacy of a 'peoples' rights' strategy is being enhanced by contemporary and projected worldwide trends. The world has moved from a bipolar political order (preserved by East–West military confrontation) towards a situation of fragmenting states and ethnopolitical flux. Marshall McLuhan predicted a global reversion to 'tribalism.' Today we see evidence for it – the shattering of the world into smaller ethno-political nations even as larger economic blocks are being formed. Concurrently, a new international climate is developing in regard to 'peoples' rights.' The United Nations has held to a longstanding tradition of non-intervention in matters that are essentially within the borders and domestic jurisdiction of any member state. But, since the signing of the Helsinki Accord (1975), there has been a marked evolution in U.N. thinking. The United Nations is coming to understand the need to interpret its charter so it can respond more effectively to the human rights of oppressed peoples within sovereign states. This need was exemplified in the case of sanctions imposed on South Africa and in the tacit approval of u.s.-led intrusions into Iraqi territory to set up safe havens for the Kurds, and also in the dispatch of peacekeepers into Yugoslavia. In these actions, the United Nations has signalled an inclination to upgrade the concern for 'peoples' rights' at the expense of national-sovereignty considerations.

Circumstances may soon force the United Nations to go beyond a moral-humanitarian basis for intervention. The United Nations cannot afford to be seen as unable to deal with ethnic conflicts within state boundaries, or it risks a world filled with Lebanons and Yugoslavias. Ethnic nationalism is already feeding on itself and could spin out of control as each ethnic secession creates new ethnic minorities and new surfaces for ethnic conflict. For example, the secession of Croatia from Serb-dominated Yugoslavia has created Serb minorities in Croatia who carry on the ethnic conflict. Fewer than 10 per cent of the world's nations are exempt from potential ethnic conflicts within their borders. The rest are multinational states. If ethnic nationalism and bloodshed are not to spin out of control, then the United Nations, with the backing of major world powers, must act soon to develop a mandate, principles, criteria, and mechanisms for arbitrating proactively between ethnic groups and host states before their claims to 'peoples' rights' escalate into genocidal wars or 'ethnic cleansing.' Put another way, the United Nations must develop the powers and capacity to forge a global civil society from the emerging aspirations by ethnic peoples to self-determination. This implies a new 'post-state,' multinational world order that emphasizes the collective rights of ethnic nationhood above the sanctity of the sovereign state.

However, if Indians are to make an effective case for their 'peoples' rights' before the United Nations and other international tribunals, they cannot afford to insulate or isolate themselves from the worldwide ethnic liberation movement. Instead of defining their liberation movement in terms of aboriginal rights, Indians must adopt the generic concept of 'peoples' rights.' They must undertake to work out their destiny within the framework of 'peoples' rights.' They must develop ideologies, political concepts, and linkages with ethnic minorities in other states that will identify and include them as part of the worldwide ethnic liberation movement. So long as Indians continue to make their appeals to the United Nations for justice in the name of aboriginal rights, they will be perceived as 'petitioners' and they will not qualify as voices representative of a significant force or movement in international politics. Until they adopt the generic concept of 'peoples' rights,' they will have problems communicating their case in international forums, and they will be at a disadvantage when they seek to effectively enlist the political forces and apparatus of the developing international movement for liberation that is currently being mounted by ethnically defined peoples in multinational states the world over. By adopting 'peoples' rights' as the design for achieving survival and well-being as *Indians*, they will have an opportunity to move their quest for justice outside the precedent-ridden and heavily biased Canadian political and judicial systems and laws, and into U.N. forums where international charters, protocols, politics, and laws prevail. If they fail to act, their cause will remain a prisoner of Canadian politics and law.

To sum up, my thesis is that aboriginal rights and constitutional entrenchment, respectively the premier ideology and the primary instrument of Indian leaders for achieving justice, have serious political, legal, cultural, and moral vulnerabilities and deficiencies. Indians are unlikely to achieve justice by insisting on entrenchment of inherent aboriginal rights in the constitution, or by appealing to Canadian courts, or by attending more First Ministers' conferences. I am not, however, advocating that Indian leaders necessarily abandon all claims to aboriginal rights. There is no harm in exploiting this concept for whatever tangible benefits can be derived from it, before these rights are completely vitiated. But it would be misguided for Indian leaders to commit themselves and the future of their people exclusively to aboriginal rights and to constitutional entrenchment as the ideology and the instrument for achieving justice.

It is understandable that Indians are committed to the concept of aboriginal rights. Not only does it conjure up a fantastic legacy of sovereignty, title to valuable real estate and perpetual rental income, but the concept of aboriginal rights also has a high emotional and spiritual valence for many Indians because it links them to their ancestors and, through their ancestors, to the Creator. Given the appeal of this heritage, it will not be easy for Indians to abandon aboriginal rights as their preferred ideology for achieving justice. None the less, they have an obligation to evaluate its strategic strengths and weaknesses in order to discern if it provides an adequate ideology for achieving justice. They must not let themselves be seduced by fantasies about the grandiose political and material benefits that it evokes.

These are not the parameters of justice implicit in the spirit and intent of the treaties negotiated by their ancestors.

Conclusion

We grow up with the idea that cause and effect are in some sort of 'symmetrical proportion.' If we apply the idea of symmetrical proportionality to the condition of destitution, misery, and hopelessness of Indians in Canada, then what is the 'proportionally equivalent' cause of this enormous tragedy? Canadians do not want to hear the true answer to this question. We have attempted to block out the truth by commencing our history with the arrival of the Europeans and filling it with distortions. But the truth is that this enormous human tragedy was caused by an equally enormous Canadian injustice. Driven by greed, successive generations of Canadians have dispossessed Indians of their birthright, sentenced them to live on small plots of land, and reduced them to a condition of destitution and dependence. In the spirit of cultural and racial superiority, we have acted in such a way as to destroy Indians culturally and socially. Canadians have transgressed all civilized standards of fair play, integrity, morality, and justice in their treatment of Indians. To vindicate our behaviour we have deliberately created laws that legalize all of these transgressions.

Such massive injustice inevitably breeds consequences. When any minority group experiences injustice at the hands of the dominant society, anger, frustration, and agony are bred. More than a century of Canadian injustice on a massive scale has induced a chronic sense of oppression among Indians, and it has had an inordinately debilitating effect on them. It has robbed them of their pride, dignity, and self-respect. It has reduced most Indians to despair and hopelessness. It has created a self-concept of 'victim.' Many have been psychologically immobilized and incapacitated with the result that they are unable to play a productive role in their communities or in Canadian society. An Indian leader expressed all of this to a recent provincial justice inquiry in these words: 'We have nothing to look forward to when we wake up in the morning. We get frustrated and scared. We don't give a damn what happens to anybody anymore because nobody gives a damn about us.'[23]

As a consequence of Canadian injustice, Indians have undergone and continue to undergo an ethno-spiritual holocaust as what remains of their cultures and their spirit are being systematically destroyed.

A foreign visitor to Indian reserves and ghettos in Canada could be excused for surmising that the goal of Canada's Indian policy is Indian genocide. The conditions that prevail are not inconsistent with purposeful genocide. In most Indian communities, conditions are so intolerable that Indians are destroying themselves through mindless violence, alcoholism, substance abuse, and suicide. The ethnospiritual holocaust of Indians in Canada is an 'atrocity in progress' and, just as all German citizens who failed to protest the persecution of Jews share responsibility for the Holocaust, on the same principle all Canadians who fail to protest their government's and their courts' injustice to Indians share responsibility for the incremental destruction of Indians.

Indian youths are emerging as the most tragic legacy of Canadian injustice to Indians. As young as age ten, many have, to all intents and purposes, effectively dropped out of school. When they enter their post-schooling years, most are unable and unmotivated to get a job. They are unprepared educationally, attitudinally, and psychologically to make constructive contributions to their own communities. From their childhood experiences of violence and destructiveness they have learned a culture of violence and destructiveness towards themselves and others. The levels of social pathology would indicate that this generation of youth has experienced a level of dehumanization even greater than that of their parents who, as children of age five or six, were forcibly taken from their parents and communities and made to attend residential schools where they were robbed of their identity and spirit. With vandalism and violence soaring on Indian reserves, this lost generation alarms Indian elders.

Their condition of dependence and powerlessness has sapped the capacity of most Indians for assertive confrontation with Canadian society. Instead, self-destructively, most turn their hostility upon themselves and upon each other. However, there is mounting evidence of a more militant mood in a growing segment of young, educated Indians. To the present time, this mood has found only occasional expression in relatively mild acts of civil disobedience and extra-legal protest. But recent events, such as the violent confrontation at Oka and Kahnewake, Quebec, should be taken as an early warning that the Indian quest for justice could turn into a quest for vengeance. Continued denial of justice to Indians could add a bloody chapter to Canadian history. The prospects for a bloody chapter were enhanced in the aftermath of the Oka and Kahnewake crisis. In complete contradiction to its high-sounding official statements on Indian policy, the Quebec government's first concrete response following the crisis was to buy several surplus army tanks from the U.S. military for the purpose of dealing with repeat events in future. There was little inclination by either the Quebec or the Canadian government to meaningfully address the injustice that led up to the crisis.

Massive injustice also holds consequences for the perpetrators. What consequences does Canada's injustice to Indians hold for Canadians? Canadians, when they admit that they have not achieved their full potential as a nation, generally attribute this failure to the fact that they live in the shadow of the United States. But, a more cogent explanation can be found in the fact they live under the dispiriting cloud of their historical and continuing injustice towards Indians. In human terms, and by any contemporary moral standard, it is not an inconsequential act to condemn unique cultural nations of peoples to such a level of powerlessness and destitution that they give up and resort to self-destructive behaviour on a massive scale. In truth, Indian lives are being sacrificed to Canadian greed. If our conscience is unaffected by the groaning sound of so many children, women, and men in anguish and despair, our humanity is impaired – a defect that will never allow us to build a humane, inspired, and united Canadian family.

The wages of injustice always are a lack of self-esteem and self-confidence. Canada will not achieve the sense of greatness to which it aspires without first rendering justice to Indians. This consideration seems too subtle to move many Canadians, or the Canadian judiciary, and it is obviously much too subtle to move Canadian politicians. Prime Minister Mulroney provided evidence for such an assertion in his approach to the Meech Lake Accord. He assumed he could spurn with impunity his moral obligation to extend constitutional justice to Indians. Elijah Harper proved him wrong, and Mulroney's miscalculation has taken Canada to the brink of disintegration. How could Mulroney expect to instil respect for Canadian nationhood when he shows so little respect for Indian nationhood?

Every nation of people has memories, and it is an axiom in human experience (individual and collective) that a proud future wants a proud past. Canada's past, its history, is summed up by its treatment of Indians. What esteeming thing can Canadian parents tell their children today about Canada's treatment of Indians? Canadians can find no positive image of themselves in their treatment of Indians. Unless the present generation of Canadians leaves a better moral legacy in its treatment of Indians than that which now prevails, their children will not be able to put their past, and hence their future, in a proud perspective. Put another way, if Canadians want to place their nation on the path to greatness, they must first render justice to Indians. They must experience an awakening of their sense of humanity towards Indians; feel the pain that Indians feel; find in themselves the virtues of decency, generosity, understanding, and respect for Indians. All thinking Canadians know that their prosperity derives largely from the colonization and destitution of Indians. Settling fairly and justly will not bankrupt Canadians. But failure to do so will corrupt the Canadian spirit for as long as justice is delayed.

One would expect enlightened Canadian leaders to be appalled and ashamed by the past record of Indian treatment, and that they would exhort Canadians to deal justly with Indians. But that has not been the case. Trudeau, who, as prime minister of Canada, assiduously sought a high pedestal for himself as champion of a 'just society,' urged Indians and Canadians to develop amnesia about past injustices to Indians. Prime Minister Mulroney offers Indians justice in exchange for compliant behaviour. Recently he asserted that the 'deep wells of sympathy [note: not justice] among the entire Canadian population' are the best guarantee that the aboriginal peoples' legitimate grievances will be justly dealt with. But, the same prime minister used the events at Oka and Kahnewake to turn Canadian public opinion against Indians, thereby causing 'the deep wells of sympathy' among the Canadian population to frost over. Canadian leaders have always preferred the exercise of power to paying the price of justice to Indians. It seems that if there is to be any prospect of justice for Indians, it will be realized only if Canadian people demand that their politicians and courts render it.

It seems reasonable that, as heirs of the Crown's 'Indian' assets, Canadians should assume the Crown's moral obligation of justice to Indians. If Canadians should come to a firm consensus that they want to render justice to Indians, they can begin to do so by honouring the spirit and intent of the treaties. After all, Canada is a product of the treaties, and although Indians made their treaties with the Crown, the sovereignty of the Crown has metamorphosed into 'sovereignty of the Canadian people.' Thus, the moral obligation to honour the spirit and intent of the treaties falls squarely on the Canadian people. The only honourable interpretation of the treaties is that they represent an enlightened agreement between peoples who trusted each other and dealt with each other in the spirit of peaceful coexistence, mutual obligation, and benefit. If Canadians accept this honourable interpretation they must reject Trudeau's premise that Indians gave away vast expanses of land for 'so much twine or so much gunpowder.' Not only is this premise unsupportable, but such a transaction would amount to theft, plunder, and fraud by the founders of the Canadian nation. That is not an inspiring premise for Canadian nationhood.

The paramount criterion and standard of justice that emerges unambiguously from the spirit and intent of the treaties is the survival and well-being of Indians as *Indians*, for all time to come. To fulfil this spirit and intent will require that Indians and Canadians forge a 'new covenant,' one that will give recognition to this standard of justice. Because the future needs of Indians cannot be foreseen, it must necessarily be a 'living covenant' – one that is open to ongoing development, refinement, and renewal, but always with the purpose of ensuring the future survival and well-being of Indians as *Indians*.

2 Policy

For officials at the Department of Indian Affairs and Northern Development (DIAND), the 1960s began as just another decade of smug bureaucratic arrogance wedded to ignorance about their Indian wards. Cultural assimilation was still considered a 'progressive policy,' and both politicians and bureaucrats were blissfully optimistic about the progress being made in that direction. Statistics showed increases in the number of Indian children receiving post-elementary schooling; federal programs to relocate Indians from reserves (and federal responsibility) to urban centres (and provincial responsibility) were deemed to be progressing at a satisfying pace; Indian friendship centres were springing up in cities to facilitate Indian relocation from reserves; there were illusions of viable economic development on reserves; studies on Indians were being commissioned and 'solutions' and new ideas were being presented (e.g., the Hawthorn Report);[1] Indian leaders were learning how to function in colonial political and bureaucratic structures; DIAND was in full control of Indians and land reserved for Indians. In short, everything was humming along smoothly for Indian Affairs.

But, following the 1968 federal election, Pierre Elliott Trudeau, the liberal-democrat, burst upon the Canadian scene, and DIAND's blissful world was shattered forever. Full of 'just society' idealism and fervour, Trudeau was determined to make a difference. As a liberal, he 'knew' what was right and good for Indians – to become 'Canadians as all other Canadians.' But, as a democrat, he was bound to consult Indians before implementing his solutions. Thus, in the year leading up to the 1969 White Paper on Indian Policy, DIAND bureaucrats, under marching orders from their political 'masters,' had to leave their comfortable offices and scurry into the remote corners of Canada, where the reserves are located, to engage Indians in 'consultations' about their future.

For Indians, this was a radically new experience. Never before had the princely mandarins from Ottawa deigned to solicit their views in such a diligent fashion. The effect of the consultation process on Indian leaders was remarkable. It raised their expectations, inspired new ideas, charged their emotions, and unleashed a tremendous pan-Indian dynamic that irrevocably changed Indian–Canadian relationships. Most consequential of all, it raised in Indian leaders a profound sense of individual and collective empowerment and political efficacy – something they had never experienced before. Later, this sense of empowerment was translated into political protest when the contents of the White Paper on Indian Policy were revealed in the fall of 1969, and Indian leaders discovered that the 'consultations' had been a total sham. None of their expressed interests, rights, needs, and aspirations had been heeded. The shock of this discovery transformed their characteristic posture of subordination and passiveness into such a fierce resistance that, in 1971, the government retracted the White Paper.

The unity and intensity of Indian opposition to the White Paper caught Canadian government officials off guard and sent them reeling in confusion. So decisive was the Indian triumph that for a full decade (the 1970s) the Canadian government lost its will and capacity to make 'Indian policy.' DIAND became bogged down in a muddle of defensive strategies: to lower Indian expectations (e.g., on sovereignty); to neutralize Indian demands (e.g., on aboriginal rights); to diffuse Indian energies (e.g., by proposing amendments to the Indian Act); to divide Indians (e.g., by making them compete for scarce funds); and to devitalize Indian leadership (e.g., by co-optation). Only in the 1980s did the government recover its balance sufficiently to again undertake new policy initiatives uniquely affecting Indians. These new initiatives included the Parliamentary Task Force on Indian Self-Government (Penner Report) in 1982; the sections 25, 35, and 37 amendments to the Constitution Act in 1982 and 1983; the First Ministers' Conferences on aboriginal matters in 1983–7; the Ministerial Task Force on Program Review (Nielsen Report) in 1986; and the Indian Self-Government Community Negotiations policy statement in 1986. By the 1990s, the government was on a policy-making 'roll' as it announced the Royal Commission on Aboriginal Peoples and the Aboriginal Constitutional Process.

What goals does the Canadian government harbour for Indian peoples in its recent spree of policy initiatives? In this chapter I review and analyse the goals of government policies towards Indians in Canada. I take the position that 'Indian policy' provides too limited a framework for understanding the conduct of Indian affairs in Canada; that the conduct of Indian affairs can be understood only as part of a much broader policy-making process in the Canadian polity, economy, and society. This broader policy-making process which impacts on Indians is identified here as the actualization of the 'national interest.' I begin my discussion with an elaboration of the 'national interest' as a policy paradigm for understanding the conduct of Indian affairs in Canada.

The 'national interest'

The Canadian 'national interest' is an artificial construct, a device of the reigning Canadian 'establishment' for asserting its political, economic, and social hegemony over the Canadian nation. It is used to create the illusion that there exists a national homogeneity of interests, and that government policies are designed to promote these interests. Thus, it serves to legitimate government policies. But, clearly, the 'national interest' is not arrived at by any rational calculations referenced to the 'national good' as defined by the majority of Canadians. More often than not, assessments and definitions of the 'national interest' are made behind closed doors – political, bureaucratic, and corporate – where only the voices of the powerful are heard.

The 'national interest' is not a well-defined or precise notion. Commonly, it denotes no more than the convergent or mediated interests of the powerful as arbitrated by the federal cabinet. None the less, the 'national interest' is an overwhelming and permanent force in Canadian policy development; it will not be denied, and it affects Indian interests in profound ways. For purposes of analysing its impact on Indian policy we must look to prevailing, economic, political, and social priorities as defined by the Canadian government. Some current 'national interest' priorities that can be seen to impact on the conduct of Indian affairs are national unity (i.e., resolving federal-provincial constitutional disputes and conciliating differences with Quebec), the national debt (i.e., controlling or 'capping' government expenditures), and resource development (i.e., removing legal constraints to corporate exploitation of oil, mineral, logging, and hydro potential).

In the following pages, I evaluate 'the national interest' as a force in Indian affairs from the perspective of Indian interests, Indian influence, and the role of Canadian politicians and bureaucrats, and in terms of 'sidestream' effects.

Indian interests

Implicit in the 'national interest' policy paradigm as presented here is the thesis that all Canadian government policies, whether they are 'Canadian' policies or 'Indian' policies, will subordinate, if not sacrifice, Indian interests to Canadian interests. This 'national interest' imperative relative to Canada's conduct of Indian affairs was already in evidence in Canada's founding charter. Although section 91 (24) of the British North America Act, 1867, which created special federal government legislative authority over Indians and lands reserved for Indians, has been construed as policy in the Indian interest – specifically, to protect Indians from provincial and private exploitation – the facts don't support this construction. If the primary rationale for section 91 (24) was to protect Indians, why did the Canadian government use its authority under this section to cede large areas of Indian land to provinces and private enterprises without Indian consent, and far below their market values? Arguably, section 91 (24) has afforded some incidental protection to Indians, but the primary reason it was enacted in 1867 was to serve the fledgling 'national interest' by creating central federal control and jurisdiction over Indians and their territories, thereby facilitating coordination of Indian policy with national military, settlement, and economic policies.

One merit of the 'national interest' policy perspective is that it exposes more fully the extent to which Indian interests, rights, needs, and aspirations are prey to government policy designs. Under section 91 (24) of the BNA Act the Canadian government is declared to be the sole trustee of Indians and lands reserved for Indians. Legally and morally, trusteeship implies that the federal government has an obligation at all times to act in the best interest of Indian peoples. This comprehensive obligation goes beyond the limited concept of the government's 'trust' or 'fiduciary' responsibility recently addressed by the courts (i.e., issues of government responsibility for competent and honest management of Indian resources and affairs, including legal liability for misuse of Indian funds and unauthorized leasing, taking, or selling of Indian land and water). The Canadian government's trust responsibility requires it, at all times, to act in the best interest of Indians within the total 'Canadian policy' framework and not just with respect to 'Indian' policies. In other words, the government's trust responsibility goes beyond an obligation merely to avoid iniquitous 'Indian' policies. It includes an obligation to ensure 'Canadian' policies do not deliberately, or even inadvertently, sacrifice

Indian interests to the Canadian interest. But, as author and executor of the Canadian 'national interest,' the government is in an ongoing fundamental conflict-of-interest position vis-à-vis Indian interests.

In this regard, 'Indian policy' has always been a misnomer. We can reasonably infer from 'Canadian policy' that it is designed to serve some sort or segment of 'Canadian' interest. But we can never infer from 'Indian policy' that it is designed to serve any 'Indian' interests. Or the contrary, 'Indian policy' has always been, and is today, a design for sacrificing Indian interests for the general 'Canadian good,' that is, the 'national interest.' Such was the case with the Indian Act (a policy for government control), the treaties (a policy for acquiring Indian lands), extending the vote (a policy for undermining Indian nationhood), education (historically a policy of 'civilization,' i.e., as-similation; however, recently, when the government faced a fiscal crunch, a redefined 'national interest' dictated a policy of capping funding for Indian post-secondary education). All of these 'Indian policies' were formulated with primary reference to the 'national interest,' not with reference to the interests, rights, needs, and aspirations of Indian people. In short 'Indian policy' has historically served as a metaphor for the Canadian 'national interest.' Nowhere is the 'national interest' written more explicitly and unambiguously than in 'Indian policy.'

The 'national interest' policy imperative has extended even to creating appropriate Indian stereotypes to rationalize and justify the 'Indian policies' designed to serve the 'national interest.' When the 'national interest' dictated the taking of Indian lands, the Indian was given the image of a 'heathen,' implying an ignorant, cruel, dirty, immoral, lazy subhuman species. This image was elaborated and validated with gruesome fictional accounts of Indian cruelty, treachery, and perversity. Such a subhuman species could have no moral claim or legal title to land that God created for his children. This Indian stereotype justified both military and missionary actions against Indians – genocide and ethnocide.

When the 'national interest' imperative required that Indians should be removed from their ancestral lands to make way for settlers and business enterprise, the image of Indians was transmuted from heathen into a childlike people, ignorant, naïve, and vulnerable to exploitation, debauching by alcohol, and abuse by unprincipled European traffickers. Such a people needed government protection, and thus the reserve system was introduced, along with the Indian Act.

When the 'national interest' imperative prescribed that Indians should be 'Canadians as all other Canadians,' they were given the image of a racial minority group, of disadvantaged citizens suffering from multiple burdens of segregation, prejudice, discrimination, inequality, and lack of individual rights. This set the scene for the 1969 White Paper that identified their special status, their aboriginal rights, and their land claims as the 'cause' of all their disadvantages, and sought to terminate these elements of the aboriginal heritage.

A recent instance of a Canadian policy initiative premised on sacrificing Indian interests to the 'national interest' imperative occurred during negotiations leading up to the ill-fated Meech Lake Accord. The 'national interest' called for Quebec to be brought into the Canadian constitutional framework. The 'trade-offs' that occurred in the Quebec–Canada conciliation process at Meech Lake resulted in the adoption of an agenda that effectively removed aboriginal self-government from the program of constitutional reform and gave approval to an amending formula that empowered each province to veto any constitutional amendment on Indian government. Had the Meech Lake Accord been enacted, these 'deals,' which were struck in the 'national interest,' would have effectively ruled out, for all time, any possibility of Indians achieving meaningful self-government.

One reason why Indian interests are readily subordinated or sacrificed to the 'national interest' is that government officials generally construe those interests as being inimical to the 'national interest.' This tendency has been most evident when dealing with Indian economic interests such as land rights, hunting, and fishing. But it is also evident in the political realm when Indians make claims to self-government, treaty rights, special status, and so on. Such claims are always interpreted by Canadian politicians and bureaucrats as threatening Canadian political sovereignty and integrity.

The Penner Committee Report (discussed later in this chapter) stands as an exception to the Canadian government's historical practice of subordinating Indian interests to the 'national interest.' This committee of Parliament worked diligently to understand Indian interests, rights, needs, and aspirations. While it did not give Indian interests full equality to the 'national interest,' it made a praiseworthy attempt to develop a policy framework for *reconciling* some key Indian interests with the 'national interest.' This report, was relegated to the waste-baskets of the bureaucracy. Its fate serves to confirm the assertion that the Canadian government is unwilling to fulfil its fiduciary responsibility to Indians. When Indian interests compete with the 'national interest,' Canadian politicians will always subordinate or sacrifice them.

Subordination of Indian interests to the 'national interest' has also been effected through judicial decisions. Jurisprudence relating to Indian rights and claims has been shaped by the 'national interest'; that is, Canadian judges make their decisions with reference to the 'national interest,' and the 'national interest' always prevails over Indian interests in all decisions of consequence. Indians have learned from experience that the courts are not above compromising historical moral and legal commitments to Indians, if necessary, to protect the 'national interest.' To cite one example among many, in *Simon* v *The Queen* (1985)[2] the Canadian Supreme Court ruled that, under section 88 of the Indian Act, when the terms of a treaty come into conflict with federal government legislation, the latter prevails. Leon Mitchell[3] cites cases in which the federal court has ruled that the Canadian government holds the authority to unilaterally alter Indian treaty rights when it enters into an agreement with a province, if the federal-provincial agreement contains terms that require the restriction of Indian rights as set out in a treaty.

For more evidence of judicial subordination of Indian interests to the Canadian 'national interest,' Indians can point to judicial rulings in regard to the Migratory Birds Convention Act, the Jay Treaty, and the decisions reached in *Sikeyea* v *The Queen* (1964), *The Queen* v *George* (1966), and *Daniels* v *White and The Queen* (1968).[4] All of these decisions, made in the 'national interest,' violated treaty covenants and Canadian moral and legal commitments to Indians in favour of the 'national interest.' In these and other cases (e.g., the *Sparrow* decision), Canadian courts have consistently held that the government, acting in the 'national interest,' has the sovereign power to regulate and extinguish aboriginal rights. The courts need not act intrusively to serve the 'national interest.' They merely take creative advantage of the obscure and vague wording in the constitution, the treaties, the laws, and the agreements. Lower-court judges who aspire to make decisions on Indian rights that will survive the appeal process need only apprehend where the 'national interest' lies, and then artfully exploit any legal vagueness to construct a ruling (preferably worded in high-sounding language) to serve the 'national interest.'

To sum up, Indian interests are always either subordinated or sacrificed to promote the 'national interest.' When the 'national interest' requires fiscal retrenchment, then Indian program budgets are capped.

When the 'national interest' requires a federal-provincial constitutional accord, then Indian self-government is removed from the constitutional agenda. When the 'national interest' dictates a reconciliation with Quebec, then the federal government's fiduciary responsibility for Indians in Quebec is abdicated. When the 'national interest' dictates resource development, then aboriginal title is extinguished.

Indian influence

Canadian policy making is always a complex political process of mediation among a variety of concerns and interests. A partial listing of these concerns and interests includes: international political and economic forces, federal-provincial mandates, cabinet priorities, economic and social exigencies, political partisanship and ideological values, regional concerns, interdepartmental rivalries, public expectations, interest-group pressures, legislative and judicial precedents, and resistance to change – a virtual snarl of competing concerns and interests. In this snarl, Indian concerns and interests have a low ranking. This has been the case ever since confederation when Indians became superfluous to Canadian military and economic concerns.

Unless confronted with an 'Indian crisis,' the time of Parliament and of Cabinet is deemed too valuable to take up for a concentrated examination of Indian interests, rights, needs, and aspirations. Arguably, the 1969 White Paper on Indian policy and the Penner Report stand as exceptions to this rule. But neither of these initiatives culminated in policy. The 1969 White Paper was recanted, and the Penner Report was shelved. More typically, when Canadian politicians, individually and collectively, assess national priorities, they are swayed by bigger, richer, more cohesive, more influential, and more compatible constituencies that come well ahead of Indians. Indians fall at the margin, if not outside the periphery, of Canadian politicians' consciousness and concerns. This was exemplified, recently, during deliberations around the Free Trade Agreement. Indian interests, rights, needs, and aspirations were not even mentioned by Canadian politicians in the debate on this historical agreement.

Although the Canadian government, mainly out of guilt, occasionally surrenders some power to Indians, and Indian leaders are getting better at frustrating Canadian politicians when they ignore Indian interests, none the less, the fact is that Indians lack the mechanisms and resources to penetrate the closed political, bureaucratic, and corporate doors behind which the 'national interest' gets defined. Even when they are admitted into the 'inner circle,' their voices are lost in the snarl of competing concerns and interests. For example, in 1975 the federal government sought to place its relations with Indians on a better footing by creating the Joint Cabinet/National Indian Brotherhood Committee as a joint policy-formulating experiment. But, three years later the experiment was terminated without having produced a single joint policy agreement.[5] A similar lack of results marked the four First Ministers' conferences that were held to deal with aboriginal constitutional matters.

The conventional means for a minority group to advance its interests – that is, by intense and targeted involvement in the political process – has not worked for aboriginal peoples. They have not been able to translate their electoral potential into political influence. For example, in the 1988 national election there were twenty-four electoral ridings in which the number of eligible aboriginal voters exceeded the margin of victory by the successful candidate.[6] Arithmetically, aboriginal voters could have decided the election outcome in most of these ridings. More than half the time in the past three decades this number of ridings could have determined which political party would form the government. For most ethnic minorities in Canada such political potential would translate into significant political muscle. But, in the case of aboriginal peoples, their potential electoral power has proved inconsequential. The reasons for this are twofold: aboriginal people, emotionally and intellectually, have not 'accepted' Canadian citizenship, thus they tend to have a very low voter turnout, and those who vote seem uninterested in voting as a block. Consequently, Canadian politicians, with few exceptions, simply disregard the Indian vote. The effect is that, politically, Indians are consigned to a status of 'citizen-minus.'

Some Indian leaders have advocated greater involvement by their people in the various levels of federal, provincial, and municipal government, by voting and by standing for election. Others have proposed formation of an independent aboriginal peoples' party to encourage aboriginal peoples to elect aboriginal representatives to the various levels of government. Still others have championed the notion of 'proportionate assured representation,' that is, a fixed number of aboriginal seats in the provincial and federal legislatures and in the Senate. The Royal Commission on Electoral Reform and Party Financing (1990) asked Indian leaders across Canada for their reaction to the idea of a constitutionally guaranteed number of seats in Parliament for aboriginal people. The chairman of the commission noted that, if aboriginal people were represented in Parliament according to their percentage of the Canadian population, they would have ten sitting members. Given the closeness of Canadian elections since 1957, ten aboriginal members voting as a block could have held the balance of power in Parliament more than half the time. While these ideas are under continuing discussion, as yet none has achieved widespread support among Indians, and none has been officially adopted as a policy priority by major Indian organizations. One underlying reason for the lack of interest is that Indians are chary of being identified as Canadian citizens. Participation in Canadian politics is viewed by many to be in conflict with their claims to historical aboriginal nationhood.

The matter of Indian representation in Canadian legislatures raises a large unanswered question: Would the Canadian 'establishment,' and Canadians generally, tolerate a political system or situation that might give Indians a parliamentary 'balance of power'; are they prepared to tolerate more than a token Indian influence in Canadian politics? Based on past behaviour it is highly unlikely that Canadian legislators would constitutionally guarantee to Indians enough seats to give them a potential 'swing vote in Parliament.' Indian leaders claim, already, to have evidence of provincial governments gerrymandering electoral boundaries to reduce the number of Indian electors in northern provincial constituencies where they have a potential 'swing' vote in provincial elections.

The lack of Indian influence in shaping the 'national interest' is not attributable to a lack of public forums or media channels to present their issues and views to the Canadian public. Indian leaders regularly have access to the Canadian public, and on a number of occasions they have gained international attention for their grievances. But such approaches have not proved very fruitful as avenues of political influence in shaping the 'national interest.' The Canadian government ignores such initiatives, or it neutralizes them with counter-claims, more 'studies,' new committees, deceptive rhetoric, and empty gestures, or it co-opts Indian leadership. However, one notable exception to this generalization occurred on 23 June 1990, when Elijah Harper, lone Indian member of the Manitoba legislature, used procedural tactics to block Manitoba's ratification of the Meech Lake Accord. Because the Accord required the ratification of all ten provincial legislatures, Harper single-handedly killed the Accord. This is not to say that Harper dispatched the 'national interest' imperative in Canadian constitutional development, but he did temporarily frustrate it – an epic achievement, all things considered.

Politicians and bureaucrats

The broader 'national interest' policy perspective on the conduct of Indian affairs helps us to answer Sally Weaver's question: 'Why in the new [Mulroney] government, is a minister [Crombie] unable to implement his own priorities when they have prime-ministerial and [Indian] constituency support?'[7] When considered within a 'national interest' policy paradigm, the influence and philosophies of individual government officials, even the most senior officials, are marginal to the conduct of Indian affairs. From time to time, senior officials in government (e.g., Chrétien, Penner, Crombie, and Nielsen), holding distinctive personal philosophies, briefly figure prominently as champions of particular 'Indian policy' designs. And, because the conduct of Indian affairs sometimes appears to conform to the personal philosophy articulated by such officials, the appearance is of causal antecedency (especially if the philosophy is articulated by the Minister of Indian Affairs). But it is a mistake to posit a causal link between the personal philosophies of senior government officials and 'Indian policy.'

As I have already said, in the snarl of competing concerns and interests out of which Canadian government decisions emerge, Indian policy is always shaped by the political, economic, and social imperatives of the evolving 'national interest.' Personal philosophies about how Indian affairs should be conducted, even if they are the philosophies of cabinet ministers, count for little. Such is especially true in the case of the DIAND, which, as a department, occupies one of the lowest rungs in the government hierarchy and where the tenancy of ministers is too brief for their personal philosophy to take root as 'departmental' philosophy. At best, their ideas briefly become part of the political discourse on the future of Indians. Therefore, it is of small consequence whether a minister of the DIAND is 'friendly' or 'hostile' to the Indians' interests. In either case, the 'national interest' prevails over their personally held priorities and philosophies.

Moreover, being 'successful politicians,' cabinet ministers are well aware of the folly of advocating policies that run counter to the 'national interest.' Thus, in respect to fundamentals, Crombie and Nielsen, although they represented profoundly different philosophic and value orientations, both pursued Indian policies that were essentially consistent with what has been acknowledged as being in the 'national interest'; that is, both advocated devolution of responsibility under a municipal style of 'Indian government' with limited *delegated* (not inherent) powers; both sought to restrain government spending by advocating greater Indian responsibility and accountability (self-reliance); and both advocated restructuring Canadian–Indian relationships to bring jurisdictional arrangements more into conformity with the constitutionally mandated roles of federal and provincial governments as these apply to Canadian citizens generally.

Media reporters with a need to simplify complex policy processes typically emphasize the personalities, personal philosophies, and ideologies of DIAND ministers and senior bureaucrats in their interpretation of Indian policy. Some scholars have made similar analyses. However, in the course of four First Ministers' Conferences on aboriginal matters, over a period of five years, the policy positions of the federal government and of the various provinces at the constitutional negotiating table did not change on any one of the fundamental issues that were under contention with aboriginal representatives (e.g., Crown sovereignty and Crown land title). Yet, during this period we witnessed a turnover of federal and provincial government officials that resulted in virtually a new slate of prime minister, premiers, and political parties they represent, and the bureaucrats who advise them. This suggests that Indian policy positions derive from a 'higher source' than the personal philosophies and values of prime ministers, premiers, cabinet ministers, or senior bureaucrats. That higher source I submit here is the 'national interest.'

'Sidestream' effects

Most members of the Canadian government will admit that government policies affecting Indians have at times been misguided, but none would agree that they were deliberately malicious. All would say they want a better life for Indians. How is it, then, that a government comprised of such well-intentioned people can foster policies that created and continue the horrendous conditions that prevail in all Indian communities? One common tendency among Indian leaders is to attribute such problems to officialdom's ignorance about Indians. While the charge of official ignorance is well founded, the 'ignorant politician/bureaucrat' rationale is not an adequate explanation for the Indian condition. This is evident on reserves where administration of programs and services has been substantially transferred from DIAND to band/tribal councils and their bureaucrats. Conditions on these reserves have not improved measurably.

If the horrendous conditions of Indians is not comprehensible as a product of sinister intentions, or lack of concern, or political and bureaucratic ignorance, then how do we explain these conditions? I have already proposed that, significantly, these conditions are a consequence of the government's subordination and sacrifice of Indian interests to the 'national interest' imperative. In this section I propose that these conditions are also attributable to unpremeditated 'sidestream' consequence of 'Canadian policies' that are designed to serve the 'national interest.' An example of such a sidestream consequence can be observed in the Canadian government's 1988 policy announcement of fiscal restraint. One of the 'casualties' of this 'Canadian policy' of fiscal restraint was funding for Indian post-secondary education. There were no sinister intentions behind this policy, nor did it uniquely sacrifice Indian interests to the 'national interest.' But, the sidestream effect of the 'Canadian policy' was that Indians, who are already at an enormous disadvantage vis-à-vis Canadians, were further victimized.

The 'sidestream' reality of the 'national interest' in government thinking could not have been more explicitly enunciated than was done by the Honourable Bill McKnight, erstwhile minister of DIAND, when, on 26 October 1988, he explained to Canadians why it was so important to bring Canada's northern comprehensive aboriginal-claims process to a quick conclusion. His explanation and rationalization emphasized two 'national interest' imperatives: the first 'national interest' theme was resource development – 'the most dramatic step to date in this comprehensive claims process was taken when agreements-in-principle were signed ... for managing and regulating onshore oil and gas development' (p. 8) – and the second, the consolidation of Canada's Arctic sovereignty – 'By resolving once and for all the claims of Native Northerners, we make the strongest possible statement for our continuing, responsible sovereignty throughout the area' (p. 13).[8] The interests, rights, needs, and aspirations of the aboriginal peoples with whom the government was negotiating the aboriginal claims, and for whom the minister carried a fiduciary responsibility, were incidental; they were relegated to the 'sidestream' of these two 'national interest' rationales for concluding the agreement.

Another example of the 'sidestream' fact in Canadian policy can be discerned in the government's abjuration of its historical policy of Indian cultural assimilation. Until the 1960s the Canadian government considered cultural assimilation to be a progressive Indian policy. The subsequent change in this policy came not as a response to Indian interests, rights, needs, and aspirations, but as a sidestream effect of Canada's policy of bilingualism and multiculturalism – a policy designed to serve the 'national interest' by conciliating Quebec separatists without offending other immigrant groups in Canada. Had the policy of bilingualism and multiculturalism been referenced to Indian interests, rights, needs, and aspirations it would have included the 'original peoples' as one of the 'founding nations' along with the English and French. It would not have lumped, as it does, Indians with the 'other' immigrant minorities.

Aboriginal leaders are not unaware of the sidestream effects of Canadian policy. The United Native Nations of BC and the Native Council of Canada were reacting to anticipated sidestream policy effects on their members when they supported the BC government in its suit against the federal government's decision to impose a cap on its transfer payments to that province. In an affidavit filed with the BC Court of Appeal, these two aboriginal groups asserted that a limit on the federal government's contribution to British Columbia under the Canada Assistance plan (a 50–50 federal-provincial cost-sharing scheme that covers welfare and social programs) would have a disproportionately negative impact on Natives because about 60 per cent of Native people living away from reserves depend on provincial social assistance. In their written argument they asserted that the limitation on transfer payments 'will make it difficult if not impossible for the province to accommodate the needs of aboriginal people living off the reserve.'[9]

So long as Indians remained solely a federal responsibility, they were somewhat shielded from the sidestream effects of provincial policies. But, with the entrenchment of their aboriginal rights in the Constitution Act, 1982, and with the growing involvement of the provinces in Indian affairs, it is inevitable that, in future, Indian interests will become increasingly vulnerable to 'provincial interests' and to the sidestream effects of provincial policies designed to serve those interests.

Summing up, in my analysis to this point, I have considered the Canadian government's conduct of Indian affairs within a 'national interest' policy paradigm. Despite its vagueness, the 'national interest' imperative provides a valid policy paradigm for understanding the conduct of Indian affairs because it carries a constant and consequential impact on Indians, even when turnover in governments occurs. Successive Canadian governments have evidenced different styles and philosophies, but all have conducted Indian affairs to serve the 'national interest'; that is, all Canadian governments, of whatever party stripe, have consistently subordinated Indian interests to the Canadian 'national interest' in their development of policy. None has developed policies with primary or coequal reference to Indian interests, rights, needs, or aspirations. The grounds for this assertion will become more evident as my analysis continues.

Institutional assimilation

The power-sharing formula worked out by the Fathers of Confederation in 1867 gave the provinces jurisdiction over education, health care, civil and property law, resource development, municipal institutions, and sales tax. It mandated the federal government to take charge of virtually everything else. But, under section 91 (24) of the British North America Act, Indians were assigned a 'special status' that gave the federal government exclusive jurisdiction over 'Indians, and land reserved for Indians.' For the past half-century the most persistent aspect of Canada's policy towards Indians has been to attenuate the 'special status' of Indians under section 91 (24). Attenuation of Indian special status is deemed to be in the 'national interest' because of the troublesome political-economic-legal liability incurred by Indian claims to aboriginal rights, treaty rights, land title and sovereignty, and by the spiralling costs of maintaining a complex of separate federal political, economic, legal and bureaucratic structures and programs to serve Indians.

Consequently, the Canadian government has placed Indian special status under assault from all sides. The most insidious and perilous assault on Indian special status is concentrated on the institutional assimilation of Indians, that is, the progressive incorporation of Indians into the political, legal, social, and economic institutional framework of Canadian society. The ultimate goal is the elimination of all institutional arrangements that set Indians apart from Canadians. For public consumption – Indian, Canadian, and international – this policy initiative is presented by the Canadian government as having the goal of moving Indians from their colonial status of collective subordination to equality through desegregation of institutional arrangements. But, in fact, institutional assimilation can be regarded as the 'final assault' in the Canadian government's historic campaign to 'civilize' Indians or, using Trudeau's euphemism to make them into 'Canadians as all other Canadians.'

Although the federal and provincial governments have conflicting perspectives as to what ought to be the constitutional mandates of their respective institutions, there is no fundamental disagreement between them over the goal of institutional assimilation of Indians. Both levels of government are fully committed to the goal of incorporating Indians into the prevailing federal and provincial political, legal, social, and economic institutional framework. Provincial governments have already cooperated extensively with the federal government in the institutional assimilation of Indians by negotiating bilateral agreements under which the provincial institutions provide education, health, welfare, economic development, and other services to Indians.

Despite the federal government's horrific record of betrayed trust, paternalism, mismanagement, and so on, Indians consider the transfer of responsibility for services to their communities from federal to provincial jurisdiction as a worrisome trend. This attitude derives from a deep concern by Indians that their special status and their aboriginal and treaty rights will be jeopardized if they come under provincial jurisdiction. The Assembly of First Nations has characterized the federal government's policy of transferring its constitutional responsibility for Indians to the provinces as inviting the 'wolves to tend the sheep.'[10]

The Canadian government's approach to institutional assimilation of Indians is multifaceted. Next, I briefly elaborate on three of the main strategies: structural integration, constitutional normalization, and individualization.

Structural integration

Structural integration has reference to the elimination of all segregated Indian institutional structures. This objective is being achieved through a two-phase government strategy. In the first place, traditional *Indian* social systems (e.g., traditional forms of self-government, redistribution and sharing, custom, and spiritually) were displaced by forcibly imposing Euro-Western political, economic, legal, and social structures and norms on Indian communities. Initially, these imposed structures were segregated from prevailing Canadian institutional structures, and placed under the control of the DIAND. While this segregated arrangement shielded Indians from the full force of cultural assimilation, it also served the important function of schooling them in how to function within Canadian models of institutional structures. In the second, and current, phase of structural integration, the Canadian government is deliberately phasing out the DIAND, the Indian Act, and the segregated system of institutional structures for Indians, and is progressively incorporating Indians into prevailing federal and provincial institutional structures.

A specific instance where the Canadian government has carried structural integration into the second phase is in education. During the first phase, Indian children were forcibly enroled in segregated federal Indian schools where they were educated according to Canadian curricula and standards. In the second phase, the federal government closed many Indian schools and entered into negotiated agreements with the provinces for provision of education to Indian children in provincial schools. Already, more than half of school-age Indian children have been transferred to provincial school systems. Under such agreements most Indian children will soon be fully assimilated into the Canadian educational system.

The Canadian government's objective of structural integration is being facilitated by Indian migration to urban centres. Prior to the Second World War, virtually all Indians lived in reserve communities, and the federal government dealt with them as a collectivity through segregated institutional structures. Today, more than a third of all Indians live in urban centres, and they are being assimilated, as individuals, into provincial institutional structures. This enormous and accelerating shift of the Indian population to urban centres has been deliberately facilitated by the federal government in order to expedite the structural integration of Indians. To this end, the federal government has instituted a number of assistance programs to lure Indians in to leaving the reserve, such as offering them relocation and housing grants. A more reprehensible federal government tactic, also purposed to expedite the structural integration of Indians, has been to allow some federal services on reserves (e.g., schools, housing, health services) to deteriorate to such a point that Indians are compelled to leave the reserve and accept provincial services.

Historically, structural segregation of Indians derived from their special status, and has buttressed it. Therefore, the Canadian government's strategy of progressive structural integration has the effect of undermining the Indians' historical claims to special status.

Constitutional normalization

Since the Second World War, the federal government has given a high priority to the 'constitutional normalization' of Indian status, that is, to vitiating the historic constitutional anomaly of section 91 (24) that assigned exclusive jurisdiction over Indians to the federal government. The goal is to bring Indian status into broad conformity with prevailing federal and provincial constitutional mandates as these apply to Canadians generally. That is what Trudeau had in mind when he introduced the 1969 White Paper. More recent evidence for this idea can be found in 'Federal-Provincial Memoranda of Agreements' – bilateral accords for the 'normalization' of the delivery of services and programs to Indians. Additional evidence can be inferred from the Nielsen Report[11] recommendation that Indian special status should be diminished by ending their exclusive relationship with the federal government.

From time to time the courts have facilitated the process of constitutional normalization with rulings that broaden the application of provincial jurisdiction over Indians. The courts have done so with reference to section 88 of the Indian Act, which subjects Indians to provincially enacted 'laws of general application,' with some exceptions. With the courts' sanction section 88 has been used by the federal and provincial governments as a licence to erode Indian special status under section 91 (24) by expanding provincial legislative jurisdiction over Indians. Interpretations of section 88, as to which provincial laws are 'laws of general application' and therefore applicable to Indians, represents a value judgment made by the courts. The history of judicial interpretation of section 88 reveals a consistent pattern of incremental expansion of the powers of the provinces over Indians; that is, the extent to which provincial laws of general application apply to Indians is constantly being broadened by the courts.

A more subtle but, none the less, consequential actuation of the idea of constitutional normalization can be found in section 35 (2) of the Constitution Act, 1982. Here Indians have been lumped together and equated with Metis in the constitutional definition of 'aboriginal peoples'. This idea was first floated by Jean Chrétien (then minister of the DIAND) during the parliamentary debates on the 1969 White Paper. Chrétien asserted that the problems of Indians could not be solved separately from those of the Metis. He offered no explanation why the legal distinction between the two groups rendered the problems of both groups intractable to improvement. With the benefit of hindsight, it is evident that Chrétien's statement signalled an emerging government policy designed to blur and undermine the special status of Indians by joining them with the Metis. The Metis do not come under section 91 (24) of the BNA Act, or under the Indian Act, or under the DIAND; they have neither treaties, nor a constitutionally grounded land base, nor a trust relationship with the federal government; they are accepted as full 'provincial citizens.' In short, the Metis meet Trudeau's 'Canadians as all other Canadians' standard. By equating the constitutional status and rights of Indians with those of the Metis ('Canadians') the governments of Canada have created the 'vagueness' that opens the door for the courts to bring Indians into conformity with prevailing federal and provincial constitutional mandates.

A most damaging implementation of the idea of constitutional normalization occurred when full Canadian citizenship and the franchise were thrust upon Indians by a unilateral declaration of the Canadian government. This constitutional 'right' was not sought by Indians and, quite contrary to democratic theory, was proclaimed without Indian consent. In effect, the right to vote in Canadian elections was imposed on Indians in the 'national interest,' to affirm Canadian sovereignty over Indians. The Canadian government touts its extension of the franchise to Indians as an 'enlightened' democratic act done in the interest of Indians, but this act holds significant adverse implications for Indian special status. Bringing Indians into the Canadian political system has had the effect of subjecting them to a process of socialization that promotes intrinsic individualism ('one person, one vote'), and it functions to channel Indian opposition to Canadian policies through the ballot-box, where they have little influence. Moreover, it lends symbolic legitimacy to the fiction that Indians have given democratic consent to Canadian sovereignty and citizenship, and that their primary commitment is to the Canadian regime. Thus, it undermines Indian claims to 'peoples' rights' under the U.N. charter.

Individualization

In the wake of independence movements by colonized third-world nations following the Second World War, the Canadian government came under growing domestic and international pressures to decolonize the Indian peoples within its borders. In this regard, the government had two options: it could grant 'peoples' rights' to Indians (i.e., the path of self-determination) or it could impose 'individual rights' on them (i.e., the path of institutional assimilation). The Canadian government, with the consent of the provincial governments, has opted to decolonize Indians by imposing individual rights. Trudeau's 1969 White Paper represents a failed 'Indian policy' approach to this goal; Trudeau's Charter of Rights and Freedoms is serving as an effective 'Canadian policy' approach to achieve the same end.

Canada's rationale for choosing 'individual rights' over 'peoples' rights' as the pathway to Indian decolonization rests partly on the premise that the concept of 'peoples' rights' deviates fundamentally from the Western-liberal principle underlying Canadian democracy that there must be no inequalities among citizens based on racial or ethnic status. As already noted, the most influential Canadian advocate of this Western-liberal principle, Trudeau, viewed Indians as a disadvantaged racial minority, and he attributed this disadvantage to their special status, which he saw as engendering a racial psychology against Indians. It is worth noting here that, although the Metis do not have a special status, they are no less victims of racism. Clearly, the Canadian racism towards Indians is not explained by Indian special status. Rather, it is a consequence of how the Canadian government has chosen to define Indians (and Metis). Indians (and Metis) are victims of racial discrimination because, historically, the Canadian government has defined Indians (and Metis) in terms of racial, rather than cultural, criteria. If we take the experience of the Metis as an indication, removing special status from Indians and providing them with individual rights will not change the racial psychology of Canadians towards Indians.

Thus, one is forced to conclude that there is a much more weighty consideration than 'Western-liberal principles' that underlies Canada's bias in favour of individual rights over peoples' rights as its design for decolonizing Indians. Aboriginal rights, treaty rights, self-determination, land claims, resource claims, reparation claims, and many other troublesome demands by Indians are made in the name of their historical special status. By imposing the Western-liberal principle of individual rights, that is, making Indians into 'Canadians as all other Canadians,' the governments of Canada can legally void most problematic Indian rights and claims because these rights and claims have no application to Indians as individuals. Clearly, the 'national interest' rather than any idealistic commitment to Western-liberal principles is what drives all eleven governments in Canada to assert that decolonization must proceed with reference to the individualistic Charter of Rights and Freedoms, and not by Indian self-determination.

Consistent with this strategy, the Canadian government, in its public policy on Indian status, insists on defining Indians as a minority group, rather than as a 'people.' A particular example of this perspective can be noted in Canada's observance of the U.N. Convention on the Elimination of all Forms of Racial Discrimination (1969). This convention requires that appropriate measures be undertaken to secure the advancement of disadvantaged racial or ethnic groups. To the degree Canada has made gestures to fulfil its obligations to Indians under this convention, it has done so within the concept of *individual* rights, not 'peoples' rights.' The declared official Canadian policy is to liberate Indians from their underprivileged 'minority group' condition through equality of *individual* opportunity.

To sum up, the imperative of the 'national interest' is dictating Canadian policies designed to attenuate Indian special status even though Indians consider this to be contrary to their interests, rights, needs, and aspirations. The government's design for achieving the end of Indian special status is through institutional assimilation, and its strategies are 'structural integration,' 'constitutional normalization,' and 'individualization.' Already the government has made great progress on all three fronts, and perhaps the process has already moved beyond the point of no return.

Pan-Indianism

Pan-Indian political mobilization in Canada occurred as a sidestream effect of colonial political, legal, and economic policies. By defining culturally diverse Indian tribes/bands as a single legal category and by imposing uniform colonial policies and structures on them (e.g., the Indian Act, the reserve system, and the DIAND), the Canadian government created a shared experience, circumstance, and condition for all Indians. Moreover, the residential school experience, to which most Indians were subjected, gave them a common language, which greatly facilitated the emergence of the pan-Indian movement. However, it took the 1969 White Paper on Indian Policy to precipitate the Indians' commonalities and discontent into a significant pan-Indian political movement. The 'consultation process' mandated by Trudeau to legitimate the 1969 White Paper engendered a feeling of empowerment among Indian leaders, and the subsequent sense of betrayal the White Paper policy evoked among all Indian leaders served to raise their consciousness about their shared colonial experience, circumstance, and condition. The frequent meetings also made them aware of their cultural commonalities, which helped to draw them together in a spiritual cause. In effect, the 1969 White Paper brought to an end a century during which the Canadian government successfully fragmented Indians into hundreds of isolated communities.

The post-1969 period saw a proliferation of pan-Indian organizations – provincial, regional, national, treaty, women, youth – all devoted to the purpose of representing and promoting their shared interests and goals, and building collective strength. The most prominent pan-Indian organization is the Assembly of First Nations, the national organization that represents status Indians in Canada.

However, while regressive Canadian Indian policies created shared interests and a common cause for Indians, they have not provided an effective glue for pan-Indian unity. Pan-Indian unity is tenuous and elusive. The reasons for this are several: there exists no historical cultural or social community at the pan-Indian level; there is no tradition of large-scale political and cultural cooperation among most Indian bands/tribes; there exist profoundly diverse, often conflicting, political and economic interests among band/tribes that cause factionalism. Moreover, pan-Indian leaders operate at a considerable social distance from the 'grass roots' constituency they are supposed to represent. In the absence of a strong connection with their constituency, pan-Indian leaders have their primary affiliation with other Indian leaders. This has led to a pattern of decision making based on 'leadership consensus' and the advice of professional consultants. This approach to decision making tends to neglect the immediate day-to-day needs and interests of 'grass roots' Indians. In consequence pan-Indian leadership functions without a mass followership.

In an effort to close the gap between themselves and the grass-roots constituency, pan-Indian leaders have made moves to restructure their organizations to give direct representation to band/tribal councils through their respective chiefs. The Assembly of First Nations comprises over six hundred chiefs. And, in an effort to generate wider appeal and commitment from their putative constituency, pan-Indian leaders have emphasized popular ideological issues of pan-Indian concern, such as sovereignty and aboriginal and treaty rights. Moreover, they have sought out high-profile international and national forums in which to confront and oppose the Canadian government on these ideological issues – at the United Nations, The Hague, the U.K. House of Lords, the First Ministers' Conferences, and so on. But, the chiefs are not 'grass roots' Indian people and, despite the popular ideological issues to which pan-Indian leaders give emphasis, the gap between themselves and the 'grass roots' Indians has not been bridged.

The Canadian government's treatment of the pan-Indian movement is revealing. When the government believed that pan-Indian organizations could be used to control Indians and to give legitimacy to its Indian policies, it volunteered generous funding, and created 'joint' committees made up of senior government officials and pan-Indian leaders, moves that were designed to co-opt pan-Indian leaders onto the 'government team.' However, as events unfolded and some pan-Indian leaders took strong public stands against its policies, the federal government expediently shifted its focus and funding away from pan-Indian organizations and processes to local band/tribal councils and initiatives. This created a divisive competition between band/tribal councils, and national Indian organizations, for political influence and government funding. The government's strategy caused pan-Indian leaders to lose control of their 'troops,' so to speak. And it significantly diminished their capacity to oppose federal and provincial government policies that are contrary to the Indian common interests.

Most recently, the Canadian government, now intent on forging a constitutional deal that will bring Quebec into the Canadian family and fearing that pan-Indian leaders might find a way to sabotage the process (as they did in the case of the Meech Lake Accord), has expediently sought a rapprochement with pan-Indian leaders. Government funds to pan-Indian organizations are flowing freely again; pan-Indian leaders have the ear of the prime minister and cabinet ministers again; Indian leaders are being co-opted onto high-level committees and commissions again; the government is offering pan-Indian leaders another fifteen minutes of fame and fortune.

In retrospect it can be seen that government policy towards the pan-Indian movement was never motivated to enhance the movement's capacity to advance Indian common interests, rights, needs, and aspirations. Consistently, the government's policy was designed to 'use' the pan-Indian movement to advance the 'national interest.'

Indian government

The concept of 'Indian government' emerges from Indian history and from Indian aspirations. Following the treaty-making process, historically independent Indian tribes found themselves within the borders of an alien state – Canada – where Canadian legislators and courts proceeded in the name of the Crown to enforce Canadian sovereignty over them. Progressively Indians were forced, against their will, into a status of total political and administrative subordination to the Canadian government. But, throughout this period, they have retained strong memories of political independence; moreover, the bitter experiences of colonialism have kept alive in their souls a vision of self-determination – a sovereign government 'of their people, by their people, for their people.' Indians claim their right to sovereign self-government as pre-existing the arrival of the Europeans, and they hold that it survives as an inherent right, bestowed upon them by the Creator. How has the Canadian government responded to Indian claims and aspirations to sovereign self-government? In the past decade the government has introduced two initiatives on Indian 'self-government'; a brief discussion of both follows.

The Penner Committee

On 22 December 1982, the Parliament of Canada appointed a special committee to act as a parliamentary task force on Indian self-government. Chaired by Keith Penner, a member of Parliament from the governing Liberal party, and composed of representatives from all political parties in the House of Commons, the special committee was mandated to review all legal and related institutional factors affecting status, development, and responsibilities of band councils on Indian reserves, and to make recommendations in respect to establishing, empowering, and funding Indian self-government. In carrying out its mandate, the committee members made a great effort to hear and heed the Indian point of view. They travelled the length and breadth of Canada to obtain first-hand information from Indian people. The committee members came away from this process of consultation with a strong conviction that the federal and provincial jurisdictional relationships within Canadian confederation must be fundamentally reordered to make room for the inherent right of Indians to self-government.

More specifically, the committee recommended that Indian 'First Nations' governments should be constitutionally recognized as a distinct order of government within the Canadian federation and that Indian people themselves should, by free choice, determine the form and structure of government they desire. They proposed that Indian governments should have full legislative and policy-making powers in such areas as social and cultural development, revenue raising, economic and commercial development, justice and law enforcement, and band/tribal membership codes, and that they should have full control over their territory and resources.

The committee recommended the phasing out of the DIAND but, to enhance Indian participation in Canadian policy decisions affecting them, it recommended establishment of a raft of new federal agencies that would give Indians access to the seats of power in the federal government. The proposed agencies include a ministry of state for Indian First Nations relations; a joint Indian–federal government panel to consider requests for recognition of Indian First Nations governments; a secretariat to facilitate Indian–federal government negotiations; a special parliamentary commission to monitor the state of Indian–Canadian government relationships; and a tribunal to adjudicate disputes between Indian governments and other Canadian governments.

The committee rejected approaches to Indian self-government that represented a mere amendment of existing arrangements within current legal assumptions, such as 'devolution' of delegated administrative authority, or amending the Indian Act. The committee held that current legal assumptions offer inadequate scope for the required fundamental reordering of relationships that would allow Indian governments to relate to other Canadian governments on a 'government to government' basis.

The Penner Committee model of Indian First Nations government implied a new meaning for the concept of 'citizen plus.' As used in the past,[12] 'citizen plus' meant Indian entitlement to all the benefits of Canadian citizenship, with some benefits added by virtue of aboriginal rights. The old meaning did not exclude Indians from the normal constraints of Canadian citizenship, such as subordination to Parliament, and an obligation to obey all Canadian laws. In the Penner Committee model, however, the notion of 'citizen plus' implies that the primary allegiance and identity of on-reserve Indians would be vested in their citizenship in Indian First Nations. While Indians would be entitled to all of the benefits and associated responsibilities of Canadian citizenship, Indian governments could selectively choose to exempt their nations from some of the unwanted features of Canadian citizenship, such as the Charter of Rights and Freedoms. In effect, the Penner Committee proposed to greatly enhance the special status of Indians in Canada and to entrench their special status in the constitution.

The Penner Committee's recommendation that Indian government be entrenched in the constitution as an inherent right, with its own legislative jurisdiction, implied the requirement to restructure existing assumptions and systems of Canadian government and law to accommodate the rights of Indians. By giving Indian rights and interests coequal status with Canadian rights and interests, the Penner Committee defied the 'national interest' imperative. Such a proposal was an anathema to the ten provincial governments and the federal government.

In his response to the Penner Report, the minister of Indian Affairs agreed with the committee's recommendation that the Indian–federal government relationship needs substantial restructuring, and even used some of the committee's rhetoric. But when he set out his government's version of the restructured relationship with reference to the inherent powers, responsibility, accountability, recognition, and funding arrangements of Indian government, it was evident that the federal government had turned its back on the Penner Report. No compromise was permissible between the 'national interest' and Indian interests on the constitutional jurisdiction of Indian government.

Community-based self-government

The Canadian government was quick to reject the Penner Committee Report; none the less, the report incited a momentum of aspirations for self-government among band/tribal Indian leaders – aspirations that the government viewed as potentially troublesome if not properly channelled. In anticipation that the First Ministers' conferences on aboriginal matters would block all attempts to define and constitutionally entrench Indian self-government, the federal government decided to develop its own legislative initiative on Indian government designed to placate Indian leaders, and to appropriately channel and limit their expectations. The legislative model of Indian self-government it chose to accomplish these ends has been titled 'Indian Self-Government Community Negotiations.'[13] The government's 'policy' statement on this legislative initiative, published in September 1989,[14] makes it quite clear that what is being offered to Indians under the guise of 'self-government' is an updated version of a very old notion titled 'devolution of responsibility.' In 1884, the Indian Advancement Act was enacted to confer 'certain privileges on the more advanced Bands of Indians of Canada with a view to training them for the exercise of municipal powers.' The present Indian government policy initiative is an updated version of the 1884 devolution agenda. It implies that the Canadian government now considers Indian leaders sufficiently schooled to begin exercising some 'municipal powers'.

The 1884 version of 'devolution' was operationalized within the Indian Act. Under the current Indian government proposal, band/

tribal councils will be freed from some of the constraints of the Indian Act. But strong continuities with past colonial practices of control over Indians still abide. This is evident in the fact that, at present, the DIAND is re-forming itself to play a close monitoring and auditing role so as to ensure that the bands/tribes that are granted 'self-government' will administer the devolved functions and associated funds in a manner that conforms to Canadian legal, political, and fiscal prescriptions and standards. Clearly, old colonial habits of paternalism and distrust are not going to disappear under 'community-based Indian self-government.' Given the high level of Canadian government control built into the proposed Indian self-government model, it is more accurately described as an 'alternative Indian Act' than as 'freedom from the Indian Act.'

If the Canadian government held as a primary concern (or even as a coequal concern to that of the 'national interest') that Indian self-government should serve the interests, rights, needs, and aspirations of Indian people, it would have made some accommodation to the basic principles of self-government put forward by Indian leaders. But none of the key jurisdictional concepts contained in Indian paradigms of self-government (e.g., 'inherent' authority versus delegated authority) appear in the Canadian government's Indian self-government model. Moreover, following the pattern by which the Royal Proclamation, the Indian Act, and the treaties were framed, the proposed Indian self-government model (outlined in the guidelines) allows Indians no role in establishing the basic principles and precepts of self-government, nor in determining the spheres and scope of their authority. The basic principles and precepts have been declared non-negotiable by the Canadian government. Under the government's model Indians are required to 'construct' their self-government from a set of approved parts. They are not being given the opportunity to derive self-government from an indigenous set of philosophies and principles.

Although the Canadian government is proceeding with its Indian self-government initiative on a 'band-by-band' basis, from the outset it was envisioned as a 'snowball' strategy; that is, government officials quite correctly anticipated that once a few key bands agreed to accept the Indian self-government offer, others would follow, in an accelerating trend. Had the government's intent been to serve Indian interest, rights, needs, and aspirations, the Canadian government could have proceeded by establishing a few pilot projects, thus allowing Indians to test this model of Indian government to see if it benefited them. But, instead, the Canadian government followed its usual strategy for putting Indians on the path it wants them to take – it held out money and a bit more authority as incentives to band/tribal councils if they would engage in the negotiation process. Next, it announced that a backlog of applications was building and it put out hints that the offer could soon be withdrawn. This clever tactic raised fears among band councils that they might be left out, and it engendered a competitive rush – a bandwagon effect – to enter the negotiation process.

At bottom, the government's Indian self-government initiative represents a strategy for diminishing Indian special status by 'normalizing' federal-provincial constitutional mandates in respect of Indians and land reserved for Indians. The idea underlying this version of 'Indian self-government' is to void the federal government's unique relationship with Indians under section 91 (24) by a series of phased shifts that will jockey federal and provincial jurisdictions and responsibilities for Indians into a 'normal' constitutional configuration – 'normal' in the sense that Indians will be dealt with as all other Canadians. The government proposes to achieve this goal by vacating certain areas of its historical constitutional jurisdiction and responsibility in favour of the provinces. Thus, the status and authority of Indian self-government will derive from federal and provincial delegated authority and legislation, and Indian governments will function as municipalities, subordinate to both federal and provincial governments.

In the past, schemes by the federal government to transfer its historic responsibility for Indians to the provinces have always met with strong opposition from both Indians and the provincial governments. This time, however, the federal government has carefully conceived its present Indian self-government initiative to overcome both sets of resistance. In order to mitigate provincial resistance the federal government has committed itself to including the provinces in any negotiations on matters of Indian self-government authority that normally fall inside the provincial constitutional mandate, even matters that, under section 91 (24), at present fall under exclusive federal jurisdiction. Moreover, the federal government has declared itself ready to enlarge provincial legislative authority over Indians in those areas that normally fall inside the provincial constitutional mandate. The provinces have always coveted such legislative authority. In order to overcome Indian opposition to such a transfer of jurisdiction to the provinces the federal government has committed itself to enlarging band/tribal councils' administrative control over their own affairs and budgets – something band/tribal councils have always craved. The federal government's strategy of dropping bread crumbs on the path they want the provinces and Indians to follow is showing promise. Already provincial governments have shown a keen interest in facilitating the community-based Indian self-government process. And, at present, 178 Indian bands/tribes have submitted formal proposals to achieve self-government, and more than 50 are close to an agreement.

The Canadian government is representing its Indian self-government initiative as if it were intended to serve Indian interests, rights, needs, and aspirations. This fiction is plausible to band/tribal councils because the proposed arrangement will allow them to administer more of their affairs and budgets. But, in fact, this version of 'Indian self-government' is a cunning strategy for serving the 'national interest.' By conforming Indian political, administrative, and legal institutions to provincial municipal–type structures, it will facilitate the next phase of institutional assimilation, that is, fully assimilating Indian governments into the provincial municipal system.

To sum up, the Canadian government's community-based Indian self-government initiative is a lure that conceals the trap of institutional assimilation. It pretends to offer self-government to Indians but, when all the smoke and mirrors are removed, it becomes clear that the proposed 'Indian self-government' constitutes no more than a reshuffling of DIAND 'desks' or functions consequent to the downsizing of DIAND. In this shuffle, the important 'desks' (those representing policy-making authority and functions) are being transferred to other federal and provincial government departments and agencies, whereas a few lesser 'desks' (those representing local administrative/clerical authority and functions) are being transferred to Indian bands/tribes and are termed 'Indian self-government.' In effect, Indians are being offered a 'franchise' to manage some local affairs, but subject to stringent 'head office' rules, conditions, and standards, and to central monitoring and controls over programs, services, and budgets.

Indian leaders must be careful not to step into the Canadian government's trap by calling the proposed transfer of some DIAND administrative/clerical functions to bands/tribes by the name of 'Indian self-government.' In the first instance, it is obviously not the sovereign self-government to which Indians aspire and which they claim as an inherent right. Second, expanded self-administration subject to such overarching external restraints does not qualify as self-government by any accepted definition. But, if Indian leaders accept the proposed transfer of DIAND administrative functions in the name of 'Indian self-government,' they will undoubtedly compromise the aboriginal right of future generations to true *Indian* self-government. The words that are used here are important. If Indian leaders accept the Canadian government's terminology they will become victims of 'the great lie' – that is, by repeating a lie often enough they will come to believe it, and future generations of Indians will come to believe they have achieved Indian self-government.

Constitutional reform

On 21 June 1991, the Canadian Parliament initiated a new round of constitutional reform by establishing a Special Joint Committee of the Senate and the House of Commons on a Renewed Canada. This new round called the 'Canada Round' is focusing on the redistribution of federal and provincial powers. Because Quebec is the single strongest advocate of decentralization of powers, much attention has been focused on the demands of that province. But, in reality, *all* of the provinces are entering into this 'new round' for the purpose of expanding their constitutional mandate at the expense of the federal government's mandate. All are elbowing for more provincial jurisdiction in the federation and, at the same time, they are jockeying to maximize their powers within the federal legislative institutions such as the Senate and the Supreme Court.

Under section 35.1 of the Constitution Act, 1982, Canadian governments are committed to the principle that aboriginal peoples will participate in discussions pertaining to constitutional amendments that relate directly to them. When the Canadian government tabled its proposals for constitutional reform before Parliament's Special Joint Committee on the Process for Amending the Constitution on 25 September 1991, they contained proposed amendments that relate directly to aboriginal peoples. Thus, the governments of Canada were constitutionally obliged to consult with the aboriginal peoples.

In consequence of this constitutional commitment, aboriginal organizations demanded adequate funding to engage their people in a process of consultation preliminary to putting forward their proposals for constitutional reform. The Canadian government acceded to these demands by mandating and funding selected national Indian, Inuit, and Metis organizations to consult their respective peoples, and to bring their proposals resulting from these consultations to the special joint committee. This process has been titled by the government 'the Aboriginal Constitutional Process' and is also known as 'the Parallel Constitutional Process.'

Under 'the Aboriginal Constitutional Process,' the Assembly of First Nations (AFN) was mandated and funded to consult Indian peoples. The AFN carried out its mandate under the title 'the First Nations Circle on the Constitution (FNCC).' The AFN's mandate was specifically to develop proposals for Indian self-government (although they were also invited to bring forward proposals on whatever other issues they wish) and to bring these to the special joint committee. The special joint committee was to examine these proposals, along with any submitted by the federal government and the provinces prior to submitting its report and recommendations to Parliament. However, the FNCC was not able to complete its consultation process with Indian people in time to place its proposals before the special joint committee prior to that committee's report to Parliament. Consequently, the special joint committee's recommendations do not take into account the views expressed by Indian people to the FNCC. In its report, the committee merely acknowledges the input of some unnamed provincial Indian leaders and AFN officials.

The essence of the federal government's proposal for constitutional reform is to be found in Part 3 of the proposals document.[15] Part 3 deals with the apportionment of constitutional sovereign powers in the Canadian federal system as set out in sections 91–5 of the Constitution Act, 1867. Significantly, only the federal and provincial governments (i.e., the 'two orders' of government) are included in this part. The aboriginal peoples didn't merit even a mention. Here we had a clear signal by the federal government that it harboured no intention of including Indian 'third order' governments in the division of constitutional sovereign powers. This made a sham of the aboriginal constitutional process that was loudly proclaimed by the Canadian government as giving Indians an opportunity to shape the constitution to reflect their rights, interests, needs, and aspirations. The money and mandate given to the AFN to consult their people on the constitution amounted to little more than a ploy to distract Indian leaders while the federal and provincial government wrangled over the division of constitutional sovereign powers.

In Part 3, the federal government has declared itself 'prepared to transfer to the provinces authority for non-national matters not specifically assigned to the federal government under the constitution or by virtue of court decision.' Any transfer of federal jurisdiction to the provinces has implications for Indians because any powers transferred to the provinces will require that Indians, in their quest for self-government, must negotiate with the provinces for the delegation of those powers (e.g., housing, job training, mining, forestry, and environmental protection). This will be the case even though Indians continue as a federal responsibility under section 91 (24) of the Constitution Act, 1867. Yet, Indians have no vote on the proposed transfer of federal jurisdiction to the provinces.

On 25 September 1991, the federal government submitted its proposals respecting aboriginal self-government to the special joint committee. Following is a summary of these proposals.

Aboriginal claims to sovereignty, to an inherent or treaty right to self-government, and to decide which laws of Canada or a province they are bound by, are all explicitly rejected.

The 'Canada Clause' that would be entrenched in S. 2 of the Constitution Act, 1867, would acknowledge that Aboriginal Peoples were historically self-governing and that their rights are recognized in Canada.

Aboriginal right to self-government within the Canadian federation would be entrenched immediately. Negotiations defining self-government would begin at once, and any agreements reached would be constitutionally protected as they are developed. After ten years, the right to self-government would be 'justiciable,' that is enforceable by the courts.

Aboriginal communities would be governed by a mixture of federal, provincial and aboriginal laws, the exact mixture to be worked out through negotiations, but failing in this, after ten years, the courts would be able to pronounce on this issue.

Aboriginal governments would be subject to the individual rights and freedoms protected by the Canadian Charter of Rights and Freedoms.

Aboriginal peoples would be given guaranteed representation in a reformed Senate.

A continuing constitutional process would be entrenched affording an opportunity to address unfinished aboriginal constitutional items. In addition, this process would review the results of negotiations on self-government during the ten-year period until the right to self-government becomes justiciable.[16]

On 28 February 1992, the Special Joint Committee on a Renewed Canada published its recommendations for constitutional renewal to the Parliament of Canada. It is noteworthy that the committee makes no recommendations for assignment of any constitutional sovereign powers to aboriginal governments ('third order of governments') in sections 91–5. The committee's recommendations pertaining to 'Aboriginal Matters' are as follows:

> The Committee recommends the entrenchment in section 35 of the *Constitution Act, 1982* of the inherent right of aboriginal peoples to self-government within Canada.
>
> The modern application of self-government will require negotiations with respect to the jurisdiction to be exercised by self-governing aboriginal communities. We recommend the entrenchment of a transition process to identify the responsibilities that will be exercised by aboriginal governments and their relationship to federal, provincial and territorial governments.
>
> We recommend that the fundamental rights and freedoms of all Canadians, including the equality of the rights of men and women, ought to receive full constitutional protection.
>
> We recommend that federal treaty obligations, fiduciary and trust responsibilities, and the provision of fiscal transfers that continue after the implementation of forms of self-government by various aboriginal groups be administered by a small bureau jointly managed by the federal government and representatives of the aboriginal peoples.
>
> We recommend:
>
> i. in order to protect the aboriginal and treaty rights which the Constitution guarantees to the aboriginal peoples of Canada, that any amendment to the Constitution of Canada directly affecting the aboriginal peoples require the consent of the aboriginal peoples of Canada prior to its implementation;
> ii. that representatives of the aboriginal peoples of Canada be invited to all future constitutional conferences relating to the matters referred to in paragraph (i); and
> iii. that the Constitution provide that a constitutional conference be convened within two years after the amendment on the inherent right of self-government of the aboriginal peoples of Canada comes into force.
>
> We recommend that the role of the Indian, Inuit and Metis peoples in the development of Canada, as well as their inherent rights as the First Peoples be recognized in the proposed Canada Clause. In addition,

the clause should contain a recognition of the right and responsibility of aboriginal peoples to protect and develop their unique cultures, languages and traditions.

We recommend:

> Guaranteed aboriginal representation in the Canadian Senate. This will be a logical extension of aboriginal self-government, and the details of this representation should be negotiated with aboriginal peoples, consistent with the relationship between numbers of seats and population applied to the distribution of Senate seats among provinces and territories.[17]

The FNCC completed its consultations with Indian peoples and published its recommendations on 13 April 1992 in a report entitled *To the Source*.[18] Subsequently, at a Special Chiefs' Assembly on the Constitution held on 23 April 1992, these recommendations were translated into a series of resolutions, adopted by consensus.[19] These resolutions defined the AFN's official constitutional position, which was presented to the Continuing Council of Ministers Responsible for Constitutional Development. The AFN's position subsumes the following elements:

- aboriginal inherent right to self-government with appropriate provision of lands and resources to operate as full governments which can meet the needs of their citizens;
- recognition (equivalent to that accorded Quebec) of First Nations peoples as distinct societies;
- bilateral sovereign nation-to-nation relationships between the Crown in Right of Canada and Treaty First Nations;
- full participation and consent of First Nations prior to alteration of any federal-provincial mandates that affect First Nations rights, interests, and jurisdictions;
- recognition of First Nations governments as a third order of government;
- a requirement that constitutional amendments which affect First Nations be subject to the consent of the First Nations;
- full and equal participation by First Nations in all First Ministers/ First Nations Leaders' Conferences;
- deletion of existing constitutional requirement of blanket First Nations compliance with federal and provincial laws, and initiation of discussions purposed to define nation-to-nation relations with

regard to the imposition of the laws of Canada on First Nations, their citizens, and their economic enterprises;
- guaranteed representation on the Supreme Court of Canada, a role in the nomination of Supreme Court judges, and representation as distinct people in a reformed Senate;
- recognition of aboriginal languages as the first official language of Canada accompanied by resources comparable to those allocated for support of the French language;
- guarantees that the natural resources upon which a First Nation depends for survival will be collectively held in trust for future generations, and that the consent of the affected First Nations is required prior to exploitation of such resources.

All of the foregoing proposals for constitutional reform, although important in identifying and framing aboriginal issues, and in staking out negotiating positions, must be deemed as 'preliminaries' to the constitutional 'main event.' The 'main event' comprised a series of multilateral meetings on the constitution, chaired by the federal minister of constitutional affairs, the Honourable Joe Clark. These multilateral meetings were attended by representatives from the federal government, nine provincial governments, the two territorial governments, and four aboriginal associations. The premier of Quebec, the Honourable Robert Bourassa, refused to participate in these meetings until satisfied that the key provisions of the failed Meech Lake Accord would be restored in any new constitutional proposals. The initial multilateral meeting was held in Ottawa, on 12 March 1992, followed by eleven further meetings, lasting a total of twenty-seven days. These meetings concluded with the 'July 7 accord.' This accord satisfied Premier Bourassa's demands regarding the restoration of the substance of the Meech Lake Accord and, consequently, he accepted an invitation to return to the constitutional negotiating table at Harrington Lake on 4 and 10 August, 1992, and again in Ottawa, 17–21 August 1992. The Ottawa meeting was chaired by Prime Minister Brian Mulroney, and, with all of the members of the 'Canadian family' present, a constitutional consensus was achieved – a 'national-unity' accord. This accomplishment led to a final meeting at Charlottetown, Prince Edward Island, on 27 and 28 August 1992, to seal the 'national-unity' accord, and to consider a process of ratification.

The following text provides a summary of the agreements affecting aboriginal peoples that resulted from the multilateral meetings prior to Quebec's participation (i.e., the 'July 7 accord'). The agreements reached with Quebec present – that is, the 'national-unity' accord, subsequently renamed the 'Charlottetown accord' – produced only four 'add-on' provisions to the 'July 7 accord' that affected aboriginal peoples. In the following text, these four additions appear after the summary of the 'July 7 accord.' As well, asterisks have been inserted to identify ideas for which a consensus to proceed with a political accord was achieved.

– The Canada Clause, which expresses fundamental Canadian values and guides the courts in their future interpretation of the constitution, is to acknowledge that aboriginal peoples have the right to promote their languages, cultures, and traditions and to ensure the integrity of their societies, and that aboriginal governments constitute one of three levels of government in Canada (federal, provincial, and aboriginal).
– The constitution is to be amended to recognize that the aboriginal peoples of Canada have the inherent right of self-government within Canada. This right is to be placed in a new section of the Constitution Act, 1982, section 35.1 (1). The recognition of this right should be interpreted in light of the recognition of aboriginal government as one of three orders of government.
– The inherent right to aboriginal self-government is to be justiciable (i.e., enforceable by the courts); however, its justiciability will be delayed for a five-year period. There is also a commitment to place the creation of special tribunals on the agenda of a future First Ministers' Conference on Aboriginal constitutional matters(*).
– There is to be an explicit statement in the constitution that the commitment to negotiate does not make the right to self-government contingent on negotiations or in any way affect the justiciability of the right of self-government, or affect existing aboriginal and treaty rights.
– All parties (federal, provincial, and aboriginal) are committed to negotiate in good faith with the objective of concluding agreements elaborating the relationship between aboriginal governments and the other orders of government. The negotiations are to focus on the implementation of the right to self-government, including issues of jurisdiction, lands and resources, and economic fiscal arrangements.
– A process of negotiation is to be set out in a political accord to guide the self-government negotiations(*). The process of negotiation is to provide that:

- all aboriginal peoples have equitable access to the process of negotiation;
- self-government negotiations are to be initiated by the aboriginal peoples, when they are prepared to do so;
- self-government agreements may provide for self-government institutions that are open to the participation of all residents in a region covered by the self-government agreement;
- there is to be an approved process for approval of aboriginal self-government agreements involving aboriginal peoples, Parliament, and, to the extent of their jurisdiction, by the legislatures of the relevant provinces;
- self-government negotiations are to take into consideration the different circumstances of the various aboriginal peoples;
- self-government agreements are to be set out in future treaties, or amendments to existing treaties, including land claims. In addition, self-government agreements could be set out in the agreement which may contain a declaration that the rights of the aboriginal peoples are treaty rights, within the meaning of section 35 (1) of the Constitution Act, 1982;
- a dispute-resolution mechanism involving mediation and arbitration is to be established to assist in the negotiation process.
- Section 25 of the Charter of Rights and Freedoms (the non-derogation clause) is to be strengthened to ensure that nothing in the charter abrogates or derogates from aboriginal treaty or other rights, and in particular rights or freedoms relating to the exercise or protection of aboriginal languages, cultures, or traditions.
- There is to be a general 'non-derogation' clause to ensure that division of power amendments will not affect the rights of aboriginal peoples and the jurisdictions and powers of aboriginal governments.
- The Canadian Charter of Rights and Freedoms is to apply immediately to governments of aboriginal peoples.
- Aboriginal governments are to have access to section 33 of the Constitution Act, 1982 (the notwithstanding clause), under conditions similar to federal and provincial governments, but which are appropriate to the circumstances of aboriginal peoples and their legislative bodies.
- Aboriginal representation in the Senate is to be guaranteed(*).
- Aboriginal senators are to have the same role and powers as other senators, plus a possible double-majority power (i.e., approval by a majority of senators voting and a majority of aboriginal senators

voting) in relation to certain matters materially affecting aboriginal people(*).

– Aboriginal representation in the House of Commons is to be pursued by Parliament in consultation with representatives of the aboriginal peoples after it has received the final report of the House of Commons Royal Commission on Electoral Reform and Party Financing(*).

– The role of aboriginal peoples' in relation to the Supreme Court is not modified in this round but is to be recorded in a political accord and is to be on the agenda of a future FMC on aboriginal issues(*):
  – provincial and territorial governments should develop a reasonable process for consulting representatives of aboriginal peoples of Canada in the preparation of lists of candidates to fill vacancies on the Supreme Court;
  – aboriginal groups should retain the right to make representations to the federal government respecting candidates to fill vacancies on the Supreme Court;
  – the federal government should examine, in consultation with aboriginal groups, the proposal that an Aboriginal Council of Elders be entitled to make submissions to the Supreme Court when the Court considers aboriginal issues.

– For greater certainty section 91 (24) of the Constitution Act, 1867, is to be amended to apply to all aboriginal peoples.

– There is to be a constitutional provision that will ensure federal and provincial laws will continue to apply until they are displaced by laws passed by governments of aboriginal peoples pursuant to their authority.

– Cultural matters within the provinces are to be a matter of exclusive provincial jurisdiction but this change should not alter the federal government's fiduciary responsibility for aboriginal people. The non-derogation provision for aboriginal people will apply to culture.

– Aboriginal governments are to be authorized to undertake affirmative-action programs for socially and economically disadvantaged individuals or groups within their jurisdiction, as well as programs for the advancement of aboriginal languages and cultures.

– All aboriginal peoples are to have access to those aboriginal and treaty rights recognized and affirmed in section 35 of the Constitution Act, 1982, that pertain to them.

– With regard to treaties the constitution is to be amended as follows:
  – treaty rights are to be interpreted in a just, broad, and liberal

manner, taking into account the spirit and intent of the treaties and the context in which they were negotiated;
- the Government of Canada is to be committed to establish and participate in good faith, in a joint process, to clarify or implement treaty rights or to rectify terms of treaties when agreed to by the parties. The provincial governments are also to be committed to participate in the treaty process when invited by the federal government and the aboriginal peoples concerned or where specified in a treaty;
- participants in the process are to have regard, among other things and where appropriate, to the spirit and intent of the treaties as understood by aboriginal peoples. It is to be confirmed that all aboriginal peoples that possess treaty rights shall have equitable access to the treaty process;
- it is to be provided that these treaty amendments shall not extend the authority of any government or legislature or affect the rights of aboriginal peoples not party to the treaty concerned.
- Matters relating to financing are to be dealt with in a political accord(*). The accord is to commit the federal and provincial governments and the governments of aboriginal peoples to:
  - promoting equal opportunity for the well-being of all aboriginal peoples;
  - furthering economic, social, and cultural development and employment opportunities to reduce disparity of opportunity among aboriginal peoples and between aboriginal peoples and other Canadians;
  - providing essential public services at levels reasonably comparable to those available to other Canadians in the vicinity;
  - providing aboriginal governments with fiscal or other resources, such as land, to assist those governments to govern their own affairs and to meet the commitments listed above, taking into account the levels of services provided to other Canadians in the vicinity and the fiscal capacity of governments of aboriginal peoples to raise revenues from their own sources;
  - the issues of financing and its possible inclusion in the constitution is to be on the agenda of the first FMC on Aboriginal constitutional matters.
- There is to be aboriginal consent to future constitutional amendments that directly affect the aboriginal peoples. The mechanism for this consent are under discussion.
- Governments of aboriginal peoples should have access to a mech-

anism to ensure that designated bilateral and multilateral agreements with federal and provincial governments are protected from unilateral change.

– Representatives of the aboriginal peoples of Canada are to be invited to participate in discussions on any item on the agenda of a FMC that directly affects the aboriginal peoples(*).

– The constitution is to be amended to provide for four future FMCs on aboriginal constitutional matters beginning no later than 1996, and following every two years thereafter.

– The issue of gender equality is to be on the agenda of future FMCs on aboriginal constitutional matters(*).

The four 'add-ons' to the 7 July accord resulting from the Charlottetown meetings are summarized below:[20]

– A contextual statement is to be inserted in the constitution as follows: the exercise of the right of self-government includes the authority of the duly constituted legislative bodies of aboriginal peoples, each within its own jurisdiction:
  – to safeguard and develop their languages, cultures, economies, identities, institutions, and traditions; and
  – to develop, maintain, and strengthen their relationship with their lands, waters, and environment so as to determine and control their development as peoples according to their own values and priorities and ensure the integrity of their societies.
  Before making any final determination of an issue arising from the inherent right of self-government, a court or tribunal should take into account the contextual statement referred to above and should enquire into the efforts that have been made to resolve the issue through negotiations and should be empowered to order the parties to take such steps as are appropriate in the circumstances to effect a negotiated resolution.

– the specific constitutional provision on the inherent right and the specific constitutional provision on the commitment to negotiate land is not to create new aboriginal rights to land or derogate from existing aboriginal or treaty rights to land, except as provided for in self-government agreements.

– A law passed by a government of aboriginal peoples or an assertion of its authority based on the inherent-right provision may not be inconsistent with those laws which are essential to the preservation of peace, order, and good government in Canada.

- The new provision to include Metis in section 91 (24) is not to
result in a reduction of existing expenditures on Indians and Inuit
or alter the fiduciary and treaty obligations of the federal government for aboriginal peoples(*).

The agreements outlined above slated to proceed via a 'political
accord' do not indicate a constitutional amendment. They merely
committed the federal and provincial governments to negotiating the
identified issues with aboriginal representatives. Although the Charlottetown Accord achieved a substantial consensus (not unanimity on
all points) among Canada's First Ministers and the aboriginal delegations, it failed in a national referendum and was rejected even in
Indian communities. However, even assuming all of the above 'agreements' are ultimately entrenched, they will not bridge the gap between the Indian leaders' conception of self-government and that held
by the federal and provincial governments. Throughout the consti-
tutional-reform process Indian leaders uncompromisingly insisted that
the aboriginal inherent right to self-government must mean a 'third
order' of government with a share of Canadian *sovereign* powers identified in sections 91–5 of the Constitution Act. In effect, they demanded a redrafting of the 'architecture' of Canadian federalism to
make room for a 'third order' of *sovereign* Indian government. However, the federal and provincial governments categorically and ada-
mantly denied this demand. Their refusal was rationalized on grounds
that to acknowledge Indian sovereign powers, even within the Canadian federation, would threaten the integrity of the Canadian state.
They agreed only to entrench a form of aboriginal inherent right to
self-government that is based on powers to be negotiated, and that
will be subject to federal and provincial sovereignty (in effect, 'contingent powers') within the framework of the Canadian federation.
Moreover, to ensure that future Indian governments will not jeopardize provincial interests and jurisdictions, Quebec insisted upon
limiting their authority and laws by requiring that they must be consistent with Canadian laws essential to the 'preservation of peace,
order, and good government in Canada.' The truth is that the gap
between the Indian leaders' stated conception of a 'third order' *sovereign* government and the version agreed to by the eleven Canadian
governments can be bridged only by smoke, mirrors, creative legal
rhetoric, empty promises, and mutual pretence.

The agreements reached in the Canada Round of constitutional
negotiations, arguably, provided just such a fantastic 'bridge.' The

governments of Canada and aboriginal leaders agreed to entrench in the constitution a justiciable aboriginal 'inherent right to self-government' as an undefined *principle* – in effect, entrenching an 'empty box' – with provision of a *process* for defining the principle. The first phase of the process involves trilateral political negotiations to be conducted, over five years, among band/tribal councils and provincial and federal governments, as to the exact meaning of aboriginal 'inherent right to self-government.' If no meeting of the minds resulted from the negotiating phase, then the process would move to the second phase – litigation. In this second phase, the Court can be asked to interpret the principle, and impose a solution. This 'empty box' stratagem is identical to that employed when 'existing aboriginal rights' was entrenched, without definition, in the Constitution Act, 1982. This is a stratagem of political expedience. It allowed aboriginal leaders and Canadian First Ministers to escape a constitutional impasse. Both sides knew that an attempt to specify the powers of aboriginal self-government would have frustrated the negotiations. Any definition of aboriginal self-government acceptable to the federal and provincial First Ministers would have been unacceptable to aboriginal leaders, and vice versa. Aboriginal leaders opted for the 'empty box' stratagem to escape the entrenchment of a repugnant definition of 'inherent right to self-government.' They believed they could get a better result through trilateral political negotiations, and, in the event political negotiations failed, through litigation.

What would Indian leaders have gained by entrenchment of the *principle* of 'inherent right to self-government,' and a *process* for defining the principle? Stripped of all illusions, they would have gained no more than a constitutional sanction to enter into a political and legal process for the purpose of empowering their hypothetical 'third order' governments. They would have moved from 'delegated' to 'negotiated' authority, with an option of litigated authority. They would not have gained 'sovereign authority. It is hardly a secret that 'political negotiations' are exercises in power politics. The party with the most power prevails. What weapons can Indian leaders bring to such negotiations? Bluff, bluster, veiled threats, begging, pleading the destitution of their people, appealing to Canadian guilt, and so on. These are not weapons of power. Thus, it is unlikely in the extreme that Indian leaders can gain the powers essential for meaningful 'third order' governments in such negotiations. A more likely scenario is that Indian leaders would experience years of frustration and ultimate disappointment in these negotiations, and then they would proceed to phase two – litigation.

Their prospects of gaining significant powers through litigation are dismal. The Court, constrained by the 'national interest' imperative, is unlikely to cause the federal and provincial governments consequential difficulty when Indians plead their cases for 'inherent right to self-government.' The Court can follow the logic and precedent it established in *Sparrow*, with regard to 'existing aboriginal rights.' That is, it can draw a distinction between the *existence* of an 'inherent right to self-government' and the *exercise* of that right. The constitutional basis for such a distinction already exists by virtue of the separation of the *principle* of aboriginal inherent rights to self-government from the *definition* of aboriginal self-government. The Court can then hold that the entrenched aboriginal 'inherent right to self-government' has an abstract, permanent quality, and that this right exists in its pre-contact 'pristine state.' But, in the same breath, it can hold that the *exercise* of that right is subject to federal and provincial sovereignty in the context of Canadian federalism. The Court may even reiterate the platitudes it used in *Sparrow* when it exhorted lower-court colleagues to 'honour the Queen,' 'hold the Crown to high standards,' and so on. It may even set standards for 'negotiations in good faith.' But, none of this can hide the fact that a ruling which holds the *exercise* of aboriginal rights to be subject to federal and provincial sovereignty in the context of Canadian federalism diminishes prospective Indian governments to a status that will amount to little more than federal-provincial municipal governments. In short, the constitutional 'empty box' holds a constitutional 'empty promise.'

The important question confronting Indian leaders is whether the constitutional 'agreements' they negotiated would have enabled their people to live and survive as *Indians*. Clearly, the 'agreements' were not framed within a concept of *Indian* principles and philosophies. They were framed within a purpose of improving the status and condition of Indian Act Indians as a deprived Canadian minority group. This is a worthy purpose, but does it yield a framework within which bands/tribes can survive as *Indians*? I will return to a further discussion of this issue in chapters 3 and 4.

It is important to note that there is a fundamental and profound philosophical difference in the way that the Canadian government and the AFN have portrayed the participation of Indians in the Canada Round of constitutional reform. The Canadian government construed

Indian participation as a commitment to Canadian sovereignty; as an 'interest group' undertaking to secure a legitimate place for themselves as citizens of Canada, and to ensure that their rights, interests, needs, and aspirations as Canadian citizens are reflected in the constitution. The AFN expressed quite a different perspective. The Chief of the AFN, Ovide Mercredi, asserted that their involvement in the process was as sovereign nations who are concerned that Canadians should entrench appropriate principles of law in their constitution that will ensure just treatment of Indian First Nations. Mercredi's publicly enunciated premise was that constitutional entrenchment of appropriate principles would provide greater assurance to Indians that Canadians will obey their own laws in regard to Indian rights. This premise denies that Indians participated as Canadian citizens, subject to Canadian sovereignty.

Whose interpretation of Indian participation will prevail when these differing perspectives are arbitrated in international forums? If Indian leaders want to maintain the option of approaching the United Nations as 'colonized peoples' seeking self-determination, then it becomes imperative they establish unambiguously and incontrovertibly that their participation in the Canadian constitutional reform process is not as an 'interest group' comprised of 'Canadian citizens' who want a role in building the new Canadian constitution, but as 'peoples' engaging in a 'nation-to-nation' transaction. At this point in the constitutional reform process it is not yet clear whether Mercredi's assertion (that Indian participation is as 'sovereign nations') represented mere negotiating rhetoric or is an assertion of principle for which the AFN is prepared to stand and fight. As we have seen in the previous chapter, when Indians seek to make a case in the U.N. forums for the right to self-determination, the Canadian government's strategy is to deny the 'peoplehood' of Indians and to insist Indians are citizens of Canada. By participating in the constitutional reform process, Indian leaders may have crossed a critical invisible line, and having crossed this line they will no longer be perceived (internationally) as colonized 'peoples' eligible for self-determination, but as disadvantaged Canadian citizens. In effect, their claim to 'peoples' rights' under the U.N. charter may have been forfeited. This contingency serves to underline the imperative that, if Indians hope to be recognized by the United Nations as 'peoples,' they need to develop ideologies, political concepts, and linkages with ethnic minorities in other states that will identify and include them as part of the worldwide ethnic liberation movement.

The Department of Indian Affairs and Northern Development

The affairs of Indians are regulated under the Indian Act, which is administered by the federal Department of Indian Affairs and Northern Development (DIAND). Under its mandate to administer the Indian Act, the DIAND has, for more than a century, controlled Indian lands, monies, business transactions, government programs, and services in Indian communities. In spite of its pervasive and extensive authority over Indians, within the Canadian government the DIAND occupies one of the lowest rungs in the political and bureaucratic hierarchies. Constantly on the defensive vis-à-vis Indians, always plagued by a poor public image, and suffering from frequent turnovers of its Ministers and senior officers, the DIAND has not been a consequential force in setting government priorities or in government decision making. Despite the DIAND's pitiful status and record, however, the government's announced policy of dismantling the DIAND, ostensibly to make way for Indian self-government, carries profound implications for Indians whose affairs it administers. I will briefly elaborate on some of these policy implications.

Band/tribal Indian leaders look upon the dismantling of the DIAND as a development that will transfer government bureaucratic authority over their people, lands, budgets, services, and programs to band/tribal councils. But, to reiterate for emphasis, this misapprehends the federal government's primary purpose in dismantling the DIAND. The primary purpose as stated before, is not to empower band/tribal councils; it is to structurally integrate Indian affairs into the generic federal and provincial government departments. In keeping with this purpose, the federal government has plans to relocate most of the DIAND's present policy and decision-making powers among a host of federal and provincial government departments and agencies, while transferring only selected local administrative/clerical responsibilities to band/tribal councils.

In effect, the dismantling of the DIAND, when taken in conjunction with the federal government's proposal to transfer all non-national 'residual' constitutional powers from itself to the provinces, will give an entirely new twist to how section 91 (24) will be administered, and it will dramatically alter the relationship of Indians to the federal government. Metaphorically speaking, the DIAND has functioned as a small wobbly Indian 'wheel' in the machinery of the federal government. Over the years, Indian leaders have discovered some of the leverage points on this wheel. Now this wheel is being disassembled into a number of tiny 'cogs' that will be dispersed and appended to wheels within wheels in the complex and confusing apparatus of federal and provincial governments. Indians will be hard-pressed to locate leverage points in this Rube Goldberg contraption.

With the loss of the DIAND and the minister through which they have historically expressed their collective will to the Cabinet, Indians' capacity to advance their collective interests, rights, needs, and aspirations will be further downgraded. In future, when intolerable decisions are taken by government, local Indian leaders will be reduced to venting their frustration by kicking the figurative equivalent of the government's 'vending machine' – the lowly civil servant. Such a limitation will take away Indians' small remaining sense of collective political efficacy. In short, even though 'Indian government' promises to increase their on-reserve administrative authority and offers a limited degree of local institutional pluralism, Indians will be left with even less scope than they have now for making their political will felt, or for advancing their collective interests within the Canadian state.

Under threat of dismemberment, the DIAND (as a collectivity) has developed a keen ambition to find ways to validate its continuing existence. This concern for survival has inspired the DIAND to envision a viable new role for itself. In effect, it is endeavouring to 'phase over' rather than 'phase out' some of its historical authority, by shifting its emphasis from service and program delivery to 'superintending' band/tribal councils as they deliver local services and programs. The DIAND planning document for 1985–9 confirms this objective. The main focus of this document is on instituting elaborate monitoring and auditing regimes to enforce Canadian government rules, regulations, and standards on Indian governments in their administration of former DIAND services, programs, and funds. This is an astute bureaucratic tactic. It promises to facilitate the government's two main policy objectives (i.e., institutional assimilation of Indians through dispersal and devolution of all 'Indian' service and program functions and setting of limits on expenditures on Indian services and programs through tight central controls), yet it allows the DIAND to survive. To gain Cabinet approval for this new role, the DIAND is vigorously promoting the notion of its indispensability as a 'middleman' between Indians and other government departments, by emphasizing its essential professional expertise in Indian political, fiscal, cultural, economic, and legal matters.

The end of Indian policy

The Canadian government is moving deliberately and systematically to end its 'Indian policy' making role. Beginning with the White Paper 'Indian policy' initiatives have proven to be a political minefield for Canadian politicians and bureaucrats. For example, the Nielsen Report caused such great public perturbations that the Mulroney government was forced into the embarrassing stratagem of publicly disowning and discrediting the report authored by the deputy prime minister, Erik Nielsen. One cabinet minister (David Crombie, minister of Indian affairs) demeaningly referred to the report as 'the entrails of policies which have been found in the waste baskets of the bureaucracy.'[21] Indian outcry over the report was so vociferous that the prime minister felt impelled to create a special cabinet committee to evaluate ongoing, government-wide aboriginal policy, and he felt pressed to publicly announce a series of high-sounding (albeit empty) promises of 'justice for Indians'.

For Indians, the sorry irony about the commotion over the Nielsen Report is that shortly after the rumpus subsided the special cabinet committee folded, having produced nothing; David Crombie departed the DIAND, having generated little more than soporific rhetoric; and the prime minister's high-sounding promises of 'justice for Indians' evanesced like the morning mist. The government's charade was effective in soothing Indian ire over the Report; none the less, for government officials it was an embarrassing and time-consuming episode. It reconfirmed the practical lesson learned from the 1969 White Paper experience, and from the Penner Report, that, in the conduct of Indian affairs, it is imprudent to articulate Indian policy proposals because the resulting reaction, whether in terms of Indian opposition or raised expectations, usually spins out of control. Today the prevailing sentiment among senior government officials is that 'only a jackass would stir up the Natives' by developing new Indian policy proposals.

The Canadian government has another compelling reason for looking to end its Indian policy-making role. Recent court decisions referenced to the Charter of Rights and Freedoms proscribe discriminatory policies aimed at Indians unless beneficial to them. Given that the DIAND was never mandated to develop policies in the Indians' interest (the DIAND's role has always been to translate the 'national interest into synergic Indian policies and administrative initiatives), and considering the horrendous conditions in which Indians live today, one must assume that the Canadian government considers itself vulnerable to a court challenge on the ground that most, if not all, of its 'Indian policies' are discriminatory towards Indians in a non-beneficial way. The only way to escape such a court challenge is to cease making new Indian policy, phase out existing Indian policies, and conduct all Indian affairs under the umbrella of 'Canadian policy,' that is, under policies not designed uniquely for Indians.

How can the Canadian government get out of making Indian policy? The need for Indian policies is occasioned primarily by the Indians' institutional segregation. In different words, Indian policy exists as a function, primarily, of the *de jure* and *de facto* separation of 'Indian affairs' from 'Canadian affairs.' This separation is legally objectified in section 91 (24) of the Constitution Act and by the Indian Act, and it is functionally objectified in the DIAND; that is, every government policy and administrative initiative taken through the DIAND comes to be defined as 'Indian policy' because the DIAND draws its mandate from the Indian Act and because it pertains uniquely to Indians. This is the case even where the DIAND implements actions that grow out of broader government policies that affect all Canadians (e.g., fiscal restraint). This dilemma would be virtually eliminated if the Indian Act were repealed and the DIAND dismantled. The administration of Indian affairs could then be fully assimilated into generic federal and provincial government departments and agencies. Once all Indian affairs are thus institutionally assimilated, Indians will become 'Canadians as all other Canadians,' and the government can administer virtually all Indian affairs under 'Canadian policy.' This will greatly diminish the government's vulnerability to legal and political charges of making policies that are prejudicial towards Indians.

For example, if Indian housing programs are merged with Canadian housing programs under Central Mortgage and Housing Corporation, and Indian alcohol and drug treatment programs are merged with Canadian alcohol and drug treatment programs under Health and Welfare, Canada, and so on, then the Canadian government no longer needs 'Indian policies' to administer Indian affairs. Indians can be dealt with as 'Canadians.' Under such an arrangement the government can cap budgets, cut back or eliminate programs and services, and, as long as it does so for all citizens, it won't run the risk of being accused of racism or victimizing Indians, or of being charged under the Charter with generating discriminatory Indian policies.

An instance of such a policy-administrative approach occurred recently (1990) when the secretary of state announced that his department would, as a 'general cutback,' reduce its subsidies to communication programs. The cutback resulted in the loss of critical funding for Indian media associations. Had these funds been administered by the DIAND, such a cutback of essential funding would have been roundly condemned as a regressive and prejudicial 'Indian policy.' The secretary of state's action did not entirely escape such routine criticism. But, because it was carried out by a 'generic' government department in the name of 'Canadian policy' (that is, it also affected subsidized Canadian publications), charges of discriminatory Indian policies were considerably muted. And, technically, the government was safe from charges that it had violated the implied proscription of the Charter of Rights and Freedoms against unbeneficial discriminatory policies aimed at Indians.

Indian self-government has been represented by the federal government as a strategy for transferring federal government jurisdiction for 'Indians, and lands reserved for Indians' to Indian people themselves. If this goal is fully realized, then section 91 (24) can be deleted and the basis for the Indian Act and the DIAND will be gone. In that context the federal government's Indian self-government initiative must be viewed as a strategy for eliminating the statutory warrant for 'Indian policy' initiatives. It will also eliminate the federal governments fiduciary (trust) responsibility for Indians. In fact, this is the purpose of another current federal government initiative titled the 'Lands, Resources and Title (LRT) Review.' Specifically, this review is conducting an examination of the Indian Act in regard to revenue and trust provisions. The end-purpose of the LRT Review is to diminish and possibly terminate the government's fiduciary (trust) obligations to Indians. As such it represents another endeavour by the government to get out of the 'Indian business.'

The Canadian government's stated goal to eliminate the Indian Act and to phase out the DIAND are fully consistent with an 'end of Indian policy' scenario. The DIAND is the only department with the critical mass of expertise, the historical mandate, and the career incentives for civil servants to generate 'Indian policy.' By abolishing the DIAND the Canadian government will deliberately destroy its own capacity for making Indian policy. Thereafter, Indian affairs will be conducted almost entirely under the aegis of Canadian policy.

Conclusion

When incidents like those as Oka and Kahnewake occur, thoughtful Canadians become interested in understanding why Indians behave as they do, but, they have little understanding about why their government behaves as it does. The 'national interest' policy paradigm presented in this chapter provides Canadians with a framework for analysing all government policies and actions affecting Indians. Such an analysis should lead thoughtful Canadians to seriously question their government over its continuing neglect of a central responsibility, that is, its constitutionally entrenched role as trustee for Indians, and its consequent moral and legal obligation to reconcile the 'national interest' with Indian interests. The government cannot evade this obligation by adopting a strategy of conducting Indian affairs under the aegis of Canadian policy.

The federal government is actively marketing the myth that its conduct of Indian affairs has progressed from colonial wardship and cultural assimilation to Indian self-government and coexistence. The reality bears little resemblance to this myth. Contemporary Indian policies, in particular the 'Indian self-government' initiative, are designed (by means of 'structural integration,' 'constitutional normalization,' and 'individualization'), to undermine and diminish, and ultimately to eliminate, Indian special status and to achieve their full institutional assimilation. The government's assimilation enterprise has not been dismantled; it has merely changed its address from 'culture' to 'institutions.'

The Canadian government's Indian self-government proposal is a deliberate, clever, and cynical exploitation of a concept that holds deep emotional significance for Indians, symbolizing their most cherished cultural aspirations. The government is using this inspiriting concept to lure Indians down a path that leads to institutional assimilation and to the termination of their special status. Under the guise of self-government, Indians are, once again, being placed on a path not of their choosing. And, in a gesture of sham munificence, the government is saying they can set the pace at which they will walk down this path.

This deception should be cause for concern to Indian leaders. Their cooperation in this charade of Indian self-government could compromise their descendant's claim to self-determination. The words 'Indian self-government' are important here. Indians must not allow themselves to be seduced into accepting the Canadian government's misleading label of 'Indian self-government' when what is being offered is no more than selective and limited local self-administration. If Indians accept the Canadian government's terminology, they will fall into the trap of 'the great lie'; that is, they and future generations will come to believe that their inherent right to self-government has been realized.

Indians, not surprisingly, evaluate all Canadian government policies from the perspective of their (Indian) interests. Thus, Indians are baffled, frustrated, and angry about recurring policies (both 'Indian' and 'Canadian') that ignore or are hurtful to their interests, rights, needs, and aspirations. An interesting instance of such a recurring policy can be found in two otherwise disparate government policy initiatives: the 1969 White Paper (an 'Indian policy' position) and the 1985 Nielsen Report (a 'Canadian policy' position). The 1969 White Paper was initiated by Trudeau's Liberal government which espoused Western-liberal ideals. The White Paper was cast in ideological-humanistic terms of equality and tolerance. The Nielsen Report was initiated by Mulroney's Conservative government which espouses fiscal stringency. The Report was cast in terms of cash-driven expedients to reduce federal government expenditures. Yet, both embody essentially the same solution to the 'Indian problem.' Both advocate the structural integration of Indians into Canadian institutional systems. Both advocate eliminating the Indians' special status and 'normalizing' federal-provincial constitutional mandates in regard to Indians. Both advocate the 'individualization' of Indians.

Understandably, Indians see such a recurring manifestation of a regressive design as emanating from a sinister 'hidden agenda,' one that is purposed towards their cultural assimilation. No doubt, 'hidden agendas' abound in government circles. Such artifices are essential to the pretensions of self-important politicians and bureaucrats. Few things bloat the political and bureaucratic ego more than an occasion to publicly deny they have a 'hidden agenda.' But, recurring regressive designs such as the institutional assimilation of Indians are much better explained by the fact that the conduct of Indian affairs is consistently structured by the constant priorities of the 'national interest' – the 'national interest' imperative is the 'hidden agenda.' The elimination of Indian special status surfaces as a recurring Canadian policy initiative because it is always deemed to be in the 'national interest' that Indians should be 'Canadians as all other Canadians.' And, while governments of different ideological stripe pursue the 'national interest' from different convictions and in different styles, none the less, in regard to Indian status, they define it essentially in the same way.

Beginning with the Indian Act, and with every subsequent Canadian or Indian policy initiative, the Canadian government has ignored, subordinated, or sacrificed Indian interests, rights, needs, and aspirations in order to advance the 'national interest.' The consequences of adhering to such a policy paradigm comprises a history of gross injustice to Indians, verging on genocide and ethnocide. But, just as important as the injustices of the past, if not more important, is what the Canadian government intends to do to Indians in the future. Implicit in the 'national interest' policy paradigm is the prospect that Indians in Canada are unlikely ever to realize justice because Indians can never achieve justice within a 'national interest' policy framework. Policies shaped by the 'national interest,' whether they are 'Indian policies' or 'Canadian policies,' will always subordinate Indian interests to Canadian interests. If Indians are to achieve justice, that is, survival and well-being as *Indians*, there must first occur a paradigmatic shift in Canadian policy making, from the imperatives of the 'national interest' to a coequal emphasis on Indian interests. That is, Canadian policies must be formed with equitable reference to, and they must be reconciled with, Indian rights, interest, needs, and aspirations. This expresses the spirit of coexistence, mutual obligation, sharing, and benefit with which the chiefs marked the treaties. It also expresses the Canadian government's trust obligations to Indians. To meet this standard will require that Canadians set aside more than a century of political, legal, and constitutional precedents; subdue their greed for Indian lands; and root out their deeply ingrained colonial attitudes of racism, paternalism, and distrust towards Indians.

3 Leadership

Today, as band/tribal councils are attaining a greater measure of self-administration and responsibility and as they aspire to self-government, the effectiveness of Indian leadership becomes decisive for the future of Indians. Effective Indian leadership represents the only and final chance for Indian people to escape their destitution, despair, and frustration, and it represents their only hope for survival and well-being as *Indians*. Indian leaders today are better educated, politically more experienced and sophisticated, and better organized to act in the interests of their people. But a new criticism is surfacing: that Indian leaders are taking on the same values and self-interests as the Department of Indian Affairs and Northern Development (DIAND) bureaucrats they are striving to replace.[1]

In this chapter I take a critical perspective on emerging structures and norms of Indian leadership. For a proper interpretation of my critique it is important to draw a distinction between Indian *leaders*, on the one hand, and the *colonial structures and norms* within which Indian leaders carry out their functions, on the other. My critique addresses the latter and the deleterious consequences that these structures and norms hold for the way Indian leaders perform their roles. It is important to emphasize that Indian leaders did not create these colonial structures and norms of leadership. These were imposed by the Canadian government. Thus, Indian leaders are not the 'effecters' of the negative consequences; like their people, they too are 'casualties' of the imposed colonial structures and norms of leadership. However, my critique implies that Indian leaders have an obligation to make plans to terminate the pernicious structures and norms before asserting self-government, and they have an obligation to work with band/tribal members to create indigenous social systems and norms of leadership that will ensure the empowerment of the people and the accountability of leaders to their people.

My critique will be distasteful to some readers because, unavoidably, it carries paternalistic overtones. But we are witness to more than a power struggle between Indian leaders and the Canadian government. We are witness to a colonized peoples' struggle for their survival and well-being as *Indians*. Concerned Canadians, who support Indian leaders in their confrontations with the Canadian government, also have an obligation to ensure that the colonial structures and norms that at present function on Indian reserves do not cause to come into existence a small Indian ruling-élite class who will use their growing control over these structures to exploit their own people. Concerned Canadians cannot close their eyes to the possibility that 'Indian self-government' may serve to cloak or to legitimate an indigenous tyranny that harms the mass of band/tribal members.

Indian leaders are faced with a daunting challenge: they must begin to correct the consequences of generations of Canadian political and bureaucratic oppression, misdeeds, mismanagement, and neglect, and they must start the process from a base of inadequate resources and powers. This challenge to Indian leadership is magnified by complex social and cultural changes that have occurred and are presently occurring in Indian communities. As the nature of their community changes, Indian leaders are confronted with difficult philosophical and political choices and decisions – choices and decisions about a fundamental restructuring of the political, economic, and social systems that at present give them their status, powers and privileges.

The following discussion is divided into two parts. In the first part, I carry out a brief overview and analysis of traditional and contemporary Indian leadership systems and values. In the second part, I identify some of the choices and decisions confronting Indian leaders in their quest for Indian self-government.

Leadership characteristics

Traditional *Indian* leadership grew out of social systems that were organized around extended kinship groups, whose relationships and duties were defined by custom and whose cultures were essentially communal. Most *Indian* societies did not differentiate power into formal specialized institutional structures. The tribal community performed all of the political, social, spiritual, and economic functions in an undifferentiated fashion. They reached decisions by a 'dialectic consensus' approach, in the equivalent of 'town-hall' meetings. In a real sense, the *people* constituted 'the government' in respect of all of its functions. There was no 'body politic,' no permanent 'political machinery,' no 'authority hierarchy.' No individual or group could unilaterally claim part of the tribe's authority or power. Power and authority were vested only in the band or tribe as a whole. Thus, the dichotomy of 'rulers' and 'ruled' did not exist between leaders and members. In short, *Indian* governments existed 'of, by, and for' the collectivity.

Although there were some exceptions, where chiefdoms had a degree of authority attached to the 'office' from which decisions flowed and through which goods and services were distributed, in most tribes power and authority were not vested in 'offices,' or in the incumbents of 'offices.' In the absence of formal institutional positions or 'offices' to legitimate their status leaders in traditional *Indian* societies had to earn and legitimate their status and influence by establishing a reputation for generosity, service, wisdom, spirituality, courage, diplomacy, dignity, loyalty, and personal magnetism.

Although social status structures existed (that is, some persons occupied honoured positions such as chief, medicine man, or elder), there was no significant 'wealth hierarchy.' In most traditional *Indian* societies, leaders achieved status and influence, not by possession of wealth, but by the distribution of it. They shared generously because this was their obligation – the structure of beliefs, values, traditions, and customs required this behaviour. In the 'potlatch,' for instance, material possessions, songs, dances, and legends were shared once a year. The hosts in a potlatch enhanced their status and influence as they shared their wealth. Significantly, such values ensured continued redistribution of wealth within a tribal community.

Traditionally, *Indian* 'elders' exerted a profound political, social, and moral influence in their communities. In a society with an oral tradition, *Indian* elders played the essential and highly valued function of transmitting the tribal customs and traditions to the younger generation. Frequently, they also played a special role in identifying band/tribal members who displayed the qualities of leadership. However, as a consequence of the colonial political and bureaucratic structures imposed on Indian communities under the provision of the Indian Act, the influential status and role of elders in Indian society has declined. Most of their influence was initially displaced by the authority of the DIAND officials; today, the political influence of elders exists as an unofficial adjunct to elected and appointed band/tribal political and bureaucratic authority. Band/tribal office-holders call on elders for advice, but sometimes their symbolic-nostalgic value is exploited by office-holders who solicit their endorsement for decisions or actions that might otherwise be questioned or opposed by the people. With few exceptions, unless they hold elected or appointed positions, elders do not play a formalized role in decision making or in the management of band/tribal affairs. More typically, today, their role is limited to a social and moral influence; to spiritual counselling and to carrying out ceremonial functions at traditional gatherings, sacred ceremonies, and public meetings.

As a rule, the leadership system of a society is rooted in its culture. Clearly, this is not the case with Indians in Canada today. They have had an alien leadership system imposed on their communities. For more than a century the Canadian government has purposefully aimed its policies and practices toward the goal of replacing traditional Indian leadership systems, philosophies, and norms, with colonial institutional structures, philosophies, and norms. In this purpose, the DIAND, acting under authority of the Indian Act, served as the paramount instrument for destroying traditional leadership systems. In the commentary that follows I address some of the major effects that DIAND and the Indian Act have had on traditional Indian leadership systems and roles.

Ruling class

Traditionally *Indian* leaders were the servants of their people. But, under colonial political and administrative structures, which are based on hierarchical authority delegated by the DIAND, Indian leaders, without choice, were cast in the role of managers of their people. In effect, traditional systems of *Indian* leadership have gradually been transformed into a ruling-class system. The process of transforming the traditional *Indian* leadership system into a ruling-class system began upon first contact with Canadian government officials. Government officials exploited the absence of formal political organization in *Indian* communities by following a practice of political and economic favouritism towards selected leading families who were willing to ally themselves with the government. Government officials would subvert the traditional system of leadership by channelling essential goods and services to band/tribes through such compliant Indian families, thus empowering them to disproportionately benefit themselves and their kinfolk and followers.

The process of transforming traditional *Indian* leadership into an indigenous ruling class was also facilitated by the colonial administrative systems imposed on Indian communities. When the government began to hire Indians for clerical functions at the local band/ tribal level, these recruits were selected from compliant leading families and were tutored in the philosophies, values, and norms of the DIAND. Moreover, the DIAND's hierarchical authority structures created opportunities and incentives for vertical mobility and for exercising official power – opportunities not present in traditional *Indian* society. This provided a base for the evolution of an indigenous political and bureaucratic ruling class in Indian communities, recruited, indoctrinated, and on the payroll of the DIAND.

Prior to the Indian Act, most *Indian* communities, when selecting their leaders, engaged in an extensive consultation process aimed at achieving consensus on the most worthy candidates for leadership positions; that is, candidates who, during their lifetime, best exemplified the personal qualities of generosity, service, wisdom, spirituality, and so on. But, beginning with the 1869 Act for Gradual Enfranchisement of Indians, the Canadian government introduced provisions for the election of chiefs in accordance with the Canadian electoral regime. These provisions were subsequently incorporated into the Indian Act of 1876. In 1884 the Indian Advancement Act was passed. This Act, which was subsequently incorporated into the Indian Act of 1906, provided for the election of six councillors who, in turn, elected a chief.

Initially, most bands/tribes resisted or were apathetic to the elective provisions of the Indian Act. This led the Department of Indian Affairs to venture imposing the elective provisions on some reserves (e.g., the Six Nations Reserve near Brantford). However, factional disputes resulted that proved troublesome to the department, causing it to allow bands/tribes to follow traditional leadership selection practices so long as the chief complied with the authority of the department. However, if a band/tribe showed resistance, the department's resident agent on the reserve would appoint his own choice of chief and councillors, and then channel the department's benefits and authority through his appointees.

In 1951 the Canadian government amended the Indian Act to provide for election of a chief and council. This amendment was not motivated by any ideal of democracy, but rather by a desire to gain greater control over Indians by removing all remnants of the traditional systems of leadership. The 1951 Indian Act gives bands the option of following a 'customary regime' instead of the 'Indian Act regime' of band council selection. Under the 'customary' option, bands are permitted some discretion in leadership selection procedures. Approximately half of the bands have adopted the 'customary' option; however, although the elective system is discretionary under this option, only a handful of bands have exercised this discretionary power to introduce traditional or original systems of leadership selection (e.g., a hereditary system of leadership selection or dispensing with voting procedures). The rest have used their discretionary power under the 'customary' option in a conformist way (e.g., to set higher age requirements for eligible voters, to extend the term of office of council, to provide for participation of off-reserve members in the band election process). In other words, with a few isolated exceptions, the 'customary' process adopted by bands is simply a variation of the 'Indian Act regime'; that is, it conforms to the standard electoral regime in Canada in all fundamental aspects. Under this elective system of leadership selection, the candidate with a simple majority of votes succeeds to leadership. This process heavily favours candidates from the largest kin groups. Smaller kin groups often feel disenfranchised by this process, which tends to divide the community into 'rulers' and 'ruled.'

Another Indian Act device which has facilitated the formation of an indigenous ruling class in many Indian communities is the provision for privitization of communal landholdings on Indian reserves. Traditionally, there was no concept of individual or private land ownership. Even the concept of individual usufructuary rights in land was in conflict with traditional practices in communal Indian tribes. Tradition held that land belonged to the Creator, and the fruits of the land were for the benefit of all living things. At the outset of the reserve system, Indian leaders, out of respect for their traditions and customs, emulated their forefathers by using reserve lands in accordance with the communal needs of all the members. But the traditional form of land-holding has changed profoundly.

(Here I should clarify that the analysis which follows does not apply equally or uniformly to all bands/tribes across Canada. In some of the Prairie provinces, bands/tribes historically have leaned more to traditional and communal forms of land tenure and have been more conservative about allotments to individuals. Also, the analysis is based on developments that are most evident in 'advanced' bands/tribes. In the government's lexicon, 'advanced,' when applied to bands/tribes, generally refers to an acquired competence to meet the DIAND's political and administrative norms and standards. Some bands/tribes lag behind, but all covet the DIAND's designation 'advanced' because of the expanded authority it yields, and they strive to qualify for it.

Therefore, 'advanced' status and the changes it implies represent the *present* of many, and the *future* of all, bands/tribes.)

Under the Constitution Act, 1867, reserve lands are held in trust by the Canadian government for the collective benefit of all band/tribal members, present and future. But the Canadian government, acting from duplicitous motives, encouraged privatization of reserve lands by issuing 'location certificates' to selected band/tribal members. The 'location certificate' gave the holder personal rights to a tract of reserve land. Under the Indian Act such *individual* allotments of communally held reserve lands are protected by Canadian law. The government's underlying motive was to encourage the 'civilization' of Indians by fostering values of individualism and private entrepreneurship. Specifically, the Indian Act (under sections 20–9) establishes a system of personal landholdings that allows individual Indians to obtain a 'Certificate of Possession' of a tract of reserve lands. The minister has also delegated by-law authority to qualifying bands, empowering them to make individual allotments to band members. Any allotment made under authority of the minister gives individual band/tribal members 'lawful possession' of the allotted land. This implies the right to exclusive personal use and occupation of the land, in accordance with band/tribal by-laws.

In practical terms 'lawful possession' is comparable to individual land title; that is, the holders of an allotment under authority of the minister can use the land as if they had individual title to it. They have the power to transfer their 'estate in land' to their heirs or to another band/tribal member, and they are entitled to compensation if deprived of it. While a number of bands/tribes do not follow the formal prescriptions of the Indian Act in regard to the Certificate of Possession, most follow a land-allotment procedure under authority of band/tribal councils that yields essentially the same outcome, that is, the privatization of landholdings on reserves.

Taking advantage of these provisions, some Indian families have been able to divert large parcels of prime communal lands to their own personal possession. This constitutes a significant deviation from traditional *Indian* values and customs. This practice has generated great inequities on many reserves. Some families have large valuable landholdings; others may have only a residential lot and many have no land to put their feet on. In 'advanced' bands/tribes, it is mainly through privatized landholdings that most families of the ruling class have achieved and maintain their status. They have translated their landholdings into political-administrative power, and they are using their political-administrative powers to protect and enhance their landholdings. In this endeavour, they are being aided and abetted by the DIAND.

Social class

The sociological forces activated by Indian Act designs for an elective system of leadership and the privatization of land, taken in conjunction with the DIAND's processes of Indian leadership co-optation, are not only giving rise to an Indian ruling class, they are also giving rise to a social-economic élite class. By undermining traditional Indian values of reciprocity and redistribution, which historically inhibited socio-economic class development in Indian communities, these forces (i.e., the elective system, privatization, bureaucratization and co-optation) are generating a two class social-economic order on most reserves: a small, virtually closed, élite class comprising influential landowners, politicians, bureaucrats, and a few entrepreneurs, and a large lower class comprising destitute, dependent, and powerless people. (It should be noted that the designation 'élite class,' as it is used here, generally implies income and wealth in the order of the Canadian middle class, although some Indian élites are considerably wealthier. In reserve communities where most members are on social assistance and destitute, it doesn't take much income or wealth for 'élite' status.)

At present, there is almost no intermediate social stratum on Indian reserves. The absence is explained by the fact that transitional classes generally emerge from employment, and the prevailing rate of unemployment on most reserves hovers between 60 and 90 per cent. Because a society on welfare has little potential to develop a transitional class, it is unlikely that a significant middle class will emerge soon on Indian reserves. If there is a potential for middle-class development in Indian communities, it lies in the slowly increasing number of Indians from the lower class who pursue advanced education. Until recently, most Indians seeking advanced education came from the élite class. However, if the Canadian government continues, undiminished, its program of subsidizing all Indians who are academically qualified for post-secondary education, more members of the Indian lower class will be prepared to step up into the present void between the élite and lower classes. But if this leads to development of an Indian middle class, it will likely be an urban phenomenon because Indian reserves afford few employment opportunities for educated Indians from the lower class.

Dichotomization of Indian societies into two social-economic classes carries some serious negative consequences for Indian communities. One of these consequences is a corresponding dichotomy of economic and political interests in Indian communities. With the élite class controlling the political agenda, lower-class interests get neglected. Elite class interests tend to be primarily 'power' not 'problem' oriented; that is, such interests are related to expanding their jurisdiction and control over band/tribal political and administrative structures. Put another way, concerns that affect the power, status, and privileges of the élite class are given preference over the problems that afflict the Indian lower class: high unemployment; excessive rates of family disintegration; alcohol and substance abuse; extraordinary levels of violence, suicide, incarceration, and so on. At present, these everyday problems and concerns of lower-class Indians receive voluble 'lip-service' from the élites, but they do not receive the priority attention and concerted action required to begin solving the massive social pathologies that prevail in most Indian communities. Even as political and fiscal authority of the Indian élite class has been in the ascendancy in reserve politics and administration over the past two decades (in 1990–1, 74.5 per cent of DIAND program expenditures were administered by band/tribal councils), the problems of the lower class are receiving scarcely more attention or a greater share of resources.

The emerging divergent class-based interests in Indian communities are creating a growing social and political chasm between the élite class and the lower class, impairing community harmony of purpose. While some dissention on Indian reserves has roots in historical kin-group alignments, increasingly political splits and strife derive from contemporary social-economic class inequities and conflicts in interests between élite and lower classes. Not infrequently, these class lines are coterminous with kin-group alignments. Moreover, because membership in the emerging élite class on reserves tends to be based primarily on heirship (although a few newcomers are drawn from the ranks of 'unconnected' educated young, a few enter by marriage, and a few rabble rousers are co-opted from the 'out circle,' these are exceptions), élites don't serve as 'role models' of success for the lower class. Because of the 'closed' character of the elite class, it is perceived as a 'barrier' to opportunity, effectively stifling lower-class aspirations, with a consequent loss of human potential.

These two social-economic classes constitute not only distinct interest groups, but, increasingly, cultural subsocieties. The lower class is rooted primarily in a culture of dependence, while the élite class is socially and subculturally rooted primarily in the élite group; that is, they represent a distinct Indian élite subculture. Although they are somewhat inhibited in the display of their wealth (that is, they dare not live too ostentatiously in terms of houses, furniture, cars, and so on, because this would provoke censure from other band/tribal members), most élites display a strong orientation towards middle-class Canadian values; that is, they have adopted notions of personal goals, competition, status, and the associated norms that are not unlike those of middle-class Canadians. In this élite subculture, the meaning of 'band/tribe' is no longer a *communal* way of life and survival. 'Band/ tribe' represents family access to political, bureaucratic, and entrepreneurial opportunities, benefits, and status. Increasingly, their goals are coming to be defined in terms of personal or family concerns and achievement. Communal values and sharing are more venerated in principle than personally practised by the élites.

Kurt Lewin has characterized minority-group leaders undergoing assimilation to the dominant culture as exercising 'leadership from the periphery.'[2] This is an apt characterization of Indian élites. Like 'successful' ethnics who disassociate themselves from their impoverished compatriots, Indian élites try to avoid uncomfortable associations and customary obligations (like sharing) that would impede their pursuit of personal goals. By distancing themselves socially and officially from the destitute members of their community, élite Indians are 'leaving' their band/tribe socially and culturally.

Contemporary band/tribal leaders petition the Canadian government for funds on a 'communal' basis, that is, by emphasizing the collective entitlements and collective destitution of their people. This approach has some of the features of an 'affirmative action' strategy, in so far as it assumes a shared status, a common fate, and an equal need by all band/tribal members. But, the notion that all members of Indian communities have a shared status, a common fate, and an equal need is not valid under the prevailing two-class system. While Indians as a collectivity represent a disadvantaged status classification in Canadian society, within that status classification one segment, the élite class, does not share in the disadvantaged economic position common to most members of the community.

Under traditional tribal 'communalism,' assistance accepted on behalf of the group must benefit first those who need it most. But the distribution of collective entitlements in Indian communities has not been equitable, nor according to need. Instead, government assistance has disproportionately benefited the élite class. Government officials regularly proclaim 'Indian gains.' But who has gained? In the past two decades, the Indian élite class, which has taken a position at the front of the Indian line in respect of economic opportunity, has prospered, but the lower class of Indian society, which needs help most, has seen very little improvement. With each new generation, unemployment, poverty, dependence, and pathologies are becoming more and more entrenched in the lower class. When an élite class takes advantage of its power to confer government monies (which are appropriated for the benefit of the collective) disproportionately upon themselves and their kin, it constitutes evidence that *Indian* philosophies, values, and communal customs no longer regulate leadership behaviour.

Within the reserve community, the emerging two-class structure has the potential to endure for many generations. The élite class has the legal right to transmit its landholdings and wealth, undiminished by taxes, to its descendants. Moreover, in the absence of a taxation system on reserves to redistribute income from land ownership and entrepreneurial activities, and with traditional customs of sharing and redistribution no longer being practised, there are virtually no legal or normative operative mechanisms for redistributing wealth from the élite class to the lower class. Given a politically entrenched élite class, that is, a ruling élite class, it seems unlikely that any mechanisms (e.g., progressive taxation) will be introduced soon that could serve as vehicles for sharing or redistribution of wealth on Indian reserves. Thus, the prospect is for growing inequities of wealth between the two classes in future. Moreover, because the ruling élite class is largely closed, and because Indian communities (unlike other North American communities) do not experience any influx of immigrant population, who can be assigned to the bottom rung of the social-economic ladder, thereby creating some 'mobility' for the existing lower class, the possibility exists that the 'two-class' stratification system on Indian reserves could attain a castelike rigidity. In effect, they would be trapped in a status of 'double caste' – within their own society and within Canadian society.

Power

Any analysis of power in Indian communities must take into account the important fact that virtually all authority and funds of band/tribal councils come through the DIAND. Thus, although band/tribal chiefs and councillors must seek the vote of their people, their mandate to govern comes from the DIAND. This puts elected Indian officials (chiefs and councillors) and the appointed bureaucrats in an inevitable position of political subordination to DIAND officials, rather than to the people who elect and appoint them. As a consequence of this historical status, Indian leaders' responsiveness and accountability to their people has not been institutionalized.

Equally noteworthy in any analysis of power on Indian reserves is the fact that, unlike political and bureaucratic structures in Canadian society, which have evolved within the framework of democratic principles of government and administration (i.e., with checks and balances), the political and bureaucratic structures on Indian reserves have evolved according to the DIAND's rigid, oppressive, authoritarian, colonial design for *controlling* Indians. These political and bureaucratic structures are a creation of the DIAND, and they conform to the colonial Indian Act. As recently as a decade ago the DIAND ran all Indian affairs through these structures like a colonial autocracy. Enlightened liberal-democratic principles, philosophies, norms, and attitudes had little place in this regime. Band/tribal councillors and bureaucrats served as 'paid help' of the DIAND. As 'students' in the DIAND's school of colonial tutelage, the Indian ruling élite class was indoctrinated with many colonial-authoritarian tendencies. Moreover, the political-bureaucratic structures through which band/tribal affairs are administered continue to require adherence to the DIAND's standards. This means that Indian bureaucrats who seek higher status, security and career enhancement must follow the DIAND's norms and conform to the DIAND's expectations because these are important criteria for measuring their merit.

As DIAND programs, services, and budgets are devolved to bands/ tribes, the day-to-day authority for these are being delegated mainly to Indian bureaucrats rather than to elected officials. Even though band/tribal councillors are authorized to remove appointed officials, the bureaucrats tend to hold a strong hand. Band/tribal council members, who generally are elected for only two years, rarely acquire the competence and confidence to take political control of the bureaucratic structures. Band/tribal bureaucrats, just as DIAND officials before them, hold the advantage of superior knowledge and expertise vis-à-vis elected band/tribal councils in the administration of programs, services, and budgets. They can manipulate band/tribal councils by mystification of process and knowledge.

By virtue of the stability of their tenure and their collaborative associations with DIAND officials, band/tribal bureaucrats have indispensable 'connections,' experience, and skills in dealing with the federal bureaucracy from which essential funds and power flow. Moreover, their 'office' accords them considerable authority over the distribution of government grants and services, as well as over band/tribal assets, and any revenues. This authority places them in a position of patronage. Band/tribal councillors must come to them for the favours they need to distribute to key kin groups in order to curry continued political support. Also, control over distribution of band/tribal benefits allows bureaucrats to gain direct influence with key kin groups, and thus build a political base independent of band/tribal council for their continued tenure. In effect, as powers are transferred to the band/tribe, it tends to shift to Indian bureaucrats who occupy the 'command posts' on the reserve.

It follows from the foregoing that the transfer of authority from the DIAND to band/tribal councils, because it is being carried out within colonial political and bureaucratic structures, is not a devolution of powers to Indian *peoples*. Rather, the structures serve to concentrate devolved powers in the hands of a small Indian ruling *élite class*, thus continuing a century-old DIAND colonial pattern in which the mass of Indians are trapped outside the decision-making process. Government 'of, by, and for the people' is not built into this colonial model. Indian ruling élites rationalize their assumption of power on the grounds that this 'prize' was wrested from a colonial regime that had no right to it. While this rationalization has some surface authenticity, in fact, this 'prize' was originally plundered by the colonial regime from *all* Indian people. It must be considered as a *communal* asset, not booty for the ruling élite class.

From the perspective of lower-class band/tribal members, the élite establishment constitutes a privileged 'in circle,' and they view themselves as relegated to the 'out circle' where they must struggle for day-to-day survival. However, while the Indian lower class may envy and resent the power and property of the ruling élite class, up to a point they accept their privileged status on grounds that they serve an essential function and carry significant responsibility. In this sense, the relationship between the two classes has symbiotic qualities: the élites use the destitution of the lower class for political leverage when negotiating with the Canadian government, while the lower class, in turn, depends on the élites to demand improvements to their welfare payments, programs (e.g., housing), and services. Moreover, to a degree the lower class feels emotionally involved with the élites because they consider them to be (like themselves) manipulated by the Canadian government. Indian élites encourage this perception by casting the DIAND as the 'external enemy.'

As Indian élites continue to assume more administrative responsibility from the DIAND, they will come to be seen in a different light. For a while they may function under suspended judgment of the lower class because it will take some time for the people to form standards by which to assess their leaders' performance under the new arrangement. But, if the hopes and expectations of the Indian lower class that self-government will lead to measurable improvement in their condition are disappointed, then they will begin to blame the ruling élites, not the DIAND, for the misery in which they must live. The 'external enemy' (i.e., the DIAND) will be transmuted into the 'internal enemy' (i.e., the ruling élites). Under these circumstances, lower-class animosities towards the ruling élites will be very personal and could soon surpass those at present directed against the DIAND. This is already the case on many U.S. Indian reservations where élite ruling-class development is more advanced. In U.S. in recent years, there have been more protests directed against tribal officials than against the Bureau of Indian Affairs.[3] This is a sure formula for chaos and self-defeat.

Accountability

The Indian ruling élite class consider self-government as the avenue to freedom from political and fiscal subordination and accountability to the DIAND. They reject external controls as paternal devices. They insist that they must be accountable only to their own electorate. But if their aspirations for self-government are realized within the framework of colonial political and bureaucratic structures, then the emerging power arrangements on Indian reserves raise serious concerns about leadership accountability. Traditional Indian governance operated under structures, customs, norms, and values that gave the people effective control over their leaders. However, after four generations of colonial rule, traditional patterns of control over leaders have disintegrated. Even if they were still operative, traditional controls were not designed for controlling a leadership that exercises powers through hierarchical, authoritarian, and legalistic systems. And the restraints – that is, the checks, balances, and sanctions that normally operate in Western-democratic societies to make political and bureaucratic incumbents accountable to the people – have not yet taken root in an Indian civic culture. Moreover, the large majority of band/tribal members are economically dependent. Living at a bare subsistence level, they are easily intimidated by suggestions that, if members don't fully support their leaders, the DIAND will take advantage by manipulating their welfare support. They fear that rocking the boat could result in a loss of their survival rations.

In the absence of traditional controls, and without a capacity on the part of the lower class for instituting alternative checks, balances, and sanctions, Indian élites, exercising authority within the framework of colonial political and bureaucratic structures, will have an open field for arbitrary behaviour. Most band/tribal councils do not make a clear distinction between the legislative and executive functions of governance; that is, frequently band councillors have executive functions. This removes the 'check' that normally exists between the legislative and executive branches. When this arrangement exists in a setting where elected officials and appointed bureaucrats often come from the same kin group, then the conditions exist for self-interested cooperation between elected and appointed officials. If the Canadian government removes its external regulation of political action and fiscal behaviour the Indian ruling élites, acting as Indian government, will be accountable only to themselves – a situation that offers all of the conditions for graft, favouritism, misuse of funds, nepotism, and so on. To use C. Wright Mills's words,[4] political immorality is a 'systematic feature' of such a political system. One could add that it is also a formula for political tyranny.

In the absence of traditional or contemporary controls over their leaders, the Indian lower class will be even more vulnerable to manipulation under the rule of their own élites than they were under the rule of DIAND officials. At least DIAND officials were subject to routine government restraints and checks, public scrutiny, and the surveillance of Indian élites. This did not eliminate incompetence, mismanagement, misappropriation of funds, and so on, but it did inhibit unchecked abuses. In the absence of any explicit initiatives by the Indian ruling élites to revitalize the traditional codes of leadership accountability, or to develop effective new codes, structures, procedures, and norms for making leadership accountable to the people, it is understandable why many Indians outside the élite circle are expressing deep misgivings about the prospect of band/tribal self-government.

Accountability of government cannot be based on the morality of political and bureaucratic incumbents, or on their ethnic or racial origin. Accountability requires an effective system of checks, balances, and sanctions. Reliance on periodic elections alone is not an adequate instrument to hold incumbent public officials accountable to the people. This is particularly true in Indian communities where the DIAND never allowed development of an Indian civic culture. It is doubtful that leadership accountability in Indian communities can be achieved without revitalizing traditional philosophies, principles, structures, and norms of leadership responsibilities, duties, and service. Unless, of course, Indians fully go the route of assimilation.

This is not to say that the Indian ruling-élite class will go entirely unchecked in its exercise of power and privilege. Although the élite class is quite homogeneous, it is not always unified. Individual and family self-interests, competition, jealousies, personality conflicts, and so on can and do create rifts within élite ranks. Discording or rivalling élites may call for accountability from each other. Occasionally there are band/tribal members from the lower class, usually educated individuals, not admitted into the élite circle, who muster a following and confront the ruling élites with demands for accountability. Depending upon the perceived threat, such a challenge is ignored, or deflected by blaming the DIAND, or it is met with minor concessions, or the challenger will be brought into the 'in circle' for a period of time, but not to represent a constituency, rather as a co-optive act to silence criticism. Such protests have not as yet effected a fundamental restructuring of the system for greater accountability.

Indian self-government

Indian communities have before them a complex challenge: that is to choose the philosophies and structures under which they will live and govern themselves. In this part of my discussion, I evaluate several themes of crucial importance for Indian self-government: sovereignty, strategy, authority structures, communalism, individual rights, and indigenous constitutions.

Sovereignty

The issue of Indian sovereignty first emerged on the international political-legal stage following the First World War, in response to the Canadian government's proposal of full Canadian citizenship for Indians. The Six Nations viewed the Canadian government's action as a ploy to undermine their historical nationhood, and they reacted by appealing, first, to King George V in 1921, and subsequently to the International Court of Justice at the Hague, on grounds that they were sovereign nations. Since then, Indians in Canada have, on many occasions, in a variety of forums, asserted that they are 'sovereign' peoples. In August 1978, the president of the National Indian Brotherhood made an official pronouncement to the Joint Senate/House of Commons Committee, asserting the 'inherent sovereignty' of Indian peoples in Canada and, in 1981, it was entrenched in 'A Declaration of the First Nations, 1981.' Indian sovereignty has been an agenda item at virtually all national Indian meetings. Recently, their demands for 'inherent sovereignty' have been transmuted by Indian leaders into a demand for the 'inherent right to self-government,' but although the label has been changed, their requisites have remained fundamentally unchanged, as has their insistence upon a 'nation to nation' relationship with the Canadian government.

For clarity, it should be noted that the Assembly of First Nations (AFN) does not use the phrase 'inherent right to self-government' to assert independent-nation statehood with international sovereignty. By 'inherent right to self-government' they mean that the right derives from their pre-contact status and history as autonomous nations and that it is not conferred by the Canadian government or the constitution. In general terms, the AFN envisions a province-like status of government within the framework of the Canadian federation (i.e., a 'third order' of government), with an official cultural status (i.e., a 'distinct society'), with protection from the intrusive effects of the Charter of Rights and Freedoms (i.e., a 'notwithstanding' type of clause). The emphasis on 'inherent sovereignty' (as distinct from 'inherent right to self-government') comes mainly from the leaders of bands/tribes that have treaties with the Canadian government. The Mohawks have been most vocal in insisting that their treaties imply a historic 'nation-to-nation' relationship. Treaty Indian nations fear that to yield on their claims to sovereignty could undermine their treaty rights.

In retrospect, their use of the concept 'sovereignty' has not served Indians well in the quest for nationhood. It has succeeded mainly in provoking federal and provincial consternation, and it has been exploited by federal and provincial governments to portray Indian demands as unreasonable and as justification for avoiding meaningful negotiations. At the United Nations, it is not generally understood that by 'sovereignty' Indians mean a third order of government within the framework of the Canadian federation. At the United Nations, Indian claims to sovereignty raise apprehension rather than support in member nations that have ethnic minorities within their borders. Moreover, from an *Indian* perspective 'sovereignty' is an inappropriate concept. It did not emerge as a 'thesis' from *Indian* culture; rather, it emerged as an 'antithesis' to Canadian claims of sovereignty over Indians. In order to deny Canadian sovereignty, Indian leaders countered with an assertion of Indian sovereignty. In effect, they adopted the Euro-Western concept of 'sovereignty' as the analogue for their traditional status of 'nationhood.' But, traditional Indian nationhood is not the same as the Euro-Western concept of sovereignty. Traditional nationhood had reference to peoples who were organized into autonomous cultural/political/economic communities; who shared a common language, customs, and history; and whose loyalties and identities were tied to the values of kin, band, and tribe. When the chiefs who marked the treaties sought a guarantee that they and their descendants would survive as *Indians*, they had in mind traditional nationhood. They did not have in mind sovereign statehood as defined in the Euro-Western lexicon.

Indian leaders' insistence on sovereignty also seems inconsistent with the current band/tribal rush to accept the federal government's 'Indian self-government' initiative, which yields only on expanded form of self-administration based on delegated authority and which will be dependent upon Canadian government grants to sustain it. This inconsistency would suggest that, perhaps, Indian leaders' demands for sovereignty are not genuine; that it is a negotiating ploy, or a defensive move by the Indian ruling élite against rabble-rousers from the 'out circle' in their own communities who might try to usurp the élites' powers under the rallying cry of 'sovereignty for the people.'

The concept of sovereignty has been used by some Indian ruling élites to imply the idea that they must not be questioned in their handling of band/tribal affairs. By operationalizing Indian sovereignty in this way, they create a restricted preserve in which they can govern their people, free from external intervention. They can drape an 'Indian flag' over their handling of political and bureaucratic authority, band/tribal funds, and communal assets. External criticism can be dismissed as paternalism and unwarranted meddling in the internal affairs of a 'sovereign nation.' As such, the claim to sovereignty exists as a fully vested symbol that can be used by irresponsible and self-serving Indian ruling élites for devious purposes. For example, in the St Regis–Akwesasne Indian reserve, sovereignty is used by a small but powerful group of 'warriors' as a pretext to protect the gambling profits of a few casino owners, despite the strong opposition of a majority of band/tribal members to such activities in their community. Some elements on the Kahnewake reserve have used a similar claim of sovereignty to protect smuggling operations bringing goods from the United States to Canada. Such applications of sovereignty open the door to the personal enrichment of a handful of people while disregarding the negative effects they hold for Indian communities.

In their attempts to define 'sovereignty,' Indian leaders have generated long lists of matters on which they demand the 'inherent right' to legislate. These matters include band/tribal membership; law and order; resources; marriage, divorce, adoption and child welfare; wills, estates, and inheritances; mental and physical health services; culture and education; housing; economic affairs and trade and commerce; taxation; communications systems; environment and wildlife; labour standards and practices – the list continues to grow. The expanding catalogue of demands leads inevitably to the question of for what purposes these powers are being sought by Indian leaders. From the beginning of this book it has been my premise that the principle of justice that should guide Indian–Canadian relationships is the survival and well-being of Indians as *Indians*. Implicit in this principle is the idea that both levels of Canadian government, as well as Indian leaders, must conceptualize Indian self-government as an instrument for the cultural survival and social well-being of Indians as *Indians*, and not as a battleground for jurisdiction, power and control. Accordingly, the power and authority of Indian government should evolve inductively from the aspirations of Indian people for survival and well-being as *Indians*; it should be a design that grows out of the ground of *Indian* cultural philosophies and principles; and it should be purposed to deal with the urgent social and economic needs that exist in Indian communities today.

Then we must ask: Is sovereignty a necessary precondition for the survival and well-being of Indians as *Indians*? Perhaps the goal of the chiefs who marked the treaties can be achieved with an authority short of sovereignty, yet which is appropriate, adequate, and secure. Arguably, the potential to maintain and develop a culture is generally fullest and most favourable when a people is sovereign. But sovereignty and cultural survival are, conceptually and practically, independent variables. For example, Canada, a sovereign state, has been culturally overwhelmed by the United States. Yet, Hutterites, a tiny communal sect within the Canadian state, have been very successful in retaining a high level of cultural uniqueness and their language. For thousands of years, Jews successfully retained and maintained their cultural uniqueness and their language within a variety of nation-states without benefit of sovereignty. Experience also reveals that several cultures can survive within one sovereign state.

It would seem that when a people are strongly enough committed to retaining their culture and language they can do so with or without benefit of sovereignty. In fact, under conditions of scarce resources, sovereignty could prove to be a handicap for cultural development. Maintaining the functions and services of sovereignty could put such a heavy drain on Indian peoples' meager resources that nothing is left over for cultural development. Considering the current cultural crisis and the condition of economic dependence in which Indians find themselves, it is arguable that their goal of survival and well-being as *Indians* would be better served if their leaders concentrated the meager resources of their people on negotiating for a concept of nationhood that is designed specifically for cultural survival and practical progress rather than engaging in a futile pursuit of a dubious political goal (sovereignty) for which they lack the requisite cultural traditions.

The implication is that Indian leaders need to reconsider their demands for province-like 'third order' governments. The prospects are unpromising that province-like status (i.e., legislative and territorial jurisdiction comparable to those of the provinces) will help Indians to survive as *Indians*. Provincial jurisdictions are designed primarily to serve regional economic-political interests. They are not designed to protect and enhance 'distinct societies,' that is, 'cultural nationhood.' We need only listen to the voices of francophones to know that provincial status is not satisfying the cultural aspirations of that 'distinct society.' To compensate for the inadequacy of provincial status, Quebec recently felt compelled to invoke the 'notwithstanding' clause to protect francophone culture and language in that province; in the Canada Round of constitutional reform, they demanded more power for the protection of francophone culture and language in that province. Even if Quebec attains the constitutional powers to which it aspires, this will do little for the cultural and linguistic protection of francophones outside Quebec's borders. A similar problem exists for urban Indians. If Indians want protection for their 'distinct societies,' they must adopt a design that transcends territorial and political jurisdictions. Neither geographical-political sovereignty, nor provincial status nor municipal status is likely to achieve the survival and well-being of all Indians as *Indians*. Such a goal is achievable only within the framework of traditional cultural nationhood.

Strategy

Indian leaders have committed themselves to achieving self-government through constitutional entrenchment and prompt definition of their 'inherent right to self-government.' In the following analysis I premise that it is premature to negotiate or litigate the definition of 'inherent right to self-government' because Indian planning for self-government hasn't progressed far enough to make clear what form and scope of jurisdiction and authority should be subsumed under their inherent right. Indians need, first, to develop and gain experience with the form of band/tribal government that will best serve their goal of survival and well-being as *Indians*. When they know what form of government best serves their interests, needs, and aspirations, then they will be in a better position to negotiate the meaning of 'inherent right to self-government' and to identify the best process (i.e., constitutional entrenchment, treaties, or some other route) for securing the required mandate. The journey to Indian government could end with a constitutional definition of their 'inherent right to self-government,' but it ought not to begin there because it forecloses against other, perhaps better, options. Moreover, a delay before entering negotiations with provincial and federal governments to define their 'inherent right to self-government' would give them time to empower their people so they could negotiate from a position of greater strength.

Indian leaders' insistence upon immediate constitutional entrenchment of their inherent right to self-government derives significantly from a preoccupation with securing the status and authority of Indian government. They hold that the authority of Indian government should have the same constitutional status and be as secure as that of the federal and provincial governments. But, even if the authority of Indian government were to be constitutionally entrenched as an inherent right, Indian governments would not achieve the same status and security as federal and provincial governments. Constitutionally, the authority of Indian government will always be 'at the pleasure' of the federal and provincial governments. These governments have the ultimate power to define and amend what they entrench. Moreover, constitutionally entrenched provisions, like treaty provisions are always at the mercy of the Canadian judiciary, which will never tolerate an interpretation of Indian government authority that is deemed to be contrary to the 'national interest.'

Perhaps Indian leaders partiality towards the constitution as the instrument for securing the authority of Indian government comes from an exaggerated notion of their potential influence on the constitutional process. Elijah Harper's role in blocking the Meech Lake Accord may have contributed to a false sense of efficacy about their constitutional prowess. In the case of their opposition to the Meech Lake Accord, Indians held a position that was shared by many Canadians: consequently, their determined opposition received much applause from Canadians. This deterred the sponsoring governments from pursuing schemes to circumvent Indian obstruction. But, Harper's successful impact on this process was a fluke of circumstance – a convergence of chance factors. It did not demonstrate any sustainable influence over the constitutional process. The hard reality is that Indian leaders are destined to participate much as 'wallflowers' at any constitutional meetings purposed to define the aboriginal inherent right to self-government.

Instead of proceeding immediately to a definition of self-government through political negotiations or litigation, Indian leaders might profitably consider an inductive-evolutionary approach to developing *Indian* nationhood. This approach could begin by negotiating a framework agreement with the federal government based on an 'expandable' mandate for Indian governments. The mandate would have as its defining parameters, the 'spirit and intent' of the chiefs who negotiated the treaties, that is, the survival and well-being of Indians as *Indians*. Broadly stated, this would mean that Indian governments would seek only such powers and autonomy as are essential for the survival and well-being of Indians as *Indians* – in other words, a 'minimalist model' of self-government. On the other side, the federal government would commit itself to vacate federal and provincial authority in jurisdictions that are inductively validated as essential for Indian survival and well-being as *Indians*, and to guarantee validated jurisdictions by treaty or (if preferable and achievable) by constitutional entrenchment. Such a framework agreement would allow each Indian community to undertake a process of evolving its own model of self-government with some assurance regarding the future.

An inductive-evolutionary approach based on a 'minimalist model' of autonomy for Indian governments is a pragmatic strategy. It would allay the worst fears of provincial governments, which presently block the path to Indian autonomy. If a reconciliation between the positions held by Indians and the provinces on the definition of 'inherent right to self-government' is achievable at all, it will have to be structured on a 'minimalist model' of Indian autonomy, in any case.

An inductive-evolutionary approach to Indian self-government, one shaped by the idea of Indian survival and well-being as *Indians*, could yield a number of important benefits to Indians. For example, it could provide Indians with an opportunity to experiment with various participatory models of Indian self-government, and to adapt traditional philosophies and principles of government to contemporary circumstances and needs. An inductive-evolutionary process of developing self-government would allow them time to gain essential knowledge and experience of traditional infrastructures, and to build up their organizational capacities within these new infrastructures to deal effectively with the large range of complex problems that prevail in Indian communities. It would provide Indian leaders with an opportunity to gain the confidence and support of their people by working together to design Indian governments to meet the day-to-day concerns of band/tribal members. And it would give them occasion and time to define working relationships of mutual benefit with other Indian governments, and with federal, provincial, and neighbouring municipal governments. When the work is complete, the decision could then be made how best to give security to the needed autonomy of Indian government, whether by way of constitutional entrenchment, treaties, or a series of federal-provincial accords, or in some other way.

Implicit in the rationale for the proposed inductive-evolutionary approach to the establishment of Indian government is the assumption that Indians need to experiment, evaluate, and gain experience with 'home-grown' culturally authentic (i.e., *Indian*) self-government. While it is true that Indians were self-governing before they were colonized, it is equally true that for more than 100 years they have not governed themselves. For four generations their chiefs and band/tribal councils have been cast in the role of collaborators and legitimators of Canadian colonial administration. This experience may have prepared leaders for the vocation of band/tribal self-administration within the existing colonial institutional structures and norms, but it has not prepared them for *Indian* self-government, if we mean by this government 'of, by and for' the collectivity. The reservoir of precolonial experience in self-government, gained from time immemorial, has been seriously depleted and needs to be replenished by experimentation and experience.

Authority structures

Indian leaders tend to view self-government in terms of taking over the DIAND's authority and structures on their reserves, and they measure Indian readiness for self-government on the basis of their own competence to manage existing programs and services within those structures. They assert that they can do a better job of managing these than is being done by DIAND bureaucrats. This is a modest assertion, but the critical issue is not whether Indian leaders can do a better job than DIAND bureaucrats, but whether Indian leaders are proposing to govern their people through the DIAND's colonial political and administrative structures and norms. This raises a critical question for Indians: Can true *Indian* government be based on authority structures and norms that are creations of the colonial Indian Act; that stand as a colonial legacy for the control of Indians; that were imposed upon Indians to facilitate the passive acceptance of ministerial authority; and that effectively preserve the concentration of power in the hands of a small ruling-élite class?

Indian leaders argue that their takeover of the colonial political and bureaucratic structures represents a positive development because it brings Indians into the decision-making process. Clearly, it is essential for Indian people to take political/administrative control over their affairs, but this objective will not be attained if the existing colonial institutional structures and norms of power and control are retained. These are designed to push most Indians outside the decision-making circle.

The fact that, under Indian self-government, the colonial authority structures will be staffed by indigenous leaders, rather than by DIAND officials, is no guarantee that the entrenched norms of paternalism, authoritarianism, self-interest, and self-aggrandizement by office-holders will be eliminated. The morality and performance of office-holders are always strongly influenced by the structures/norms and reward systems that prevail in the organizations in which they serve. Indian leaders are neither more nor less susceptible than their DIAND predecessors to the influence of their office. Therefore, if the existing hierarchical authority structures, norms, and personal reward systems are retained, there are strong reasons to assume that Indian office-holders will perform much as their DIAND predecessors did – particularly since most of the Indian élites who will assume positions of power within these structures have already undergone indoctrination into the prevailing norms of these colonial institutions. Virtually all of their political and administrative experience and skills have been gained within these institutional structures and norms. Moreover, they have had the 'benefit' of four generations of role-modelling by DIAND officials.

So long as band/tribal leaders were on the 'outside' they were vociferously critical of the imposed colonial structures and norms. But now that they are poised to succeed to the long-coveted powers held by DIAND officials, they no longer seem so eager to change the structures and norms in a fundamental way. They have shown little inclination to develop plans for re-creating and revitalizing traditional models and norms of *Indian* government. In fact, there is very little evidence that they have any conception of self-government other than to take over and perpetuate the existing colonial political and bureaucratic structures and norms. Their primary concern and ambition seems to be to gain control over the hierarchical and authoritarian colonial institutional structures through which DIAND has historically exercised power and authority in their communities. A concurrent concern is to enhance the powers and resources vested in these local structures.

If the goal of Indian leaders is government 'of, by, and for' the collectivity, then the first step in their quest for self-government should not be to take over the existing colonial political and bureaucratic institutional structures, but to engage their people in planning and developing political and administrative structures and norms consistent with traditional philosophies and principles, i.e., structures that will empower the people and that facilitate their full participation in band/tribal decision making and problem solving. Should Indian government be developed within the framework of existing colonial political and bureaucratic structures, predictably it will destroy what remains of the 'communal' fabric of their societies. Such structures are culturally disabling to communal societies because the hierarchical authoritarian approach to problem solving is contrary to the traditional egalitarian and participatory approach.

Given the predictable political, social, and cultural catastrophe that will follow for Indian people from the existing colonial design of political and bureaucratic administration, why do band/tribal leaders in Canada want to retain the existing colonial institutional structures? The reasons are several. One is that they are hesitant to change the structures because they fear reprisal from federal and provincial governments, from which authority and money flow to them. Their fear is justified since both levels of government have served notice that they will delegate their authority and money to band/tribal councils only if these are administered through 'approved' structures. For Canadian governments and the business sector, it is convenient to deal with political and bureaucratic structures on the Indian side that mirror their own structures. As a result a significant external force is directed at Indian leaders to maintain the existing institutional structures and norms, at least for those functions that interface directly with Canadian governments and the business sector.

Another reason is that Indian leaders have 'grown up' within these structures; they feel 'at home' in the colonial hierarchical political and bureaucratic structures. All of their experience in the exercise of leadership has been gained in hierarchical structures where authority derives from 'the office' and not from personal qualities. Thus, they know how to exercise only authority that derives from incumbency in 'office.' The habits of mind that go with these offices are so deeply ingrained that Indian leaders feel more secure within these structures than with working for change.

A third reason derives more directly from self-interest and self-protection. There is uncertainty about what consequences might result if the colonial institutional structures were replaced by 'traditional' structures. What would the lower class expect of their leaders? Would they expect a return to consensus politics, 'sharing,' and communalism? The ruling élites are understandably reluctant to surrender the status and privileges they have gained, and they feel threatened by the envy and hostility directed at their status, wealth, and power by the deprived members of their communities. All of these factors create a strong self-interest in the ruling-élite class to strengthen their control over the existing colonial political and bureaucratic structures, rather than reform them.

The Canadian government has already started the process of devolving some control over its century-old colonial administration into the hands of Indian ruling élites. In this scenario the historical subordination of Indians by DIAND officials on the basis of race soon may be transmuted into subordination of the Indian lower class by the indigenous ruling-élite class. In effect, the transfer of the DIAND's power to local bands/tribes within the framework of the colonial political and bureaucratic structures could represent little more than a transfer of paternalism – a shift from 'functional racism' (i.e., DIAND paternalism) to 'functional élitism' (i.e., indigenous-élite-class paternalism) or a move from racial to class oppression.

In many former colonies in Africa the ruling-élite class has chosen to rule through the colonial structures that were in place at the time of their liberation, instead of working with the people to establish indigenous structures of leadership and accountability. The result is that today most of these nations are ruled under authoritarian systems of government. The possibility that Indian self-government will also result in authoritarian systems of government and in continuing victimization of the Indian lower class must be a cause for serious concern by all. While the identification that exists between Indian élites and the Indian lower class may soften some of the worst tendencies of the present system, it will not emancipate the Indian lower class. If the existing colonial structures and norms are retained, 'Indian self-government' will stand for sovereignty of the Indian ruling élites, not for self-determination of the Indian people. The ruling élites will be empowered, but not the Indian people. If the rationale for Indian government is *decolonization* of Indian people, power must go to the people.

The desire to retain their positions of power and privilege has motivated some Indian leaders to engage in a deception of their people. The deception is this: that by changing the *incumbents* of the colonial institutional structures on the reserves from 'white' to 'red' they will have achieved *Indian* government. Some leaders delude lower-class Indians and perhaps themselves by alluding to vague plans for grafting some traditional customs and practices onto the existing colonial structures. The effect is that many Indians assume that, under 'Indian government,' they will be governed and live in accordance with traditional philosophies and principles. But there is no hard evidence that traditional philosophies and principles are fundamental to the leaders' vision of Indian government.

It may be that, after more than a century, during which Indian leaders had little scope, incentive, and purpose for leadership other than that offered by the DIAND, they have become so acculturated to the DIAND's structures and norms that they no longer have the vision, will, or capacity to reconstruct their political and administrative structures based on traditional philosophies and principles; that is, they prefer to work out the future of their people within DIAND's colonial philosophies, principles, and structures. And perhaps the Indian lower class also is resigned to living within the existing colonial parameters. This suggestion is prompted by the observation that, although factionalism exists on Indian reserves, there no longer seems to be much dispute over the fundamental legitimacy of the selection process of leaders, or over their authority, or over the structures and norms within which they exercise their powers. When these matters are disputed, as a rule it is on similar grounds and from similar motives as when such challenges are made in Canadian communities. There is thus the suggestion that a high degree of political acculturation exists among the lower class as well as among the élite class. Perhaps the long habituation of both classes to colonial rule has functionally and psychologically incapacitated them to such an extent that revival of the traditional systems and norms of government is no longer a realistic goal.

Communalism

Indian communities confront another fundamental decision: in regard to band/tribal lands and assets, will they be 'communal' or 'privatized' societies? The Canadian public has a perception of Indian bands/tribes as communal societies. This perception derives, in part, from the traditional *Indian* practice of communalism; in part, from the fact that the Canadian government holds reserve lands in trust for the Indian band/tribe as a collectivity; and, in part, from the immediate post-treaty era when, for a while, *all* band/tribal members held an undivided interest in their reserve lands. Even today, each band/tribe has land that still constitutes a communally shared asset, a fact that in a limited way, preserves a public facade of communalism as part of the contemporary Indian norm system. But, on many reserves, particularly the 'advanced' reserves, much of the best land is claimed under certificates of possession (or a facsimile) as though it were privately owned by individuals or families. Such privatization amounts to an *internal* 'allotment' system and makes a fiction of claims that reserve lands and assets are communal property, for the benefit of all band/tribal members equally.

Privatization of reserve lands is in contravention not only of traditional philosophies and principles but also of the spirit and intent of the chiefs who marked the treaties. They intended that reserve lands be held for the communal benefit of *all* Indians, including generations yet to come. On a few reserves, where the internal allotment system is in its infancy, this intent is still meaningful – all members hold an equal share in their ancestral communal estate and assets. But, on 'advanced' reserves, where the practice of privatization has matured, communally owned land has diminished to such a degree that, even though there is a lot of 'vacant land,' much of it is privatized, leaving no room to accommodate, for example, band/tribal members whose Indian status was restored under Bill C-31. In so far as reserve lands are legally held in trust by the Canadian government, for the benefit of all Indians, landless and land-poor band/tribal members have a moral, and perhaps a legal case for claiming that the Canadian government has betrayed its fiduciary obligation to them by permitting privatization of reserve lands, and thus is guilty of cheating them and their descendents of their rightful inheritance.

The Indian élite class defends privatization as an appropriate way of distributing the 'common wealth.' They rationalize private use of land as a beneficial utilization of collective ownership. But privatization of finite communal lands cannot be deemed an acceptable mode of distributing the 'common wealth' when it leaves many band/tribal members with little or no land, and their share of the communal estate greatly diminished without any compensation for their loss. And it is particularly unfair when (as is the case on Indian reserves) there is no requirement or provision for redistributing the income earned on privatized land through taxation. An offensive corollary of privatization is that, as unallocated land gets into short supply, it builds band/tribal resistance to accepting all legitimate descendents (e.g., Indian women and their children whose status was restored under Bill C-31) as equal heirs of the 'common wealth.' This represents a betrayal of a traditional principle that all band/tribal members are entitled to an equal share in the fruits of the land and in the benefits that the community has to offer.

Land-poor and landless Indians question the rights of some families to large landholdings, while they will never have any or very little. They would like to see an equitable redistribution, or a return of all reserve land to communal status. Under the Indian Act, the band/tribe has the power to acquire the 'estate in land' of an individual landholder. But it is highly unlikely that redistribution of land, or a return to communal landholding, would be advocated by any band/tribal council because those who own the land also hold the power. They do not want to return to the traditional system of *communal* land ownership that would require them to turn over their private landholdings and enterprises to the band/tribe, and to forfeit the source of their power and wealth. On the contrary, they are keen to retain some form of the present *collective* trust that provides legal and political protection for their private holdings and shields them from most federal and provincial taxation. On 22 April 1991, the 'Chiefs' Steering Committee' presented to the Honourable Tom Siddon, minister of DIAND, a First Nations' proposal entitled 'New Optional Land Legislation.' This proposal was conceived as an alternative to the Indian Act. It is significant that two key provisions in this proposal are designed to affirm the practice of private landholdings within a collective trust: one is designed to guarantee existing individual interests in reserve lands; the other provides for appeal and redress mechanisms to protect individual interests in reserve lands.[5]

The minister of Indian affairs has the prerogative to intervene on behalf of those Indians whose communal inheritance has been plundered by privatization but is unlikely to do so, given that the individual allotment of communally held reserve land originated from the Canadian government's Indian policy. Moreover, any intervention by the minister to effect a redistribution of land on reserves would be swiftly and forcefully condemned by Indian élites on grounds of paternalism and infringement of Indian sovereignty.

Continued privatization and the consequent erosion of communalism could undermine the ideological and moral force of Indian claims to aboriginal title and special status. Such is the case because aboriginal title and special status can be claimed as an aboriginal right only on behalf of the collectively defined band/tribe. It follows, therefore, that when virtually all of the communal assets are transformed into unequally distributed individual benefits the legitimacy of Indian claims to collective aboriginal title and special status is morally and ideologically suspect. In effect, when the pretense of communal ownership is stripped away, we have 'land title' being claimed as an aboriginal right for *personal* possession and use. But a personal claim does not qualify as an aboriginal right. Thus, when Indian leaders make land claims and demand title to ancestral lands on behalf of the band/tribe, lands destined to be privatized, they are acting in contravention of the collective-communal concept on which aboriginal rights are based. And when ancestral communal lands are privatized so as to disproportionately enrich an élite class, the moral-humanitarian force of Indian claims made in the name of collective aboriginal rights is diminished further. It prompts the question 'Should the concept of aboriginal rights be preserved when it is unlikely that the collective-communal heritage will be equitably shared?'

As we will read in the next chapter, on 'culture,' the concept of communal land embodies important traditional cultural philosophies and principles (e.g., sharing, equality, and spiritual relationship to the land). Privatization of land ownership undermines these basic phi-losophies and principles. Although Indian leaders still cast their land claims in terms of a collective cultural-spiritual mission for the sur-vival of *Indians*, the trend towards privatization increases the likeli-hood that the sequel of present and pending land-claims settlements will serve to subvert, not nurture, the survival and well-being of *Indians*. As communal properties become privatized, traditional com-munal social norms and forms are modified, and the holders of prop-erty become 'privatized' in their values, attitudes, and behaviours. A change ensues in their relationship to their community and to the land. Their sense of obligation to their community fades as private property and wealth reduce their dependence upon their community. And as communal land is transformed into an individual possession, the spiritual affinity to land becomes transmuted into a commercial relationship. In effect, land becomes 'real estate,' and an object of intense internal band/tribal disputations and politics. It ceases to serve as a symbol for the spiritual unity of the communal group.

Today, 'advancing' Indian bands/tribes are drifting at an acceler-ating pace into 'privatization' of their remaining communal land-holdings and assets.[6] Traditional philosophies and principles are progressively losing their legitimacy as restraints on privatization. Concomitantly, private property and wealth have taken on a signif-icance and allure they did not have in *Indian* societies. In effect, a community value base for privatization of communal assets has taken firm root. Indian élites are pushing privatization of landownership to the limits permitted by the Indian Act, and some want to move be-yond the act. But, if the erosion of traditional *Indian* values of sharing, equality, and a spiritual relationship to the land is to be halted and reversed, Indian élites must commit themselves to the communal model of their ancestors. In so far as *Indian* cultures are a design for communal living, it is impossible to revitalize traditional culture with-out reversing privatization of Indian lands.

Individual rights

Indian leaders declare that Trudeau's Western-liberal vision of Can-ada, as expressed in the Charter of Rights and Freedoms, threatens once again, much as it did in the 1969 White Paper on Indian Policy, the cultural, political, and social survival of Indians as *Indians*. Section 24(1) of the Charter provides that 'anyone whose rights or freedoms, as guaranteed by this Charter, have been infringed or denied may apply to a court of competent jurisdiction to obtain such remedy as the court considers appropriate and just in the circumstances.' The federal government has given clear indications in its community-based Indian government initiative and in its constitutional proposals that it intends to require Indian governments, their indigenous constitutions, and their by-laws to be consistent with the Charter of Rights and Freedoms. This intention has raised serious misgivings among Indian leaders over how the individualistic provisions of the Charter will impact on their communities. They discern a fourfold peril in this Trudeauian legacy.

First, Indian leaders view the extension of the Charter into their communities as undermining Indian sovereignty. They cite the principle of sovereignty that individual rights are defined by each state and are specific and limited to each state. Under this principle it is not permissible for an individual to apply the guarantee of rights of one state as a demand against another state; no state has an obligation or a prerogative to interfere in the individual's relationship with his or her state of citizenship. Indian leaders hold that when individual members of bands/tribes have the right to appeal to external laws, or when the actions of Indian band/tribal governments are subject to external judicial review for fidelity to the Charter, Indian governments would lose the power to control their members.

Second, Indian leaders profess a concern that imposition of the Charter will have an unwanted *normative* effect in their communities. The traditional customs and normative expectations within an Indian community held that an individual's rights were subordinate to the collective welfare. A series of Charter-based judicial decisions in favour of individual interests over community interests could lead to a 'snowballing' of individualism, and the cultural disintegration of their communal societies.

Third, they express fear that the Charter's long-term effects will be comparable to those of the U.S. Allotment Act (which had as its purpose to break up the reserved land system) by giving individual Indians legal (proprietary) title to pieces of reserve lands that could then be sold to non-members. Thus, Indian special status and aboriginal and treaty rights would be delegitimized and Indians would be placed on the path to assimilation.

Fourth, Indian leaders voice angst that the Charter's provisions on egalitarian rights (i.e., section 15[1], 'equality before and under the law, equal protection of the law, and equal benefit of the law') could undermine their jurisdiction to determine their own membership criteria. The Charter elevates the concept of equality to a paramount constitutional principle, thus Indian leaders see a threat to their section 25 collective rights should these two constitutional principles come into conflict. They fear that Canadian courts could interpret the Charter's 'equality' provision as a mandate to give Canadians and Indians an equal right to membership in band/tribal political, economic, and social institutions, and equal access to a share in Indian lands and benefits.

In short, Indian leaders oppose imposition of the Charter's provision in their communities on the grounds that the Charter violates Indian sovereignty, compromises their traditional values and customs, undermines their aboriginal and treaty rights, and jeopardizes their jurisdiction over band/tribal membership criteria.

It is inappropriate to infer from their opposition to the extension of the Charter's provisions into their communities that Indian leaders have a universalized disregard for the individual band/tribal member's human rights. Indian leaders do not propose that their people be exempted from the Charter's benefits and responsibilities when they function in the Canadian political-economic-social context. As a colonized people with experience of religious persecution, government-sanctioned abduction of their children, suppression of their languages and traditions, and so on, still fresh in their memories, they are well able to appreciate the value of provisions in the constitution that will protect their people from abuse by the Canadian state. They also need and want the protection of the Charter as they seek employment, accommodation, and services in the Canadian mainstream. Proof of this need and want can be found in the annual reports published by federal and provincial human-rights commissions. Indians are greatly overrepresented among those presenting grievances to such bodies.

But Indian leaders have not evidenced a comparable concern for the protection of individual band/tribal members from injustice and abuse within their own communities. The notion that Indians need protection for their human rights from the Canadian government and society, but do not need protection from injustice and abuse by their own government and communities, is unsupportable. The introduction of 'Indian self-government' does not obviate the need to protect band/tribal members from injustice and abuse; it merely moves it to another level. Although it is appropriate that our primary focus should be on the injustice inherent in the Canadian–Indian relationship, we cannot close our eyes to the potential for injustice *within* Indian communities under Indian self-government. Oppression can occur in any social/political context, and such oppression has the universal quality of human destruction, whether it is done by alien or by indigenous authority. Without effective protection for their human dignity, individual band/tribal members will be defenceless against oppression by their own governments and communities.

If Indian leaders want their governments and communities to be shielded from the Charter, and thereby to avert a situation where their members can seek remedy for injustice and abuse by reference to external laws and interventions, then they are morally obliged to first put in place alternative indigenous guarantees. And unless such guarantees are seen by a great majority of band/tribal members as effective and acceptable protection from injustice and abuse by their government and community, the Canadian government is morally bound to extend the provisions of the Charter into Indian communities. It cannot in good conscience leave individual Indians feeling vulnerable to potential injustice and abuse by their own governments and communities.

Traditional *Indian* societies had a fundamentally different theory of the individual in relation to the community from that implied in Western-liberal ideology. Whereas Western-liberal ideology defines the individual in this relationship primarily in terms of legal rights, *Indian* cultures defined the individual primarily in terms of duties and obligations to the collectivity. The collective well-being of the band/tribe was placed above individual self-interest. Individuals had their purpose and interest in the community. Members of the community were expected to subordinate individualism, to respect the customs and traditions of the community. Everyone was expected to work for the welfare of the community. In turn, the members could expect the tribe/band to provide for their needs. These customs engendered mutual loyalty and held the community together.

However, despite the profoundly divergent theories of the individual in relation to society, both ideological systems – *Indian* and Western-liberal – are fundamentally committed to the principle that every individual is entitled to *human dignity*. In effect, the two ideological systems represent two different pathways to the same goal – human dignity for all. Whereas, in Western-liberal societies, human dignity is protected by a system of legal rights, in *Indian* societies, human dignity was protected by a well-elaborated system of positively stated duties and obligations that were entrenched in tribal customs and traditions. If all members of the tribe abided by the customs and traditions, then, as a logical outcome, each member was assured of personal security, equality, self-worth, personal autonomy, justice, fraternity, provision of basic needs – in short, human dignity.

Under their traditional indigenous systems of communalism and decision by consensus, individual Indians did not stand in need of 'Charter-type' protection of their human dignity against their government and community. In tribal societies, *the people* constituted the government; all members were entitled to participate in decision making for the common good. In such a society there is less potential for offences against the individual and not the same need for individual protection from the abuse of authority. But, as a consequence of more than a century of Canadian government colonial policies of destroying traditional Indian customs, values, and social systems, and supplanting them with Euro-Canadian hierarchical political, economic, and social institutions, norms, and values, tribal customs and traditions have become largely inoperative and no longer guarantee the human dignity of individual members within their communities.

Not only are the traditional customs, values, and social systems that protected the personal autonomy, justice, equality, personal security, etc. (that is, human dignity) of individual members inoperative but, during more than a century of colonial rule, Indian societies had little exposure to Western-democratic principles of human rights. Colonial administrators had a low regard for the human rights of Indians, and, today, many of the DIAND's colonial authoritarian traditions are built into the norms of reserve political and bureaucratic structures, which Indian leaders seek to take over. Under these circumstances the potential for abuse of individual human dignity by Indian government is great, and it is heightened by the absence of an informed and efficacious public within Indian communities.

Moreover, Indian communities that once were very homogeneous in terms of philosophies, principles, values, beliefs, meanings, perceptions, and so on, now evidence a considerable degree of social diversity and divergence. As a result, conditions conducive to the abuse of individual human dignity have been created within their communities. One example is freedom of religion. Traditionally, there were no 'religious differences' within the *Indian* community – religion was an integral and indistinguishable part of the community's normative system (i.e., customs and traditions), to which all members were committed. Under these circumstances religious freedom was not a manifest 'human dignity' issue. What we might view as religious dissent was viewed by Indian communities as social nonconformity and was dealt with as violations of community norms are treated in any society. However, freedom of religion became a human-dignity issue when some members of the Indian community converted to non-Indian religions. Under circumstances of religious diversity, punishment inflicted on individuals for nonconformity to the community's customs and traditions represents a denial of individual religious freedom, and hence human dignity. In the United States, where Indian communities have had a measure of self-government for some time, some tribes have denied the right to use communal property to members who reject the tribal religious customs.[7]

Without some form of protection, other freedoms, such as freedom of expression, also could be jeopardized. For example, William Wuttonee, a member of the Red Pheasant Reserve in Saskatchewan, was barred from returning to his reserve for speaking in support of the 1969 White Paper on Indian Policy. The bar was not removed until he recanted his support. More recently, some bands/tribes have barred Indian women who married non-Indians from living on their reserves, despite the legal restoration of their Indian status under Bill C-31. They did so on the grounds that the collective interests of the band/tribe had priority over the individual rights of the women concerned. In part, this priority was motivated by practical difficulties of accommodating the influx of reinstated women and children on reserves. But reinstated women are also charging their chiefs and councils, most of whom are male, with prejudice and an unwillingness to respect the human dignity of women. A similar charge of unwillingness to deal with violation of human dignity has been made against chiefs and councils by Indian women resident on reserves who have been physically and sexually abused by their husbands and other men.

What is the best approach to achieving the needed protection for human dignity under Indian government? The U.S. Congress sought to deal with this issue by enacting the Indian Bill of Rights as part of the Civil Rights Act, 1968. The U.S. Indian Bill of Rights is, in effect, an extension of the American Bill of Rights. This bill enumerates specific human rights that are not to be abridged by tribal governments, which has the effect of extending the Western-liberal principle of individual rights into Indian communities. Today, there is much evidence that the individualistic provision of this act are divisive and destructive of Indian communalism in the United States. However, it is important to emphasize that the problems encountered with the U.S. Indian Bill of Rights arise not from any inherent incompatibility between protection of human dignity and communalism. They derive from the process by which the U.S. Congress undertook to protect the human dignity of Indians; that is, the bill did not emerge from the philosophies and principles of *Indian* communal cultures. Instead, the U.S. Congress sought to guarantee human dignity for Indians in their communities by imposing on communal societies individual legal rights, based on philosophies and principles of Western-liberal individualism. This makes about as much sense as our seeking to guarantee human dignity in Canada by imposing on our individualistic society *Indian* customs and traditions that spell out a comprehensive set of duties and responsibilities for all Canadian citizens.

The consequent problems on U.S. Indian reservations should serve as a caution against imposing the Canadian Charter's standards of Western-liberal individualism on Indians in Canada. If the Charter is imposed on Indian communities, then inevitably the two sets of incompatible standards – Western-liberal individualism and traditional Indian communalism – will not only create tension and conflict within Indian communities but will destroy what is left of, and close the door on, communalism. The challenge is how to protect the human dignity of individual Indians without foreclosing the traditional communal political, cultural, and social futures of Indian communities. This is not a matter of 'balancing' communal rights with individual rights. The challenge is one of exercising community power in a way that is consistent with *Indian* communal cultural traditions, yet protects individual human dignity. Meeting such a challenge presupposes that Indians must have the opportunity to define guarantees of individual human dignity consistently with traditional communal values, cultural patterns, and collective needs. In other words they must have the opportunity to tailor their own 'charter of human dignity.' Such a charter could protect individuals without compromising the integrity of their traditional communal social compact.

One difficulty with a proposal that Indians be allowed to tailor their own charters of human dignity is that Canadian federalism in its present configuration is not designed to accommodate this kind of pluralism. Canadian federalism at present is designed to accommodate pluralism based on 'individualism,' not on 'communalism.' Thus, accommodation within the structure of the Canadian federal state of an Indian charter of human dignity based on communalism engenders unique and complex social, political, economic, legal, constitutional, and practical difficulties. By contrast, the Québécois (also a 'distinct society') are rooted in the Euro-Western norms of individualism, and they experience relatively few contradictions (Bill 178, the 'language bill,' excepted) between their collective rights and the individualistic provisions of the Charter.

In the absence of an effective constitutional guarantee for the collective cultural-linguistic rights of Indians, a 'make-do' solution to the conflict between Charter rights and Indian communal rights may lie in an accord structured on a 'notwithstanding' option. The 'notwithstanding' clause is a design for protecting the supremacy of provincial legislatures; it is an inadequate instrument for the protection of cultural rights, but it would allow Indian communities to selectively exempt themselves from Charter provisions where these threaten the integrity of *Indian* culture and where effective indigenous protection for human dignity is well established.[8] This expedient could provide a framework for satisfying Canada's legitimate concerns for protection of Indian human dignity under Indian self-government, yet provide Indians with a shield for their communal cultures and their autonomy in areas critical for their survival as *Indians*.

However, considerable caution must be exercised in designing such a provision. Indian women have pointed out that the 'notwithstanding' option empowers Indian governments in a way that lends itself to abuse of their rights. They have expressed a deep concern that their equality rights could be jeopardized by any constitutional provision that allows male-dominated Indian governments to circumvent the Charter of Rights and Freedoms by invoking the 'notwithstanding' clause. Their valid concerns could be met by including in the accord a requirement that Indian governments must hold referenda within their communities and must show a substantial (e.g., 75 per cent) consensus of band/tribal members before exercising the 'notwithstanding' option. By entrenching such a requirement in the constitution the Canadian government could place the protection of Indian human dignity in the hands of all Indian people, including women. Incidental or inadvertent injustice to individual Indians could be minimized by including a provision that would allow band/tribal members to appeal 'exempted' rights to federal and provincial courts, subject to the sanction of Indian government.

All societies, including the Canadian state, routinely limit individual rights according to the needs of the collectivity – that is, the price of group protection and benefits. Arguably, the power to limit individual rights poses less of a threat in the hands of a subordinate group, such as Indians in Canada, than when such a power is exercised by a state government, such as Canada's. If a band/tribal member feels that Indian government is failing to protect the individual member's dignity, or if individual band/tribal members do not want to subordinate their rights to the strictures of their collectivity, they can escape the paternalism of their community by opting out, knowing they have Canadian citizenship to fall back on. No analogous escape is readily available to the Canadian citizen. Obviously, such a 'love us or leave us' approach represents a drastic 'solution' from the perspective of the individual who must forfeit identification with the group, along with any benefits or privileges that group membership confers. But, given that such an 'escape' is available to Indians, then is it reasonable to insist that the individual rights of a member should be permitted to take priority over group rights when the member insists upon stressing individual rights to the point of threatening the survival of the group?

Canadian courts have had difficulty deciding questions of Indian individual rights versus collective rights because the underlying principle is not adequately dealt with in law. Under the constitutional-legal concepts of aboriginal and treaty rights, Indians are able to assert certain collective, or peoples' rights against the Canadian state. Simultaneously, as citizens of Canada, Indians can assert their individual rights, which are protected for all Canadians under section 15 of the Charter of Rights and Freedoms. The only exception is the shielding of aboriginal collective rights (section 25) from the Charter's provision in matters that are constitutionally mandated to Indian governments. In practical terms, this exemption means that, in respect to matters that are constitutionally mandated to Indian governments, individual Indians' recourse to appeal would not extend to the federal or provincial judicial systems.

Are Indians morally obliged to adopt the Western-liberal doctrine of individual rights, as embodied in the Canadian Charter of Rights and Freedoms, as their standard of protection for human dignity? Put another way, is the validity and morality of an *Indian* approach to human dignity to be tested against Western-liberal cultural principles and philosophies of individual rights? A look around us reveals that the Western-liberal approach leaves many Canadian citizens without human dignity. To insist that Indians must adopt the Western-liberal approach would be consistent with Canadian ethnocentrism towards Indians, going back to the founding of this nation. It would re-create the scenario of colonial religious missions, only this time Western-liberal 'fundamentalists' become the new wave of zealots, exhibiting the same attitudes of arrogance, intolerance, and 'true-believer' conviction that they, not the Indian people, must be the ultimate arbiters of what is 'good and right' for Indians.

It is possible and perhaps likely that at some future time the Charter of Rights and Freedoms may assume greater relevance for Indians in terms of their 'internal' relationships. If Indians continue the present trend away from communalism towards privatization, and if they choose to govern themselves through impersonal, specialized, hierarchical institutional systems on their reserves, then the individual-rights provisions of the Charter will become as essential in Indian communities as they are in Canadian society. In this regard, an accord structured on a 'notwithstanding' clause, as mentioned earlier, could serve a flexible function: it could provide a framework for gradual transition to effective indigenous guarantees of human dignity; or for gradual transition to Charter-based legal guarantees of human rights. But any move, whether towards indigenous guarantees of human dignity or towards Charter-based legal guarantees of human rights, must be a decision involving *all* of the Indian people. It would be cultural imperialism, short-sighted, paternalistic, and counterproductive for the Canadian government to impose its standard of Western-liberal individual legal rights on Indian communities because of ethnocentrism, or based on some political principle, or because of a psychological need to exercise sovereignty and cultural hegemony over Indians.

Indigenous constitutions

In its *Guidelines*[9] for 'community-based self-government negotiations,' the Canadian government ostensibly offers Indian bands/tribes an opportunity to escape some of the constraints of the Indian Act by allowing them to develop 'indigenous constitutions for self-government.' However, it sets out a number of restrictive rules and conditions that must be followed in developing these constitutions. A review of these rules and conditions reveals they are designed primarily to ensure continued 'Indian Act–like' control by the Canadian government over the political and bureaucratic functions that are being devolved from the DIAND to Indian bands/tribes. What the Canadian government is proposing in its 'guidelines' is obviously not a constitution of Indian 'nationhood.' A constitution of Indian nationhood must grow out of the cultural and social aspirations and needs of the Indian people. It cannot be 'prescribed' by the Canadian government.

Thomas Paine has said, 'A constitution is not an act of government but of a people. A constitution comes before a government and the government is only a creature of a constitution.' This statement implies that the most fundamental requirement of Indian self-government is that the constitution that defines it must derive from the will of band/tribal members. It cannot be prescribed by the Canadian government. Nor can it be the work of the Indian élite class. It must be an act of self-determination by *all* of the band/tribal members. In this regard, Indian leaders can learn from the mistakes of the prime minister of Canada, the Right Honourable Brian Mulroney, in his handling of the Meech Lake Accord. Mulroney tried to amend the Canadian constitution by 'executive decision,' behind closed doors, without involving the Canadian people. The end-result of Mulroney's misguided scheming was a divided people and a nation on the brink of disintegration. Mulroney's mistake underlines the fact that a constitution is not important in and of itself. What is important is that the constitution is 'of the people, by the people, and for the people.'

A participatory process of constitutional development is important for Indian people because their constitutions will determine the character of the future Indian nations. Making a constitution involves all the key 'decisions of nationhood,'[10] decisions that will provide a framework for defining Indian identity and the sort of society the people want to build. It involves defining the duties and responsibilities of individual members, their relationship to each other and to their government. It also involves identifying the cultural values and social systems (whether communal or privatized) under which the people want to live. It means choosing their desired form of government; defining its structures, powers, and responsibilities; and specifying how decisions will be made. A participatory constitution-making process will also allow band/tribal members to develop their own expectations regarding the status, power, role, and accountability of their leaders, rather than continue with a form of leadership that was designed by the colonial government to further its interests and to control Indians. If Indian people are not fully involved in their indigenous constitution-making process, they will be left out of these crucial 'decisions of nationhood' and, in effect, they will be denied their most important aboriginal right. The 'decisions of nationhood' affect future generations; therefore, they require critical evaluations of goals, means, and the future consequences of these decisions. Although Indians cannot re-create their past, they can reimagine their future. They can forge constitutions that grow out of their traditional philosophies and principles, and that will provide frameworks within which their cultures can evolve in a dynamic interrelationship with a changing world, to meet their aspirations for well-being and survival as *Indians*.

In order to achieve a meaningful standard of participation by band/tribal members, the process of indigenous constitution-making must involve much more than merely mimicking the Canadian charade of 'public hearings,' 'consultations' on a constitution drafted by experts, a referendum, followed by legislative ratification, all within an 'urgent' time-frame. Constitution making demands a self-conscious and deliberate process of full, free, intensive and extensive discussion by all the people, and must result in a substantial consensus. However, before such meaningful public participation will be possible in Indian communities a networking system for discussion and consultation must be established. It will also be necessary to create a conducive climate and the requisite motivation for full intensive 'grass roots' involvement; that is, band/tribal members must be convinced that they have a stake in their constitution and that their views will be taken seriously.

Achieving a meaningful standard of participation constitutes a huge and time-consuming task, but it must be done if Indians leaders hope to achieve viable Indian self-government. Ultimately, the viability of Indian governments will depend upon their legitimacy in the minds of Indian people, not upon entrenchment of an inherent right to self-government in the Canadian constitution. An Indian government's capacity to generate support for the difficult decisions that lie ahead, will hinge not on its Canadian constitutional authority or jurisdiction, but on whether the Indian people consider the mandate, the power, the goals, the leadership, the philosophies and principles of their government to be legitimate. Loyalty cannot be imposed either by the Canadian constitution or by Indian government; it must emerge from the affection and affinity that Indian people have for their leaders, for their government, and for their constitution. If Indian government engenders the trust and loyalty of band/tribal members, then they will be less disposed to press for the right to appeal to an outside authority when an Indian government decision goes contrary to their individual self-interest. They will be more willing to subordinate self-interest to the interest of the collectivity. But, if the Indian people are left out of the constitution-making process and the 'decisions of nationhood,' they will not respond sacrificially when they are called upon to support difficult decisions taken by their government.

An authentic participatory process of constitution making could serve a number of other important complementary functions. It could provide the occasion for reconstructing and restoring traditional horizontal networks or 'circles' of people for *ongoing*, face-to-face consultations in regard to community problems, concerns, and goals. A shift to such a traditional participatory form of democracy, in which the people would bring together ideas, knowledge, experience, and information for the purpose of collectively arriving at the best decision, would yield a sense of efficacy, empowerment, belonging, contributing, and mutual nurturing, which is now desperately lacking in Indian communities. It would give participants a sense of 'ownership' in Indian government and its decisions. In traditional *Indian* societies, where such participation occurred, a strong identification and bond existed between the individual, the community and its leaders.

But the most important benefit that could come from a participatory constitution-making process is the empowerment of lower-class Indians. Indian élites today are in a position where they can, if they choose, rule without the popular support of, and without accountability to, band/tribal members; that is, they can take advantage of the powerlessness and apathy of their people and continue to rule over their people in collaboration with, and through the powers and resources delegated to them by, the DIAND. But this approach to Indian government will not give Indian leaders the needed political clout to meaningfully influence the 'national interest' paradigm within which the Canadian government conducts Indian affairs.

The lack of Indian 'people power' is most stark, and most adverse to their interests, when Indian leaders negotiate with Canadian governments. Despite their public visibility and bravado, Indian leaders lack real significance and force in these negotiations. Lacking 'people power' to back them up, Indian leaders are generally reduced to rhetoric of vilification, bluster and bluff, posturing, begging, playing victim, and appealing to the Canadian sense of guilt. If Indian leaders are to exercise *real* power when they negotiate the meaning of 'inherent self-government,' they must stop looking to the Canadian government to legitimate their authority and start looking to their people. True *Indian* self-government will not occur by delegation or devolution of authority from the DIAND. Unless their power comes from their people, Indian leaders will continue to be ignored 'at the pleasure of' the Canadian government.

However, a powerless people cannot empower their government. Thus, if Indian leaders choose to derive their power from their people, they face a formidable task: to draw the mass of alienated and apathetic members of the lower class into the decision-making process within their communities. During a century of colonial rule, Indian people have acquired a deep sense of alienation, cynicism, and submissiveness towards authority, and resignation and apathy about their future. To overcome this mind-set, the people will need to be tutored in effective political attitudes, skills, and experience. This can come only from ongoing participation and influence in the decision-making process in their communities. It will also require complete self-re-socialization by Indian politicians and bureaucrats to traditional attitudes of service and accountability to their people. Only such a process can achieve the decolonization and emancipation of the Indian lower class. If Indian self-government entails only the devolution of power to the Indian ruling-élite class then only the élite class will be decolonized. The powerlessness of the lower class will continue, and the consequences of this powerlessness – despair, alcoholism, violence, suicide, etc., etc. – will continue as well.

In the decade following the 1969 White Paper, the rhetoric of Indian leaders contained many expressions of interest in and concern for the aspirations and ideas of the 'grass roots' Indian people. Candidates for Indian leadership positions were obliged to 'prove' they were in touch with 'grass roots' Indians. Competing leadership candidates impugned each other's worthiness for Indian leadership positions with accusations of being out-of-touch with the 'grass-roots people.' Regional and national Indian organizations were structured and restructured, ostensibly to enhance 'grass roots' input. Today, one rarely hears the phrase 'grass-roots people' from the lips of Indian leaders. The 'ethnic' criterion of Indian leadership legitimacy has subtly shifted from being in touch with the 'grass-roots people' to the criterion of being in touch with 'elders.' Seemingly, the 'grass-roots people' have lost their relevance to the political process.

In the past, Indian leaders have failed to take advantage of opportunities to give their people a sense of empowerment. This was the case on the occasion of the patriation of the Canadian constitution, again in the period leading up to, and during, the First Minister's conferences on Indian matters, and, most recently in the aboriginal constitutional process. Perhaps the most notable missed opportunity presented itself in the immediate aftermath of the 1969 White Paper on Indian Policy. It was my good fortune to be conducting research (for my doctoral thesis) into Indian leadership and nationalism at the height of Indian reaction to the 1969 White Paper. As I interviewed Indian leaders from coast to coast, and from the 49th to the 60th parallels, I observed their excitement as they were emotionally and intellectually energized by the experience of effective confrontations with Canadian government officials and by their sense of pan-Indian togetherness. When they succeeded in forcing the Canadian government to retreat from the policies of the White Paper, they felt a great sense of accomplishment and victory. What I was witnessing was the feeling of empowerment being experienced by Indian leaders. But, sadly, Indian leaders (despite their rhetorical emphasis on 'grass roots' Indians) were unable to translate this achievement into a victory that 'grass roots' Indian people could claim as theirs, and to inspire them with the same feeling of empowerment. It is my view that Indian leaders have failed to translate their considerable achievements into 'grass roots' victories because they neglected to involve their people fully in the struggle. Only a thin layer of Indian society has participated – the leaders and their entourage – and that layer has been the only beneficiary of the experience of empowerment.

This is not to deny that 'grass-roots' Indians were aware of the significant achievements of their leaders, or that they shared in the pride, excitement and satisfaction of the victory over the colonial power. These were high and heady days for all Indians in Canada, but the 'grass-roots Indians' could experience the game and the victory only as spectators. It was a triumph of Indian leaders', not the peoples' victory. Elijah Harper's great victory in blocking the Meech Lake Accord, and Ovide Mercredi's triumph at Charlottetown, similarly, were not translated into an achievement that Indians from the lower class could claim for themselves. Those who had a TV set experienced this event much as most Canadians who were in Harper's or Mercredi's cheering section.

The greatest challenge confronting Indian leaders in the transition to self-government is to inspire and mobilize their people to undertake the monumental task of moving from colonial subordination to true *Indian* government. Indian leaders' fitness for self-government will be signalled not by their ability to outshine the DIAND officials in the administration of the colonial political and bureaucratic institutional structures on their reserves, but by their willingness to invest the time and effort needed to overcome the alienation, cynicism, submissiveness, and apathy of the Indian lower class and to involve them fully in self-government. When it comes to self-government, Indian leaders need to be aware of and to challenge their own imbedded paternalism, acquired under DIAND tutelage.

Today, Indian leaders are presented with the best opportunity yet to empower their people. They can take advantage of the opening provided by the community-based self-government process to engage their people in a meaningful process of participatory constitution making. They can take the constitution-making process out of the hands of the DIAND and use it for the purpose of founding true *Indian* governments, which will govern at 'the pleasure of the Indian people.' Such a process has the potential to yield Indian governments that can serve as a symbol of solidarity, group pride, and loyalty – the essential ingredients of empowerment. Metaphorically, I am talking about the willingness of soldiers to risk their lives for their nation. With such a commitment by the people, Indian nationhood will have become real and Indians will survive as *Indians*. Without such a commitment, Indian government will be a 'paper tiger.'

Conclusion

The Indian élite class argues its readiness for self-government on the basis that it is more competent than the DIAND to administer on-reserve programs and services. But traditional *Indian* government was not based on an effective *élite group*. Government by consensus required an effective *people*. Thus, readiness for *Indian* government is indicated not by the presence of an élite class that can effectively administer the affairs of the people, but by the presence of an empowered people who can govern themselves and hold their leaders to accountability.

Before the Indian Act, Indian *people* were effective at governing themselves. But dreadful things have happened to them. During more than a century of colonial rule they have had no opportunity to govern themselves. For four generations they have been denied the opportunity to express their will as to how, and in accordance with which philosophies and principles, they will be governed. During this time Indian people have become alienated, cynical, and apathetic. In consequence, a great majority of Indian people have been psychologically disenfranchised and incapacitated from self-government. Their leaders, in turn, have been devitalized by the powerlessness of their people.

In this chapter I have proposed that, in order to surmount these handicaps, Indian leaders need to adopt a paradigm of mutual empowerment with their people. The adoption of such a paradigm calls for significant changes in the approach to Indian self-government. I have broadly outlined an indigenous constitutional process designed to open the door to Indian peoples' awareness of their lost power and to place them on the path to re-empowerment. For such a process of re-empowerment to occur, Indian leaders must, first, cut the umbilical cord to the DIAND whence they have always derived their authority, and they must graft it on to their people. In effect, they must make Indian government into an extension of the people.

Implicit in the proposed paradigm of mutual empowerment is the requirement that Indian leaders must cast themselves in the role of working *with* their people, not *on behalf* of their people. No one can deny that Indian leaders have worked hard *on behalf* of their people. They have worked for better housing, schooling, health and welfare services, and so on. But, when Indian leaders work *on behalf* of their people, they tend to draw their political power from the horrendous plight of their people – their destitution – not from the power of the people. It is an 'exploitative' rather than a 'representative' role relationship. This habit serves to reinforce the peoples' sense of victimhood; it does not nurture their sense of participation and power in addressing the problems, needs, and visions of their community. Until structures and processes for empowerment of the people are in place, Indian self-government will be no more than a metaphor for empowerment of the ruling-élite class. This poses a threat to, rather than a promise of, emancipation for the Indian lower class, and it jeopardizes the survival and well-being of Indians as *Indians*.

Indian leaders who demand more power have a moral obligation to justify their demands by working with their people to develop a coherent political program for guaranteeing individual human dignity, and for achieving a better world for their people. Such a political program will be achieved only if Indian leaders become much more concerned with rebuilding the spirit of their people, re-establishing the 'community,' healing families and individuals. If Indian government is to achieve the survival and well-being of Indians as *Indians*, they must have healthy people and empowered people.

For Indians seeking self-government, one of the first questions must be what to do about the colonial political and administrative structures and norms imposed on their communities by the DIAND? The expedience of insinuating some 'Indian' cultural forms into existing colonial institutional structures to give them an Indian 'spin,' and then staffing these colonial structures with Indians, will provide no more than an *Indian* façade to self-government. In reality, it represents a complete and total rupture with traditional *Indian* philosophies and principles. Under such a colonial model, Indian self-government will mean little more than a changing of the guard, a shift from 'functional racism' to 'functional élitism,' from racial to class oppression.

The DIAND's colonial political and administrative structures are designed for the division of the Indian community into 'rulers' and 'ruled,' into an élite class and a lower class. The traditional structures of communalism, with the associated systems of redistribution, consensual decision making, and accountability averted such divisions and still stand as a viable model for Indians in restructuring their governments today. But restructuring their governments according to traditional philosophies and principles will be a complex undertaking in cultural adaptation and development. Indians must carefully consider the complexities of such a venture. What worked for their ancestors may not work today. There are internal and external factors that will limit the possibilities. Internally, for example, although some functions can still be carried out within a 'holistic' framework, their circumstances may necessitate institutional differentiation with regard to religion, education, and politics. Externally, also, there are 'realities' that did not exist in traditional times that may require 'alien' political and administrative structures and norms.

The recent events at Oka, and other less-publicized incidents of 'grass roots' protest at many other locations across Canada raise the question: Are there in the ranks of emerging Indian leadership any Louis Riels? or any Gandhis? Individuals who have concluded that neither the Canadian government nor their own leadership is responding adequately to the needs of their people, and that there is no hope of justice at the end of the path they are now on? Individuals who will translate the 'grass roots' Indians' sense of despair, frustration, bitterness, and injustice into a decisive confrontation against Canadians, and even against their own élite class? In the past, Indian leaders in Canada have typically cooperated with their colonizers. Although often under vociferous vocal protest, they have more or less collaborated with and acquiesced to colonial authority. There have been no consequential underground or insurgent movements against colonial oppression. But, clearly, the conditions are ripe for the emergence of such movements. When they emerge, will they turn into another Riel tragedy?

On a small scale, Oka represented a Riel-like tragedy. There are many other reserves in the country where the Indian sense of injustice and frustration is festering like a boil that could break out on any day with violent consequences. If Indian protest movements emerge, it is unlikely that they will be led by the ruling-élite class. Indian élites have shown little inclination to risk their positions and income by 'biting the hand that feeds them.' If such movements emerge, they are likely to find their leaders among the growing number of educated Indians from the lower class. A study conducted in the spring of 1981 among Indian university students revealed that many hold attitudes and values supportive of such movements, even to the point of violence.[11]

In closing this chapter, it is appropriate to place Indian leadership in context. Indian leaders presently perform many essential functions on behalf of their people, and they articulate some of the central values and key interests of their community. Their task is an unenviable and virtually unmanageable one. They have inherited from the DIAND almost insoluble problems of social pathology, and they have inadequate information and resources for dealing with these problems. They are constantly placed in a position where they must create illusions to maintain their positions. For the DIAND they create the illusion that their people are united behind them. For their people they create the illusion of having influence with the DIAND, and that all things will get better when they achieve self-government.

Moreover, the imposed colonial political and bureaucratic structures and Canadian policies trap Indian leaders into the priorities and limitations of these structures; that is, budget ceilings, DIAND rules and regulations, program organization, career incentives, and so on orient their attention away from the calamitous problems of alcoholism, suicide, violence, family disintegration, and incarceration that are destroying the lower class. Even if élites do not believe in the existing colonial system, they may feel they must work within it because, if they undermine its legal, political, historical, cultural, constitutional legitimacy, they could lose their special status and rights.

Clearly, Indian leaders confront daunting challenges. These challenges are magnified by the truth that their people will survive as

Indians only if they, the leaders, make a totally selfless commitment of heart, mind, body, and soul to the survival of traditional philosophies, principles, social systems, and languages. There are leaders who already have such a commitment; they are exceptions to the broad generalizations contained in this chapter about the corrupting effects of colonialism on Indian leadership. That is, they are *Indian* leaders with a vision and a mission to put their people on the path to survival and well-being as *Indians*. If the leaders' engagement with their people is selfless and authentic, then the people will respond. But, if the leaders fail their people, then the historic tragedy of *Indians* will be complete and final.

4 Culture

The measure and validity of a culture is determined by its efficacy as a design for surviving and living. By this standard *Indian* cultures in Canada are in a state of crisis. Moreover, this cultural crisis is so grave that Indians will not survive as *Indians* unless they initiate immediate and intensive measures to revitalize their traditional cultural philosophies, principles, social and normative systems, and languages.

Many will reject such an expression of angst as alarmist, if not nonsensical. They dismiss such a concern by pointing out that the imminent demise of *Indian* cultures has been falsely predicted for more than one hundred years, and that, despite the most intensive efforts of successive Canadian governments to assimilate them, Indians continue to survive as distinct peoples. But those who are sanguine about the present state or the future of *Indian* cultures are making a fundamental mistake – they misconstrue the fact of Indian non-assimilation, that is, Indian distinctness, as evidence of *Indian* cultural survival. They overlook the reality that Indian distinctness derives from a variety of circumstances other than traditional cultural bases: they are a colonized people, they live on isolated reserves, they have special constitutional status, they are subject to special legislation, they are legally defined as Indians, their affairs are separately administered by the Department of Indian Affairs and Northern Development (DIAND), they are economically dependent upon the Canadian government, they are destitute, they experience racism, and so on. All of these factors, and others besides, have played a consequential role in the persistence of Indians as distinct peoples. But Indian distinctness that derives from these factors falls outside the framework of *Indian* cultures. In fact, the Canadian government has imposed on Indians a mode of surviving and living that has devastated *Indian* cultures.

The most persuasive evidence for the assertion that *Indian* cultures are in a state of crisis can be found within their own communities. When problems of living increase to epidemic proportions, as they have in most Indian communities, it is not a consequence of individual inadequacies. It signals a significant failing of *Indian* cultures as designs for living. It indicates that traditional values, norms, customs, and social systems have lost their relevance, their legitimacy, and hence their capacity for maintaining social order within their communities. In this chapter I analyse, first, the causes and, then, the consequences of the crisis of *Indian* cultures; next I proceed to make some proposals for achieving the goal of Indian survival as *Indians*.

Cultural crisis: Causes

The crisis of *Indian* cultures has been precipitated by at least three major causal factors: (1) the systematic forced cultural assimilation to which Indians have been subjected; (2) the loss of their traditional means of subsistence; and (3) their social, political, and economic isolation from the world external to their reserve communities. I deal briefly with each of these three factors.

Forced assimilation

For well over a century *Indian* cultures have been subjected to constant aggression by Canadian governments through the educational system, the law, and so on. The tragic experience and consequences of this aggression are already well documented in the literature and will be only briefly reiterated here. Harold Cardinal[1] has spoken eloquently of a 'lost generation,' describing a generation of Indians who, at a tender age, were abducted by government agents from their families and placed in parochial residential schools, where they were subjected to aggressive religious proselytizing; where they were taught to devalue their traditional spirituality, values, and norms; and where they were prohibited from speaking their indigenous languages. Additionally, their communities experienced punitive legal prohibitions against traditional spiritual expressions, ceremonies, and other cultural practices. One consequence of this policy of individual assimilation and collective cultural repression was that a number of traditional cultural practices disappeared for want of transmission to new generations, thus creating cultural voids.

Another aspect of forced assimilation has been the compelled displacement of *Indian* social and normative systems by colonial institutional forms and norms in all Indian communities. Indians were not permitted to remold their traditional social systems to fit new circumstances and needs. Rather, their traditional social systems were systematically destroyed. Specific instances of such a destruction occurred with the imposition of the Indian Act 'elective system' of band/tribal councils and the infliction of the DIAND's hierarchical administrative system upon Indians. Traditionally, Indian societies had emphasized the precepts of equality, accountability of leaders to the people, a participatory-consensual form of decision making, and the integration of spiritual and governing elements. But the imposed elective system of government and the hierarchical administrative structures gave rise to an indigenous/élite social class; it redirected accountability of Indian leaders from the people to the DIAND; the people were pushed to the periphery of decision making; and the spiritual dimension was replaced by a legalistic approach in the governing function. In effect, traditional political and social systems collapsed and Indians were forced to assimilate into colonial political, economic, and legal institutional structures. Moreover, the churches pursued a similar pattern of inflexibly forcing Indians into structures and values that allowed for no modification to fit *Indian* customs and world-views.

The assimilation of Indians by forcing them into colonial institutional structures and norms has been the most persistent objective of Canada's long-term Indian policy. This intent has at different times been cloaked in various altruistic guises, ranging from the missionary imperative to 'civilize' Indians, to the Trudeauian artifice of extending 'equality' or 'full citizenship' to Indians by removing their special status. Today, institutional assimilation is being pursued with renewed vigour under the guise of 'Indian self-government.' The federal government is using the subterfuge of offering Indians 'self-government' to mount a new legislative, administrative, and constitutional assault, designed to phase out the existing segregated system for administering Indian affairs and to fully incorporate Indians into Canada's political, economic, and legal structures.

No one can deny that the systematic destruction of cultural patterns, beliefs, and social and normative systems and structures to which, for over a century, Indians were subjected by the Canadian government has had a devastating impact on *Indian* cultures – far beyond that which normally results from voluntary contact with a dominant group. But, however destructive the forced cultural and institutional assimilation may have been, an even more devastating consequence for Indian cultures has resulted from the loss of their traditional means of subsistence.

Loss of subsistence

Unable to foresee what lay ahead, and beguiled by the Crown's empty promises and by their own ethnocentrism, Indian treaty makers envisioned a cultural future not unlike their cultural past; that is, they assumed their descendants would continue to survive primarily by traditional means of hunting, fishing, and gathering, and that they would continue to live according to traditional values and customs. Consistent with this vision of their future, they placed great weight on securing Crown guarantees for their traditional means of subsistence. This is not to say that Indian treaty makers were oblivious to the potential negative impacts that sharing their lands with the Europeans would have on their cultures. Most anticipated that the influx of settlers would impact negatively on their traditional food supply and that they would need to supplement the yields obtained from their traditional pursuits. That is why they insisted on including treaty articles requiring the Crown to provide them with some livestock, seed, and other agricultural items. They expected to accommodate these supplementary modes of subsistence within the framework of their traditional philosophies, principles, and social and normative systems; however, events did not follow the course they anticipated.

Immediately upon conclusion of the treaty-making process, the colonial government proceeded to construe the treaties as licences to allot Indian lands to the provinces for settlement and for corporate resource exploitation. When the settlers and entrepreneurs began arriving in large numbers and occupied the land, the Indians' natural environment and the traditional means of subsistence for which *Indian* cultures were designed were destroyed. Moreover, federal and provincial governments began to enact legislation that restricted or denied the hunting, fishing, and gathering rights of Indians on their ancestral lands. When the colonial government actualized the treaty covenants in this way, Indians experienced a sudden, severe, and disastrous erosion of their traditional means of subsistence and way of life. Adequate land and wildlife were fundamental to *Indian* cultures. More than most other cultures, theirs were founded on a practical and spiritual relationship to the land and wildlife. Expropriation of their traditional modes of subsistence disrupted this relationship, and in consequence the foundations and force of *Indian* cultures began to crumble. In effect, the treaties became instruments of Indian cultural extinguishment.

Isolation

Following the signing of the treaties, Indians were placed in a state of limbo. For more than one hundred years, the Indian Act segregated and isolated Indians geographically (by the reserve system), socially (by prejudice and discrimination), politically (by a colonial system of administration), and legally (by the constitution and the Indian Act) from the world external to their reserves. Some argue that this enforced isolation sheltered Indians from being overwhelmed by the acculturating forces of Canadian society. While this notion has some merit, a much more persuasive analysis is that Canada's policy of isolating Indians dealt their cultures a crippling blow.

The first and foremost function of a culture is to satisfy the basic needs of the group for living and surviving. While a culture is more than that, it can't be less; as a minimum requirement, a culture must embody the essential values, knowledge, organization, experience, technology skills, and so on that will ensure the survival of the group in its environment. *Indian* cultures were significantly formed for living and surviving in their natural environment and, prior to the arrival of the Europeans, Indians possessed an effective design for surviving and living in their environment, premised on subsistence by hunting, fishing, and gathering. The effectiveness of their design is evidenced by the fact that European frontiersmen overcame their enormous ethnocentrism and readily adopted cultural traits from Indians.

However, for a culture to remain viable and effective as a design for surviving and living, it requires continuous development and adaptation to the surrounding environment. Rather than provide Indians with opportunities to gain experience in coping with their changing environment and to establish themselves in viable economic endeavours, the Canadian government passed laws to incarcerate Indians on their reserves and to prohibit them from engaging in a variety of commercial activities such as selling agricultural products off reserve. The consequences of Canada's policy of isolating Indians on small reserves for more than one hundred years has been to deny them the motive and opportunity to adapt and develop their traditional cultures as effective designs for living and surviving in the changing world around them. This has precipitated a cultural crisis.

Cultural crisis: Consequences

The accumulated effect of the Canadian government's Indian policies was to inflict massive devastation on *Indian* cultures. Forced assimilation effected a systematic destruction of cultural patterns, beliefs, and social and normative systems and structures, incurring cultural voids. Loss of their traditional base of self-sufficiency, which had confirmed the value of their cultures as designs for living and surviving in their natural world, destroyed the efficiency of their traditional cultures. Forced isolation from the rest of the world denied them the opportunity to adapt and develop their traditional cultures as effective designs for living and surviving in the encroaching new world. Below, I analyse the consequences of the devastation inflicted on *Indian* cultures as 'culture of dependence' and 'deculturation.'

Culture of dependence

The combined effect of cutting Indians off from their traditional base of subsistence and isolating them from the rest of the world was to degrade them, taking them from a state of economic self-sufficiency and independence to one of economic dependence upon government social assistance. In part, this dependence was precipitated by the suddenness with which their traditional economy collapsed. But a more decisive factor was the Canadian government's 'Indian policy,' which, in effect, constituted a framework for transition from Indian economic self-sufficiency and independence to dependence. As their traditional means of subsistence disappeared, causing Indians to experience an insufficiency of basic requirements for survival, the Canadian government made up the shortfall not with opportunities for economic self-sufficiency, but with handouts. That is, the Canadian government effectively designed all Indian programs and services on the premise of Indian dependence. Thus life on Indian reserves came to be systematically patterned for living and surviving in a condition of dependence upon social assistance. Following the Second World War, the introduction of universal social programs, such as family allowances, further affirmed and entrenched large-scale dependence in Indian communities.

Confirmation for the assertion that the traditional Indian economy has been supplanted by dependence on the Canadian government can be found in the extraordinary levels of people living on social assistance in almost all Indian communities. Approximately 60 to 70 per cent of Indians living on reserves are chronically unemployed and must survive on social welfare. In most Indian communities traditional means of subsistence – hunting, fishing, and gathering – if they exist at all, have been relegated to a minor form of supplemental subsistence activity or a nostalgic hobby. At the same time, on most reserves more than 90 per cent of band/tribal council operating funds come from Canadian government grants.

The lengthy experience of individual and collective economic dependence has profoundly influenced the Indians' cultural adaptation to their world. Instead of adapting their traditional cultures to an industrializing world, Indian communities have been forced to adapt their cultures to a dependent form of surviving and living. By force of circumstances, their cultures, their social and normative systems, have become designs for surviving on government grants and social assistance rather than by their own productivity. In consequence, their identity and self-concept have been significantly formed within a framework of structural, social, and psychological dependence. This leads to my premise that the extended process of individual and collective interaction with a state of dependence has generated an Indian 'culture of dependence,' and that the cultural transmission that occurs in Indian communities today is, significantly, that of a 'culture of dependence.'

One study of people living in destitution has identified what the author refers to as a 'culture of poverty.'[2] This term refers to a system of values, motivations, and norms of behaviour adapted for survival in poverty-stricken circumstances. Most Indians live in a state of poverty, and they have developed systems of values, motivations, and norms of behaviour adapted to this circumstance. But it would be a misjudgment to represent Indian distinctiveness in terms of a 'culture of poverty.' Persons who survive by working at minimum wages are poor, but not dependent. One who ekes out a bare living on income from beer cans gathered in roadside ditches is poor, but not dependent. By contemporary standards Indians have always been poor; they had few possessions and lived in spare circumstances. To explain the inordinate levels of apathy and social pathology in Indian communities one must look beyond their condition of poverty to their condition of dependence. The Indians' 'culture of dependence' manifests not only their experience of chronic economic dependence, but also their experience with colonial oppression, paternalism, ethnocentrism, ethnocidal residential schools, injustice, imprisonment, and so on. All have played a significant role in shaping their culture of dependence. Today, the culture of dependence, more than their traditional cultures, constitutes the principal source of Indian identity.

The 'culture of dependence' evidences some continuities with *Indian* cultures, which is why some mistake it for *Indian* culture. For example, traditional value configurations such as equality and sharing continue to be acclaimed, even in the context of dependence. But, under conditions of dependence, these have become twisted into the equality of shared powerlessness, shared victimization, hopelessness, loss of self-esteem and role function, apathy, alienation, and destitution. Whereas traditional cultures placed a heavy emphasis on each member's obligation to contribute to the survival of the communal group, the culture of dependence, under the influence of social welfare, has an individualizing effect by emphasizing personal survival over the survival of the community. Typically, within the framework of dependence, most traditional role and status structures have been destroyed.

To sum up, although many Indians retain a sense of Indian identity, it is misleading to infer the existence of strong traditional cultures from this sense of identity. This identity is only tenuously rooted in traditional philosophies and principles. Today, Indian distinctiveness and identity are rooted significantly in the culture of dependence. The culture of dependence holds attraction for individual Indians because it offers a durable sense of social community.

Deculturation

Under the compounded impact of forced cultural and institutional assimilation, economic dependence, and isolation, *Indian* cultures have undergone a process of cultural degeneration or 'deculturation'; that is, many traditional social systems, normative patterns, and practices of surviving and living have disappeared as a result of government repression, and others have progressively been rendered irrelevant by dependence, leaving cultural voids which have gone unfilled. Thus, while the 'traditional ways' are still being acclaimed in Indian communities, in fact many traditional values have ceased to be part of the practical culture in any meaningful sense. The loss of consequential traditional cultural traits and patterns, without replacement by new functional forms, has undermined the Indians' means for maintaining social order within their communities.

Evidence for such deculturation can be observed in the uncommonly high levels of alcoholism, substance abuse, suicide, violence, family disruption, sexual abuse, child neglect, theft, vandalism, and so on which prevail within Indian communities. Testifying about crime and vandalism on his Easterville reserve, Chief Alpheus Brass told the judges sitting on Manitoba's Aboriginal Justice Inquiry that, before the destruction of their traditional way of life, 'we would have had no reason to speak to any inquiry about crime and violence. We had no crime or vandalism. Our elders were respected. Our young people had a future. We didn't have alcohol or drug abuse.'[3] In their report, the inquiry commissioners state that Indian offender/Indian victim violence and abuse in Indian communities has reached epidemic proportions. Crime rates on Indian reserves are almost ten times higher than in the rest of Manitoba; homicide rates are thirty-six times higher. Increasingly, this violence involves the victimization of those with least power – children, women, and the elderly. The report states further that such victimization, particularly sexual abuse of minors and women, is coming to be viewed as the norm in many Indian communities. In effect, their only sanctuary from a hostile and prejudiced Canadian society has become an unsafe place for children, women, and the elderly.

Such breakdowns in social order within Indian communities are generally explained as the result of maltreatment of Indian males by a racist society. Although the fact of Canadian racism toward Indians cannot be denied, any analysis of victimization of Indian women and children by Indian men based only on Canadian racism is deficient. The problem is significantly attributable to cultural degeneration. Traditionally, social order within *Indian* communities was maintained by social and normative systems that held members accountable for their behaviour and its consequences upon other persons and the community at large. But traditional *Indian* social and normative systems no longer function to instil sufficient social and moral accountability to inhibit band/tribal members from becoming seriously troublesome to their kin and others.

The failure of *Indian* cultures to function as agencies of social order within their communities can also be seen to contribute to Indian problems with the Canadian criminal-justice system. As their indigenous norms and customs fail to maintain order, Indians increasingly call upon Canadian law enforcement and courts to maintain order within their communities, thereby making themselves vulnerable to the pervasive ignorance, bias, and racism of the Canadian criminal-justice system. Because of ignorance, bias, and racism in the Canadian criminal-justice system, Indian leaders are calling on the government to establish a separate Indian criminal-justice system. But the solution to social disorder in Indian communities does not lie there. There is no reason to believe that a separate Indian criminal-justice system, of itself, will significantly reduce the problems of social disorder within Indian communities. While a separate system can deliver a more just, more acceptable, service to Indians than is being provided by Canadian police and criminal courts, unless it is accompanied by revitalization and relegitimation of traditional values and norms of social control, a separate Indian law-enforcement and justice system cannot significantly impact the problems of social disorder that presently prevail in Indian communities. A few tribes/bands that have begun to focus their energies on revitalizing and relegitimating their traditional cultures have experienced success in reducing the rates of violence and vandalism in their communities. But there is, as yet, no reliable evidence that a separate Indian law-enforcement and justice system can produce such a result.

To sum up, the massive forces of forced assimilation, loss of traditional means of subsistence, and isolation have reduced *Indian* cultures into patchworks of remnants and voids. The result is a cultural crisis manifested by a breakdown of social order in Indian communities.

Cultural revitalization

In recent times a growing number of Indians have become increasingly troubled over the degeneration of their traditional cultures. This concern has kindled their interest in 'cultural revivalism.' However, their efforts at cultural revival have focused primarily on the expressive-ritualistic aspects of their traditional cultures, that is, ceremonies, songs, dances, art, traditional legends, art works and so on. These expressive-ritualistic elements have undergone a renascence of sorts. Today, more Indians are taking an interest in sacred societies, in participation in sweet grass and sweat-lodge ceremonies, in attending pow-wows and putting up a tepee. Although expressive-ritualistic activities are important elements of a culture, a culture reduced to its expressive-ritualistic function is inadequate as a design for surviving and living. Moreover, the expressive-ritualistic function of Indian cultures is no longer in a reciprocal or holistic relationship with their practical culture. That is, Indian expressive-ritualistic culture no longer serves to celebrate the success of their traditional way of surviving and living, as it once did; it serves only a segmented function as a basis for spiritual identity and fraternity. Traditional values and norms that defined their ancestors' way of life, such as communalism, sharing, mutual aid, equality, and decision by consensus, no longer define contemporary day-to-day practical cultures in Indian communities. They define idealized mythical cultures from an earlier time.

As their traditional cultures fail to meet their needs for living and surviving in the contemporary world, Indians are confronted with four options; (1) they can forfeit their traditional cultures and assimilate into Euro-Western culture; (2) they can resign themselves to living in the culture of dependence; (3) they can try to constrict their life within the limits of the faded fragments that remain of their traditional cultures; or (4) they can revitalize their traditional cultures by adaptation and development so they will serve as effective designs for surviving and living in the contemporary world. On the assumption that the first three options are unacceptable, my discussion here focuses on adapting and developing *Indian* cultures to serve as efficient designs for surviving and living in the broad economic, political, and social context of their time.

Adaptation and development

As used here, cultural adaptation and development refer to the maximization of the potentialities of a community by enhancing the effectiveness of its culture as a 'blueprint' for living and surviving in its environment. Because of the 'survival' imperative, in a changing world, every culture requires continuous adaptation and development. Effective cultural adaptation and development require a plan and much effort. A community that fails to maintain the efficacy of its culture by ongoing adaptation and development to meet changing circumstances becomes vulnerable to acculturating forces, and to the cultural defection (assimilation) of its members, who look to other cultures for better answers. This expresses the experience of Indians in Canada who, individually and collectively, are increasingly being lured into the orbit of Euro-Western cultural patterns. Unless their traditional cultures are upgraded into more effective designs for surviving and living in the contemporary and emerging world, Indian communities will not be able to hold their members. To stem the growing tide of individual assimilation and collective acculturation, *Indian* cultures and social systems must be adapted and developed to better accommodate the changing circumstances, needs, and aspirations of the people.

Historically, Indians have not lacked the norm of cultural adaptation to changing circumstances. In past, they adapted their cultures quite readily to change, and they absorbed ideas and practices that they felt would enhance their survival prospects or enrich their lives. This readiness to adapt was evident during the fur-trade era, when a number of Indian tribes successfully adapted their traditional cultural patterns to new circumstances. The record also shows that in the early stages of reserve life a number of tribes successfully incorporated herding, farming, and new technologies into their cultural patterns to supplement their traditional means of subsistence. During this time *Indian* cultures continued as vibrant and effective designs for surviving and living in their changing environment. But the process of Indian cultural adaptation to the changing world around them came to an abrupt end when the Canadian government introduced perverse policies that denied Indians the right to practise their traditional way of life, supplanted their traditional means of subsistence by dependence, and isolated them from new world realities. Because 'incarcerated' people have little opportunity to adapt and develop their cultures, Indians, who were confined to their reserves, had little opportunity to update their cultures to meet the changes that were occuring in the outside world.

It is worth noting that, despite the constraints, a few Indian bands/ tribes have experienced a measure of success in adapting their traditional values and behaviour patterns for surviving and living in the world beyond their reserves. For example, some Huron and Iroquois bands in Quebec and Ontario, and some coastal tribes (e.g., Tsimshian) in British Columbia, provide evidence of successful cultural adaptations (distinguished from acculturation) to living and surviving in the Canadian economic mainstream, following loss of their traditional means of subsistence. Any explanation for differential results among various bands/tribes in adapting their traditional cultures to the mainstream is complex. *Indian* tribal cultures are diverse and one can only speculate about different degrees of cultural disruption and compatibility with Euro-Western cultures, and opportunity. For example, some coastal bands/tribes subsisted primarily on fishing, and their cultures were less disrupted by the colonial land grab. Also, some traditional tribal cultures that legitimated a more individualistic (versus communal) value orientation are more congruent with the values of Canadian society and, hence, more adaptable to it. Alternatively, 'opportunity' must also be considered a key variable. Indian communities that experienced less geographical isolation from the

Canadian mainstream had better opportunities to make appropriate adaptations.

I should clarify that my assertion here isn't that Indians have failed to make any cultural adaptations to changing circumstances. Clearly, the experience of colonialism and the loss of their traditional means of subsistence have required them to forge new cultural responses. My assertion is that, out of exigency, these were adaptations to a condition of dependence, not to survival in the changing world around them. Moreover, Indians cannot escape the culture of dependence without first escaping their condition of dependence. *Indian* cultures will never function as effective designs for surviving and living in the contemporary world so long as Indians remain in a state of dependence. Even eliminating poverty, if it is done within the framework of dependence (i.e., more generous social assistance), will not free them from the culture of dependence. The only escape lies in working for their living.

Because a culture is inseparable from the day's work, if Indians fail to adapt and develop their traditional cultures for working in the modern world, individual Indians can succeed in the Canadian mainstream only if they assimilate to Euro-Western values. Clearly, they cannot succeed within the culture of dependence. The implication here is that if Indians do not adapt and develop their traditional cultures for living and surviving in the modern world, then those Indians who choose to work in the Canadian mainstream will of necessity become alienated from what remains of their traditional cultures, and they will abandon them for the more efficient Canadian cultural patterns. Myths of past cultural greatness or superiority will not hold members' loyalties. As Indians' contact with the Canadian mainstream increases, their cultural affinities will be determined more by comparative evaluations of cultural efficiency than by myths of past cultural superiority. Increasingly, this will be the trend especially for young and urban Indians who, like other Canadians, have acquired cravings for cars, clothes, and other material and service goods.

Just as the natural world was an essential part of their ancestor's environment, the Canadian economy, polity, and society have become an essential part of contemporary Indians' environment. If Indians are to live and survive as *Indians* in the modern economic, political, and social environment, then they must adapt and develop their traditional cultures with reference to that environment. The connection between that environment and their traditional cultures must be direct and extensive. For example, adaptation of traditional cultures to the Canadian economy must extend to the development of Indian human resources in terms of education and skill requirements. In so far as their cultures must provide the necessary motivation to participate and succeed in the Canadian mainstream this will profoundly affect other aspects of the traditional culture such as customs and attitudes.

To sum up, if Indians are to survive as *Indians*, then their cultures must receive more than ritual acclaim that relegates them to the status of a totem. Although a totem can elicit powerful emotions, it cannot serve as a practical design for living and surviving in the modern world. If *Indian* cultures are to serve as efficient designs for living and surviving, then each generation has an obligation to contribute to their ongoing adaptation and development, otherwise the next generation will inherit the previous generation's neglect.

Theory and effectuation

In order to fix anything we need to know how it works. The process of cultural change, however, is not entirely intelligible. Cultural adaptation and development are complex concepts, involving the diffuse interaction of many variables. On the one hand, the process is not one of chance factors and circumstances. On the other hand, it cannot be understood as entirely a process of deliberate and logical decisions. Logically, we 'know' that at one time humans pre-existed culture; but, today, we are born into a culture, and culture exerts control over human society; that is, culture can be seen to make humans what they are and to think and behave as they do. Conversely, from desires for improvement, or in response to changing needs and circumstances, human societies can and do creatively impact their cultures by adding to, deleting from, and reforming their cultural heritage. Some scholars have theorized that a cultural practice will be retained if it is functional and it will be discarded if it is dysfunctional for surviving and living. But, in real life, retention of functional cultural practices and elimination of dysfunctional practices occur more by trial and error than by design. So there are many exceptions to this 'functionalist' rule, even though the essential value of a culture is its efficiency as a design for surviving and living. To paraphrase Karl Marx: humans make their own culture, but they don't make it just as they please.

Some scholars take a deterministic or fatalistic perspective in regard to cultural change: they hold that human intervention has no effect; that culture is subject only to its own DNA-like' laws of self-generation and natural evolution. The logic underlying assertions of 'cultural fatalism' appears to be that, because we don't fully understand the causal dynamics of cultural change, and because we cannot absolutely control it, cultural change must be regarded as an autonomous and self-guiding process. In fact, very little cultural change is unrelated to some sort of causal factor and, not infrequently, the deliberate actions of humans can be seen to be the cause of change. It is irrational to view the changes that have occurred in *Indian* cultures as a result of 'DNA-like' laws of self-generation and natural evolution, rather than as a consequence of forced acculturation, deliberate destruction of traditional means of subsistence, and compelled isolation within a framework of dependence. Should Indians decide to sit back and leave cultural change to take its 'natural course,' cultural assimilation will be inevitable because that is the 'natural course' on which the government of Canada has placed them.

In this discussion, I assume that although Indians are subject to the constraints and limitations of their resources and their political, economic, and social environment, within these constraints and limitations lie many degrees of latitude for creativity in initiating and guiding their cultural adaptation and development so as to achieve the sort of cultural community they want to be in future. For example, they can shape their cultures by planned socialization of their youth. Stated negatively, aspects of their *Indian* culture that are *not* transmitted to the next generation will cease to be part of their culture. Stated positively, because the process of socialization is always selective and interpretive, if bands/tribes can achieve a consensus about what their cultures 'ought to be,' they can, through a long term process of deliberately designed socialization exercise considerable influence over the future shape of their cultures. Of course, such an assertion implies that Indians must have the opportunity to play a creative and guiding role in adapting and developing their cultures according to their aspirations and judgments about the best way to live and survive. In short, if Indians want to live and survive as *Indians*, careful planning and a collective will are required to achieve such a goal. All social-system resources must be involved, and Indians must have the social-political 'space' to work out their cultural destiny.

Indian leaders have an essential role to play in Indian cultural revitalization. Jules Henry has stated: 'All great cultures, and those moving in the direction of greatness, have an elite which might be called the *cultural maximizers*, whose function is to maintain and push further the culture's greatness and integration ... The functions of a cultural maximizer include organization (i.e., maintaining the level of integration of the culture as it is) and contributing certain qualitative features necessary to the continuance of cultural life.'[4] The need for Indian leaders to act as cultural maximizers is particularly critical today. At present, the mass of Indians are too demoralized to effect a cultural renaissance. But Indian leaders are not demoralized, and they must find a way of re-empowering their people to meet this challenge. For only if cultural adaptation and development have the support and commitment of 'grass roots' Indians can it be successful. There must be ongoing consultations between the 'cultural maximizers' and the 'grass roots' people; otherwise, the people will not accept and legitimize the new culture and it will have no force. In effect, new 'cultural constitutions' must be negotiated within Indian communities. Unless Indian leaders undertake this challenge it is doubtful that Indians can survive and live as *Indians*. If they choose to allow cultural change to occur spontaneously in the 'spirit of the times,' that is, if they continue to let cultural change occur as a series of unplanned, ad hoc deletions and additions – whatever is convenient – then the extinction of *Indian* cultures will occur as a legacy of contemporary Indian leaders' neglect.

How well are Indian leaders playing the role of cultural maximizers? The assessment is not a positive one. They have placed more emphasis on politics than on cultural adaptation and development. Many, when they speak about traditional culture, are not describing their personal culture. Many are, culturally speaking, 'leaving their people'; that is, they are finding 'personal solutions' to the inadequacy of *Indian* cultures and the culture of dependence by detaching themselves from the community and adopting an Indian élite subculture, or the culture of Canadian society. Once they are acculturated, Indian leaders have little incentive to act as 'cultural maximizers,' that is, to revitalize *Indian* cultures, because they, personally, do not need them for surviving or living. The result is a culturally bifurcated Indian community: an élite composed largely of acculturated individuals, and the mass trapped in a culture of dependence.

Philosophies and principles

Cultures embody a set of premises about the purpose, value, and meaning of life. For Indians, these premises are derived from unwritten covenants the Creator communicated to their ancestors. The covenants comprehend a number of fundamental philosophies and principles that gave coherence and unity to *Indian* values, beliefs, social systems, customs, and traditions. These fundamental philosophies and principles emphasized an organic, holistic concept of the world; spiritual and harmonious relationships to the land and all life forms; communalism; personal duties and responsibilities to the band/ tribe; social and economic justice, equality, and sharing; universal and consensual participation in decision making; personal autonomy; human dignity; and so on.

My premise in the following discussion is that if Indians are to survive and live as *Indians*, the process of cultural adaptation and development must be guided by the philosophies and principles inherent in their covenants; that is, their cultures and their identities must be revitalized within a framework of traditional philosophies and principles. This speaks to the need to bridge the past and the present in such a way as to allow Indians to be part of the twentieth century without betraying the fundamental philosophies and principles of the ancient covenants. Such a bridge can be built only by close cooperation between Indian 'elders' and the youth. The elders have the essential role of ensuring that the cultural chain linking the ancient covenants to the present is not broken, that is, of maintaining integrity with fundamental *Indian* philosophies and principles. The youth have the essential role of ensuring that the fundamental philosophies and principles are interpreted for relevance to their surviving and living needs in the contemporary social, economic, and political circumstances.

In the Indian lexicon, 'cultural authenticity' has come to be defined largely in terms of ancient customs and traditions. Customs and traditions emphasize behavioural imperatives and speak to the regulation of activities and relationships. Defining cultural authenticity in this way involves some serious drawbacks. Inherent in such customs and traditions are the limitations of the time and place in which they were conceived. It follows that, if a culture's authenticity is defined by a body of ancient prescriptive customs and traditions, rather than by broad philosophies and principles, the degrees of freedom for cultural adaptation and development will be greatly constricted. Such is especially the case if the authenticating customs and traditions are perceived as *sacred* behavioural prescriptions of the Creator. Sacred prescriptive customs and traditions that cannot be reconciled with contemporary needs for surviving and living become a curse for those who must abide by them.

If Indians are to survive and live as *Indians*, then the process of cultural adaptation and development cannot be constrained by pre-scriptive customs and traditions conceived in another time and place. Put another way, Indians need an escape from the constraints of outdated customs and traditions. The avenue of escape here lies in an intellectual abstraction of the fundamental philosophies and prin-ciples underlying their ancient customs and traditions, that is, in breaking free of the belief that their fundamental philosophies and principles can and must exist only as expressed in their ancient cus-toms and traditions. Once they are free from this constraint, then the traditional philosophies and principles can be translated into contem-porary pragmatic ethics, morality, norms, and customs to meet the needs for surviving and living in their changing environment.

Because participants in a culture generally are not aware of the basic premises embodied in their cultural heritage, Indians will need to identify and study in depth the fundamental philosophies and principles that underlie their traditional customs and traditions, and to develop new knowledge (i.e., ethics, morality, norms, customs) within the framework of those philosophies and principles. This must be their first priority of cultural adaptation and development: to derive a framework of traditional fundamental philosophies and principles that will serve as a guide in adapting and developing their cultures for surviving and living in the contemporary world.

This framework of philosophies and principles could be entrenched in indigenous constitutions, that is they could codify in secular form their ancient sacred covenant. Such a constitution will allow Indians to evaluate and, as necessary, amend their customs and traditions to fit emerging needs and aspirations, but to do so within the framework of their traditional philosophies and principles. This process implies both continuity and change: continuity of fundamental philosophies and principles and change as ancient customs and traditions are recast to fit contemporary needs. Thus, the door to the future will be opened without turning their backs on the past. The process of redesigning ancient customs and traditions for contemporary realities within a framework of traditional philosophies and principles will not be easy. But, through trial and error, such a process can produce efficient new cultural forms.

It is worth noting that *Indian* cultural adaptation and development can proceed only from where Indian cultures stand today; that is, adaptation and development must contend with the culture of de-pendence and with the acculturation that has already occurred. This means that, in order to revitalize *Indian* cultures, Indians must psychologically and intellectually break out of the culture of dependence in which they have been trapped, free themselves of the Euro-Western value system into which they have been assimilated, and purge the 'deviant' colonial political and administrative institutions and norms that have been imposed on them.

Defining cultural authenticity on the basis of abstract and codified traditional philosophies and principles that are translated into pragmatic ethics, morality, norms, and customs to meet their living and surviving needs in their contemporary environment will give *Indian* cultures greater 'portability.' This holds particular relevance for urban Indians. Urban Indians need a culture that allows them to live and survive in their setting without having to forfeit their identification with their cultural heritage. A culture that prescribes outdated customary and traditional behavioural imperatives can never flourish in a city.

The Jewish people provide a remarkable example of a society that has preserved its identity as a cultural group based on a set of codified philosophies and principles. The Jewish people have experienced massive social and geographical disruptions; they have survived thousands of years of enslavement and persecution; fragmentation into small groups scattered over all continents and dispersed into virtually all cultures of the world; three thousand years without the protection of national boundaries or political sovereignty; and the Holocaust. Throughout this experience they have preserved the continuity of their traditional fundamental philosophies and principles. Jews started as a tribal people with a spiritually defined cultural identity that was based on a covenant between themselves and the Creator. This covenant has been a 'constant' in maintaining their sense of cultural identity and their will to survive as Jews. It has stood as a barrier between them and assimilation into other cultures.

Yet, throughout its history, Jewish culture while remaining true to its traditional fundamental philosophies and principles, has undergone continuous adaptation and development to maintain its effectiveness as a blueprint for surviving and living in a variety of changing political, economic, and social circumstances and environments. Although custom and tradition serve important functions in Jewish culture, the Jewish identity is defined essentially by enduring philosophies and principles. As necessary, customs and traditions have been adapted for coping with the changing world around them (e.g., modern science and industrialization) without compromising the authenticity of traditional fundamental philosophies and principles. If Jewish 'ancients' were to reappear today, they might not recognize all of the customs and traditions, but they would probably feel comfortable with the fundamental philosophies and principles that have guided Jewish cultural adaptation and development through the ages, enabling their descendants to live and survive as Jews.

Although the Indians' struggle to preserve their cultures and national identities cannot be directly equated with that of the Jews, it is occurring under conditions that bear a number of similarities to those historically experienced by Jews. Indians are a tribal people and have experienced forced social and geographic disruptions, colonial oppression and exploitation, fragmentation into small bands, dispersion over an entire continent, and an ethno-spiritual holocaust. Thus, the survival of Jewish culture may be instructive for the survival of *Indian* cultures. Particularly worthy of attention is the Jewish emphasis on fundamental philosophies and principles as their guiding framework for cultural adaptation and development in a variety of changing political, economic, and social settings.

Can Indians adapt their cultures to their contemporary environment without forfeiting their *Indian-ness*? It is a mistake to view the crisis in *Indian* cultures as deriving from an inherent incompatibility between the requirements of the modern industrial world, on the one hand, and traditional philosophies and principles, on the other. There is no inherent reason why traditional fundamental philosophies and principles need be compromised by cultural adaptation and development for contemporary needs. None the less, if Indians want to survive as *Indians*, they need be wary of all temptations to deviate from the fundamental philosophies and principles embodied in their ancient covenants. History may hold a lesson in this regard. A deviation of tragic consequence occurred when Indians allowed themselves to be seduced into the fur trade. When Indians engaged in the fur trade, a fundamental principle – that all living things are sacred and are not to be killed except to satisfy life's necessity – was transgressed. They acted like the Europeans, that is, as profiteering 'wasters' of living things. In this action *Indians*, for commercial gain, forfeited their spiritual relationship with other living things, and by this transgression they became collaborators in their colonization and subsequent cultural disintegration.

Today, there is evidence that Indians are being seduced by the Canadian government into forfeiting yet another fundamental principle: their spiritual relationship to the land. Evidence for this allegation is strongest in the present trend towards privatization of communal Indian lands. Indian élites seem to have lost sight of the traditional spiritual meaning of land as the basis for their communal society and as the collective link to their ancestors and the covenant. Cultural confusion is also evident in the way bands/tribes pursue their land claims. Every land-claim negotiation involves cash in lieu of land as a large part of the settlement. It would appear that the traditional spiritual relationship to land is being supplanted by a commercial relationship to real-estate. Unquestionably, Indians are entitled to restitution, but they must take care that they do not seek restitution in the form of alien goods that will subvert their traditional philosophies and principles. They must seek it in a form that will serve their survival and well-being as *Indians* for generations to come. Indians can live and survive as *Indians* only if they value land in the same way as their ancestors did – as a communal, spiritual heritage.

Language and cultural transmission

Language derives from the shared experiences, feelings, values, and ideas of a people over a very long period of their existence; it reflects and conditions the thought patterns and world-views of a people. For example, most *Indian* languages classify most things as animate, that is, as having a spirit. This conditioned the way they related to animals, plants, and the land, and it engendered a world-view that emphasized the harmony of nature.

When a language dies a world-view is lost. Thus, Indians cannot fully survive as *Indians* without retaining their languages. They cannot fully understand or experience the philosophies, principles, and social and normative systems of their ancestors without their languages. They may don traditional dress and participate in the traditional dances, but without their languages they cannot think or feel the same spiritual relationship with the land and all life forms thereon that their ancestors did. Only through their indigenous languages can today's Indians fully access the knowledge, wisdom, sentiments, and meanings offered by their cultural heritage. In short, without their languages they cannot fully restore their traditional identity or nationhood.

Today, Indians charge the Canadian government with destruction of their indigenous languages and cultures, and they denounce the government for failing to provide for Indian language and cultural instruction to their children as part of the school curriculum. Clearly, the Canadian government committed a great crime against Indians and their cultures when it forced Indian children at ages five to fifteen to attend residential schools where they were severely punished by their teachers if they spoke their indigenous language. The long years spent in residential schools subverted the parents' human right to teach the tribal language to their children. In consequence, the main vehicle of *Indian* cultural expression was critically impaired. To revive their languages and cultures Indian leaders demand constitutional guarantees and funding comparable to that given to Canadian francophones. But, even if they were to achieve such constitutional guarantees and funding, it would not revive their languages and cultures. Reviving *Indian* languages and cultures is primarily a matter of motivation. A language and a culture will survive only when a cultural community is sufficiently motivated to preserve them.

There are many opportunities for reviving *Indian* languages and cultures that lie outside the parameters of constitutional guarantees, more money, and formal instruction in schools. Specifically, Indians can make much more of an effort to keep their indigenous language alive in their homes and communities. Increasingly, the first and only language spoken in Indian homes and their communities is English. The 1981 Census reported that only 46 per cent of on-reserve Indians and 18 per cent of urban Indians spoke their indigenous language.[5] By neglecting to instruct their children in their indigenous languages and cultures, Indian parents are collaborating in the assimilation of their own children. If Indians are to live and survive as *Indians*, then Indian parents, leaders, and elders must double and redouble their efforts to teach their children their indigenous languages and cultures through informal and formal interaction and role modelling in the home and in the community. Constitutional guarantees, more money, and Indian language and cultural instruction in Canadian schools will be ineffective, unless the family and the community become effective mechanisms for transmitting their languages and cultures. If they fail to propagate their languages and cultures in the home and the community, then their identity will be lost and their children will not live and survive as *Indians*.

Linguistic and cultural transmission or socialization has particular significance in the case of a society with an oral tradition. In a literate society languages, philosophies, and principles can be permanently recorded and thus retained in the written 'memory' for reference and even revival by future generations. However, oral societies such as most bands/tribes in Canada have a much more limited capacity for storing and transmitting their cultures to succeeding generations, and any part of a language or culture that is not transmitted to even *one* succeeding generation is forever lost. Thus, in *Indian* societies each generation has a crucial responsibility to serve as an 'oral bridge' for linguistic and cultural transmission. Any generation that fails to fulfil this obligation denies all future generations their rightful heritage, their most important aboriginal right.

At present, the 'oral bridge' in most Indian communities is in imminent danger of collapse. The menace to the 'oral bridge' is threefold: (1) the loss of function and status of 'elders,' resulting from the imposition of colonial institutions, has seriously disrupted the oral tradition; (2) elders who were brought up in the oral tradition are vanishing from the scene; and (3) as the present generation of Indian youths become literate in the English or French language, the oral tradition is losing its legitimacy and force. Distinct from what is being transmitted, the oral tradition in and of itself serves essential functions in maintaining *Indian* identity, a sense of community, and personal continuity with the past. Thus, the loss of their oral tradition will leave another void in *Indian* cultures.

The present state of their oral tradition poses the immediate peril that *Indian* languages and traditional philosophies and principles will recede and disappear from memory before they are preserved in literature. If the fundamental philosophies and principles derived from the ancients are not preserved in a body of humanistic literature – poetry, essays, legend, history – that gives expression to the *Indian* soul, in their indigenous languages, future generations of Indians will be cheated out of an important part of their cultural heritage. Such a literature is needed to infuse and inspire the young with a sense of devotion and responsibility towards their languages and cultures.

In the absence of written *Indian* languages, Indian youths in Canada must learn their traditional philosophies and principles in English or French. But these languages cannot adequately express the sentiments, concepts, subtleties,and ambiguities of *Indian* world-views and thought. Nor do they yield the same sense of *Indian* identity and community of feeling. In order to make it possible to produce an authentic *Indian* humanistic literature, every 'linguistic family' must set about to write an indigenous dictionary and grammar so that their fundamental philosophies and principles can be codified in their native languages. Indian bands/tribes could greatly enhance their capacities to carry out such a monumental task if they cultivated closer ties with university- and college-based Native American Studies programs. An example of a significant contribution emanating from such a program is provided by the work of Professor Don Frantz, of the University of Lethbridge. With cooperation from the Blackfoot community, Professor Frantz and Norma Jean Russell have compiled a Blackfoot dictionary and a Blackfoot grammar.[6]

But for many Indian communities time is running out as the 'elders' who can contribute to such an undertaking in their native tongue are vanishing from the scene. The window of opportunity has narrowed to less than a generation. With the passing of the traditional elders, who are the repositories of the knowledge and expertise gained from centuries of trial, error, and observation, Indians will lose the essential 'oral bridge' to their past. And if nothing is done to preserve the cultural past for tomorrow, then the culture that will be transmitted to future generations of Indians will be the culture of dependence or the culture of Canadian society. The *Indian* cultural future will have been forever lost.

Urban Indians

For urban Indians a crucial question is: How will *Indian* nationhood be defined? It is a premise of this discussion that for urban Indians to retain an *Indian* identity they must be included in the definition of *Indian* nationhood, and if they are to be included, then the significant boundaries of *Indian* nationhood cannot be race or territory, but must be culture. Such a definition is consistent with traditional *Indian* nationhood. Traditional *Indian* nations were not defined by race or territorial boundaries; they existed and functioned as cultural communities.

Most urban Indians identify themselves as originating from a certain band/tribe and reserve. The band/tribe and reserve hold great significance for them. They are the source of their spirituality, the link with their ancestors and the communal way of life. The reserve is all that remains of their ancestral lands. Strong links with their band/tribal community are important if they are to maintain an *Indian* identity. 'Strong links' has reference to cultural, social, and political connections between urban Indians (including those whose Indian status was restored under Bill C-31) and their band/tribal community of origin.

Strong cultural links between reserve and urban Indians are important for another reason. It is unlikely that many tribes/bands can survive as *Indians* unless they forge strong cultural links between their urban and reserve communities. This assessment is prompted by recent and projected demographic trends indicating that an accelerating proportion of the total Indian population is migrating to urban centres. Over time, the centre of Indian cultural influence may be located in the city. Thus, the fate of *Indian* cultures may be decided by urban Indians. Thus, it is imperative that reserve-based Indians forge strong cultural linkages, in effect form one cultural community with their urban kin, and that both participate in the revitalization of their cultures. Both urban and reserve-based Indians have essential contributions to make to the vital enterprise of cultural adaptation and development. They can complement each other's experience and resources in the process of adapting and developing the fundamental *Indian* philosophies and principles for surviving and living in the contemporary world. This does not imply total uniformity of urban and rural *Indian* cultures. All cultures of the world have urban and rural variations, showing unique adaptations for the different environments. But, for band/tribal *Indian* cultures, these must be variations of style only, not of fundamental philosophies or principles.

Despite the great differences between an urban setting and a reserve setting, Indians in both environments at present experience virtually the same unconscionable level of social pathologies, that is, high rates of unemployment, alcoholism, drug abuse, violence, family disruption, suicide, and so on. Most urban Indians live as transients, on welfare, in ghetto conditions, in the most destitute of circumstances. In small part, the social disorganization of urban Indians derives from the disruption all rural migrants to the city tend to experience. But Indian migrants more than any other cultural group have problems in making a successful urban adjustment. The main reason for this failure is not one of individual shortcomings; rather, it derives from a cultural handicap. Like their kin on the reserves, most urban Indians live and survive within the framework of the culture of dependence, which is as inadequate a design for surviving and living in the city as for doing so on the reserve.

Urban Indians who participate successfully in the Canadian mainstream cannot escape becoming part of the Canadian class structure. This structure cannot be replicated or carried over into their reserve communal societies; none the less, *Indian* cultures must be able to accommodate the success of urban Indians or they will become psychologically estranged and alienated from their people and cultures. Today, acculturation is a necessary price urban Indians must pay for success in an urban setting. Thus, the challenge is to adapt and develop *Indian* cultures for success in urban settings. Unless *Indian* cultures are adapted and developed for successful urban living, Indians will be forced to choose between cultural assimilation or to continue living in the culture of dependence. If *Indian* cultures were made into effective designs for successful urban living, it would serve to affirm the value of their traditional cultures and identity, and it would stem the tide of acculturation and assimilation.

Pan-Indians

The term 'Indian' serves the Canadian government as a convenient political-legal-administrative categorization of the culturally diverse first peoples of Canada. An accidental designation, it expressed what the colonizers were conditioned to see (i.e., colour or race) at the time of first contact with the people indigenous to this continent. However, the term 'Indian' should not be taken to imply a historical pan-tribal *cultural* identity or unity. This is not to say that the diverse Indian communities, historically, did not evidence many cultural similarities. Most tribal cultures were built upon a face-to-face base, with their relationships, behaviour, and activities regulated by custom and tradition. Therefore, most indigenous tribes/bands were predisposed to organize their social systems holistically. While there is evidence of some functional differentiation in their social organization, with few exceptions they did not separate functions into specialized institutions. Spirituality, for example, was not organized into a specialized religious institution separate from other functions; rather, it permeated the customs, traditions, and norms that governed all tribal functions. Moreover, because their survival was so directly dependent upon their natural environment, most Indian tribes/bands held a spiritually rooted respect for the land and all life forms. They viewed themselves as one part of the natural order, related to all other beings and things, and they emphasized harmony and unity with this universe. Because the survival of most tribes/bands depended on cooperation among their members, they emphasized kinship relations, mutual aid, generosity, and cooperation within the community. Additional pan-tribal similarities could be observed in the practice of social and political egalitarianism, a strong commitment to consensual decision making, personal autonomy, and respect for elders.

But these cultural similarities among the tribes/bands in Canada did not add up to a pan-Indian community or unified cultural identity. Although some regional alliances were formed among bands and tribes on the BC Pacific Northwest coast, and in eastern Canada by the Iroquois, a unified identity beyond the tribe was rarely needed and was rarely developed. In short, the category of 'Indian,' as defined in the Indian Act and as entrenched in the constitution, while it encompasses pan-tribal cultural similarities, does not derive from any historic unified pan-Indian cultural identity.

Yet, it cannot be denied that the category 'Indian,' as defined in the Indian Act, does represent a collective identity for the indigenous peoples of Canada today. This identity, however, derives from 'post-contact' experiences. In particular, it derives from their common experience as colonized peoples. The cumulative shared experiences and effects of colonization (i.e., cultural repression, forced assimilation, political oppression, theft of ancestral lands, injustice, maladministration, dependence, poverty, racism and so on), compounded by the imposition of separate laws (the Indian Act), a separate administrative system (the DIAND), the reserve system, the boarding-school experience (which gave them a shared language), as well as other shared circumstances, have created a remarkably uniform political, legal, economic, and social environment for all Indians. This uniformity is characterized, chiefly, by their condition of dependence. These common social-political-economic-legal-administrative experiences of colonialism and their condition of dependence have had a profound impact upon Indian attitudes, world-views, motivations, and behaviours. And, while different bands/tribes have responded in varying ways to these common experiences, a high level of post-contact pan-Indian cultural homogeneity has resulted. This homogeneity, defined primarily by the culture of dependence rather than by their historic cultural similarities, provides the pan-Indian identity.

The development of a pan-Indian community is most evident among urban Indians, but it is also evident among the élite class of Indians who manage a variety of pan-Indian political-economic interests. These urban Indians and Indian élites have more opportunity and incentive for intertribal contact, which facilitates building a pan-Indian social-cultural community. Evidence for the existence of such a social-cultural community can be observed in the popularization of intertribal participation in pow-wows, 'sweats,' sweetgrass, and other ceremonial gatherings, and in intermarriages. Although, currently, the most prominent manifestation of the pan-Indian movement is political, it is conceivable that, in future, these social-cultural groupings could evolve into a unified pan-Indian ethnic identity based on a melding of their pre-contact cultural commonalities and post-contact experiences of colonization.

The pan-Indian movement is envisioned by many as an instrument of Indian unity that has the potential to enhance the survival and well-being of *Indians*. But there may be an irreconcilable contradiction between the concepts of *Indian*-ness and pan-Indianism. Before there can be a successful pan-Indian movement, there must, first, exist a unified pan-Indian cultural identity. Without such a unified identity, it would be almost impossible to sustain political cohesion. Such a unified identity requires symbols and a socio-cultural system that transcends traditional band/tribal cultural boundaries. The required transcending symbols and socio-cultural systems can be achieved only by subordinating, muting, and blurring traditional band/tribal cultural boundaries and uniqueness. Herein lies a dilemma for Indians: if pan-Indianism is to serve as an effective instrument for enhancing the survival and well-being of Indians, it will be at the expense of *Indian*-ness, because in order to prevail it must foster a non-tribal Indian cultural identity.

Assimilation to pan-Indianism could greatly enhance the political and social capacities and resources required to sustain a distinctive identity (and such an identity would do considerably less violence to traditional tribal philosophies and principles than assimilation to Canadian society); none the less, pan-Indianism represents a form of 'extinction' for historical band/tribal *Indian* cultures and social systems. Thus, Indians need to consider carefully whether they want a pan-Indian identity for their children. They need also to give thought to the possibility that a pan-Indian ethnic community may not be sustainable over the long term because it lacks a historical cultural base, historical language, loyalty, and so on. It could well turn out to be a 'way station' on the road to gradual and complete assimilation into Canadian society, or it could trap them in the culture of dependence. Moreover, within the concept of 'pan-Indianism,' Indian claims to aboriginal rights and to nationhood lose much of their historical, legal, political, and moral justification because there exists no historical cultural basis for a claim to nationhood at the pan-Indian level. A claim to nationhood at the pan-Indian level would necessarily have to be based upon the race-referenced status criteria of the Indian Act, and this is unacceptable.

The Canadian government, by its formal recognition and funding of pan-Indian organizations, has actively encouraged the development of a pan-Indian movement. Perhaps, it has done so because pan-Indianism fits the legal, administrative, and racial status–determining criteria in the Indian Act, conforms to the constitutional definition of Indian, and facilitates political-bureaucratic control and management of Indian affairs. However, pan-Indianism has a significant potential to cause political problems for the Canadian government. If Indian political organization was limited to band/tribal entities, Indians would be fragmented into so many little parts that their influence could easily be nullified.

Resistance to change

The failure of Indians to adapt and develop their cultures to new world realities is not the result of any inherent cultural deficiency. As already noted, historically Indians have evidenced a strong norm and capacity to adapt their cultures to changing circumstances and to enhance their cultures as designs for surviving and living. Thus, I have attributed the failure of Indians to adapt and develop their cultures for surviving and living in today's world to Canadian government policies that forced assimilation on Indians, destroyed their traditional means of subsistence, and imposed isolation on them. But within Indian communities there also is resistance to cultural adaptation and development – voices that speak from a posture of siege, calling for a 'fortress' against the influences of the outside world. What follows is a brief analysis of two indigenous attitudinal constraints to cultural adaptation and development that I call 'false hope' and 'sanctity of custom and traditions.'

Many Indians believe the best solution to their tragic cultural and social plight is to be found in a return to their past world. Disconnected from contemporary and emerging realities, they cling to a 'false hope' of restoring their traditional way of life by re-establishing their historical natural environment and traditional modes of subsistence. This 'false hope' is based on the assumption that large tracts of their lost lands will be restored to them under aboriginal rights, treaties, and land claims; their nationhood will be regained; and, once again, they will live a traditional lifestyle of hunting, fishing, and gathering. This 'false hope' is often articulated when Indian leaders press their comprehensive land claims with the Canadian government, and when they seek political support within their own community.

In times past, some groups of Indians have attempted to actualize this 'false hope' as an escape from the afflictions of their destitution and social pathologies. Such a mind-set provided the compelling motivation for the Chief Small Boy venture. In 1971, Chief Small Boy of Hobbema, Alberta, fled with a group of followers to the Rocky

Mountains in an idealistic and desperate attempt to escape the horrific conditions on their reserve. Chief Small Boy sought to revitalize the tribe's traditional culture by re-establishing their spiritual and sub-sistence relationship to the land and wildlife. Although the spiritual aspect of Chief Small Boy's venture was symbolically very meaningful for many Indians, his design could not satisfy the day-to-day sub-sistence imperatives of the group, and thus it failed on practical grounds.

Those who insist that *Indian* cultural survival is inextricably linked to the traditional means of subsistence – that is, hunting, fishing, and gathering – are not doing their peoples or their cultures a service. By insisting on such a linkage, they are, in effect, asserting that *Indian* culture will become irrelevant, and *Indian* identity will disappear, unless their traditional economy is restored. Such an assertion carries the ultimate prospect of cultural defeatism and despair. In the 'real world,' the bottom line is that Canada will not redesign its industrial society to make room for the traditional ways of *Indian* life. In effect, Indians are confronted with a political, economic, and social envi-ronment beyond their powers to change or escape. The trend is al-ready very evident. While individual Indians from a few bands/tribes in the northern regions of Canada's provinces still rely on hunting, fishing, and gathering to supplement their social-assistance incomes, for members of bands/tribes living in the southern regions this is not a viable lifestyle. Thus, any strategy for preserving the authenticity of *Indian* cultures that is based on restoring traditional economies is doomed to certain failure. If Indians are to survive as *Indians* their cultures must be more than a mere correlate of their traditional and outmoded means of subsistence. They must be flexible, evolving de-signs for living and surviving in an industrialized world.

A more promising approach to Indian survival as *Indians* is, as I have proposed, to root their identities and the authenticity of their cultures in their traditional philosophies and principles, not in ancient modes of subsistence. Only the traditional philosophies and principles can ensure the survival of authentic *Indian* world-views and social systems. The failure of Chief Small Boy's venture to meet the sub-sistence imperatives of his group is not to be taken as a measure of the virtue, viability, or the contemporary relevance of the traditional philosophies and principles. It merely demonstrated the futility of any effort to rehabilitate the traditional culture by restoring the tra-ditional means of subsistence. Those who cling to the 'false hope' that their traditional economy can be restored through aboriginal rights, treaties, or land claims are inhibiting the survival of Indians as *Indians*. Without cultural adaptation and development to fit the new world, Indians are doomed to continue living and surviving in a culture of dependence with its associated sense of apathy and defeatism.

I turn now to 'sanctity of custom and traditions' as an indigenous attitudinal constraint on *Indian* cultural adaptation and development. Indians have a profound and abiding emotional commitment to the sanctity of their ancient customs and traditions. This commitment is nourished by their nostalgia for an idyllic past; by ethnocentrism; by their consciousness of kind and sense of community; and by the affirmation it provides for their aboriginal and treaty rights. However, their commitment to their ancient customs and traditions goes beyond mere nostalgia, ethnocentrism, community, and political/legal utility. They consider these customs and traditions to be an essential spiritual link to their ancestors and, through their ancestors, to the covenant and the creator.

In the ancient myths, their customs and traditions are received by their ancestors from the Creator, and they represent the Creator's sacred blueprint for the tribe's survival and living. Chief Seattle expressed this belief to the governor of Washington Territory, as follows: 'Our religion is the traditions of our ancestors – the dreams of old men, given them in solemn hours of night by the Great Spirit; and the vision of our sachems; and it is written in the hearts of our people.'[7] In this belief system, customs and traditions are considered as sacred prescriptions rather than as secular designs for living and surviving. This idea finds expression in the 'holistic' nature of traditional Indian cultures – that is, the spiritual dimension integral to all aspects of their cultures. This sacred quality of their ancient customs and traditions creates an equation in which any cultural change becomes problematic. It also has the effect of steering cultural revitalization movements in the direction of religious fundamentalism, that is, where the main goal is to revive *original* customs and traditions, and to oppose all cultural change as sacrilegious (e.g., the Delaware revitalization movement of the early 1760s). Thus, by assigning a sacred value to the customs and traditions, not only is change inhibited but deficiencies in the culture may be rationalized and represented as virtues.

In so far as survival of a people depends upon their ability to make dynamic and creative responses to a changing environment, any society that rigidly confines itself to its ancestral customs and traditions because of cultural deification, sentences itself to ultimate extinction or assimilation. In a world of great stability, or in a utopia where everything is perfect, little cultural change is required and a static culture may be tolerable. Perhaps the pre-contact world of Indians can be described as utopian and as having great stability. But, in the rapidly changing and imperfect world in which they live today, Indians must be free to adapt and develop their cultures to changing needs.

Indians must defend their cultures, not with 'sacred' fences, but by opening their cultures to new ideas. However, in advocating 'cultural liberalism,' that is, removing the fence of sacredness, I emphasize the need to first establish a foundation and framework of traditional fundamental philosophies and principles. The challenge of living and surviving as *Indians* is to reformulate the ancient customs and traditions without compromising the enduring truths (i.e., the traditional philosophies and principles) that these customs and traditions were designed, in their time, to express. It is in these enduring truths that Indians must seek the authenticity and essence of *Indian*-ness, not in the residue of outdated customs and traditions. When these enduring truths are established as a foundation and framework, Indians can then proceed to creatively reshape and revitalize their cultural houses to meet their needs in the contemporary world, without fear of compromising the Creator's blueprint. There can be no contradiction between the Creator's law and the right of a people to survive. The Creator would not have given their ancestors a law that would hinder their descendants' survival. The implication is that each generation carries an obligation for cultural adaptation and development.

Indians are at present involved in a process of separating out the expressive traits of their culture (e.g., art, music, dance, costumes, ceremonies, and rituals) from the seamless whole of their traditional culture. From among these expressive traits they are selecting some practices (e.g., the sweat lodge, peace pipe, sweetgrass ceremonies, and sun dance) that they deem to be essentially spiritual in significance, and they are intent on preserving these as a sacred ancestral inheritance. Perhaps by compartmentalizing the sacred in this way they will feel greater freedom to adapt and develop their cultures for surviving and living in today's world, knowing that at least a part of their identity is immutably rooted in their sacred traditions.

Political dimensions

The survival of Indians as *Indians* subsumes a number of diverse political considerations. In the following pages I discuss some of these considerations: cultural alliances, sovereignty, social organization, multiculturalism, the Indian Act, and band/tribal membership.

Cultural alliances

Indians in Canada have historically comprised a multiplicity of tribes/bands representing seven cultural areas and twelve linguistic 'families' (each with a number of distinct dialects).[8] Within this multilinguistic, multicultural mosaic there existed differences in social and normative systems predicated largely on food supply and ecology. For example, fishing communities had a fairly predictable and dependable food supply, and it was accessible to individual families. By contrast, Plains Indians had to follow their food supply and band/tribal members had to cooperate in the hunt for food. Consequently, each developed different social/economic/political organizations, customs, and traditions. *Within* each of the seven cultural areas and twelve linguistic families, however, there existed uniformities and affinities in fundamental cultural philosophies and principles.

Upon this historical mosaic of cultural-linguistic families, successive Canadian governments have imposed a number of divisive legal definitions. Under Canada's Indian policies, these cultural-linguistic families have been divided into 'status–non-status,' 'treaty–non-treaty,' 'reserve-urban,' 'band members and non-members,' and a full range of combinations and permutations of these and some additional categories. These categories of Indians have been further fragmented into more than six hundred bands. By effective force of Canadian political, legal, and administrative categorization, the primary Indian identities of today conform to the diverse colonial definitions, rather than to any cultural-linguistic 'families.' This predominance of Canadian legal-political-administrative definitions over cultural-linguistic definitions has divided Indians who historically shared a cultural-linguistic heritage into factions, and it has fragmented their resources and efforts to adapt and develop their cultures and to maintain their languages.

My purpose in presenting this brief overview is to propose that, in order to save their cultures and languages, Indian peoples must initiate a process of building cultural and linguistic alliances that transcend and override the legal definitions and social-political boundaries imposed upon them by the Canadian government. They must transcend their band/tribal social-political barriers and ethnocentricities in order to pool resources and forces within the historic cultural-linguistic families for a united venture purposed to revitalize their traditional cultures and languages. This does not require a corresponding political union; that is, there is no need to reorganize the existing 'political units' (bands/tribes) to conform geographically, demographically, or jurisdictionally with the cultural alliances or areas of cultural and linguistic cooperation. The bands/tribes could continue to be the defining political unit. But an endeavour to forge inter-band/tribal cultural and linguistic alliances will require band/tribal councils to create appropriate structures for joining their resources and forces in a formal, concerted effort.

The idea of inter-band/tribal cooperation is not new. In a number of contemporary instances, several bands/tribal have organized themselves, politically and administratively, into 'tribal councils' for the purpose of promoting treaty rights, or achieving efficiencies in program and service delivery. For example, the Dakota-Ojibway Tribal Council is a formal unification of seven bands with a total of approximately seven thousand members in southern Manitoba. It was formed to achieve efficiencies in the delivery of child-welfare services, policing, fire protection, and so on. But such initiatives have been motivated by political-administrative considerations, not by *cultural* goals. Consequently, these cooperative ventures have had only minor implications for cultural development.

It is worth emphasizing that, although the proposed cultural alliances would serve as a basis for primary cultural identity and loyalty, such alliances are not to be equated with 'pan-Indianism,' as this term is generally used. Pan-Indianism implies the development of a new cultural form based largely on the common experience of colonialism. Under the proposed cultural alliances, bands/tribes would work cooperatively to develop their cultural affinity within the framework of shared traditional philosophies and principles. Such alliances would demand fewer cultural compromises from bands/tribes than a pan-Indian approach. The proposed alliances would have a great advantage over the current band or tribal political units in their capacity to provide the essential 'critical mass' of people and resources needed to adapt, develop, and maintain a culture and a language.

Sovereignty

On the agenda of Indian leaders, cultural concerns have been subordinated to political concerns, as is evident in their constitutional posture, which is dominated by political, not cultural, goals. Their stated constitutional positions conceptualize the Indian future primarily in terms of self-government and political nationhood. Cultural goals are viewed as contingent upon achieving their political goals. But the survival of Indians as *Indians* depends primarily upon cultural revitalization within a framework of traditional philosophies and principles, not upon political sovereignty. Put another way, revitalized *Indian* cultures are a prerequisite for political sovereignty, rather than the reverse. Jewish culture survived for thousands of years without benefit of political sovereignty. But the Jewish state would have been impossible without the survival of Jewish culture. If sovereign Indian states came into existence today, without cultural revitalization, most would have only their 'race,' and the culture of dependence as the primary basis for their nationhood.

Historical experience affirms that *Indian* cultures are vulnerable to destruction and, therefore, in need of protection. What is not so clear is what sort of protection they need. On the one hand, political sovereignty is neither a necessary nor a sufficient condition for *Indian* cultural survival; on the other hand, external legislative-constitutional provisions that encumber or constrain *Indian* cultural adaptation and development doom *Indian* survival. For Indians to survive as *Indians* they must be shielded from the application of Canadian laws that undermine their capacity to adapt and develop their cultures. A charter of collective cultural rights, entrenched in the constitution, could provide such a shield.

However, one must question whether sovereignty is necessary or even conducive to their survival as *Indians* in Canada. Arguably, sovereignty provides a people with the greatest control over their cultural development. But (as I have proposed in chapter 3), under conditions of scarce resources, which describes the Indian situation, sovereignty could prove a handicap for cultural development. Maintaining the functions and services of sovereign nationhood could prove to be such a tremendous drain on the Indians' limited resources that nothing will be left over for cultural adaptation and development. Indian leaders need to give careful consideration to how much political autonomy is actually needed and beneficial for the survival of Indians as *Indians*.

Social organization

There exists a fundamental reciprocal and interdependent relationship between a society's social organization and its cultural philosophies and principles. A change in one compels a change in the other. This is evident in the deculturation and acculturation of Indians that has occurred consequent to the imposition of colonial administrative structures on Indian reserves. When Indians were denied the right and opportunity to maintain a social organization in a pattern consistent with their traditional philosophies and principles, it caused the relevant cultural values and norms to erode and collapse with disastrous consequences for social control in Indian communities. The process of deculturation and acculturation will not be stemmed when Indian leaders assume full control over the colonial administrative structures on their reserves, because the hierarchical authority and specialized institutions through which they will govern are incompatible with *Indian* philosophies and principles; they are based upon Euro-Western philosophies and principles. *Indian* social organizations grew out of philosophies and principles of communalism, sharing, spirituality and a holistic design.

In other words, there exists a fundamental contradiction between traditional *Indian* cultural philosophies and principles and the colonial social organization that has been imposed upon them. If traditional philosophies and principles are to be restored then it will require a corresponding re-creation of traditional social systems. Conversely, if traditional social systems are to be re-created, then traditional philosophies and principles must be restored. In the absence of *Indian* cultural revitalization, the colonial social organization that has been imposed upon Indian communities, will continue to evolve according to Euro-Western philosophies and principles. Unless the colonial political and administrative system is supplanted with traditional social systems, the deculturation and acculturation of Indians will continue.

In so far as the Indian ruling-élites have a vested interest in retaining the existing colonial political and bureaucratic systems, it is reasonable to expect resistance from them to any meaningful movement to revitalize *Indian* philosophies and principles. Such is the case because revitalization of *Indian* cultures would require a reciprocal reform of the colonial system through which the élites at present exercise their powers, and from which they derive their status and privileges. By clinging to the colonial political and administrative system on their reserves, the Indian ruling-élites are discouraging the revitalization of traditional philosophies and principles, and the survival of Indians as *Indians*.

Indian leaders argue that the process of establishing social systems based on traditional philosophies and principles must await achievement of political autonomy. But the process of building a social system based on traditional indigenous philosophies and principles need not, and should not, await political autonomy, especially given the unlikelihood that the political autonomy which they envision will ever be realized. The process of building legitimate indigenous social systems based on traditional philosophies and principles could begin immediately through voluntary organizations. A number of needful areas can be readily identified: shelters for abused women and children, suicide- and alcoholism- prevention programs, parent-teacher associations, cultural and linguistic instructional programs, youth recreational activities, and a variety of other endeavours that would enhance the structure and functioning of the family and the community, and that would foster the physical, social, and emotional well-being of children.

Such voluntary associations are notably lacking or grossly inadequate in Indian communities, despite a great and urgent need for them. If such voluntary organizations were to take root in Indian communities, they could offer full scope to all band/tribal members to put into practice the traditional fundamental philosophies and principles of personal duties and responsibilities to the communal group, of sharing, of spiritual and harmonious relationships, of justice and human dignity, and so on. Moreover, voluntary organizations could provide a mechanism for restoring the traditional connection between generosity and an individual's advancement to a leadership position in the community's hierarchy of social prestige and esteem. Through such a process Indian communities could kick-start the reciprocal dynamic that exists between revitalization of their traditional philosophies and principles and re-creation of their traditional social systems.

Canadian multiculturalism

Under Canada's policy of multiculturalism, overt forced cultural assimilation of Indians has been discontinued, and an official stance of tolerance for cultural diversity has been adopted. When Canada's policy of multiculturalism was introduced in 1971, then prime minister Pierre Trudeau told the House of Commons:

> There cannot be one cultural policy for Canadians of British and French origin, another for the original peoples, and yet a third for all others. For although there are two official languages, there is no official culture, nor does any ethnic group take precedence over any other ...

We are free to be ourselves. But, this cannot be left to chance. It must be fostered and pursued actively. If freedom of choice is in danger for some ethnic groups, it is in danger for all. It is the policy of this government to eliminate any such danger and to safeguard this freedom.[9]

Unfortunately, Trudeau's high-sounding proclamation of free cultural choice shrouds a shabby reality: under Canada's multicultural policy the price of free cultural choice is considerably higher for the first peoples, the Indians, than it is for the 'citizens plus,' the 'founding nations' – namely, the British and French – or even for most other immigrant groups. Canadian laws, institutional structures, and norms are based on *individualism*; thus they are compatible with British, French, and most other immigrant cultures, but they are alien to Indian *communal* cultures. The price to Indians who accept Trudeau's invitation to 'be themselves,' that is, live according to their traditional *Indian* cultures, is to forfeit the opportunity to participate as equals in the Canadian mainstream. Stated positively, Trudeau's liberal-Western model of multiculturalism requires Indians to become 'Canadians as all other Canadians' if they want equal opportunity in the Canadian mainstream. This is not a formula for the survival of Indians as *Indians*.

The current Canadian multicultural paradigm as defined in section 27 of the Constitution Act casts the issue of *Indian* cultural survival in very superficial terms, that is, in terms of removing legal prohibitions against the expressive-symbolic elements of *Indian* cultures (e.g., religious expression, language, and ceremony), and entrenching the *individual* right of Indians to preserve and practise these expressive-symbolic elements. However, if Indians are to survive as *Indians* this cannot occur within the framework of multiculturalism and individual rights as currently defined in the constitution. Indians must have collective cultural and linguistic rights and they must be empowered to develop and maintain essential political and social systems that fit consistently with their traditional fundamental philosophies and principles.

In line with their claims to sovereignty, Indian leaders demand entrenchment of their collective cultural-linguistic rights as an inherent authority of Indian self-government. While constitutional entrenchment of such authority for Indian governments would yield some room in the Canadian federation for the adaptation and development of *Indian* cultures and languages, we have already witnessed that a geographic-political approach to the guarantee of cultural-linguistic rights does not provide protection for the collective rights of francophones outside Quebec. It is even less likely that such an approach will provide protection for the cultural-linguistic rights of Indians living off their reserves. On the same grounds, the 'notwithstanding' clause, which was framed to protect provincial legislative supremacy and which is accessible only to constitutionally recognized Indian governments, will provide no protection for the cultural-linguistic rights of Indians who live in urban centres. Because it is construed in case-specific and 'negative' terms, the 'notwithstanding' clause is seriously inadequate as protection for the cultural-linguistic rights, even of those who live within reserve boundaries. Moreover, invoking this clause to protect cultural-linguistic rights carries a potential risk for abuse of individual rights by Indian governments.

What constitutional steps can Canada take that will allow Indians to survive as *Indians*? Obviously, any steps in this direction will require a monumental will on the part of Canadians and their politicians. Assuming such a will can be mustered, one way to guarantee the cultural-linguistic rights of *Indians* (and of francophones) in Canada would be to entrench a 'charter of collective cultural-linguistic rights.' Such a charter would be framed to guarantee the collective right of a 'people' or 'nation' to their culture, language, and social systems as an inherent unconditional and inalienable right. It would be purposed to guarantee the cultural survival of Indians as *Indians* (and of French Canadians as francophones); that is, it would be purposed to enhance and protect the cultural rights of cultural 'nations' or 'peoples,' not the political powers and autonomy of territorial governments (as the Canada Round of constitutional amendments was designed to do). Obviously, there are nearly overwhelming complexities in drafting such a charter, among them, establishing criteria of eligibility for cultural 'nationhood' or 'peoplehood' status and defining the rights and mutual responsibilities of the Canadian state and the eligible cultural 'nations' or 'peoples' The anticipated outcome of such a charter would be a Canadian state comprising a federation of anglophone, francophone, and aboriginal cultural 'nations' or 'peoples,' with the last-named grouped into a number of cultural 'families.' Such a multinational concept has always been unacceptable to most Canadians. But, a far-sighted analysis may prove it to be a lesser 'evil' than risking the genocidal solutions currently being played out in other multi-ethnic states.

One would expect Canadians to show great empathy for Indian cultural concerns. After all, cultural insecurity is a ubiquitous Canadian malady. It affects francophones in Canada, anglophones in Quebec, and immigrant minorities across Canada. Moreover, all 'good' Canadians are paranoid about U.S. cultural hegemony. Driven by this justifiable paranoia, the government of Canada has adopted a wide array of protective measures. For example, 'Canadian culture' regulations stipulate Canadian content in magazines, books, broadcasting, television, and movies, and prohibit foreign control of Canadian cultural institutions. Yet, when it comes to Indian aspirations and appeals to allow them to safeguard their endangered cultures, the Canadian government, and Canadians generally, evidence very little understanding or sympathy. In fact, the Canadian government consistently lobbies against every initiative by Indians to achieve protection for their cultures in international charters and conventions. Therefore, it has been the consistent thesis of this discourse that Indians cannot rely on the Canadian constitution, the Canadian courts, the Canadian government, the Canadian people, or Canadian money for the preservation of their cultures and languages. At best, Indians can hope only that Canadian courts and the Canadian government will not revert to regressive rulings and policies designed to assimilate them. *Indian* cultural survival will come only from cultural revitalization, a task for which Indians must assume full custody and full responsibility.

The Indian Act

The Indian Act does not define who is an Indian, only who will be recognized, legally, as having Indian status under the act; none the less, the act has had profound implications for Indian identity because, until the 1985 amendment to the Indian Act, band membership was an automatic corollary of Indian status. In effect, the status-determining criteria embodied in the Indian Act determined band/tribal membership and Indian identity, in so far as Indians draw their identity from band/tribal membership.

How is Indian status determined under the Indian Act? The Canadian government originated its pre-1985 Indian status/band membership lists (the Indian registry) primarily on the basis of biological ancestry and pre-contact band membership, without any stated cultural standard. The text of the Indian Act does not explicitly cite race (i.e., shared physical characteristics) as a criterion of Indian status–determination; it employs, instead, the language of biological ancestry or descent. And while originally *Indian* culture could reasonably be inferred from biological ancestry and pre-contact band member-ship, over several generations, without reference to cultural standards, the Indian Act status-defining criteria have become tantamount to a racial system defined by blood; that is, in practice, the Indian Act criterion of biological ancestry has functioned as a proxy for race, not as a proxy for culture.

The only exception to the blood-based status-defining criteria can be found in section 12(1)(b) of the pre-1985 Indian Act. In this section, the Canadian government arbitrarily imposed a patrilineal status-determining criterion by stipulating that a wife's status follows that of her husband. In other words, an Indian woman who married a non-Indian man lost Indian status, and a non-Indian woman who married an Indian man gained Indian status. If, from the start, 'blood' (i.e. biological ancestry) had been the exclusive and consistent cri-terion for Indian status, then the Indian registry would have omitted non-Indian women who 'married in' and included Indian women who 'married out.' It would also have included Indians who forfeited their status when they became 'enfranchised' (that is, removed from the list because of military service, education, or in exchange for certain other rights) and Indians who were omitted from the original registry through oversight or by design. But these additions and deletions would not have significantly altered the essential 'racial' composition of the Indian registry today.

In short, although the Indian status-determining criteria embodied in the Indian Act were not derived from any explicit or consistent principle of 'race,' the effect of the act's status-determining criteria has been such as to create and perpetuate a racial category. And because *Indian* culture was never incorporated in the Indian Act cri-teria for Indian status determination, *Indian* culture has never been a criterion for band/tribal membership determination. In effect, the Indian Act status-determining criteria have served to preserve the race while neglecting the culture. Its criteria have created racial commu-nities while disregarding cultural communities.

It is interesting to note that the neglect of cultural standards in the status-defining criteria of the Indian Act has drawn very little attention from Indian bands/tribes. The gender-discrimination provision (sec-tion 12[1][b]), however, which revoked the status of Indian women who 'married out,' has drawn much attention and protest from the women affected and from women's rights advocates generally. The issue of whether section 12(1)(b) constituted gender discrimination in violation of the Canadian Bill of Rights was brought before the Supreme Court of Canada, and the Court rendered its decision in 1974, upholding the section.[10] Subsequently, in 1980, Sandra Lovelace, a Maliseit Indian woman whose Indian status had been revoked under this discriminatory provision, brought her grievance before the U.N. Human Rights Committee. In its ruling in 1981, the committee declared Canada in contravention of article 27 of the U.N. Charter of Rights. In response to this censure by the United Nations, the Canadian government introduced an amendment to the Indian Act (Bill C-31, 1985) that repealed section 12 (1)(b). This amendment was designed to abate the Canadian government's immediate embarrassment for being in contravention of the U.N. Charter of Rights, and of its own Charter of Rights and Freedoms (1982).

The effect of the 1985 amendment to the Indian Act has been to create a new Indian registry. The new registry will comprise all persons listed on the pre-1985 registry, plus those achieving reinstatement under Bill C-31. The first-generation descendants of these reinstated Indians may also be eligible for Indian status, but are not automatically eligible for band membership. Descendants of reinstated Indian women born *prior* to 17 April 1985 are eligible for Indian status if they have *two* Indian-status grandparents (i.e., the 'half-descent rule'), while descendants of reinstated Indian men are eligible if they have one Indian-status grandparent (i.e., the 'quarter-descent' rule). The 'half-descent' rule applies to all descendants of 'reinstatees' born *after* 17 April 1985. The quarter and half 'descent' criteria are a transitional anomaly in the act; that is, they will disappear over the long term as they apply only to the descendants of reinstatees who are without band-membership status. Underage children of a reinstated woman have the right to reside with their mother on her reserve, but no such right is stipulated for the husband or for overage children.

In order to bring the act into conformity with the provisions of the U.N. Charter and the Canadian Charter of Rights and Freedoms, and to ease bureaucratic bookkeeping, the 1985 amendment provides that, in future, no one listed on the registry will lose his or her status involuntarily, whether by marriage or any other event. Moreover, any and all future descendants of those listed on the registry will have Indian status as a birthright, regardless of the status of the other parent. However, non-status persons (male or female) who 'marry in' will not be eligible for Indian status. In other words, neither race nor gender, nor culture, will be used to establish eligibility for Indian status. Simply stated, 'status begets status,' ad infinitum. By omitting any reference to biological ancestry, the Indian Act amendment has removed the last historical hint that Indian status carries any cultural significance, but this does not change the essential racial composition of the Indian registry.

Band membership

Under the Indian Act, prior to 1985, band/tribal membership automatically followed from 'Indian status,' in turn, band/tribal membership legally entitled a member to reside on the reserve (albeit, the actual opportunity to reside on the reserve was always subject to availability of housing and other facilities). Under the 1985 revisions of the act, Indian status has been separated from band/tribal membership. The federal government continues to determine 'Indian status,' but bands/tribes are now empowered to develop and implement their own criteria (i.e., 'membership codes') for accepting new members. The government has represented its motive for this legislation as purposed to devolve control over membership to band/tribal councils. Indeed, it has that effect, but the government's action was more self-serving than progressive. Anticipating that restoration of Indian status (and, hence, band/tribal membership) to large numbers of Indian women and their descendants under Bill C-31 would generate intense conflicts over who would be admitted to residence on the reserve, the federal government deftly devolved the authority over membership determination (and, hence, eligibility for admission to reserve residence) to band/tribal councils – let them take the heat for accepting or denying reserve residence to reinstated Indian women and their descendants. Had the federal government sincerely wanted to empower band/tribal councils it would have devolved control over Indian status–determining criteria.

Bands/tribes were given up to two years to formulate their membership codes. If they neglected to do so during this period, the provisions of the 1985 Indian Act stipulate that until such time as a band/tribe develops its own membership codes (in accordance with section 10 of the act), all those who are reinstated under Bill C-31 are eligible for band membership and that band/tribal membership will continue to follow automatically from Indian status. In other words, any Indian bands/tribes that have not developed membership codes, by default, are obliged to accept to membership all reinstatees under Bill C-31 until such time as they develop such codes. Such is the case because band/tribal powers with respect to membership determination are only 'forward looking' from the time they develop their own membership codes; that is, they cannot remove from band/tribal membership anyone who acquired the right of membership by virtue of achieving Indian status before they developed their membership code. Indian leaders have always resented the Canadian government's control over Indian status–determining criteria; none the less, when the question of whether section 12(1)(b) constituted gender discrimination came before the Supreme Court of Canada in 1973, the National Indian Brotherhood, representing the interests of all Indian bands/tribes, intervened on the side of the Canadian government, in support of this section of the act. They did so, they said, out of a concern that, if the Court ruled this section to be discriminatory, the whole Indian Act would be vulnerable on grounds of racial discrimination, and they were not ready to accept a repeal of the Indian Act. Following Lovelace's victory at the United Nations in 1981, the Assembly of First Nations belatedly (1983) issued a statement in which it supported the U.N. ruling.[11] Simultaneously, it emphasized the Indians' aboriginal right to control their own membership ('citizenship'). In the same context, it gave assurances that, when Indians develop their criteria of band/tribal membership, they will have as their goal cultural survival, and their criteria will not be sexist or racist.

The 1985 amendment of the Indian Act, allowing Indian communities to set their own membership criteria, has raised one of the most significant and thorny issues in the Indians' history of dealing with their own identity: how to define the criteria of membership in their communities. Band/tribes are now empowered to begin building the kind of community they want. For example, bands/tribes can use their new authority to establish membership criteria based upon authentic cultural criteria instead of Indian Act criteria. This development places Indian communities in a position where they now need to consider very carefully what sort of societies they want to be. What will be the primary basis for the identity of band/tribal members? How Indians resolve the question, 'Who shall be eligible for band/tribal membership?' carries significant consequences for their survival as *Indians*.

Before the original Indian Act of 1876, band/tribal membership–determination and identity was not a problematic issue for Indians. Although they organized themselves on kin-group lines, their concept of themselves was as a 'cultural family.' The sacred trust of the band/tribe was to preserve, by oral transmission and by practice, the philosophies and principles enshrined in the Creator's covenant.

An identity not based on the Creator's covenant would not have been considered worth preserving. Today, however, the determination of band/tribal membership and identity has assumed some disturbing complexities.

Traditionally, the 'aboriginal heritage' existed as a seamless whole; that is, the obligations and the benefits of band/tribal membership were inextricably linked. Respect for band/tribal traditions and fulfilment of the customary duties and responsibilities were the only legitimate basis for a claim to the benefits a band/tribe could offer, and members who did not fulfil their cultural obligations to the community were denied the benefits of band/tribal membership. In contrast, the benefits of band/tribal membership were oft-times extended to strangers who showed a willingness to respect band/tribal traditions and to fulfil the customary duties and responsibilities to the community. But today the 'seamless whole' of the aboriginal heritage has been rent in two; that is, band/tribal members can and do claim the benefits of membership without respecting tribal traditions or fulfilling their customary duties and responsibilities to the community. This uncoupling of band/tribal benefits from cultural obligations poses a serious jeopardy for *Indian* cultural survival.

The forces that are engendering the split between cultural obligations and the benefits of band/tribal membership derive from Euro-Western conventions and jurisprudence regarding 'patrimony' (i.e., property passed down in a direct line of biological descent). Under Euro-Western conventions and jurisprudence regarding 'patrimony,' Indians, as descendants of the 'first people,' are deemed to have a qualified claim to their ancestral heritage (i.e., use of the land and other entitlements). It is within this Euro-Western framework of 'patrimony' (not entitlement by virtue of cultural or political nationhood) that the Canadian government has chosen to negotiate Indian claims to their ancestral lands and other entitlements. Accordingly, Indian eligibility for making claims to their ancestral heritage is being judged on the conventional criteria for claiming an inheritance, that is, on the basis of biological ancestry (or 'Indian status,' as defined in the Indian Act), not on the basis of cultural criteria.[12]

It is worth noting that several exceptional circumstances associated with Indian claims to their ancestral heritage, fall outside of the normal Euro-Western conventions regarding patrimony. One is that Indians claim their ancestral heritage as band/tribal collectives, not as individuals. Another is that their claim comprises more than tangible estates, such as land; other claimed entitlements subsume intangibles, such as an inherent aboriginal right to self-government. Moreover, Indians are required to prove and negotiate their claims to their ancestral heritage after a hiatus of several generations, during which time their ancestral heritage was denied by the Canadian government. These unique circumstances give an awkward legal 'spin' to Indian claims to their ancestral heritage, but the Canadian government is, none the less, determined to process these claims within the framework of 'patrimony,' not as a settlement with cultural (or political) nations.

The Canadian government's 'patrimonial' strategy is evident in its insistence that the validity of Indian claims must be judged by the conventional criteria for claiming an inheritance; that is, Indians must prove biological ancestry and ancestral possession of the lands and any other entitlements, or their claim is denied. The 'patrimonial' strategy is also confirmed by the government's insistence that the 'intangibles' of the Indian patrimony, such as aboriginal rights, are extinguished once the 'inheritance' has been settled.

On the one hand, Indian leaders have gone along with the Euro-Western model of patrimony by dutifully basing their various claims on biological ancestry and ancestral possession, rather than on cultural (or political) nationhood. On the other hand, they want to negotiate their claims within a 'non-extinguishment' treaty-making process, meaning the 'intangibles' (i.e., aboriginal rights) of their ancestral heritage are inalienable and must endure in perpetuity.[13] Because such a model falls outside the conventional Euro-Western 'patrimonial' model, the government has firmly rejected it.

Within the tradition of communal *Indian* cultures, there exists a norm of equitable distribution of band/tribal benefits among all qualifying members of the community. In the context of communal sharing, and of a finite patrimony (e.g., limited reserve land and other entitlements), the norm of equitable distribution engenders a 'zero-sum' dynamic; that is, the per-capita share of communal benefits (assets and other entitlements) is diluted as the membership grows. As a result of this zero-sum dynamic, band/tribal membership has become a divisive issue among Indians. It has induced a very conservative attitude by bands/tribes towards eligibility for reserve residence – conservative to the point where legitimate co-heirs to the ancestral patrimony are denied residence in their communities and their rightful share of the ancestral heritage.

Evidence for such a conservative effect and the consequent divisiveness surfaced recently in response to Bill C-31, which restored

Indian status to approximately 100,000 Indians (mostly women and their descendants), thus making them eligible for band/tribal membership. Many band/tribal councils opposed Bill C-31 on grounds that their ancestral heritage (i.e., reserve lands and treaty benefits, etc.) is inadequate to provide their present membership with an acceptable standard of living. Therefore, they could not accommodate additional members. This resulted in a squabble among blood heirs over their ancestral heritage. The squabble over this heritage is complicated by 'privatization,' that is, the Indian Act provision under which communal benefits (assets and entitlements) are being transformed into individual benefits. The Indian élite class, which benefits disproportionately from privatization, is motivated by a powerful class-based interest to protect their bloated share of band/tribal assets from potential diminishment by claims from any additional 'heirs.' Consistent with this self-interest, then, they are committed to preserving the status quo.

The Canadian government's policy of executing the Indian heritage within the framework of patrimony can be seen to be antagonistic to *Indian* survival because the 'zero-sum' dynamic to which it gives rise discourages reserve residents from adopting cultural criteria of band/tribal membership. Their concern is that if membership criteria are defined according to *cultural* standards the potential exists that the door would be opened to an unlimited number of people who would be entitled to reserve residence, thereby devaluing every current band/tribal member's share of the ancestral heritage. But unless *Indian* cultural criteria form the foundation of band/tribal membership qualifications, *Indian* cultures will lose their force as a basis for Indian identity. Moreover, if *Indian* cultural criteria are not used as the basis for band/tribal membership determination, what will be the basis? At least one Indian band, the Sechelt band in British Columbia (the first band in Canada to have achieved 'self-government'), has incorporated 'social acceptance' as a necessary condition for membership. Candidates for membership must achieve endorsement by a majority of band voters, and a minimum 50 per cent voter turnout is required. According to the most recent report, all who have sought band membership under this membership code have failed.

The zero-sum dynamic created by the Canadian government's policy of executing the Indians' heritage within the framework of a patrimony may predispose many bands/tribes to continue the pre-1985 Indian Act precedent of giving primary emphasis to biological ancestral criteria of membership determination, which tend to transmute into racial criteria of 'blood quantum.' Moreover, they will do so from the same self-interests that motivated the Canadian government – to limit the number of Indians who can claim a patrimony – and for reasons of bureaucratic efficiency. On the other side, many Indians who seek band/tribal membership may be motivated by the lure of present and anticipated patrimonial benefits that accrue to band/tribal members, not by cultural affinity. It is ironical that the 'patrimony' that yields much more misery than benefits to Indians should be the cause of so much divisiveness and cultural disruption in Indian communities.

Some Indian leaders appear to believe that biological-ancestral criteria can be used in the service of cultural survival. But this is a misguided notion. From experience we know that biological-ancestral based systems of membership determination inevitably transmute into race-based systems. Such systems perpetuate racial survival, but they offer no assurances that cultural integrity and viability will be preserved. Biological-ancestral criteria may deny membership to people who are deeply committed to *Indian* culture and community, and they may admit to membership people who have no commitment to preserving the traditional cultural heritage, or may even be committed to corrupting traditional philosophies and principles (such as communalism) for their personal enrichment. Biological-ancestral membership eligibility criteria are poor instruments for achieving a community committed to living and surviving as *Indians*. A culture does not need an expression of race to survive. Identification of a culture with race merely imprisons the culture within racial boundaries.

Indian cultural integrity and viability will be best served when band/ tribal membership is defined by cultural criteria. Representations of such criteria were proposed by Ernest Benedict: 'accept the idea of communality, learn the language, respect the customs, have reverence for the spiritual goals, be of good character and be committed to the betterment of the community.'[14] Such a culturally based system of membership determination would eliminate the confusing and factionalizing system that invidiously classifies Indians into 'regular Indians' (i.e., patrilineal descendants from ancestry recognized as members at the original enrolment of the band/tribe), 'C-31 Indians' (i.e., Indian women who lost their status by marriage to non-Indians and were reinstated under the 1985 Indian Act amendment), 'section 6(1) Indians' (i.e., Indians with two status-Indian parents), 'section 6(2) Indians' (i.e., Indians with only one status-Indian parent), status

Indians with band membership, status Indians without band membership, and non-status Indians with band membership.

Biological ancestral-based membership eligibility criteria, whether administered by the Canadian government or by Indian bands/tribes, will have the effect of sustaining and promoting racism by both Canadians and Indians. Self or other identification that emphasizes collective categorization and nomenclature such as 'ancestry,' 'descent,' and 'blood-quantum' facilitates 'seeing' race. As such, it can serve only one purpose, and that is to intensify prejudice, discrimination, inequality, subordination, and hatred. Separation of Indians and Canadians on the fiction of race is morally unconscionable. Membership criteria that effect such a separation do not merit constitutional or legislative protection as an aboriginal right, or as a definition for Indian 'citizenship.'

Under the U.N. Charter, Indians have a compelling 'peoples' right' to *cultural* nationhood. But this claim will be defined as an issue of human rights only if Indians can claim this right in the name of *cultural*, not *racial*, communities. Therefore, if Indians want to safeguard their 'peoples' right' to cultural nationhood, they must survive as *cultural*, not *racial*, communities. If Indians should allow their cultural distinctiveness (philosophies, principles, languages, etc.) to disappear, then their historical, legal, and moral justification for cultural nationhood will also disappear. Distinctiveness based on the culture of dependence will not qualify as a legitimate claim to nationhood.

The threat to their claim to cultural nationhood is not hypothetical. After more than a century of forced assimilation, loss of the means of subsistence, and isolation, their warrant for a claim to cultural nationhood has fallen into serious jeopardy. This situation underlines the urgent need for an *Indian* cultural renaissance. Indian peoples must develop their impoverished and tattered cultures fully enough so they do not have to resort to biological-ancestral-racial criteria to sustain their identities. If they want to maintain international moral legitimacy for their claims to nationhood, they must adopt cultural criteria of membership and abandon biological-ancestral-racial membership criteria that have their roots in the colonial Indian Act.

According to the ancient covenant, the ancestral legacy, including both the tangibles (e.g., use of the land) and the intangibles (e.g., self-government), is a 'communal' birthright that is willed to all *Indians*, including future generations. Indian Act Indians may have a *legal* claim to the ancestral legacy because the Canadian government has so decreed. But, according to the covenant, only *Indians* have a moral and spiritual claim to the ancestral legacy. The intent of the chiefs who marked the treaties was not to benefit a select group of Indian Act Indians, but to fulfil their obligation to the covenant by negotiating an arrangement that would ensure the survival and well-being of Indians as *Indians* for all time to come.

Conclusion

In a speech at Kew Gardens, in London, in 1990, Prince Charles, heir to the British throne, acknowledged the importance of aboriginal cultures for the welfare of all mankind. Referring to the aboriginal peoples' vast knowledge of the ecosystem, he said: 'Generations of observation and trial and error have honed their judgment in a process as rigorous as any laboratory testing. These people are accomplished environmental scientists and for us to call them 'primitive' is both perverse and patronizing.'

As blueprints for survival and living, Indian cultures have much more to offer than ecological insights. But Prince Charles understood his subject. Aboriginal cultures have much to offer to societies that have deluded themselves into believing their technology supersedes the natural world and, acting under this delusion, have impaired the ozone layer, turned the atmosphere into a greenhouse, polluted the earth's waters, and are destroying the rain forests. Aboriginal cultures, uniquely, are the repositories of much knowledge and experience linking humanity to the natural environment. *Indian* cultures in North America taught an empathetic relationship with the natural world that did not permit possession, manipulation, exploitation, and profiteering from it. They understood the ecological imperative of humankind's interdependence with the wholeness of life on earth; that there are no boundaries that insulate human welfare from the global natural environment that sustains them. At this crucial time of world ecological crisis, *Indian* cultures can provide humankind with the philosophies, principles, and language (concepts) that will enable us to think and believe that the oxygen we breathe was produced by vegetation on another continent, and the water we drink was evaporated from distant seas. Such philosophies and principles are essential for the survival of humankind.

Cultures grow out of the imaginations and the historical experiences of human communities freely interacting with their respectice environments. Because the variables of 'imagination,' 'experience,' and 'environment' are never fully replicated again, every culture is unique in its design for living and surviving. Thus, every culture adds a unique dimension to human civilization. Cultural diversity is not merely an aesthetic good; it represents a 'survival kit' as humankind faces the awesome challenges of the future. At Kew Gardens, Prince Charles articulated this very idea. He recognized the essential truth that humankind's best safeguard against extinction is to be found in the 'reservoir' of knowledge that derives from cultural diversity. We cannot know when we may need the experience, knowledge and understanding that can be gained from a particular culture.

Unfortunately, Canadians have inherited the British and French colonial legacy of ethnocentrism-in-the-service-of-imperialism. The hallmark of this legacy is a convenient belief that 'civilization' is a hierarchical phenomenon in which cultures are ranked from 'primitive' to 'advanced.' When operationalizing this belief, Canadians, like the British and French 'founders' of this nation, place their culture at the top rung and relegate *Indian* cultures to the bottom rung, as unworthy of preservation. It is illogical to rank cultures according to some contrived hierarchy of 'civilization.' Only in the world of unthinking ethnocentrists and bigots does it seem logical to do so. It is possible to value one's own culture without devaluing the cultures of others. All humankind would be better served if Canadians could conceive of cultures in egalitarian terms, with each culture considered a consequential and beneficial part of the whole. The way to enrich civilization is not to 'civilize' Indians by forcing them to adopt the 'top rung' culture, but by valuing the diversity that *Indian* cultures can contribute to world civilization. Within such a conception of cultures, *Indian* cultures would be esteemed for the knowledge they have to offer, and would be nurtured, not denigrated, feared, or brought to extinction.

Such a conception of cultures and civilization does not preclude an evaluation of a particular culture's performance. Although there exists no universal rational calculus for evaluating the worth of a culture, every culture must have a capacity to provide for the basic needs of the community, to maintain social order, and to inspire cultural loyalty by its adherents. Such an evaluation would confirm that, although Indians are not in need of 'civilization,' their cultures are in a state of crisis and in need of adaptation and development. Forced assimilation, isolation, and destruction of their natural environment and the traditional means of subsistence for which their cultures were designed has undermined the foundations of *Indian* cultures. In the words of Chief Dan George, Indians 'are living on the dying embers

of a dying culture.'[15] Pre-contact *Indian* cultures, unmatched as designs for living and surviving in the natural environment, have been
supplanted by a culture of dependence, that is, a blueprint for survival
premised on social assistance.

At present, more than half of Canada's Indian population are under
eighteen years of age. Except for the 'expressive' aspect of their traditional cultures, most are receiving virtually no exposure to fundamental *Indian* philosophies and principles. Indian elders who should
play the essential role of interpretation and transmission of traditional
philosophies and principles have been largely relegated to symbolic
functions, which they perform in a language most youths do not
understand. Even the expressive culture is coming under increasing
pressure as it must compete with the values and appeal of North
American pop culture for the minds of Indian young people.

Indians have come to a crossroad in their history: they can deceive
themselves that the 'culture of dependence' represents *Indian* culture
and cling to the identity it provides them, they can assimilate into
Canadian society, they can be satisfied with a residual expressive
culture, or they can set out on a course of cultural revitalization. Right
now, the historic stage appears set for the extinction of *Indian* cultures.
But a cultural crisis should not be a signal for despair, it should be a
call to action. *Indian* cultures are not dead. They continue to survive
latently in the traditional philosophies and principles. The extinction
of *Indian* cultures is inevitable only if Indians think it is inevitable
(or if they assume that the survival of their cultures is inevitable).
Although the current generation of Indians bears little responsibility
for the present cultural crisis, they must assume full responsibility for
the future of their cultures. The challenge they face is to adapt and
develop their traditional cultures for living and surviving in the contemporary economic, political, and social world in which they find
themselves. This is a daunting task, but not an impossible one. It is
impossible only if they never undertake it. However, it will not be
accomplished as long as Indian aspirations for their cultural survival
remain at the level of sentiment.

The historic experience of forced assimilation has impelled many
Indians to adopt a fortress mentality regarding their cultures. But an
effective culture can emerge only from a process of adaptation and
development in response to a society's ongoing experience, needs,
and aspirations while in interaction with the real world. This cannot
be accomplished within a fortress or a prison. In a changing world,

cultural isolation leads to cultural obsolescence, which in turn condemns future generations to ever-deepening dependence.

Indian cultures can still be transformed into a positive force, but if Indians hope to survive as *Indians* they cannot make up their cultures as they go along. First, they must develop a clear vision and consensus about who they want to be, culturally, in future. Then they must realistically assess the damage that has been done (and continues to be done) to their traditional cultures by their state of dependence and by acculturation. Finally, they must critically evaluate what needs to be done and mobilize to get it done if they are to become what they want to be, culturally. Throughout, this process must involve all members of the community and must be conducted within the framework of traditional fundamental philosophies and principles. Such a process of cultural revitalization will necessitate a purge of corrupting colonial institutions, and of traits derived from the culture of dependence and from Euro-Western acculturation.

The future of *Indian* nationhood depends upon cultural revitalization. *Indian* nationhood cannot be erected on a culture of dependence, or on the basis of Western values with an Indian 'spin,' or on the basis of a residual 'expressive' culture; these provide only an illusion of *Indian* culture. Nor will *Indian* nationhood be achieved by self-government, land claims, or treaties, or by any of the other claims Indians are making of the Canadian government. Nor will viable *Indian* nationhood spring from constitutional concessions by Canada's governments. At bottom, the fate of *Indian* nationhood rests in Indian hands. If *Indian* nationhood is to be realized, then the present generation of Indians must reignite the cultural 'fire' that was entrusted to their ancestors from time immemorial and keep it burning for future generations.

Will Indians survive as nations or as a race? In the absence of viable *Indian* cultures, race may be the only identity under which Indians can claim special status and aboriginal rights. Without *Indian* cultures, future generations of Indians may be sentenced to live in the oppressive prison-house of race, in which membership criteria will be based on fractions of blood, and their relationship with Canadian society will be defined by mutual racism.

Implied in Prince Charles's speech at Kew Gardens is his belief that *Indian* cultures deserve a status of prominence in the cultural mosaic that composes world civilization. As a vision of the future, *Indian* cultures have much to offer the world. Already, Indians cite, with justifiable pride, the numerous contributions of their cultures to Euro-Western societies. But Indians will not survive as *Indians* based on past cultural contributions. Nor can they be satisfied with merely 'dumping' their cultures into the mainstream and becoming part of the 'melting-pot.' The blending of their cultural traits and patterns with those of Euro-Western cultures would be comparable to a litre of red dye being added to the St Lawrence River. It would be a travesty if the great *Indian* cultures should vanish in this manner. Moreover, it would betray the trust of the 'ancients' and the aboriginal rights of future generations of Indians.

Also implied in Prince Charles's statement is the message that all Canadians bear a moral obligation, not only to Indians, but to all humankind for the survival of *Indian* cultures, because the loss of the wisdom contained in *Indian* cultures is not just an Indian loss. The loss goes beyond the band/tribe to all humankind. It is morally re-prehensible for Canadians, whether by design or inadvertence, to bring about the extinction of *Indian* cultures. The moral case for *Indian* cultural survival is particularly compelling because *Indian* cultures have no other homeland. By contrast, all of the immigrant cultures in Canada have a secure base in their mother countries.

If Indians are to fulfil their sacred trust to safeguard their traditional cultures, then opportunity as much as commitment is a necessary condition. In their present condition of powerlessness, destitution, and dependence, Indians are in a weak position to revitalize their traditional cultures. Historically, cultures have not survived under the yoke of dependence. Canadians must enable Indians to escape their condition of dependence, and recognize the jurisdictional space they require to re-create their social systems consistently with their tra-ditional fundamental philosophies and principles. To this end, Ca-nadians must acknowledge and honour the inherent and inalienable right of Indians to live and survive as *Indians*. More than Canadian money and constitutional guarantees are involved here; the survival of *Indian* cultures is more dependent upon Canadians understanding the value of, and showing respect for, *Indian* cultures than upon money and constitutional guarantees. Most Canadians treat *Indian* cultures with contempt or as museum pieces. If Canadians will fulfil their obligations to Indians and their cultures, the rewards for this will be substantial: it will yield a richer cultural mosaic that enhances

Canadian life, the human spirit, and humankind's chances for survival. But, if Canadians fail to fulfil their obligations, then they will have effectively entrenched Indian 'race,' not *Indian* 'culture,' in the Canadian constitution.

（

5 Economy

Indian economic dependence upon Canadian society is generally perceived in terms of the majority of individual Indians who survive on government welfare cheques. But this perception overlooks Indian collective dependence. Band/tribal political, bureaucratic, health, educational, and social service infrastructures are also dependent upon Canadian government grants. An Indian economy of sorts exists on many reserves: some ranching and agriculture; sundry arts, crafts, and tourist businesses; occasional lumbering and guiding; a little hunting and fishing; and sometimes a manufacturing operation. But reserve-based enterprises play a minor or insignificant role as a source of personal incomes and general revenue for all but a handful of bands/tribes. Preponderantly, the economic base on most Indian reserves consists of social welfare and various types of government grants. Unlike most Canadians, who have benefited from growth in the Canadian economy through improved wages or business income, most Indians are unemployed and exist outside the Canadian wage and business economy. For them improvement of their economic situation occurs only when Canadian governments consent to raise welfare payments or increase grants to bands/tribes.

Economic dependence has caused social malfunction in Indian societies. Privation is part of the cause, but the main problem is that lack of productive employment has undermined traditional role and status relationships, especially for male members, most of whom have lost their important role of food provider for their family or kin group. They are denied an opportunity to validate their self-worth by contributing to the survival and well-being of their family and community through work. The idleness of unemployment has devastated morale and undermined *Indian* cultures. This, in turn, has bred extraordinary levels of social pathologies. Broken homes, child neglect and abuse, foetal alcohol syndrome children, malnutrition, drunkenness, vandalism, violence, suicide, and repeated incarceration are day-to-day realities in many Indian homes.

The economic prospects of Indians grows more grim with each generation. Until Confederation, no public funds were required for Indian support. A few bands/tribes continued to be self-supporting until the 1950s. Today, many Indians are second- and third-generation dependents, on permanent social assistance, and their numbers have increased with each generation. But the worst may lie ahead. Because they receive an inferior quality of education, and because of economic, racial, and cultural barriers, Indian children experience progressive failure, resulting in a school drop-out rate in excess of 70 per cent. As hopelessness and apathy grow, and as the gap widens between their educational achievement and that required by an increasingly complex technological-industrial world, Indian dependence will become more and more impervious to solution.

Without fundamental changes to the economic policies that have created Indian dependence, and the consequent social pathologies, Indians cannot survive as *Indians*. Yet, the need for long-term planning for a better economic future for Indian peoples is not being effectively addressed. Although the issue of Indian dependence is the focus of frequent lip-service and some fragmentary policy initiatives by federal and provincial governments and by Indian leaders, by and large the three parties typically assume a predictable pattern of self-serving political postures: the federal government emphasizes capping its costs by shifting an increasing share of its historic fiscal obligations to the provinces; the provincial governments resist assuming any additional fiscal responsibilities and cite the federal government's constitutional mandate under section 91 (24); and Indian leaders typically press their demands for more control over, and an expansive increase in, financial assistance from both levels of governments. But there is little evidence of a concerted, resolute, tripartite effort to develop a long-term, coherent, design for liberating lower-class Indians from their state of dependence and destitution.

The neglect goes on despite the fact that economic dependence is the central and dominating fact of Indian cultural, political, and social life. Moreover, it is the principal feature of Indian–Canadian political and social intercourse, breeding resentment and fostering ugly stereotypes on both sides. On the Canadian government side, Indian dependence has resulted in the entrenchment of a system and attitude of colonial paternalism. On the other side, it has induced Indians to view the solution to their disadvantaged economic condition primarily in social-assistance terms; that is, they consistently assume that the solution to their problem lies in the Canadian government allocating more generous funding to provide for their needs. This perspective is evident in a paper submitted to the U.N. Human Rights Commission by the Grand Council of the Crees. Drawing attention to problems of overcrowding and inadequate housing, they assert 'that Canada's entire indigenous housing backlog could have been eliminated if the money spent for the 15 days of the Calgary Olympics had been allocated instead to the construction of indigenous housing.'[1]

Implicit in this complaint is the assumption that the solution to their housing shortage lies in larger government grants, not in fuller employment that would enable their people to provide for their own housing. Such an assumption would be unacceptable to the Canadian public if it came from any other minority group. It serves to show the degree to which Indian dependence is accepted as 'normal' by both Canadians and Indians.

Government policy

Why are Indians today in a state of dependence? The blame for this does not fall on the dependent Indian population. They did not choose this way of living. Rather, it is rooted in Canadian policies and attitudes. Successive Canadian governments brought about this result by interfering with the normal evolution of the Indian economy. If the Indian economy had been allowed to follow the normal course of economies, the decline of their traditional means of subsistence would have been compensated for with other forms of self-sufficiency. In a land of opportunity alternative forms of subsistence, such as farming, ranching, industry, would gradually have supplanted traditional Indian means of hunting, fishing, and gathering. But the Canadian government erected barriers to such an evolutionary process. Specifically, Indians were prohibited from engaging in a variety of commercial activities, such as selling agricultural products off reserve. In effect, they were denied the opportunity to participate in the Canadian market economy. Some early attempts by Indians to establish farming and ranching operations on reserves were sabotaged by the government by reneging on treaty agreements to deliver cattle, seed, and agricultural equipment. This policy course was taken because it gave the government greater control over Indians, it pleased Canadian farmers, and it offered administrative convenience.

During the era of fur-trade relations with Indians, the 'national interest' was well served by Indian participation as 'producers' in the Canadian economy. But when settler agriculture, resource extraction, land speculation, and industrial development superseded the fur trade in economic importance, traditional *Indian* economic pursuits, such as hunting, fishing, and gathering, were deemed by the Canadian government to be not only inconsequential, but a hindrance to de-velopment of the new economy. The Canadian government's solution to this problem was to compel Indians to engage in treaty negotiations purposed to free as much Indian land as quickly as possible, for more profitable economic pursuits. By diverting Indian lands away from the economic interests and benefit of Indians, and for the benefit of Canadians, Indian opportunities to expand or modernize their econ-omies were first narrowed and then foreclosed. When the Indians' traditional means of subsistence had been destroyed by settlement of their lands, and when they could no longer feed or clothe themselves, the Canadian government, under the hypocritical guise of benevo-lence and Christian charity, transformed them into dependent wards by introducing a social-welfare system as the primary and permanent economic base of support in virtually all Indian reserves. Thus, In-dians were transformed from a state of economic self-sufficiency and independence to a condition of total dependence and destitution, in effect being made economic prisoners on tiny reserves.

Historically, the Canadian government's Indian policies have been designed to serve the 'national interest'. Consistent with its definition of the 'national interest,' the main thrust of the Canadian govern-ment's current fiscal strategy in regard to Indians is to control costs to the federal treasury. Over the past four decades, federal spending on Indian affairs has increased dramatically as the Indian population has grown, as their self-sufficiency has declined, and as the acceptable standard of social services in Canada has been raised and expanded. From the Canadian government's perspective, costs for services to Indians have got out of hand and must be controlled. The Canadian government is seeking to control these spiralling costs to the federal treasury by segregating its 'strictly legal' (i.e., constitutional and treaty) obligations to Indians from the rest of its assistance to Indians. In essence, the government's game-plan is to transfer the cost of its 'statutory' and 'humanitarian assistance' to Indians (estimated at 75 per cent of its present allocations to Indians) to the provinces. This design was made explicit in the Nielsen Report, which advocated placing federal government programs to Indians under a budget cap, with the expectation that Indian funding requirements above the cap would be foisted on the provinces. This design would not only shift significant fiscal responsibility for Indians to the provinces, but also bring funding arrangements for Indians into greater conformity with existing federal and provincial constitutional mandates generally.

A concurrent aim of the Canadian government is to control its 'strictly legal' fiscal obligation to Indians by imposing a discipline of greater fiscal restraint on band/tribal councils. It is pursuing this objective under the guise of 'self-government' for Indians. Under this mantle the government is devolving to band/tribal councils responsibility for services and programs on reserves under budget caps. The underlying plan is to make the same amount of money go farther by requiring band/tribal councils to be more restrained, judicious, and efficient in their spending. In effect, under 'self-government,' the reserve will change from a DIAND-administered enclave of dependence and destitution to a fiscally 'leaner' band/tribal council managed enclave of dependence and destitution.

In short, without regard to the morality of capping funding at a time when Indian need for services and programs is increasing, the Canadian government's primary concern and its 'economic strategy' is to control costs to the federal treasury. It proposes to achieve this goal by grafting an auxiliary fiscal 'umbilical cord' from Indians to the provincial treasuries, and by imposing greater economic restraint and efficiency upon band/tribal councils. Obviously, this policy is not designed to liberate Indians from their state of dependence and destitution through economic development. Historically less than 10 per cent of the Canadian government's appropriations for Indian affairs has been directed to economic development and job creation, and there is no evidence in the government's present and proposed funding structures that suggests a serious interest in improving Indian economic self-sufficiency and independence.

Indian goals

On the agenda of Indian leaders, economic concerns have been subordinated to political concerns. This emphasis on political concerns derives, in part, from Indian leaders' intense involvement and preoccupation over the past two decades with such issues as the 1969 White Paper, the entrenchment of aboriginal rights in the constitution, the expectations for self-government created by the Penner Report, the subsequent four First Ministers' conferences on defining aboriginal rights, the community-based Indian self-government initiative, the

Nielsen Report, the Meech Lake Accord, and, at present, the Royal Commission on Aboriginal Affairs, and the Aboriginal Constitutional Process. These issues have roused Indian leaders to an expanded political consciousness and have swollen their political aspirations almost to the point of crowding out concerns for achieving economic independence and self-sufficiency of their people.

In part, Indian leaders' neglect of economic independence and self-sufficiency concerns derive from the absence (despite the destitution of most of their people) of any real economic exigency. Whereas the leadership in third-world nations, concurrent with their emergence from colonialism, were overwhelmed by the task of providing for the basic survival needs of their citizens, Indian leaders can neglect economic concerns in the sure knowledge that the Canadian government has the resources and a constitutional, political, and moral obligation to provide their people with a 'reasonable' standard of living. In this context, Indian leaders can defer economic-development concerns without disastrous consequences for their people.

However, it should not be inferred from what I have said that Indian leaders have no concern or concept of economic development for their communities. Many Indian leaders have articulated notions of band/tribal economic development. Basically, their concept of economic development embodies a tripodal design: one part is based on a revitalized traditional economy (i.e., hunting, fishing, and gathering); another part is based on modern reserve economic development (i.e., agriculture, business, industry, resource extraction and tourism); and the third part is based on expanded government grants (i.e., transfer and equalization grants, corporate tax transfers, federal-provincial shared-cost programs, block grants, and so on). In the following pages I briefly describe and evaluate each of these three parts of the tripodal economic design as a general strategy for Indian economic development.

Traditional economy

Indians have a strong preference for economic development that will confirm and complement their cultural traditions and identity. Consistent with this preference, Indian leaders advocate an economic system in which a significant part of band/tribal income would be derived from traditional pursuits of hunting, fishing, and gathering. This form of economic activity requires an adequate land base and foodstocks. Advocates of a traditional economy propose to achieve the needed land base and foodstocks within the framework of land-claims settlements; revitalized or new treaties; and constitutionally entrenched provisions that will acknowledge their aboriginal rights to freely hunt, fish, and gather on their reserve lands, and on un-occupied Crown lands, in all seasons. Their attitude is that since the Canadian government's policies destroyed their traditional economy, it now has a responsibility to provide the land and foodstocks that will enable them to re-establish their traditional means of subsistence.

Unfortunately, negotiations of their land claims, treaty, and constitutional rights hold no reasonable prospect for an outcome that will allow development of the band/tribal traditional economy to a meaningful level. The additional land that can realistically be expected to be transferred to Indians through future land-claims settlements and under treaties will have only a marginal impact on Indian traditional economic development. While a few remote northern bands/tribes still derive part of their subsistence from traditional means, even these derive the largest part of their income from government social assistance. In the settled southern parts of Canada, traditional pursuits hold little economic import for most bands/tribes. The foodstocks available on their reserves and on proximate unoccupied Crown lands can never be large enough for traditional means of livelihood to amount to more than symbolic significance.

Moreover, federal and provincial wildlife-conservation legislation has greatly limited the freedom of Indians to pursue their traditional economic activities. And recent court decisions have placed a very narrow interpretation on their aboriginal right to hunt, fish, and gather. Generally, the courts have limited the exercise of these rights to the purposes for which they were exercised by their ancestors – that is, for food, ceremony, and social purposes – not for commercial purposes on a meaningful scale. The structure of legal precedent, and the implication of the *Sparrow* decision for interpreting aboriginal rights pursuant to section 35(i), make it highly unlikely that future courts will read into aboriginal rights a significant commercial entitlement. Most assuredly, no entitlement that holds significant negative consequences for the 'national interest,' will be acknowledged.

Overall, economic development within the concept of tribal traditional economies has very limited potential for contributing to Indian economic well-being. Those who advocate an economy based on traditional Indian pursuits do so partly from nostalgia for an idyllic era in Indian history. But such aspirations are out of touch with present and future realities and can become a great liability for the survival and well-being of Indians as *Indians*. Unrealistic insistence upon restoring an economy that cannot be re-created carries the legacy of continuing dependence, defeat, and hopelessness for the mass of Indians.

Reserve economy

Most local Indian leaders consider a reserve-based economy as an essential constituent of self-government. Towards this end, they press the Canadian government to allocate more money for on-reserve economic development and to adopt policies that will diminish present obstacles to on-reserve economic development. One of the obstacles to on-reserve economic development derives from the 'protective' provisions in the Indian Act. The act (section 98) states that Indian lands cannot be provided as chattel security for a loan. Not being allowed to use reserve lands as chattel security means that Indians are greatly handicapped in borrowing money from conventional sources, such as banks. However, this provision of the Indian Act merely legalizes what most Indians insist upon – that is, protection of their lands from the risk of possible seizure in the event of a loan default. In other words, although Indians need equity capital for on-reserve economic development, they don't want to put up (and are legally prohibited from putting up) their reserve lands as collateral security. This effectively denies them access to the large pools of capital required for on-reserve economic development.

In order to offset the Indians' handicap of not being able to borrow capital through a conventional chattel-security relationship, the federal government has established economic development funds uniquely purposed for development of Indian commercial, industrial, and resource enterprises. The Canadian government allocated $873.7 million to such a fund for the period 1989–94. An impressive array of government agencies (the Canadian Aboriginal Economic Development Strategy and the departments of Indian Affairs and Northern Development, Industry Science and Technology, and Employment and Immigration Canada) have been mandated to make the strategy work. It should be pointed out that the concept of government funding for Indian commercial, industrial, and resource development is not new. Because the reserve is not the location of choice for manufacturing firms, the DIAND has, on numerous past occasions, sought to bring labour-intensive manufacturing ventures to reserves by offering generous incentives and subsidy packages to private corporations to cover the cost of physical plants, equipment, and training of personnel.

Whenever a new industry is introduced into a reserve setting under the government's fiscal incentive policy, it is accompanied by much public fanfare from the DIAND and band/tribe officials. The event is hailed as a historic occasion and described as ushering in a new era of employment and prosperity for the band/tribe. Then, typically, a few years later, the enterprise falls into financial difficulty, and the government doesn't want to expend the monies required to bail it out. But, to save face, appease Indians, and for social objectives, it will frequently keep non-viable economic enterprises afloat for a while, usually on a reduced scale, by continuing government subsidies. Characteristically, local Indian leaders attribute the high failure rate of government-sponsored business ventures to DIAND bungling. They believe they could do better if they were given a free hand and control over planning, implementation, and management of on-reserve economic development. Consistent with this belief they conceive of self-government as including the takeover and direction of economic development on their reserves.

Although the rhetoric of those who promote on-reserve economic development always stresses job creation, despite the significant cumulative sums of money expended to introduce economic development onto Indian reserves (e.g., manufacturing, tourist enterprises, handicrafts, farming, and ranching), such ventures, even where they have succeeded, with rare exceptions have provided only tokenistic employment opportunities for reserve dwellers. The natural increase in band/tribal labour supply far exceeds the jobs created by such ventures. The level of unemployment on most reserves (60 to 90 per cent) has remained relatively constant, even with out-migration.

While the Indian Act presents some significant impediments to on-reserve economic development, there exists a much more fundamental constraint to the viability of such development. It is this: the reserve system was created to clear Indians out of the way of Canadian economic development. Hence, most reserve were located on small, remote, unproductive pieces of land. Of the approximately 600 Indian bands, no more than a score have the economic potential to sustain their present population at an acceptable standard of living through reserve-based economic development. The few exceptions have got lucky and struck wealth in the form of natural resources, or they sit on valuable real estate because urban-industrial areas have grown up adjacent to their reserves. But the overwhelming majority of reserves are located in areas with no prospect that they can develop an economic base adequate to support more than a fraction of their existing population, never mind the projected increases in population.

The potential for on-reserve economic development is further circumscribed by diseconomics of scale. The average band population is approximately 550; more than 80 per cent have fewer than 1,000. Designs to overcome diseconomics of scale through cooperative pan-Indian arrangements are hindered by geographical dispersion, isolation of bands from each other, and a variety of cultural/political barriers. Other handicaps to on-reserve economic development are high transportation costs and inadequate infrastructures. Moreover, a 'segregated,' government-subsidized, Indian economy, as represented by the reserve-based design, makes Indians extremely vulnerable to competing interests in the Canadian economy. A segregated Indian economy would always be peripheral and expendable, and the first 'to go,' in an economic recession. Jobs in such a discrete structural arrangement would have little security.

This is not to deny that most, if not all, reserves could provide a livelihood for more families than is the case at present. Well-planned and -capitalized on-reserve economic-development projects could improve employment opportunities for many reserve communities. Furthermore, business development designed to take advantage of band/ tribal consumer spending could keep some of the 90 per cent of social-assistance dollars Indians currently spend off their reserves, recirculating that money in their communities. The result would be the creation of some additional jobs. Also, instead of leasing some of their best agricultural and commercial lands to outside entrepreneurs, as some bands now do, they could develop more of their own farming and business ventures, thus creating jobs and income on the reserve.

But, overall, on-reserve economic developments hold prospects for only marginal improvement to the present on-reserve employment situation. Even under the most optimistic, but realistic, assumptions regarding land and cash-claim settlements and government equity-capital programs, on-reserve economic development potentially can offer employment to only a minority of on-reserve residents. If job creation is premised on on-reserve economic development, the majority of reserves will never be more than ghettos of unemployment; their economies will be dominated by government-funded welfare and public-service sectors. The hard fact is that their populations have already grown far beyond the level that most reserves can sustain, even if exploited to their full potential.

Even if reserves were magically brought up to the standard of economic development that prevails in most Canadian rural communities of comparable size, it would not result in the lower levels of unemployment that prevail in Canadian rural communities. Rural Canadians have accepted the reality that they must move to where the jobs are because jobs rarely move to their communities. Thus, unemployment levels in such communities are held down by depopulation from massive out-migration to urban centres. However, urban migration from reserves has not resulted in depopulation. In the past two decades the numbers on reserves have increased from 188,513 to 293,204.

It is easy to understand why on-reserve economic development holds great appeal for the local Indian élite class. When Canadian government economic-development money is given in the form of aid, whether to an individual entrepreneur or to the band/tribal council, the rules and procedures by which such funds are allocated disproportionately enrich the élite class. They are in a position to take advantage of the opportunities presented because they have the power, the connections, the skills, and the educational qualifications. Thus, economic advancement, promoted within the tax sheltered framework of on-reserve development, serves primarily to enhance the powers and privileges of the Indian élite class. The benefits that trickle down to the lower class are so small that they appear to have no measurable impact on Indian unemployment, dependence, or destitution.

Grant economy

Indian leaders advocate the concept that the Canadian government owes Indian peoples an expanding 'annuity in perpetuity' for the land that has been taken from them. Some leaders characterize this debt as a 'non-extinguishment settlement.' Under such a settlement, Indians continue to retain aboriginal title to their ancestral territories, and the Canadian government is obliged to pay an annual rent for the lands now possessed and exploited by Canadians. Other Indian leaders put forward the notion that Indians are entitled to a proportionate share of the national wealth and that, like the provinces, Indian governments are entitled to regional economic development funds, transfer payments, equalization grants, resource revenue sharing, and so on. In both concepts, the bottom line is that the Canadian government is morally and legally obligated to provide Indians with adequate funding to sustain them at a standard comparable to that of Canadians. Advocates of this design propose to overcome the obvious paternalism inherent in such a funding arrangement by insisting that the funding must be guaranteed and unconditional, which implies full band/tribal control over their budgeting processes, without accountability to the funding agent – that is, the Canadian government.

In response to band/tribal leaders' demands for control over their budgeting processes, the federal government has introduced a multitiered 'spectrum' of funding options. Each tier in the spectrum provides for an increment of more local control over the band/tribal budgeting process. While falling far short of meeting Indian leaders' demands for a guaranteed, unconditional funding arrangement, without accountability to the Canadian government, the multitiered scheme, does allow bands/tribes to progress to higher levels of fiscal autonomy. Funding options included in the spectrum are: 'contribution arrangements' (i.e., requiring accountability to the DIAND at a detailed level on program delivery and expenditure of funds); 'flexible transfer payments' (i.e., local delivery of programs based on annual fixed budgets, and specific terms and conditions); 'alternative funding arrangements' (i.e., local delivery of programs based on one- to five-year budgets and with a measure of local discretion in program planning and funding priorities); self-government' (i.e., local delivery of programs based on one- to five-year fixed budgets for approved community plans). Only bands/tribes that 'qualify' following an assessment process are approved by DIAND officials to progress from one tier to the next. Moreover, even the top-tier funding options require after-the-fact accountability. Bands/tribes must provide program reports to the DIAND, proving they have met specified standards, and they must submit adequate audits.

Even if band/tribal leaders were successful in persuading the Canadian government to give them all the money they want, and on their own terms, more money and more control over budgets will not yield economic independence, nor will it ameliorate the high levels of social pathology in Indian communities. Proof of this assertion can be found in a report prepared for the DIAND in October 1984, by Dion Resources Consulting Services, Ltd. (Joe Dion, owner, is an Alberta Cree, a former chief of the Kehewin Band in Alberta, and was president of the Indian Association of Alberta from 1977 to 1980). Dion's report provides evidence that oil and gas wealth on Indian reserves is causing more social problems than it is solving. Suicide, alcoholism, drug abuse, broken families, and other serious social disruptions increased *because* of the wealth produced by re-source development in reserve communities that were part of the study. Wealth is not the answer, just as poverty is not the problem.

There is another problem inherent in a 'grant economy.' The Ca-nadian government's rationale for providing economic-development grants to Indian communities rests partly on the 'affirmative action' doctrine that members of some groups, which are 'unequal,' should be treated preferentially to compensate for the disadvantages they experience. But not all members of Indian communities suffer equally from inequality. This raises the issue of how best to ameliorate the collective inequality of Indians. By directing compensatory measures to the group as a whole? or to destitute members of the group as individuals? If compensatory government grants are directed to the band/tribe as a whole, there is a justifiable concern that the benefits will go disproportionately to the ruling-élite class, while those who need it most will get little or nothing. Under such an arrangement the well-being of the collectivity is not well served.

Any economic strategy based on massive Canadian government support, however it is labelled, will not liberate Indians from their state of economic dependence. Government grants provide few Indian jobs. They only make it possible to survive (barely) without jobs. Any increase in the level of government funding within the framework of a 'grant economy' can only increase the degree of Indian dependence.

Economy and self-government

A fundamental fault with the tripodal economic model is that it is a design primarily to maximize band/tribal council political jurisdiction over Indian lands and Indian people, not to achieve Indian economic self-sufficiency and independence. Band/tribal leaders assume that Indian economic self-sufficiency and independence will follow from political autonomy. But, in fact it works the other way around: band/tribal political autonomy depends upon achieving economic self-suf-ficiency and independence. To achieve meaningful political auton-omy, Indian governments must have the capacity to generate a substantial part of their revenue base from the productivity of their citizens. It is difficult to imagine how Indian governments can achieve meaningful political autonomy when approximately 70 per cent of band/tribal members are unemployed, and when 90 per cent or more of band/tribal operating revenue on most reserves comes from Ca-nadian government grants. No matter how generous Canadian government funding is, or how government grants are labelled and structured, or how completely band/tribal councils control their budgetary process, it will not alter their fundamental relationship of political and economic subordination to the Canadian government. Simply stated, meaningful Indian self-government cannot be achieved within the tripodal economic model because it offers no possibility for economic self-sufficiency and independence.

A practical demonstration of the devitalizing effect that dependence on government grants has on Indian political autonomy was provided by a unique event in 1975. In that year, the Annual Assembly of the Union of British Columbia Indian Chiefs (UBCIC) voted 132 to 2, with 41 abstentions, to protest Canadian injustice to their people by refusing all government funding. The consequence of this action was chaos and embarrassment for bands/tribes as they quickly ran out of operating funds. After some judicious second thoughts, the band/tribal chiefs' resolve collapsed, and they meekly solicited reinstatement of government funding. This rash action seriously undermined the legitimacy of the UBCIC and imparted the lesson that Indian political autonomy cannot be achieved within the framework of dependence upon Canadian government grants.

A model that emphasizes dependence on Canadian government grants, in any form, also raises serious concerns about Indian government accountability. Accountability invariably goes to the holder of the purse. Dependence on Canadian government grants predisposes band/tribal councils to concede accountability to DIAND officials instead of to their electorate. This tendency is exacerbated by the fact that Indian leaders, for most of the past century, have been in a relationship of collaboration, from a subordinate status, with their funding agent, the DIAND. The prospect that the Canadian government will ever put its money on a stump and run, as local Indian leaders are asking it to do, is extremely remote. Such conduct would fly in the face of custom and tradition that have been deeply rooted in government cultures from time immemorial. In order that band/tribal councils are to become accountable to their electorate – the essence of self-government – significant revenues must be derived from Indian constituents.

To sum up, the preceding discussion expresses the judgment that the tripodal economic design being championed by band/tribal leaders offers Indians no prospect of liberation from their state of dependence and destitution. While the tripodal design may hold a modest potential to improve the present economic condition of a few Indians, it offers no prospect of creating the jobs needed to deliver the mass of Indians from their condition of dependence and destitution. Because their reserves were not created for modern-day economic viability, fewer than a score of the approximately 600 Indian bands/ tribes can be deemed to have the land, location, and resources needed to achieve a decent standard of living within the tripodal framework. And, predictably, on the vast majority of reserves the dependence and destitution of Indians will continue to grow as the disparity increases between the carrying capacity of their reserves and their rapidly increasing populations.

An alternative design

It is the thesis of the discussion that follows that the economic self-sufficiency and independence needed for Indian self-government necessarily lie with the Indian people, but not within reserve borders. Positively stated, only by becoming an integral part of the Canadian mainstream economy and labour market can Indians achieve the economic self-sufficiency and independence needed for meaningful self-government. To achieve full participation will require that reserve Indian populations break out of the segmental communities in which they have been trapped for more than a century by government policies. And, like rural Canadian populations, their surplus labour must relocate from reserves to where the jobs are. The challenge I attempt to address here is to outline a design that will enable Indians to achieve economic self-sufficiency and independence through full participation in the Canadian economic mainstream, but within a purpose of survival and well-being as *Indians*.

As it is used here, 'economic self-sufficiency' refers to an economic system capable of providing an acceptable standard of living, based on productive employment, for most members of a band/tribe. 'Economic independence' refers to a revenue-generating capacity, based on productive employment of band/tribal members, sufficient to sustain, at acceptable standards, all essential band/tribal self-governing infrastructures, facilities, and services. For Indians to achieve economic self-sufficiency and economic independence requires some fundamental changes in present political, economic, and social arrangements and attitudes, in both Indian and Canadian societies; changes that must accommodate present Indian realities within the framework of *Indian* philosophies and principles.

Despite the importance of economic self-sufficiency and independence for the survival and well-being of 'Indians,' neither the Canadian government nor Indian leaders have shown sufficient interest to develop a coherent conceptual framework for achieving such a goal. In the modest degree to which the Canadian government has shown an interest in Indian economic self-sufficiency and independence, its initiatives have been ad hoc, tokenistic, and most have centred on providing capital funding for Indian élites to establish small businesses, not on employing the large numbers of unemployed lower-class Indians in productive work. Small-business development is the main thrust of the Canadian Aboriginal Economic Development Strategy, which recently was allocated more than $750 million over a five-year period. Such a strategy puts more money in the pockets of élite Indians, but it is not an effective strategy for achieving broad-based Indian employment. Occasionally, the minister of the DIAND will announce with much fanfare new initiatives to train Indians for participation in the workforce, but these initiatives have amounted to little more than public-relations gestures. They have not resulted in statistically meaningful reductions in unemployment for Indians. On-reserve Indian unemployment rates remain relatively static, at near 70 per cent.

On the other side, band/tribal leaders occasionally express concern over the exclusion of their people from the Canadian labour force, but there is little evidence of serious interest in developing a coherent plan for achieving economic self-sufficiency by integrating their people into the Canadian labour force. In fact, their advocacy of the tripodal economic model suggests an implicit acceptance of the historical status quo that segregates Indians, as a collectivity, and imprisons them in a structure of dependence outside the Canadian labour force. As a consequence of little interest shown by Canadian politicians and by Indian leaders in achieving economic self-sufficiency, most Indians are confronted with two options: stay on the reserve and collect welfare, or move to the city and collect welfare.

My premise is that to attain economic self-sufficiency and independence Indians must participate fully, at all levels, in the mainstream Canadian economy. But to achieve such a level of participation will require that Canadian society, the business sector, and governments be accepting and supportive of Indians entering the mainstream economy and labour force. It will also require that Indian communities be socially, politically, and culturally supportive of their members who must leave the reserve to find employment. These requirements represent a formidable challenge.

It is important to note that, in regard to achieving economic self-sufficiency and independence, Indians are a quite different case from the formerly colonized third-world nations. To the extent they neglect this difference, the strategy of Indian leaders for achieving economic self-sufficiency and independence is fundamentally flawed. Indian leaders consider sovereignty as a pre-condition for achieving economic self-sufficiency and independence. In this regard, they pattern their strategy after the model of formerly colonized third-world nations. But this is a false analogy. Before their liberation from colonialism, third-world nations were being bled dry by exploitation of their labour and resources. Sovereignty was necessary for them to be able to free themselves from exploitation and to build their economies to feed their people. This is not the case with Indians in Canada. Indians, although colonized, are not exploited, in the same Marxian sense. Their problem is not that their labour is being exploited but that they are *excluded* from the Canadian economy. Moreover, quite unlike formerly colonized third-world nations, Indians in Canada do not need to develop an indigenous economy to feed their people. They live in the midst of a state that is already highly developed in economic terms. The problem they confront is to overcome the internal and external social, cultural, and political barriers that preclude and exclude them from full participation in the economy of one of the richest nations in the world. For this, they do not need sovereignty. In fact, sovereignty may serve merely to heighten the barriers to full participation in the mainstream Canadian economy.

Below, I deal with Indian economic self-sufficiency and economic independence, in that order. Under 'self-sufficiency,' I deal, first, with social, cultural, and political barriers to self-sufficiency *internal* to the reserve community and, second, with political and social barriers to self-sufficiency *external* to the reserve community.

Economic self-sufficiency

As I have already said, in rural Canadian communities the surplus labour force leaves home to find work. They leave areas of little or no opportunity – the farm, the small town, the depressed region – for areas of better opportunity. This prompts the question: What is it about Indian communities that inhibits a similar pattern of out-migration from destitute reserves to find work in the mainstream economy? Lack of education and marketable skills, emotional ties to kinship and friendship groups, preference for rural environs – these are all inhibiting factors, but similar inhibiting factors have also prevailed in rural Canadian communities. The explanation is more complex. In Canadian communities the surplus labour force leaves home to find work because the socio-cultural ethos in their communities impels them to do so. Individual motivation to leave home to find work derives significantly from community expectations that everyone should be productive, and from a need to satisfy socially conditioned personal goals and wants. Put another way, although the decision to leave home to find work is ultimately an individual one, the collective community's attitudes and expectations – that is, the meaning the community gives to leaving home for employment elsewhere – exert a deeply felt influence on the individual who must contemplate such a move. The influence is felt early in a person's life and has a profound impact on individual attitudes about preparation for such a move (e.g., education).

Applying this understanding to Indians, if the surplus labour force on Indian reserves is to leave for areas of better opportunity, then there must first emerge a supportive socio-cultural ethos for such behaviour within Indian communities. Simply stated, if the community interprets leaving the reserve to find employment as disloyalty to the group, or if traditional communal values carry a negative sanction of the personal goals implied in leaving, then the individual will be reluctant to leave the reserve, even if staying means living in dire conditions of dependence and destitution. At present, virtually all reserve communities lack the attribute of actively supporting and engendering participation by their members in the Canadian mainstream economy. Instead, there is an informal, yet potent, social ethos in most Indian communities that defines members who permanently leave the reserve as living in an undesirable state, from both the individual's and the community's perspective. This is evident in the fact that community boundaries are reinforced by a tendency to derogate and define as 'aliens' (e.g., 'apples') individuals who permanently leave the reserve to pursue a career.

If Indians are to participate fully in the mainstream economy, then reserve communities need to construe off-reserve employment in such a way that leaving, even for personal improvement and advancement, is not regarded as contrary to community interests but, rather, as advancing those interests. In other words, if Indian communities are to follow the pattern of Canadian communities in which surplus labour leaves home to find work, then the social ethos in reserve communities will have to change from one that deters participation in the mainstream Canadian economy to one that actively impels the unemployed to relocate to areas of opportunity. And the community must provide continuing social, cultural, and political support to those who make such a move.

In part, resistance in reserve communities to participation in the mainstream Canadian economy derives from an anxious concern that such participation is the pathway to cultural assimilation. For example, Indian leaders tend to define the options open to their people as a dichotomous choice: on-reserve employment and cultural integrity, or employment in the mainstream and cultural disruption followed by assimilation. This view was given typical expression by Roy Fox, chief of the Blood Tribe, in his ceremonial announcement of a $65 million government-funded project to allow irrigation of reserve lands. Chief Fox underlined that this project would provide opportunity for tribe members to remain on the reserve, where they would be sheltered from the cultural disruptions and assimilation that result from off-reserve migration.[2]

The perception that Indian participation in the Canadian workforce leads to cultural disruption and to assimilation has a basis in fact. An Indian's success in the Canadian economy is usually achieved at significant cost of cultural and kin-group ties. But, when Indian leaders advocate on-reserve economic development as a defensive strategy for averting cultural disruption and assimilation, they tacitly make two questionable assumptions: (1) that on-reserve employment will safeguard Indians against cultural disruption and assimilation; and (2) that off-reserve employment must inevitably lead to disruption and assimilation. Both assumptions are problematical.

Considering the first assumption, modern economic development on reserves alters traditional modes of subsistence; introduces new social arrangements; changes traditional communal patterns of fulfilling social and customary obligations; rearranges traditional status, prestige, and power arrangements; disrupts traditional age and gender relationships; and transforms the function of production from meeting needs to complying with market forces and consumer motives. Moreover, individualism, competition, legal-rational authority, emphasis on technical qualifications – the hallmarks of capitalism – are all integral to most on-reserve economic developments. Finally, on-reserve economic development represents a potential cultural and political 'Trojan Horse' for Indian communities as collectivities because large-scale economic developments and technologies carry the risk of dominating small communities and distorting *Indian* cultural and political goals.

In regard to the second assumption, it is a fact that, at present, Indians who permanently leave their reserve community to take up careers in the mainstream economy in effect have to forfeit kinship relationships and the rights, benefits, and obligations of membership in their bands. Being deprived of social relationships, rights, benefits, and obligations leads to a loss of identification with their community and culture and, ultimately, leads to assimilation. But estrangement and assimilation are not a *necessary* outcome of participation in the mainstream economy. These derive significantly from the lack of even elementary structures of reserve–urban social, cultural, and political linkages. And, they derive, as I said in chapter 4, from a failure to adapt and develop *Indian* cultures for urban living. If effective reserve–urban structural linkages existed, and if *Indian* cultures were adapted and developed for urban living, then Indians could permanently leave their reserve community for employment without having to experience cultural disruption and assimilation.

The point to be taken from all of this is that economic segregation does not safeguard *Indian* culture, nor does participation in the mainstream economy necessarily lead to assimilation. The survival of *Indian* cultures does not hinge on whether economic development occurs on or off the reserve. It hinges on whether individual participation in the economy occurs in a framework of traditional philosophies and principles. That is, Indian participation in the economy, wherever it occurs, must proceed hand-in-hand with *Indian* cultural adaptation and development.

Band/tribal leaders have a key role to play in the development of a community social ethos that is supportive of their members' participation in the mainstream Canadian economy. But much more is required of them than merely to bemoan the lack of off-reserve employment opportunities, or to suggest that unemployed Indians may have to consider leaving home to find work. Indian leaders have a responsibility to develop a viable strategy that will help their people to psychologically free themselves from the notion that the reserve represents the essence of Indian culture and that becoming part of the mainstream economy represents forfeiture of that culture. Implied in such a strategy is a need to redesign customs and traditions so they facilitate participation in the mainstream economy. However, as chapter 4 emphasizes, for such redesigned customs and traditions to have

Indian authenticity they must be consistent with fundamental *Indian* philosophies and principles. In this regard, leaving the reserve for the purpose of taking employment could be readily construed as an obligation consistent with traditional philosophies and principles because it enhances the survival and well-being of the community. By investing such a construction with the full force of a community expectation, it could induce a dramatic shift from the prevailing notion that unemployment on a reserve is inevitable (and therefore tolerable) to an attitude that every employable Indian has an obligation to work and, if necessary, to leave the reserve to find work, in order to contribute to the survival and well-being of the community.

Another requisite to achieving an effective community social ethos for Indian participation in the economic mainstream are structures that maximize cultural, social, and political connections between urban Indians and their community of origin. At present, band/tribal members who permanently leave the reserve for employment have to forfeit their cultural ties, their kinship relationships, their communal benefits, and their right to full participation in the political life of their community. Here, the challenge to band/tribal leaders is to establish effective and durable reserve-urban structures and linkages that will enable those who leave the reserve to continue their cultural, political, and social ties with their home community. Well-conceived structural linkages would do much to lower individual resistance to leaving the reserve for employment opportunities, and would reduce pressures on those who permanently leave the reserve, to assimilate into Canadian Society.

Already more than one-third of Indians live off-reserve. Current demographic trends indicate that soon a majority of Indians will be living in urban centres. At present, the primary linkage between these communities is provided by Indians moving back and forth between reserve and city. Such a transient pattern is extremely disruptive for families with school-age children and for career progress. Well-developed reserve–urban Indian structural linkages would enable urban Indians to participate fully in the Canadian economy without feeling themselves to be any less *Indian* culturally, socially, and politically than those who live on the reserve.

Finally, an ethos for participation will prove difficult to develop so long as the operative 'benefit system' remains stacked in favour of staying on the reserve. In particular, provisions of the Indian Act that exempt income earned by Indians on the reserve from taxation creates a significant inequity between on-reserve and off-reserve employment. Similarly, social services, housing, and rights to communal assets claimable by Indians also favour reserve residents over off-reserve residents. These benefit differentials act as a strong deterrent to seeking off-reserve employment. Partly because of benefit advantages in favour of reserve residence, more than 30 per cent of approximately 100,000 Indians who had their status restored under Bill C-31 want to take up residence on the reserve, thereby adding to the already high unemployment rate on reserves.

To date, there has been little advocacy by band/tribal leaders to reduce reserve–urban Indian benefit differentials. Instead, as part of their 'Indian government' initiative, local Indian leaders are currently making demands that would have the effect of creating even greater benefit differentials in favour of reserve residents – more and better services, a separate law-enforcement and justice system, better housing, and so on. While any effort to improve the quality of reserve life must be commended, unless Indian leaders use their influence, and make an equal effort, to achieve commensurable improvements in the quality of life for their urban kin, the outcome, predictably, will be increasing overpopulation and growing unemployment on reserves, both of which are contrary to the goals of achieving economic self-sufficiency. Yet today, urban Indians are neglected on the policy agendas of band/tribal leaders. Band/tribal leaders pay scant attention to the fate of their urban kin. Occasionally they express concern over high levels of urban Indian unemployment, inadequate housing, prejudice, discrimination, and so on, but they rarely use their office or influence in a concerted undertaking to support, protect, or enhance the well-being of urban Indians.

My discussion moves now to a consideration of barriers to Indian self-sufficiency that lie *external* to the reserve community that is, barriers that lie within Canadian society, polity, and economy. Successful participation by Indians in the Canadian economy is impossible without the opportunity to do so. Band/tribal leaders will be stymied in their efforts to develop a social ethos in their communities that is supportive of participation in the Canadian economy unless there first exists a reasonable expectation among their people that they will be accepted for employment in the mainstream economy. Such is obviously not the case today. Unlike most Canadians from rural communities who find work in urban centres, Indians experience urban migration without benefit of employment opportunities. Despite significant Indian migration from reserves to urban centres since the Second World War Indian unemployment on reserves has worsened.

Moreover, most Indians who have migrated to the city have moved from reserve unemployment, destitution and despair to urban unemployment destitution and despair. The latter is the worse fate because living on welfare on the reserve, among kinfolk who also are living on welfare, is preferable to being treated as 'welfare lepers' in urban slum ghettos.

To understand why urbanization has not served to reduce Indian unemployment, one must apprehend the circumstances surrounding Indian migration to urban areas. Most Indians migrated to urban areas in response to federal government incentives and disincentives, not from a compelling social-cultural ethos to find work and fulfil personal goals. 'Incentives' included federal government relocation allowances, living allowances, training allowances, and so on, for Indians who moved to the city. 'Disincentives' took the form of government neglect of reserve housing, schools, and other services. The federal government never conceived these schemes as designs for employing the surplus labour on Indian reserves. In all of these schemes, the primary goal of the federal government was to reduce the cost of its reserve Indian welfare burden by transferring fiscal responsibility to the provinces and municipalities for as many Indians as possible. When these 'relocated' Indians arrived in the city, they lacked adequate education, cultural preparation, and financial resources, and they were confronted with massive racism. Once the relocated Indians met the provincial/municipal residence requirements for social assistance and services, they were effectively abandoned by the federal government. Because relocation and training were conceived as 'ends,' and not as 'means to an end' (i.e., jobs), this scheme produced urban Indian welfare ghettos (sometimes called urban 'reserves'), but not employment. If the goal of the federal government's Indian urbanization policy had been to reduce Indian unemployment by bringing Indians into the mainstream economy, the government would have acted deliberately and forcefully to ensure that migrating Indians had the preparation and opportunity to participate successfully in the urban labour force. For example, a meaningful investment in employer-centred internship, work/training, and apprenticeship programs would have betokened a more genuine concern for Indian employment.

Do Indians have opportunity equal to that of Canadians when competing for jobs in the mainstream economy? High urban Indian unemployment rates significantly reflect unequal job opportunities. In part, the problem of unequal employment opportunities derives from unequal educational opportunities. Underfunded and unequal schools with inferior resources are characteristic of reserve-based educational systems. And prejudice is characteristic of the provincial public school systems where they attend. Motivation is also a problem because, from the start, Indian children have dismal prospects that an education will yield a job. As if these handicaps are not enough, the Mulroney government initiated a policy to cap funding for post-secondary education for Indians, in effect foreclosing equal opportunities for jobs in the Canadian economic mainstream. Without equal education a 'participation ethos' on Indian reserves will be wasted. However, surmounting the barriers to Indian participation in the Canadian economy is more fundamental and complex than merely providing equal educational opportunity to Indians. To attain equality of job opportunity for Indians will require a virtual 'sea change' in Canadian government policies, and in public attitudes.

As a first step towards full and equal participation by Indians in the Canadian economy, Canadians and their governments must create a climate of trust. A history of Canadian deception, theft, and betrayal has resulted in a collective and individual Indian attitude of distrust towards the dominant society. This distrust is translated into a profound reluctance to enter the Canadian social and economic mainstream. Such reluctance is easily understood: Which of us would walk a second time with someone who mugged us on the previous walk? Before venturing on a second walk, one would expect, as a minimum, an apology backed up by appropriate restitution and some meaningful guarantee that it wouldn't happen again. Unless Canadians and their governments apologize to Indians for the injustice inflicted on them; make good on Indian land claims, aboriginal, and treaty rights; and provide adequate constitutional guarantees of justice in future, Indians will remain distrustful and apprehensive about participating in the mainstream society and economy.

Another formidable barrier to Indian participation in the economic mainstream derives from Canadian racism. At present, when Indians look to the reserve for employment they see hopelessness, and when they look to the Canadian mainstream they see an insurmountable wall of Canadian racism. It is illustrative that the Canadian government agency Central Mortgage and Housing Corporation feels compelled to keep a low profile on its urban Indian housing program to forestall delegations of Canadian urban residents from agitating to keep Indians out of their neighbourhoods. Indians and Canadians live in separate worlds and, in the context of existing racism, they are being driven farther apart as contact between them increases. To date, contact has served only to promote greater misunderstanding, prejudice and conflict. Most Indians avoid this problem by staying on the reserve or in urban ghettos. The 'Canadian wall' of racism, which keeps Indians out of the economic mainstream, is so high and dense that there is no quick or easy way to tear it down.

The Canadian solution to this problem of prejudice is often expressed in terms of 'tolerance' of racial differences and 'Charter protection' of individual rights and equality. But in order to remove the barriers to Indian participation in the mainstream economy, Canadians and their eleven governments must go beyond tolerance of racial differences and Charter protection of individual rights and equality. Indians cannot successfully participate in the mainstream economy within the concept of 'tolerance,' that is, tolerance for a racial group that is perceived in terms of negative social and cultural attributes. Such 'tolerance' always seems to regress into 'intolerance.' Full participation can occur only within a climate of respect for *Indian* cultures, identities, and aspirations. *Indian* cultures must be esteemed by Canadians as a valued part of the Canadian cultural heritage and as a vital component in the mosaic of world civilizations. Unless this is done, Canadians will be unable to break free of the psychology of racism and accept Indians as peoples of worth and as their equals. Until this is done, the Charter, other legislation, and the courts will prove ineffectual in guaranteeing the individual rights and equality of Indians when they participate in the Canadian mainstream, even under the most zealous law enforcement.

The experience of Japanese people in Canadian society provides reason for some optimism that the 'Canadian wall' of racism that keeps Indians out of the mainstream can be overcome. The achievement of Japanese Canadians would indicate that skin colour is not an irrevocable barrier to full participation in the Canadian economic mainstream. But, clearly, a massive and multifaceted effort will be required to break down the historical 'Canadian wall' of racism against Indians. The Canadian government needs to envision an undertaking, on the scale of a 'Marshall Plan,' involving the collaborative mobilization of resources and efforts by the federal and provincial governments, urban municipalities, the full spectrum of the private business sector, the educational establishment, unions, churches, and the general public, in a concerted effort to bring Indians into full and equal participation in the Canadian workforce. A government that can find many millions of dollars to shape public opinion on the Free Trade Agreement and on the Goods and Services Tax should surely be able to commit sufficient resources to begin tearing down the 'Canadian wall' of racism against Indians. This represents a formidable challenge, but it holds the only viable solution to Canada's most enduring and pressing human and moral problem. The question is, do Canadians and their governments have the moral will to implement the needed changes?

If Canadians remove the barriers of injustice and prejudice against Indians, and if Indians remove the social-cultural-psychological barriers within their own communities to off-reserve employment, it is possible, if taken too far, that population depletion could threaten the viability of small reserve communities. To avert such a possibility it is important that employment opportunities on each reserve are sufficient and attractive enough to retain an essential core of residents to ensure the political and cultural viability of the community. Consistent with this imperative, the design for Indian self-sufficiency through participation in the mainstream Canadian economy presented here affirms the objective of maximizing on-reserve employment opportunities, so that as many Indians as possible, who want to, can remain on the reserve. But, such economic development must occur within the framework of conventional economic development criteria. Past government initiatives to encourage on-reserve economic development through various forms of subsidies have attracted only marginal enterprisers and enterprises, most of which ended in failure. Their only effect has been to raise false expectations and disappointment, thereby setting back the time when Indians would seriously consider full participation in the mainstream economy.

Economic independence

Given that the revenue potential from on-reserve economic activity is inadequate to sustain, at acceptable standards, all essential band/ tribal government infrastructures, facilities, and services, how can Indian communities free themselves from dependence on government grants and achieve economic independence? In this section I frame an answer to this question by proposing a design that would empower Indian governments to raise revenue from the employment and business income of their members. Briefly stated, the design proposes that, subject to appropriate stipulations, the federal government should vacate, in favour of Indian governments, all of its present jurisdictions relating to income taxation of Indian employment and business income. Under the proposed design, entitlement of Indian governments to the federal government's portion of such income tax revenue would be protected by treaty arrangements that cannot be terminated or changed without agreement by both sides. Under this design the federal government would merely provide a tax-collection service for bands/tribes; it would surrender its proprietary claim to Indian income-tax revenues.

One stipulation under this design would be that Indian governments must tax *all* income earned by their members (whether it is earned on or off the reserve) at the prevailing federal income-tax rates. In effect, this would create a 'tax neutral' (i.e., no rate differential) status for all Indians, whether resident on or off the reserve and whether working for Indian-owned or Canadian enterprises. (Such a taxation system would also create income-tax parity between Indians and Canadians in respect to the federal rates of income tax). Under such a 'tax neutral' design there would be no tax incentive for band/tribal members to seek employment on the reserve. The design could be vulnerable to abuse by bands/tribes, which, conceivably, might be tempted to recruit wealthy 'members' or restrict membership to those with an income above a specified minimum. However, such temptations could be adequately controlled by stipulating that wealth or income could not form part of a band/tribal membership code.

An Indian claim to the federal portion of their band/tribal members' income tax can be justified on several grounds, among them the universal standard of justice which holds that those who urgently need it have the right to withhold the fruits of their labour for their own survival. No one can deny that Indians have an urgent need. Arguably, the Indian claim to the federal portion of their income tax could also be based on Indian aboriginal and treaty rights to economic independence. Their historical aboriginal right to revenues derived from the labour of their own members has not been extinguished with a 'clearly and plainly stated intent.' Canadians, who have benefited immensely from what formerly were Indian lands, lands that once yielded economic self-sufficiency and independence to Indians, should not begrudge Indians the right to raise revenue from their labours sufficient to support self-government, without subjecting their members to double taxation. Moreover, as 'trustee' for Indians, the Canadian government has a legal and moral obligation to assist Indian people and their governments in replacing their traditional economic base (which it has taken from them) with another economic base.

The legal precedent for a unique tax status for Indian peoples is already well established. At present, Indians are exempted from all federal and provincial tax laws on their personal and real property situated on a reserve. Since income is deemed to be personal property, Indians are exempted from paying federal and provincial taxes on income they earn on the reserve and when working off reserve for a reserve-based employer. This exemption has been upheld by Canadian courts.[3] Their tax-exempt status has its legal base in the Indian Act (sections 87 and 90), but may also be protected by section 35(1) of the Constitution Act, 1982.

While implementation of the proposed taxation design would presently incur a negligible loss of tax revenue to the federal treasury (approximately $65 million),[4] in the long term, as Indian employment levels rise (partly in response to the tax revenue incentive that the proposed 'participation/taxation' design holds for bands/tribes), it could produce significant savings for the federal treasury at the same time that it generates significant revenue for Indian governments. The assertion of a potential federal government 'saving' is referenced to the fact that, under the Constitution Act, 1867, and the treaties, Indians are guaranteed a right to live on the reserve. This guarantee has created an obligation on the part of the federal government to provide Indians who are band/tribal members and who choose to live on the reserve with a reasonable standard of living. Already this obligation incurs a sizeable annual cost to the federal treasury (approximately $4.5 billion in 1992), and this cost has been rising precipitously. Over the last nine years, the number of social-assistance dependents among Indians has increased by nearly 65 per cent, from 88,000 in 1981–2 to more than 145,000 in 1990–1, and there is no sign of a let-up. The projected future costs to the federal treasury of this legal obligation are so daunting that the federal government has introduced budget caps and is seeking to transfer more of its fiscal responsibility to the provinces, which are resisting such a transfer. In this context, every unemployed Indian who is spurred under the proposed design to find off-reserve employment does not represent a loss of tax revenue to the federal treasury. Rather, he or she represents a significant saving in social-assistance payments and other legal obligations.

If the proposed 'participation/taxation' design proved to be successful to the degree that it raised Indian employment levels to the prevailing Canadian level (and no other objective is morally defensible), then the potential income-tax revenue that would be generated for bands/tribes could exceed $1 billion,[5] and the Indian social-assistance burden to the federal treasury could potentially decrease from $460 million to $145 million, that is, an annual saving of $315 million.[6] Additionally, of course, there would be considerable sidestream gains to the federal treasury from lower rates of social pathologies in Indian communities and lower costs of social services. Moreover, the Indian reserve and Canadian economies would both benefit from increased consumer spending. In effect, by fostering higher rates of Indian employment, the proposed design creates a financial equation of 'expanding sum'; that is, every aspect of Indian existence could be improved while federal spending on Indians decreased.

The proposed ceding of federal income-tax revenue to Indian governments is not intended, at least not inceptively, as a surrogate for current government grants or fiscal transfers to Indian communities. As invisioned here, any augmented revenues generated by such taxation should not initially reduce the current level of federal grant contribution to bands/tribes; however, the federal government would gain from lower social-welfare assistance to individual Indians as a result of improved employment levels. The new tax revenue could be applied by band/tribal councils to close the gap between Indian and Canadian services, infrastructures, housing, and so on. After a period of time, however, as Indian employment rates and personal incomes approach equivalence to those of Canadians, at some appropriate point existing fiscal arrangements could be renegotiated; that is, the income-tax revenue generated for band/tribal coffers would justify the phasing-in of 'revenue offsets' reducing government grants. Such 'offsets' could be applied to bands/tribes selectively, taking into account local needs, deficiencies, and aspirations. But, any 'offset' formula would have to take into account the need to maintain a positive incentive for band/tribal communities to encourage their members to participate in the mainstream economy. Moreover, such 'offsets' could not affect any categorical services and assistance that the federal government is constitutionally mandated to provide to Canadian citizens, such as unemployment insurance, family allowance, and old age pensions.

Currently, some Indian bands/tribes, with the encouragement of the Canadian government, are moving to establish an independent revenue base by levying taxes on property located within their reserve boundaries. Bill C-115, an 'Indian Act Amendment on Taxation' (also known as the 'Kamloops Amendment'), which was proclaimed on 28 June 1988, established the power of band/tribal councils to levy taxes on property on reserves, including leasehold developments. The Canadian government is hopeful that property taxes generated under

Bill C-115 will have the effect of moderating band/tribal demands on its treasury. Subsequent to enactment of Bill C-115 the Indian Taxation Advisory Board was established in 1989. This government-sponsored and -funded 'Indian controlled' national entity was created by the federal government to legitimate and facilitate Indian property-taxation initiatives by assisting band/tribal councils in setting up appropriate tax by-laws. It also functions as a lobby group for changes in provincial laws and policies to make more room for taxation by bands/tribes.

In respect to the provinces, the proposed 'participation/taxation' design as envisioned here, would require that Indians working on or off the reserve pay all income, consumer, and other taxes to the provinces at the rates paid by other provincial residents; that is, there would be provincial tax parity between Indians working on or off the reserve, and with Canadian provincial citizens. In return, Indian governments would be entitled to imbursement by the provinces for all provincially mandated services and programs offered on the reserves, on the per-capita or usage basis applied in municipalities. Individual Indians would have the option of accessing services on or off the reserve.

At present, provincial governments are coming under increasing constitutional and political pressure to assume the same funding responsibility for bands/tribes within their borders as they do for provincial municipalities. There is no constitutional prohibition against the provinces bringing Indian governments into the framework of provincial funding under terms acceptable to Indians. No doubt, such a design represents a complex legislative and administrative challenge, more so because the design must give Indian governments the autonomy to plan and operate on-reserve services in a way that is responsive to the interests, needs, and aspirations of their constituency. This runs contrary to the provincial-municipal relationship, where acceptance of substantial revenue from the provincial government normally implies a high level of provincial control through conditions and standards that must be met to qualify for provincial funding.

Under the current constitutional division of powers, the provincial and federal governments control the terms under which Indian–provincial relations will be governed. Thus, the onus falls on provincial and federal governments to engage in bilateral and trilateral negotiations with Indians to find mutually acceptable terms and modes by which provincial funds could be transferred to bands/tribes, and by which constitutionally mandated provincial services would be provided or imbursed on reserves. This would have to be accomplished within a framework that would not place Indian governments in a position of political, fiscal, or legal subordination to provincial governments. In structuring these terms and their budgets, Indian governments might choose to segregate their revenue so that essential as well as politically and culturally sensitive functions could be totally financed from 'Indian' revenue (i.e., Indian income taxes, reserve property taxes, band/tribal resource revenue, etc.), while other less-sensitive functions could be funded by revenue transferred from provincial and federal governments.

Because of the nature of the Canadian federal system, the provinces carry a great moral responsibility to advance the economic self-sufficiency and independence of Indians. Provincial governments have an extensive constitutional mandate over economic development within their borders. At present, more than 90 per cent of the Canadian labour force and most resources come under provincial jurisdiction, and it is a safe bet that the provincial 'jurisdictional moon' will wax under future constitutional reforms. Besides, provincial financial resources and revenues are generally in better shape than those of the federal government. Also, Indian economic development will depend significantly upon provincial infrastructures. Education and legislative protection against discrimination in employment, accommodation, services, and so on, are constitutionally mandated to the provincial governments. In sum, the future evolution of Indian economic self-sufficiency and independence will be profoundly influenced by provincial government comportment.

Provincial governments frequently express concern about the immediate and long-term economic and social future of the Indian population within their borders. Large and serious problems of Indian social pathology have already surfaced in most urban centres, where they become the responsibility of provincial and municipal governments. Already some provinces bear significant costs of health, education, welfare, and other services to urban Indian populations. Projected birth rates and the escalating tempo of Indian migration to urban centres are giving some provincial and urban officials cause for trepidation that their fiscal and institutional capability to cope with the pending problems will be overwhelmed unless major ameliorative initiatives are taken quickly. Thus, provincial governments have a huge stake in spurring Indian economic self-sufficiency and independence.

Provincial and federal opposition to the proposed 'participation/

taxation' design may derive from a misperception by the public that the implied requirements will subtract from their piece of the economic pie. This misperception could arise because Canadians seem to be oblivious to the fact that non-participation by Indians in the Canadian economy represents a huge loss of productive capacity, and thus of their contribution to Canada. Converting current non-productive Indian human resources to full productivity would increase the total store of benefits to all Canadians.

Indian opposition to the proposed model may derive from an understandable hesitation by band/tribal leaders to accept any design that requires them to pay provincial or any other taxes. They feel that they get a poor return for the taxes they now pay. Moreover, they oppose any intrusion of provincial taxing authority into their jurisdiction. The present ambition of band/tribal leaders is to expand section 87 of the Indian Act so as to eliminate all provincial taxing powers on Indians. For example, Indian leaders advocate that Indians should be exempted from paying provincial taxes on such items as gasoline, tobacco, alcohol, and hotel rooms because the Indians' right to general exemption from such taxation was never extinguished.

But the pathway to Indian economic independence is not via the route of more tax exemptions. Demands by band/tribal leaders that the spiralling costs of services to their communities be paid for with the taxes of Canadians, at the same time as they clamour for more tax exemptions for themselves, no matter how they rationalize it, cannot be sustained in the Canadian political arena. From the perspective of the tax-paying Canadian public, Indian élites' claims to tax exemptions under aboriginal and treaty rights represents the ultimate tax dodge. Indians collectively would have a much more acceptable-to-the-public claim to a share in provincial and federal financial resources if, individually, they all shared in the burden of taxation and on the same basis as Canadians.

Benefits

If the eleven Canadian governments and Indian leaders were to accept the proposed 'participation/taxation' design and adopt it as a strategy for enhancing Indian economic independence through self-sufficiency, potentially, a variety of significant beneficial fiscal, political, cultural, and social impacts for the future of Indian nationhood could result.

In fiscal terms, an agreement by Indians to pay provincial taxes on goods and services and on income earned on reserves in exchange for entitlement to all provincial grants and benefits that are now available to provincial municipalities and citizens would be in the interests of the lower class who constitute the great majority of band/ tribal members. Current exemptions from provincial income taxes benefit primarily a small élite class on each reserve. The Indian lower class (i.e., those who are unemployed and on welfare) do not earn a taxable income and they already pay most provincial sales taxes. Collectively, Indians would gain much more from provincial funding entitlements than the sum of what élite Indians would be required to pay in provincial income taxes. Moreover, under the proposed taxation design, Indian governments could move out of their current plight, where they must beg the provinces for money, and assume a more dignified status, where they could hold the provincial government politically and legally accountable for economic assistance.

At present, most Indians are in a relationship of 'citizen minus' relative to provincial services and programs; that is, Indians living on reserves are not considered to be provincial citizens in terms of eligibility for provincial services and programs, and those living off-reserves are caught in a trap of confusion caused by provincial-municipal rules governing Indian eligibility for social assistance and other programs. Federal-provincial intergovernmental disputes over who is responsible for services to off-reserve Indians have brought considerable suffering to migrant Indians. In some instances, essential assistance and services, including medical care, have been denied them, because 'residency' or other eligibility requirements of the province or of a municipality were not met or could not be proved to have been met. If Indians agreed to pay all provincial taxes, they would have the same entitlements to provincial services as Canadian provincial citizens. Removal of current 'legal' barriers, which exclude Indians from provincial services, would also open the door to begin ameliorating other barriers, such as 'attitudinal' exclusions (e.g., prejudice and discrimination), 'cultural' exclusions (e.g., conflicting values and norms), and exclusion based on lack of knowledge by Indians of available provincial services, all of which now deter even 'eligible' Indians from accessing provincial services.

I have noted previously that a critical issue in Indian government is accountability of leaders to their people. Accountability by Indian government to Indian people is difficult to effect when the Canadian government is virtually the sole source of Indian governments' revenues. At present, all levels of Indian leadership – local, provincial, national – are dependent on government funding. In effect, they are on the government's payroll. However, if a significant part of Indian governments' revenues were to be generated from a tax-paying Indian electorate, such an arrangement would inevitably shift Indian leadership accountability to the people. Moreover, employment in the mainstream economy would foster the development of an urban Indian middle class. Within a structure of formalized reserve–urban political, economic, cultural, and social integration such as I have proposed, the urban Indian middle class, by virtue of being tax-paying supporters of Indian government, would have the right to vote in band/tribal council elections, run for elected office, compete for bureaucratic positions, and so on. Thus, they could challenge the political and bureaucratic hegemony of reserve-based ruling élites.

A nation's political capacity is significantly enhanced if the self-sufficiency of its people rests on a stable economic base. A high level of full-time employment through participation at all levels of the Canadian mainstream economy would strengthen and stabilize the economic foundations of Indian nationhood. Moreover, large-scale participation in the Canadian economy would enhance Indian political influence in shaping the Canadian 'national interest' and, thus, the policies that carry a 'sidestream' impact on them. Additionally, the willingness of band/tribal members to provide from their own pockets the resources needed to operate Indian government would carry significant political meaning in the Canadian context as a measure of mass Indian support and loyalty for their leadership. All of these factors, combined, would serve to empower Indian government in federal and provincial politics, and in government-to-government relations.

All Canadian governments and the Canadian people have a huge vested interest in the success of Indian self-government – 'success' meaning progress towards economic self-sufficiency and independence and, hence, reduced costs to federal and provincial treasuries. In fact, current federal and provincial government opposition to the concept of Indian government derives significantly from the anticipated high cost of such governments to their respective treasuries. By achieving higher levels of self-support, Indian communities would demonstrate to the two levels of Canadian government that Indian government will not have a negative impact on their revenue flows. Thus, Indians would have a more credible claim to self-government, and Canadian governments would be less resistant to constitutionalizing the powers and guarantees needed for Indians to live and survive as *Indians*.

Participation in the mainstream economy would provide individual Indians with greatly expanded opportunities to develop as business managers, trained technicians, and professionals. From a traditional *Indian* perspective it is important that such human-resource development should have not only an 'individual benefit' but a 'community benefit' as well. Unless there is a collective benefit to the band/tribe, Indian communities are reluctant to encourage their members to acquire 'marketable skills.' The proposed structure of formal reserve–urban Indian political, economic, social, and cultural linkages would create a complex in which the human resources developed by Indian participation in the mainstream could return to the reserve and directly benefit Indian communities by contributing their expertise to community development. And those who did not return to the reserve would benefit the community by their contribution of income-tax revenue. Conversely, Indian governments by receiving tax revenue from their urban members would have a great obligation to use their influence and powers to act as advocates for the interests and well-being of urban Indians.

Another benefit relates directly to on-reserve economic development. Band/tribal leaders often criticize the federal government for spending too little on reserve-based economic development when compared to what is spent on social welfare in their communities. But, given the 'zero-sum/catch 22' fiscal world in which the deficit-ridden federal government now operates, the Indian welfare load must be reduced before more money will be available to spend on reserve-based economic development. Under the 'participation/taxation' design proposed here, a higher proportion of band/tribal members would be encouraged to become self-supporting, thereby allowing the federal government to allocate more of its grant monies towards on-reserve economic development. Moreover, expanded off-reserve employment would enhance on-reserve economic development by the income-tax revenue it would bring to the reserve. Additional money would be brought to the reserve through kin and other channels, thereby improving the viability of on-reserve business ventures.

The proposed design also holds beneficial implications for bands/tribes in establishing their membership criteria. Under the present 'zero-sum' fiscal arrangement, bands/tribes operate under capped government grants. This motivates current band/tribal members to establish very conservative membership codes in order to protect the per-capita share of their benefits. Evidence for such a conservative tendency was found recently in the reluctance or resistance of many bands/tribes to allow Bill C-31 Indians membership. To do so would mean cutting an already inadequate 'pie' into still smaller pieces. The proposed 'participation/taxation' design, however, would create an 'expanding-sum game' in regard to new band/tribal memberships; that is, by fostering higher rates of employment and, hence, tax revenues, the bands'/tribes' potential income and cumulative wealth would increase as their employed membership grows. This would diminish the present motivation for adopting conservative membership determination criteria such as 'popularity tests' or 'blood-quantum' measurements, and would make room for cultural criteria. Concurrently, by creating on-reserve versus off-reserve tax and benefits neutrality, the proposed design would diminish the extraordinary incentives for Indians to seek band/tribal membership for reasons of economic benefit or advantage, rather than for reasons of cultural affinity.

Important also, the proposed 'participation/taxation' design invites Indians to consider carefully how the traditional fundamental principle of redistributing and sharing wealth and income is to be operationalized in their communities. What mode of redistribution and sharing do they want to implement? Traditionally, Indians had customs that obligated band/tribal members to contribute to the survival and well-being of the community. This custom served to seal bonds among members and mitigated against divisive social-class disparities. The practices of redistribution and sharing were rooted in deeply held cultural and spiritual values and were deemed obligatory. Any band/tribal member who consistently neglected to fulfil this obligation lost the right to share in the group's benefits and protection.

Clearly, Indians have departed from their traditional communal system of redistributing and sharing wealth and income. Indians, today, have moved far in the direction of individualizing and privatizing income, (including welfare income); wealth, and communal assets. Voluntary sharing is not working as a mechanism of redistribution. The loss of traditional customs of redistribution and sharing has resulted in a two-class socio-economic system on most reserves, consisting of a small élite class and a large, destitute lower class. Under the proposed 'participation/taxation' design, traditional philosophies and principles of sharing and contributing to their community could again define Indian cultures. By creating a 'public treasury' through taxation, band/tribal members would have the opportunity to fulfil the traditional obligation of contributing to their communities through sharing, and Indian governments would have a mechanism and the means for meeting the needs of destitute members and advancing the well-being of the collectivity. By requiring Indian élites to share part of their good fortune with their less-fortunate kin, the proposed design would serve as a unifying force in the Indian community.

Finally, the proposed design for economic self-sufficiency and independence through 'participation/taxation' also has the potential to yield some important social benefits to Indians. High unemployment levels and the welfare system have robbed Indians, especially males, of their productive roles. The result has been a tragedy for Indians in terms of social disorganization and social pathologies. Participation in the mainstream would not only give Indians an opportunity to develop their individual productive and creative capacities, but enable them to validate their self-worth and enhance their image in both Indian and Canadian societies. As well, it would provide the means for enjoyment of goods, activities, and facilities that define success and human dignity. Such a development offers a potential for alleviating many of the social pathologies that beset Indian communities today.

Conclusion

Indian economic self-sufficiency and independence will never be more than an illusion if Indian economic development is premised on the tripodal economic model of traditional subsistence pursuits, on-reserve economic development, and government grants. There exists a large discrepancy between the level of economic self-sufficiency and independence this model can provide and Indian leaders' aspirations for self-government.

Indian leaders who advocate a return to the traditional economy of hunting, gathering, and fishing rhetorically insist that the Canadian government must provide them with a land base adequate for such an economy. However, the notion of an 'adequate land base' is so vague as to be meaningless. Even under the most optimistic, but realistic, assumptions regarding settlements of land claims and access to vacant 'Crown lands,' there will never be a land base adequate to sustain more than a tokenistic traditional economy except, perhaps, for a handful of remote bands/tribes. Moreover, the future of a traditional economy grows more unpromising as a rapidly increasing Indian population outgrows the carrying capacity of reserves. Indian leaders who give legitimacy to the traditional economy as a solution to their condition of dependence, destitution, and social pathologies do their people a great disservice, predisposing them to endure their present condition of unemployment, welfare, and destitution in anticipation of the mythical day when full settlement of their rights, claims and self-government will restore their traditional way of life.

Equally misguided is the vision of achieving economic self-sufficiency and independence based on reserve economic development. Reserves were created to isolate Indians, not for their economic self-sufficiency and independence. While there is more or less scope for expanding on-reserve economic activity (depending on the reserve), overall the concept of government-capitalized and -subsidized reserve economic development, whether by collective band/tribal ventures or by individual entrepreneurship, has a dismal history and holds bleak prospects. Under even the most optimistic, but reasonable, assumptions, the vision of reserve-based economic self-sufficiency and independence is a sure formula for perpetuating the condition of Indian unemployment, dependence, destitution, and all of the associated misery and social pathologies that currently prevail on virtually all Indian reserves. Those who promote the myth of reserve-based economic self-sufficiency and independence are contributing to the problem of Indian dependence, not to its solution. They serve merely to raise the false hope that this is the pathway to getting the jobs that unemployed Indians want. This false hope inhibits Indians from beginning the essential process of solving the huge and growing problem of reserve-based unemployment. But, perhaps a worse outcome for any band/tribe, would be to realize great commercial value in its reserve. The worst fate that can befall a defenceless people is proof of great value in their lands: oil, gold, strategic location, and so on. Such value attracts the interest of the powerful as blood attracts sharks. Indians need not learn this lesson again.

The notion that Indian nationhood can be sustained on Canadian government grants (however these grants may be labelled) is the most problematic component of the tripodal economic model. The contradiction implicit in this notion could not be more blandly (albeit unconsciously) expressed than in the following excerpt taken from a speech by Benjamin Reifel. Reifel is a Sioux Indian, a former U.S. commissioner of Indian Affairs. His basic premise is espoused by many contemporary Indian leaders in Canada: 'If a recommendation is made to the President of the U.S., it should ask for enough money for each reservation to honestly provide a standard of living that will support tribal sovereignty and self-rule. Then, we can proudly say, this is our culture and we are taking care of ourselves.'[7] Commissioner Reifel's statement conjures up an Indian world that cannot and ought never to exist. Any proposal that Indian political autonomy and cultures should be financed by another government makes a mockery of Indian nationhood. It is a manifestation of the 'culture of dependence' in the political sphere. Such an arrangement is a design for continued colonial subordination and paternalism. What government will guarantee to pay for another government's autonomy and culture without chains attached? It is impractical and indefensible to plan the political, economic, and cultural future of Indian people based on the assumption that, because Indians were here first, the 'late-comers' have an obligation, in perpetuity, to provide whatever operating funds are needed to support Indian governments, citizens, and cultures.

One of the keys to autonomous Indian governments is *sustainability* of their economic base. Herein lies a major infirmity of the tripodal economic model. Canadians are growing increasingly impatient and unwilling to pay the growing cost of Indian dependence. Already, the Canadian government has declared the escalating level of its grant assistance to Indians politically and economically unsustainable, and it has implemented a process of capping such assistance. But, even in the unlikely event that government grants were increased to a level at which Indian communities could attain parity of services, infrastructure, living standards, and so on, any concept of Indian government that is based almost entirely on Canadian government grants condemns Indians to a political status and a culture of dependence, with all of the associated social pathologies.

In short, the tripodal economic model is inherently deficient because it holds no reasonable prospect for economic self-sufficiency and independence for Indians. To achieve economic self-sufficiency and independence, Indian leaders must broaden their economic concerns beyond the current narrow political-fiscal purpose of achieving larger government grants, and gaining more control over their band/tribal budgets. They need to consider an expanded economic model that will bring the employment and business opportunities afforded by the Canadian economy into the service of achieving economic self-sufficiency and independence through unemployment for their people.

The 'participation/taxation' design for achieving Indian economic self-sufficiency and independence that has been proposed in this chapter is premised on the idea that economic self-sufficiency can be achieved only through full participation in the mainstream Canadian economy, and that Indian economic independence can be achieved only through revenues generated from productive employment of Indian people – that is, through self-sufficiency. It envisions a future in which large numbers and proportions of Indians will leave their reserves and derive their livelihood from participation in the mainstream economy. Implementation of such a design represents a formidable challenge for Indians and Canadians alike. To enable Indians to participate in the mainstream economy on the basis of equal motivation, preparation, opportunity, and social acceptance will require a major change in Indian–Canadian relationships and attitudes, which will require a massive, multifaceted, Indian–Canadian joint venture.

On the Indian side, there is a need to develop the supportive social ethos and the formal structural linkages that will enable Indians to participate in the economic mainstream without loss of their political, economic, cultural, and social relationships to their home community. Implied in this design is a need for Indians to carefully consider their conception of Indian nationhood. Is Indian nationhood to be conceived of as an instrument for accommodating, on the reserve, all band/tribal members who wish to live there? Given the very limited land and resources, high birth rates, and impoverished circumstances, such a conception is unfeasible. Already there is strong resistance to the admission of Bill C-31 Indians, legitimate heirs to the ancestral aboriginal inheritance, to band/tribal membership. Assuming that at some point all Indian land claims are settled or terminated, and the cash has been spent, and conditions remain as they are now – a likely scenario – what then? Under such a conception of Indian nationhood the reserve would become primarily a welfare haven, a trust territory, a racial ghetto, practising a culture of dependence. It is not a design for the survival and well-being of Indians as *Indians*.

The proposed 'participation/taxation' design posits an alternative conception of nationhood; that of a traditional cultural nation in which *Indians* carry their nationhood 'on their backs.' This conception of nationhood implies a significant change from Indian leaders' current Euro-Western conception, which defines Indian nationhood in terms of political and territorial sovereignty. Under the traditional cultural conception of nationhood, the reserve would be valued, first and foremost, as sacred, ancestral, communal land. Under such a conception, Indian government becomes defined as the steward of the sacred, ancestral, communal and cultural inheritance, and it is charged with responsibility for sustaining this inheritance and the traditional culture for all (reserve and urban) Indians for generations to come. When the primary purpose of Indian government is the survival and well-being of *all* Indians as *Indians*, then urban Indians must have the same interest and stake in Indian government and Indian reserves as do reserve Indians.

Under the cultural conception of *Indian* nationhood, the challenge to Indian governments is to enhance the productive and creative potential of the people, on and off the reserve, within a framework of traditional *Indian* cultural philosophies and principles. Such a cultural conception of nationhood must not be construed as implying that Indians should relent in their aggressive pursuit of their ancestral inheritance, that is, their land claims, treaty and aboriginal rights, and other entitlements. Nor should they relent in their pressure for appropriately conceived economic development on their reserves. However, such settlements and economic development, must be pursued within a framework of survival and well-being as *Indians*, not from band/tribal leaders' aspirations for maximum political jurisdiction and power over Indian lands and Indian people.

On the other side, Canadians, and their eleven governments, have a decisive role to play if Indians are to survive as *Indians*. Canadians do not owe Indians a living, but, having destroyed their traditional economic self-sufficiency and independence, they owe Indians the opportunity to make their living in the mainstream economy at the same levels of employment and income as Canadians. Anything less is not morally defensible. This opportunity is at present being denied Indians. Correcting this problem will require that Canadians and their governments muster up the moral and political will to deal justly with Indians. The 'Canadian wall' of racism against Indians must be torn down. Doing so will require an extensive and intensive effort that goes beyond 'tolerant racism.' The racial image of Indians must be replaced with an image of cultural and human worth, thus enabling Canadians, psychologically, to accept Indians as people of value, as equals, and as co-workers.

Epilogue

The task of decolonizing Indians is complex, and it is made more so by the dissimulative rhetoric of the Canadian government and the extravagant rhetoric of Indian leaders. Such rhetoric makes it difficult to come to a discerning understanding of the two agendas. Instead of reacting to the rhetoric on both sides, my discussion has been conducted within a broad framework purposed to promote the survival and well-being of Indians as *Indians*. In this regard, it stresses five imperatives: moral justice for Indians; Canadian policies that treat Indian rights, interests, aspirations, and needs co-equally to the 'national interest'; Indian leadership that is committed to Indian government 'of, by, and for' the people; revitalized *Indian* cultures, languages, and social systems that are adapted and developed within the framework of traditional philosophies and principles; and economic self-sufficiency and independence achieved through employment in the Canadian mainstream. These five imperatives cannot be perceived as discrete ends in themselves. They are inseparably linked to each other. In this book I have tried to conceive of each imperative in such a way that it can be synthesized with the others to form an internally consistent paradigm for justice, that is, the survival and well-being of Indians as *Indians*.

The imperative of justice thus stands as the corner-stone of my paradigm. Justice is the only corrective that can heal the hurt and dispel the distrust that is felt in Indian communities. This healing and rebuilding of trust must occur before there can be any real progress towards an effective relationship between Indians and Canadians. But, at present, Canadians are following their politicians away from justice for Indians. Despite the entrenchment of aboriginal and treaty rights in the Constitution Act, 1982, the Canadian government is continuing on the path of political expediency, not justice towards Indians. And the Canadian judiciary is interpreting section 35(1) of the Constitution Act so as to reinforce the colonial legal structures that deny moral justice for Indians. In this book I have propounded the thesis that the only way Indians can escape the Canadian constitutional prison of injustice is to abandon the ideology of aboriginal rights and the instrumentality of the constitution by which they have pursued justice. Instead, they need to adopt the spirit and intent of the treaties (i.e., the well-being and survival of *Indians*) as their ideology, and the U.N.Charter guarantee of peoples' rights as their instrumentality, for achieving justice. Doing so would position them to catch the wave of ethnic liberation that is building worldwide.

The Canadian government and Canadian courts, historically, have consistently subordinated or sacrificed Indian rights, interests, needs, and aspirations to the Canadian 'national interest.' The consequences of this policy paradigm have been tragic for Indians, reducing them to a condition of powerlessness, dependence, destitution, and despair. The survival and well-being of Indians as *Indians* cannot be achieved within such a policy framework. Justice for Indians is possible only if the Canadian government will live up to the obligations of the fiduciary role it has arrogated to itself in regard to Indians; that is, it must treat Indian rights, interests, needs, and aspirations as co-equal to those of Canadians, and it must reconcile the two. Such an orientation may inconvenience Canadians, and it may cost Canadians, but it does not threaten the survival and well-being of Canadians.

The actions of present-day Indian leaders are pivotal for the survival and well-being of Indians as *Indians*. Indian leaders must consider and plan for the future with realism and with great care. They must not wait for the Canadian governments to define their future. Indian leaders must become convinced that the future of their people depends more upon their own actions than on the actions of Canadian governments; that they have the potential to inspire their people to realize the future of their choosing. To realize this potential, Indian leaders must first place themselves outside the control of the Canadian governments. This will be possible only if they discard the colonial political and bureaucratic structures that have been imposed upon them, and if they work to empower, unify, and heal their people. They must work together with their people as equals to develop an image of their future, and together with their people they must make the 'decisions of nationhood' that will move them towards that future. Working upwards from the 'grass-roots people,' they must relearn how to govern themselves according to traditional philosophies and principles. This can be accomplished only if Indian leaders will passionately and selflessly commit themselves to the cause.

For Indians to realize their full cultural potential, Indian leaders must think in terms larger than political power and monetary compensation for past victimization. Unless they develop a cultural conception of Indian nationhood, future generations of Indians will be assimilated while retaining only a sense of injustice and a memory of a lost cause. They will have to seek out accounts by anthropologists, and go to museums, to learn about their traditional philosophies and principles. In this regard, Indians today stand before a fast fading window of opportunity to tap the knowledge and expertise of their 'elders' in the essential task of rediscovering their traditional fundamental cultural philosophies, principles, languages and social systems. Failing in this, Indians will remain trapped in a culture of dependence and they will be confined in a racial prison, without a moral claim to nationhood.

The economic choices that Indian leaders make for their people will have profound implications for their survival and well-being as *Indians*. If Indian leaders should opt for self-government based on the tripodal model of traditional economic pursuits, on-reserve economic development, and Canadian government grants, then, predictably, Indians will always remain dependent upon social assistance from the Canadian government. The 'participation/taxation' design presented in this book offers a way out of the trap of dependence, based on revenue generated by full participation in the mainstream Canadian economy. But participation in the mainstream would be a model for ethnocide if it were not accompanied by cultural adaptation and development within a framework of traditional philosophies and principles. A beneficial side-effect of the 'participatory/taxation' model would be to create opportunities in the Indian lower class for upward mobility. In a context of formal structural linkages between reserve and urban Indian communities, middle-class development would impel the ruling-élite class on reserves to become more open and accountable to their constituents.

My purpose in writing this book has been to bring new insights and perspectives to a discourse on the survival and well-being of Indians as *Indians*. And this is a good time in the history of Indian–Canadian relations for new approaches. Indians and Canadians have never been more aware of each other, nor more politically interactive. I am well aware that I have taken a number of risks in this book, among them, that my contribution will be misinterpreted, or deemed irrelevant, or wrong-headed, or too ambitious, or all of the above. There may be some readers who, from personal biases or prejudices, will selectively agree or disagree with some things I have said. Some may object to my broad-based and severe indictment of Canadian society, Canadian government, and Canadian courts. Others may resent what they consider to be unkind, unfounded, and misguided criticisms of Indian leadership, their motives, and their goals, by someone who has not experienced their pain and oppression.

I hope there will be readers who will take reasoned exception to the ideas, analyses, and solutions presented in this book, for I wrote this book to provoke debate on a matter of crucial significance, a matter that may well turn out to be the most troublesome item on the Canadian agenda in what remains of this century. If my ideas fail to provoke debate, my book will have missed the mark, for it is out of the clash of ideas that good solutions are conceived. But even as readers take exception or disagree with my ideas, assertions, interpretations, and proposed remedies, I hope the spirit and intent of this book will resonate with all who share my concern over justice denied to Indians, over the unconscionable conditions in which the great majority of Indians live, and for the survival of *Indians*. Each of us has the capacity to do something about this injustice. If readers take issue with my ideas with the purpose of achieving justice for Indians, I will consider my efforts well rewarded.

Appendices

Appendix 1

The Royal Proclamation of 1763:
Comment and Excerpt

The Royal Proclamation established the boundaries of Quebec and the American colonies. It was proclaimed by the British Crown (King George III) for the purpose of maintaining peace, law, and order on the frontier. It asserted Crown sovereignty over Indians and their lands and Crown title (legal, proprietary title) in all Indian lands, acknowledging only an 'aboriginal interest' (i.e., a usufructuary/possessory right) by Indians in their ancestral Lands. The Royal Proclamation established the legal framework for Indian surrender, by treaty, of their aboriginal rights in most of their ancestral lands.

And whereas it is just and reasonable, and essential to our Interests, and the Security of our Colonies, that the several Nations or Tribes of Indians with whom We are connected, and who live under our Protection, should not be molested or disturbed in the Possession of such Parts of our Dominions and Territories as not having been ceded to or purchased by Us, are reserved to them, or any of them, as their Hunting Grounds. – We do therefore, with the Advice of our Privy Council, declare it to be our Royal Will and Pleasure, that no Governor or Commander in Chief in any of our Colonies of Quebec, East Florida, or West Florida, do presume, upon any Pretence whatever, to grant Warrants of Survey, or pass any Patents for Lands beyond the Bounds of their respective Governments, as described in their Commissions; as also that no Governor, or Commander in Chief in any of our other Colonies or Plantations in America do presume for the present, and until our further Pleasure be known, to grant Warrants of Survey, or pass Patents for any Lands beyond the Heads or Sources of any of the Rivers which fall into the Atlantic Ocean from the West and North West, or upon any Lands whatever, which, not having been ceded to or purchased by Us as aforesaid, are reserved to the said Indians, or any of them.

And We do further declare it to be Our Royal Will and Pleasure, for the present as aforesaid, to reserve under our Sovereignty, Protection and Dominion, for the use of the said Indians, all the Lands and Territories not included within the Limits of Our said Three new Governments or within the Limits of the Territory granted to the Hudson's Bay Company, as also all the Lands and Territories lying to the Westward of the Sources of the Rivers which fall into the Sea from the West and North West as aforesaid.

And We do hereby strictly forbid, on Pain of our Displeasure, all our loving Subjects from making any Purchases or Settlements whatever, or taking Possession of any of the Lands above reserved, without our special leave and Licence for that purpose first obtained.

And We do Further strictly enjoin and require all Persons whatever who have either wilfully or inadvertently seated themselves upon any Lands within the Countries above described, or upon any other Lands which, not having been ceded to or purchased by Us, are still reserved to the said Indians as aforesaid, forthwith to remove themselves from such settlements.

And whereas great Frauds and Abuses have been committed in purchasing Lands of the Indians to the great Prejudice of our Interests and to the great Dissatisfaction of the said Indians; in order therefore to prevent such Irregularities for the future, and to the end that the Indians may be convinced of our Justice and determined Resolution to remove all reasonable Cause of Discontent, We do, with the Advice of our Privy Council, strictly enjoin and require, that no private Person do presume to make any Purchase from the said Indians of any Lands reserved to the said Indians, within those parts of our Colonies where We have thought proper to allow Settlement; but that if at any Time any of the said Indians should be inclined to dispose of the said Lands, the same shall be Purchased only for Us in our Name, at some public Meeting or Assembly of the said Indians, to be held for that Purpose by the Governor or Commander in Chief of our Colony respectively within which they shall lie; and in case they shall lie within the limits of any Proprietary Government, they shall be purchased only for the Use and in the name of such Proprietaries, conformable to such Directions and Instructions as we or they shall think proper to give for that Purpose; and we do, by the Advice of our Privy Council, declare and enjoin that the Trade with the said Indians shall be free and open to all other Subjects whatever, provided that every Person who may incline to Trade with the said Indians do take out a Licence for carrying on such Trade from the Governor or the Commander in Chief of any of Our Colonies respectively where such Person shall reside, and also give Security to observe such Regulations as We shall at any Time think fit, by ourselves or by our Commissaries to be appointed for this Purpose, to direct and appoint for the Benefit of the said Trade.

And we do hereby authorize, enjoin, and require the Governors and Commanders in Chief of all our Colonies respectively, as well those under Our immediate Government as those under the Government and Direction of Proprietaries, to grant such Licences without Fee or Reward, taking especial Care to insert therein a Condition, that such licence shall be void, and the Security forfeited in case the Person to whom the same is granted shall refuse or neglect to observe such Regulations as We shall think proper to prescribe as aforesaid.

And we do further expressly enjoin and require all Officers whatever, as well Military as those Employed in the Management and Direction of Indian Affairs, within the Territories reserved as aforesaid for the use of the said Indians, to seize and apprehend all Persons whatever, who standing charged with Treason, Misprisions of Treason, Murders, or other Felonies or Misdemeanors, shall fly from Justice and take Refuge in the said Territory, and to send them under a proper guard to the Colony where the Crime was committed of which they stand accused, in order to take their Trial for the same.

Given at our Court of St James', the 7th Day of October, 1763, in the Third Year of our Reign.

GOD SAVE THE KING

Appendix 2

The Treaties:
Summary and Chronology

The treaties have their origin in the legal framework created by the Royal Proclamation of 1763. The legal framework comprised certain principles: (1) legal proprietary title was vested in the Crown; (2) the Crown recognized a usufructuary/ possessory (aboriginal) right by Indians in their ancestral lands (that is, use and benefit, not ownership); (3) Indian usufructuary/possessory (aboriginal) right in the land could be surrendered (or sold) only to the Crown; (4) if at any time Indians should wish to surrender their usufructuary/possessory rights in their ancestral lands, the Crown would purchase such rights at a public assembly of the Indians concerned.

Treaties are generally categorized as 'pre-Confederation' and 'post-Confederation.' Pre-Confederation treaties were negotiated during an era in which the British were contending with the Indians, the French, and the Americans over issues of territorial control. Consequently, these treaties were significantly shaped by military and strategic considerations. By the late 1830s, the British Crown had obtained surrenders, by treaties, of a strip of land about 700 miles in length and 200 miles in breadth, straddling the St Lawrence River from Ottawa to the tip of the Gaspé Peninsula – that is, most of Upper Canada. In 1850, two treaties covering large areas in southern Ontario (the Robinson/Huron and the Robinson/Superior) were concluded. Pre-Confederation treaty-making came to a close with two treaties signed, in 1854 and 1862, respectively, covering the Bruce peninsula and part of Manitoulin Island on Lake Huron.

The post-Confederation treaties (also called the 'numbered' treaties: 1–11) were concluded in the period from 1871 to 1929, and they cover the remainder of Ontario; all of Manitoba, Saskatchewan, and Alberta; portions of BC, the Yukon, and the western part of the Northwest Territories. The provisions of the two Robinson treaties served as models for the post-Confederation treaties, but the motivations of the two treaty-making participants had changed profoundly. On the Crown's side, the post-Confederation treaties were driven by issues of economic development (i.e., agriculture, exploitation of resources, land speculation, and commerce). Thus, the Crown's purpose was to remove Indians from their ancestral lands by negotiating surrender of their aboriginal interests and to confine them on reserves. On the Indian side, the post-Confederation treaties were motivated by a deep concern for their survival and well-being as *Indians*.

The content varied from treaty to treaty, but most treaties made provision for reserve lands, for some assistance in respect to hunting and fishing (e.g., guns, ammunition, fishing gear), agriculture (e.g., implements, seeds, animals), education (e.g., schools, supplies, teachers), and some economic development. One treaty (no. 6) also made provision for health services (i.e., a 'medicine chest'). Treaties included provision for Indians to retain exclusive hunting, fishing, and gathering rights on their reserves, and hunting rights in their traditional hunting areas in unoccupied lands surrendered to the Crown. Treaties often included entitlements to annual cash payments (i.e., 'annuities'), and rights to minerals under reserve lands.

In spite of the legal principles set out in the Royal Proclamation, in large areas of Canada, including most of BC and Quebec and parts of the Maritimes, many bands/tribes were not compensated for the dispossession of aboriginal rights in their ancestral lands. The explanation for the Crown's failure to follow the treaty-making process with Indians in Quebec and parts of the Maritimes is that those areas were passed from French to British control with a history of non-recognition of Indian title by the French. In BC, there was an effort, after Union in 1871, by the federal government to have the issue of aboriginal title negotiated, but the province of BC refused to cooperate.

Bands/tribes from these 'non-treaty' areas are currently stepping up their political and legal campaign to authenticate their historical aboriginal rights in their ancestral lands, with the objective of recovering their lands and/or receiving fair compensation for the loss of their rights in these lands. Since, under the Royal Proclamation, all bands/tribes are entitled to negotiate treaties, there exist considerable legal incentives for the delinquent provinces and the federal government to bring this unfinished business to some sort of conclusion.

Towards this end, the federal government has announced a policy of negotiating settlements of 'comprehensive' land claims (i.e., where at present no treaty agreement exists), as well as 'specific' land claims (i.e., where the federal government has not fulfilled its treaty obligations). Recently, British Columbia has expressed a more forthcoming attitude towards Indian land claims within its provincial borders. In Quebec, the James Bay and Northern Quebec Agreement (1975) and the Northeastern Quebec Agreement (1978) represent 'treaty-like' agreements. In the former agreement, 13,696 square kilometres of land was set aside for the exclusive use of approximately 10,000 Cree and Inuit. The agreement gave the Cree and Inuit communities exclusive hunting, fishing, and trapping rights in adjacent unoccupied ancestral territories, and granted them a measure of local control over health, education, and other matters in their communities. The agreement also included a 'benefits package' totalling $267.5 million in cash and $226.3 million in additional programs to be paid for by the province. In return, the Cree and Inuit peoples surrendered their aboriginal rights in 'the territory of Quebec.' Under the Northeastern Quebec Agreement, the Naskapi Indians of Schefferville, Quebec, signed a complementary deal with the province of Quebec.

Chronology of the pre-Confederation treaties

1670	British officials are directed to enter into 'Peace and Friendship' treaties with Indian people of North America
1725–8	Treaty of Peace and Friendship is signed between the British Crown and the Penobscott, Narridgwack, St Johns, and Cape Sables tribes
1752	The East Coast Micmacs subscribe to the terms of the 1725–8 treaty agreement
1763	The Royal Proclamation
1779	The Micmacs (between Cape Tormentine and the Bay of Chaleur) ratify 1752 treaty
1784–1850	Almost all of Upper Canada is cleared of Indian title under about twenty-four 'purchases or surrenders' (and the two Robinson Treaties of 1850)
1817	The Saulteaux and Cree sign a treaty. Purpose: extinction of Indian title to the area covered by the Red River Colony
1850	Robinson Superior Treaty with Ojibewa Indians of Lake Superior. Purpose: conveyance of land to Crown
	Robinson Huron Treaty with Ojibewa Indians of Lake Huron. Purpose: as above
1862	Manitoulin Island Treaty with Ottawa and Chippewa. Purpose: 'settle and improve the country'

Chronology of the post-Confederation treaties

1871	Treaties 1 and 2 with Chippewa and Swampy Cree Indians in

regards to southern Manitoba and southeastern Saskatchewan. Purpose: 'peaceful settlement and immigration'

1873   Treaty 3 (Northwest Angle Treaty) with Saulteaux Tribe of Ojibeway Indians in regards to northwestern Ontario/southeastern Manitoba. Purpose: as above, and 'other suitable purposes'

1874   Treaty 4 with Cree and Saulteaux tribes of Indians in regards to southern Saskatchewan and portion of Manitoba and Alberta. Purpose: as for treaties 1 and 2, and for 'trade and other purposes'

1875   Treaty 5 with Saulteaux and Swampy Cree tribes of Indians in regard to central and northern Manitoba. Purpose: as for Treaty 3

1876   Treaty 6 with Plains and Wood Cree and other tribes of Indians in regards to central Saskatchewan and Alberta. Purpose: as above

1877   Treaty 7 with Blackfeet, Blood, Peigan, Sarcee, and Stony Indian tribes in regard to southern Alberta. Purpose: 'to open the land for settlement and such other purposes'

1899   Treaty 8 with Cree, Beaver, and Chipewayan Indians in regard to northern Alberta, northwestern Saskatchewan, northeastern British Columbia, southeastern Mackenzie Valley. Purpose: as above, and for 'immigration, trade, travel, mining, lumbering, and such other purposes'

1905   Treaty 9 ('James Bay [Ontario] Treaty') with Ojibeway and Cree Indians in regard to central northern Ontario. Purpose: as above

1906   Treaty 10 with Chewayan, Cree, and other Indians in regards to northern Saskatchewan and a portion of Alberta. Purpose: as above

1908–10   Adhesions to Treaty 5 (see above). Purpose: to complete its coverage in what is now northern Manitoba

1921   Treaty 11 with Slave, Dogrib, Loucheux, Hare, and other Indians in regards to Mackenzie Valley and southeastern Portion of the Yukon. Purpose: as for Treaty 8

1923   Chippewa Treaty and Mississauga Treaty in regards to portions of Ontario east and south of Georgian Bay. Purpose: surrender of hunting, fishing, and trapping rights in the Province of Ontario

1929–30   Adhesions to Treaty 9 (see above). Purpose: complete its coverage in northern Ontario

1956   Adhesion to Treaty 6 (see above). Purpose: complete its coverage in Alberta and Saskatchewan

Recent treaty-like agreements

1975   James Bay and Northern Quebec Agreement with Cree Indians and Inuit of Quebec in regards to northwestern and northern Quebec. Purpose: to effect a surrender of Indian title to Northern Quebec for major hydro-electric development

1978   Northeastern Quebec Agreement with Naskapi Indians of Schefferville, Quebec, in regards to portion of north-central Quebec. Purpose: as above

1984   Inuvialuit Final Agreement with Inuit of Western Arctic in regards to northern portion of western Northwest Territories. Purpose: to disencumber lands for resource exploitation

Source: *Indian Treaties in Historical Perspective*, prepared by George Brown and Ron Maguire for Research Branch, Department of Indian and Northern Affairs (Ottawa, 1979), iv–xvi

Appendix 3

The Indian Act: Historical Summary and Selected Sections

The Indian Act grew out of Province of Canada legislation entitled 'An Act for the Gradual Civilization of the Indian Tribes of Canada' (1857). Subsequent to the Constitution Act, 1867, (also known as the BNA Act), which gave the federal government legislative authority with respect to 'Indians and lands reserved for Indians' (section 91[24]), the Canadian Parliament enacted the Indian Act in 1876. The Indian Act established the legal framework for the federal government to exercise its authority under section 91 (24) of the Constitution Act, 1867. In effect, it provided a legal basis for the colonial administration of Indians and their reserves. Although the Indian Act provisions sometimes imply a guarantee of 'benefits' and 'rights' to Indians (e.g., section 18, the use and benefit from reserve land; section 61, the use and benefit of Indian monies; and section 7, the right to vote and stand for nomination in council elections), these are merely the 'benefits' and 'rights' of colonial wards, and they exist at the pleasure of the governor in council (section 4). The main purpose of the Indian Act is to control and regulate the lives of Indians.

The Indian Act has undergone periodic amendment and occasional revision. Significant amendments were made in 1880 (to offer the privilege of enfranchisement to 'advanced' bands/tribes); 1884 (to introduce band/tribal government by council instead of by chief); 1920 (to empower the federal government to unilaterally enfranchise Indians); 1951 (to provide for an elective system of band/tribal government; to increase provincial legislative authority over Indians [section 88]; and, to allow more delegation of band/tribal administrative responsibility); and 1985 (to repeal section 12 (1)(b) so as to comply with the International Covenant on Civil and Political Rights and to bring the act into conformity with the Canadian Charter of Rights and Freedoms [Bill C-31]). The act is currently undergoing an intensive examination (Lands, Revenue, and Trust Review) with the goal of diminishing the Canadian government's fiduciary responsibility for Indians. Moreover, the Canadian government's 'Indian self-government' initiative is another strategy intended to diminish the federal government's obligations under the act by transferring more responsibility to band/tribal councils and to the provinces.

The sections of the Indian Act selected for inclusion in this appendix pertain to the status-determination criteria as these were defined in the act prior to 1985 and as they stand following the 1985 Amendment (Bill C-31; see Appendix 7). Of particular interest is Indian Act, 1978, section 12 (1)(b), which denied Indian status to Indian women who married non-Indians. The legality of section 12 (1)(b) was tested before the Supreme Court of Canada (*Attorney General of Canada* v *Lavell*, 1974). Jeanette Lavell, an Ojibwa woman, who had married a non-Indian, contested this section on the grounds that it discriminated on the basis of gender, and therefore contravened the Canadian Bill of Rights. The Supreme Court found against Lavell, ruling that the Indian Act took precedence over the Bill of Rights. Subsequently, Sandra Lovelace, a Maliseit woman from the Tobigue Reserve who had lost her right to live on the reserve when she married a non-Indian, presented her case to the U.N. Human Rights Committee (*Lovelace* v *The Government of Canada*, 1980). The United Nations declared that this section of the Indian Act violated the International Covenant on Civil and Political Rights. This U.N. censure shamed the Canadian government into amending the act so as to remove the worst aspects of gender discrimination (see below, Indian Act, 1989, sections 6 and 7).

Indian Act, 1978: sections 11 and 12

11.(1) Subject to section 12, a person is entitled to be registered if that person

(a) on the 26th day of May 1874 was, for the purposes of *An Act providing for the organization of the Department of the Secretary of State of Canada, and for the management of Indian and Ordnance Lands*, being chapter 42 of the Statutes of Canada, 1868, as amended by section 6 of chapter 6 of the Statutes of Canada, 1869, and section 8 of chapter 21 of the Statutes of Canada, 1874, considered to be entitled to hold, use or enjoy the lands and other immovable property belonging to or appropriated to the use of the various tribes, bands or bodies of Indians in Canada;

(b) is a member of a band

(i) for whose use and benefit, in common, lands have been set apart or since the 26th day of May 1874, have been agreed by treaty to be set apart, or

Persons entitled to be registered

(ii) that has been declared by the Governor in Council to be a band for the purposes of this Act;

(c) is a male person who is a direct descendant in the male line of a male person described in paragraph (a) or (b);

(d) is the legitimate child of

(i) a male person described in paragraph (a) or (b), or

(ii) a person described in paragraph (c);

(e) is the illegitimate child of a female person described in paragraph (a), (b) or (d); or

(f) is the wife or widow of a person who is entitled to be registered by virtue of paragraph (a), (b), (c), (d) or (e).

(2) Paragraph (1)(e) applies only to persons born after the 13th day of August 1956. R.S., c. 149, s. 11; 1956, c. 40, s. 3. *Exception*

12.(1) The following persons are not entitled to be registered, namely, *Persons not entitled to be registered*

(a) a person who

(i) has received or has been allotted half-breed lands or money scrip,

(ii) is a descendant of a person described in subparagraph (i),

(iii) is enfranchised, or

(iv) is a person born of a marriage entered into after the 4th day of September 1951 and has attained the age of twenty-one years, whose mother and whose father's mother are not persons described in paragraph 11(1)(a), (b) or (d) or entitled to be registered by virtue of paragraph 11(1)(e),

unless, being a woman, that person is the wife or widow of a person described in section 11, and

(b) a woman who married a person who is not an Indian, unless that woman is subsequently the wife or widow of a person described in section 11.

(2) The addition to a Band List of the name of an illegitimate child described in paragraph 11(1)(e) may be protested at any time within twelve months after the addition, and if upon the protest it is decided that the father of the child was not an Indian, the child is not entitled to be registered under that paragraph. *Protest re illegitimate child*

(3) The Minister may issue to any Indian to whom this Act ceases to apply, a certificate to that effect. *Certificate*

(4) Subparagraphs (1)(a)(i) and (ii) do not apply to a person who *Exception*

(a) pursuant to this Act is registered as an Indian on the 13th day of August 1958, or

(b) is a descendant of a person described in paragraph (a) of this subsection.

(5) Subsection (2) applies only to persons born after the 13th day of August 1956. R.S., c. 149, s. 12; 1956, c. 40, ss. 3, 4; 1958, c. 19, s. 1.

Idem

Indian Act, 1989: sections 6 and 7

6.(1) Subject to section 7, a person is entitled to be registered if

Persons entitled to be registered

(a) that person was registered or entitled to be registered immediately prior to April 17, 1985;

(b) that person is a member of a body of persons that has been declared by the Governor in Council on or after April 17, 1985 to be a band for the purposes of this Act;

(c) the name of that person was omitted or deleted from the Indian Register, or from a band list prior to September 4, 1951, under subparagraph 12(1)(a)(iv), paragraph 12(1)(b) or subsection 12(2) or under subparagraph 12(1)(a)(iii) pursuant to an order made under subsection 109(2), as each provision read immediately prior to April 17, 1985, or under any former provision of this Act relating to the same subject-matter as any of those provisions;

(d) the name of that person was omitted or deleted from the Indian Register, or from a band list prior to September 4, 1951, under subparagraph 12(1)(a)(iii) pursuant to an order made under subsection 109(1), as each provision read immediately prior to April 17, 1985, or under any former provision of this Act relating to the same subject-matter as any of those provisions;

(e) the name of that person was omitted or deleted from the Indian Register, or from a band list prior to September 4, 1951,

(i) under section 13, as it read immediately prior to September 4, 1951, or under any former provision of this Act relating to the same subject-matter as that section, or

(ii) under section 111, as it read immediately prior to July 1, 1920, or under any former provision of this Act relating to the same subject-matter as that section; or

(f) that person is a person both of whose parents are or, if no longer living, were at the time of death entitled to be registered under this section.

(2) Subject to section 7, a person is entitled to be registered if that person is a person one of whose parents is or, if no longer living, was at the time of death entitled to be registered under subsection (1). *Idem*

(3) For the purposes of paragraph (1)(f) and subsection (2), *Deeming provision*

(a) a person who was no longer living immediately prior to April 17, 1985 but who was at the time of death entitled to be registered shall be deemed to be entitled to be registered under paragraph (1)(a); and

(b) a person described in paragraph (1)(c), (d), (e) or (f) or subsection (2) and who was no longer living on April 17, 1985 shall be deemed to be entitled to be registered under that provision.

R.S., 1985, c. I-5, s. 6; R.S., 1985, c. 32 (1st Supp.), s. 4, c. 43 (4th Supp.), s. 1.

7.(1) The following persons are not entitled to be registered: *Persons not entitled to be registered*

(a) a person who was registered under paragraph 11(1)(f), as it read immediately prior to April 17, 1985, or under any former provision of this Act relating to the same subject-matter as that paragraph, and whose name was subsequently omitted or deleted from the Indian Register under this Act; or

(b) a person who is the child of a person who was registered or entitled to be registered under paragraph 11(1)(f), as it read immediately prior to April 17, 1985, or under any former provision of this Act relating to the same subject-matter as that paragraph, and is also the child of a person who is not entitled to be registered.

(2) Paragraph (1)(a) does not apply in respect of a female person who was, at any time prior to being registered under paragraph 11(1)(f), entitled to be registered under any other provision of this Act. *Exception*

(3) Paragraph (1)(b) does not apply in respect of the child of a female person who was, at any time prior to being registered under paragraph 11(1)(f), entitled to be registered under any other provision of this Act. *Idem*

R.S., 1985, c. I-5, s. 7; R.S., 1985, c. 32 (1st Supp.), s. 4.

Appendix 4

The Department of Indian Affairs and Northern Development (DIAND): Summary and Table

The locus of responsibility in government for Indian affairs has changed according to prevailing colonial priorities and interests. Around the time of the Royal Proclamation of 1763 and for a while thereafter, when the major concern of the British was to create military alliances with key Indian bands and tribes against the French, and later the Americans, the conduct of Indian affairs was placed in the hands of the military. It remained in the hands of military (or quasi-military) authorities until 1830. By this time the major priority of the British Colonial Office had changed to one of settling the land for agricultural and commercial development. Pursuant to the Royal Proclamation, land settlement required treaty negotiations with Indians for the surrender of their aboriginal rights in their ancestral lands. In response to this change in priorities, the locus of responsibility for Indian affairs was shifted into the hands of civil authorities, who were charged with the task of negotiating and enforcing treaty conditions, and 'civilizing' Indians.

The birth of 'Indian Affairs' as a separate department followed shortly after the passage of the Indian Act. A separate department was established in the ministry of the interior in 1880. Since that time, depending on the purposes of the Canadian government of the day, Indian Affairs has been expediently shifted from one federal government ministry to another – Mines and Resources (1936–49); Citizenship and Immigration (1949–65); Northern Affairs and Natural Resources (1965) – and in 1966 it was renamed the Department of Indian Affairs and Northern Development (DIAND) (also known as Indian and Northern Affairs Canada [INAC]).

Historically, the DIAND and its antecedents have been responsible for the administration of the Indian Act. As such, they have functioned as a microcosm of colonial government for Indians, controlling virtually every aspect of life on Indian reserves: health, welfare, education, economic development, housing, employment, funding, budgets, and so on. Additionally, the mandate of the DIAND has been to develop Indian policy, and to deal with land claims, trust obligations, the development of Indian self-

TABLE 1
Department of Indian Affairs and Northern Development operating and non-budg-
etary expenditures and revenues, 1990–1

OPERATING EXPENDITURES	
Indian and Inuit Affairs	258,332,033
Northern Affairs	64,739,676
Administration	50,941,531
Capital expenditures	
Indian and Inuit Affairs	9,697,810
Northern Affairs	2,548,094
Grants, contributions, and other transfer payments	
Indian and Inuit Affairs	2,264,663,748
Northern Affairs	36,137,343
Territorial government	964,670,137
TOTAL	3,651,730,372
REVENUES	
Indian and Inuit Affairs	15,474,609
Northern Affairs	27,931,224
Administration	238,583
TOTAL	43,644,416
NON-BUDGETARY EXPENDITURES	
Loans, investments and advances	23,686,310
Indian and Inuit Affairs	(182,240)
Northern Affairs	
TOTAL	23,504,070

Source: Indian and Northern Affairs Canada, Annual Report, 1990–1 74

government, and so on. At no time in the history of the DIAND has its per-
sonnel, resources and competence been equal to the task that was thrust
upon it. The evidence for this assertion can be found in the squalid living
conditions and tragic levels of social pathology that exist on virtually every
Indian reserve.

Today, under the federal government's policy of Indian institutional assimilation, the DIAND has been mandated to work itself out of existence. It
has been charged with the task of transferring its decision-making functions and associated authority to other federal and provincial government
departments and agencies, with some community-management functions
and responsibilities to be devolved to bands/tribes under the name of 'In-

dian self-government.' Already the DIAND has shrunk from a peak of more than 6,000 employees in 1984–5 to fewer than 4,000 in 1990–1. This shrinkage has occurred even though, during that time span, the budget for Indian affairs has increased by almost 50 per cent, and the Indian population for which it has overall responsibility has increased (naturally and as a result of Bill C-31 reinstatements) by approximately 50 per cent.

But, the DIAND will not disappear without resistance. The department's organization comprises a formidable array of assistant deputy ministers resting on top of layer upon layer of directors general, regional directors, directors, and senior administrators, exercising their authority through nine regional offices and some forty district offices. And it is the conduit through which massive amounts of money flow (1990–1: $3,651,730,372) to fund Indian programs and services. This must be considered a formidable contender for survival..

Appendix 5

First Ministers' Conferences (FMCs) on Aboriginal Constitutional Matters: Summary

Section 35.1 of the Constitution Act, 1982, commits the federal and provincial governments of Canada to the principle that aboriginal peoples would be invited to participate in discussion on amendments to the constitution on matters which related directly to them. Aboriginal peoples have had an opportunity to test the worth of this principle through four First Ministers' conferences.

The ostensible purpose of the FMCs was to fulfil a promise made to aboriginal peoples by Canada's eleven governments, on the occasion of the patriation of the constitution, to define 'existing aboriginal and treaty rights' as entrenched in section 35(1) of the Constitution Act. The initial FMC was held 15–16 March 1983. Four invited delegations representing aboriginal peoples were in attendance: the Assembly of First Nations (for status Indians); the Inuit Committee on National Issues (for the Inuit of Canada); the Metis National Council (for the Metis people); and the Native Council of Canada (for non-status Indians). This meeting produced the Constitutional Amendment Proclamation, 1983 (see Appendix 10), but it did not define section 35(1). During the course of the following three FMCs (1984, 1985, and 1987), the governments of Canada, on one side, and the aboriginal peoples, on the other were unable to bridge their different views of 'existing aboriginal and treaty rights.'

Beginning with the conference in 1984, the focal issue of all FMC agendas was constitutional recognition of the aboriginal peoples' right to self-government. What emerged in these conferences were two irreconcilable positions on the nature and scope of Indian self-government. Indian leaders asserted that their people have an inherent pre-existing right to self-determination, which they demanded that the First Ministers entrench in the constitution. The First Ministers asserted that the aboriginal right to self-government was subject to complete control by federal and provincial legislatures; that is, aboriginal governments could exercise only those powers explicitly delegated to them by the federal and provincial governments.

At the March 1984 FMC, the federal government advanced a proposal, which, if accepted, would have committed Canada's eleven governments to the establishment of Indian self-government in accordance with federal and provincial legislation. Under this proposal, aboriginal governments would have exercised delegated powers only. This proposal was unacceptable to the aboriginal leaders and to several provincial governments, and was rejected. At the next FMC, in April 1985, the federal government tabled what became known as the 'contingent right' proposal. Under this proposal the principle of an aboriginal right to self-government was to be constitutionally entrenched, subject to the condition that the definition of aboriginal self-government would be worked out through tripartite negotiations (federal, provincial, aboriginal), and would have to be approved by Parliament and the respective provincial legislatures. This proposal stood to receive the required provincial support for a constitutional amendment (that is, seven provinces representing more than 50 per cent of the Canadian population), and it received the support of the Metis and Inuit representatives. But it failed to gain the support of the Indian representatives, and was not enacted.

The final FMC, held in March 1987, also ended in stalemate over the nature and scope of power for aboriginal governments. The federal government again tabled a proposal to recognize the aboriginal right to self-government, again requiring that the powers of aboriginal governments be worked out through tripartite negotiated agreements. A number of provincial governments objected on the grounds that aboriginal self-government must be defined *before* entrenchment. Indian representatives also objected, insisting on a 'third order' of government, that is, with a constitutionally mandated inherent jurisdiction, not unlike the provinces (see Appendix 11). No mutually acceptable compromise could be found.

What can we learn from four tests of the constitutional principle that aboriginal peoples will participate in discussion on amendments to the constitution on matters that directly relate to them? The 1983 FMC yielded an accord, but the issues involved were hardly contentious. The following three FMCs yielded nothing, because the issue under discussion (the inherent right of aboriginal peoples to self-government) brought out the fundamental differences that exist between the two sides. The aboriginal representatives and the Canadian governments, each came to the FMCs with their prerehearsed scripts, and they spoke at each other as though from two isolation booths. The two sides started with a huge gap and moved farther apart.

Appendix 6

The Meech Lake Accord: Summary

Canada achieved self-governing ('dominion') status under the provisions of the Constitution Act, 1867, (the BNA Act). But, this act vested the British Parliament with the exclusive power to amend the constitution. When Canada was formally recognized as a self-governing nation by the Statute of Westminster (1931), because the federal and provincial governments could not agree among themselves on a formula for amending the constitution, any amendments that Canadians wanted to make were required to go through the British Parliament.

This became a source of increasing embarrassment, and a number of efforts (1927, 1935–6, 1950, 1960/1, and 1971) were made, all unsuccessful, to achieve agreement on a constitutional amendment formula. In 1980–1, then prime minister, P.E. Trudeau made a proposal to patriate the constitution (that is, to bring it 'home'), along with a Charter of Rights and Freedoms. After much political manoeuvring and some compromises, the federal government and nine provincial governments agreed to the terms of an accord for patriating the constitution along with a charter. The government of Quebec alone refused to sign the accord because it did not provide for the cultural and political integrity of the Québécois. Stated in practical political terms, it did not give Quebec (or any single province) veto power in respect to future constitutional amendments.

On 30 April 1987, Canada's First Ministers met at Meech Lake, Quebec, to consider proposals purposed to bring Quebec into full participation in Canada's constitutional family. The proposals considered at this meeting were the product of negotiations that had their official beginning in July 1986. When the final text of the Meech Lake Agreement was unanimously approved by the eleven First Ministers in Ottawa, on 3 June 1987, it embodied eight elements of constitutional change. At the same time, the First Ministers also unanimously approved a companion 'political accord' that committed them to lay the resolution containing the proposed amendments before their respective legislative bodies as soon as possible, and no later than June 1990. This allowed three years from the start of the legal process for all necessary legislative approvals.

The eight areas of proposed constitutional amendment are summarized below:

1 *Quebec's distinct Society*: Recognize that French-speaking Canadians constitute 'a fundamental characteristic of Canada,' and that Quebec constitutes 'a distinct society' within Canada.
2 *Senate appointments*: adopted a procedure for filling Senate vacancies from a list of names submitted by the government of the province to which the Senate vacancy relates.
3 *Immigration*: provided that immigration is a concurrent federal-provincial power with federal paramountcy. It committed the federal government to negotiate an immigration agreement with any province that requested it. It also provided that such an agreement could be constitutionally protected and gave each province concerned veto power over any change to its agreement.
4 *Supreme Court of Canada*: required the federal government to make Supreme Court appointments from a list of names proposed by the provinces, and that at least three of the nine Supreme Court Justices would be from names proposed by Quebec.
5 *Spending power*: required the federal government to provide reasonable compensation to any provincial government that chooses not to participate in new national shared-cost programs in areas of provincial jurisdiction, if that province provides a corresponding program.
6 *Conferences on the economy and other matters*: required the prime minister to convene, once a year, a First Ministers' Conference on the Canadian economy and other appropriate matters.
7 *Amending formula*: required unanimous consent for changes to national institutions, for the creation of new provinces, and for changes to the amending formula.
8 *Constitutional conferences*: required the prime minister to convene a First Ministers' Conference at least once a year. The agenda to include Senate reforms, fisheries, and other matters agreed upon.

Indian leaders mounted strong opposition to the Meech Lake Accord and, in a scenario reminiscent of David and Goliath, Elijah Harper, the lone Indian member of the Manitoba Legislature, slew the Accord. This remarkable feat was made possible by a unique conjunction of opportunity and personal courage. Harper took advantage of a procedural rule of the Manitoba legislature that required unanimous consent by all members in the legislature for the Accord to be put to a vote within the stipulated time frame. By denying unanimous consent, and thereby disallowing a Manitoba legislative vote on the Accord, the standard of unanimous approval by all provinces prior to June 1990 could not be met. Consequently, the Accord died.

The impact on Indians of the Meech Lake Accord would have been that constitutional entrenchment of Indian government as an aboriginal right because it represents 'a change to national institutions,' would have required unanimous consent of all eleven Canadian governments, a most unlikely scenario.

It is important to note that Indian leaders had no quarrel with bringing Quebec into the Canadian constitutional fold. In fact, they favoured such a move. They opposed the Meech Lake Accord because they believed the requirement of 'unanimous consent' would effectively close the door on 'third order' Indian governments. Moreover, the Accord ignored the reality that Indians too were 'distinct societies', with collective rights. Furthermore, they were angered by the fact they were not invited to participate in the deliberations leading up to the Accord, and by the readiness of the First Ministers to give unanimous concessions to Quebec's demands; yet, during four FMCs, the ministers had shown no political will to come to terms with aboriginal demands.

Indian leaders also expressed a great concern that the Accord did not protect Indians from the potential consequences of decentralization of the federal constitutional mandate to the provinces. And they objected to their omission from participation in the future First Ministers' conferences that were provided for by the Meech Lake Accord, even though the proposed agenda for these conferences included issues that vitally affected them. In short, Indians opposed the Meech Lake Accord because it acknowledged none of their rights, interests, needs, or aspirations. Thus, the Accord was scuttled, and Canada was thrown into a constitutional and political crisis.

Appendix 7

Bill C-31: Summary

On 28 June 1985, the federal government passed Bill C-31 ('an Act to amend the Indian Act'). The government had a political and a legal motive for passing the amendment. The political motive was provided by the U.N. Human Rights Committee, which had embarrassed the Canadian government before the world community by declaring that Canada was in violation of the International Covenant on Civil and Political Rights for denying Indian status to Indian women who married non-Indians (*Sandra Lovelace* v *The Government of Canada*). The government's legal motive for enacting Bill C-31 derived from an imperative need to bring the Indian Act into conformity with the Charter of Rights and Freedoms, which had come into effect on 17 April 1982 and declared that every person is 'equal before and under the law, and has the right to the equal protection and equal benefit of the law without discrimination and in particular without discrimination based on ... sex,' and other enumerated grounds (section 15). Thus, Bill C-31 was enacted to avert further U.N. censure or domestic legal challenges pursuant to the Charter by removing all discriminatory provisions from the Indian Act.

Specifically, Bill C-31 embodies a 'reinstatement component' that applies to any 'Indian person who lost or was denied status because of the discriminatory sections of the previous Act.' The amendment offers opportunity of reinstatement to (1) women who lost status upon marriage to a non Indian under section 12 1(b) of the Indian Act; (2) individuals who lost or were denied status through other discriminating clauses in the Indian Act; (3) individuals who lost status through enfranchisement (a process that existed in the old act whereby a person must give up status in order to be eligible for certain other rights); and (4) children of people in the first three categories. When the government framed Bill C-31, it estimated that, including descendants, approximately 72,000 individuals would be eligible for reinstatement and that anywhere from 10 to 20 per cent (i.e., 7,000 to 14,000) would seek reinstatement. However, in excess of 100,000 individuals have made application for reinstatement, and estimates are that 80,000 to 100,000 may be eligible for registration as Indians. Not only are eligible individuals seeking reinstatement of their Indian status, but many are seeking to return to the reserve to claim their rightful heritage and to take advantage of the benefits and services associated with band/tribal membership.

At the band/tribal level, the potential influx of Bill C-31 individuals threatens to overwhelm existing fiscal resources (e.g., social assistance) and infrastructures (e.g., housing, educational services, social services, medical care facilities, and land). In effect, it is making an already horrendous situation on reserves even worse.

Ironically, despite the amendments, which were intended to remove discrimination, the Indian Act today still contains explicit forms of gender discrimination. Although the act has eliminated discrimination faced by Indian women who lost status by marrying non-Indians, it passes the discrimination on to their descendants. For example, the children of a reinstated Indian woman can pass on Indian status to their offspring only if they marry a registered Indian, whereas the children of a reinstated Indian man can pass on Indian status to their offspring even if they marry a non-Indian.

Bill C-31 has created a new potentiality for discrimination because it separates the designation 'Indian status' from that of 'Band membership.' Under the pre-1985 act, Indian status and band membership were legally synonymous, and the federal government established the prerequisites and ruled on individual eligibility for status and membership designation. Under the amended act the federal government has retained the right to establish the prerequisites and eligibility for Indian-status designation, but it has empowered Indian bands/tribes to enact their own membership codes if they so desire. This creates a circumstance in which membership codes can be designed so as to deny membership and the associated benefits to status Indians, especially women, who have had their Indian status restored under Bill C-31. Some reinstatees have already experienced such discrimination.

Appendix 8

The Ministerial Task Force on Program Review ('The Nielsen Report' and 'The Buffalo Jump of the 1980s'): Summary

On 4 September 1984, the Progressive Conservative party, with Brian Mulroney as its leader, was elected to form the federal government. The Conservative party had run its election campaign on a platform of reduced expenditures and a reduced national deficit. In order to give a measure of substance to this campaign promise, the prime minister appointed his deputy prime minister, the Honourable Erik Nielsen, to head a ministerial task force to undertake a comprehensive review of all government programs, with the objective of reducing federal government expenditures. When it was completed (in March 1986) this review yielded twenty-one volumes of analyses, recommendations, and conclusions. The entire review was conducted behind a dense wall of secrecy, thereby creating a good deal of curiosity and speculations about political intrigue. It was predictable that when a summary of one of these secret reviews, a sixty-one-page document entitled *Memorandum to Cabinet: Report of the Ministerial Task Force on Native Programs*, was leaked to the media, it would achieve instant 'celebrity status' and become the focus of intense (media, political, and academic) scrutiny.

In the *Memorandum*, the task force placed 1985–6 expenditures on Indian and Native programs at $3 billion, and estimated that this cost would rise to $5.05 billion by 1990–1. This estimate was exclusive of the added costs that would be incurred by the reinstatement of Indians under Bill C-31, nor did it include projected housing requirements or the cost of comprehensive land-claims settlements.

The *Memorandum* broke down these expenditures into three categories: expenditures that the federal government is legally obligated to pay (25 per cent); expenditures for what would normally be provincial and municipal services, but are paid for by the federal government due to its responsibility for 'Indians, and lands reserved for Indians' under section 91(24) of the BNA Act, 1867 (40 per cent); and discretionary expenditures on social policy decisions (35 per cent). As an aside, the authors of the *Memorandum* noted that Indian have come to regard all 100 per cent of these expenditures as 'rights.'

Consistent with its mandate to come forward with recommendations for cutting federal government costs, the task force produced policy and program prescriptions designed to reduce federal government expenditures on Indians. Referencing its policy recommendations to its threefold fiscal classification scheme, it recommended a gradual transfer to the provinces of all 'provincial and municipal' costs (40 per cent) and all 'discretionary expenditures' (35 per cent), leaving the federal government with responsibility for only its 'strictly legal' obligations (25 per cent).

The task force took the position that such a major fiscal restructuring demanded a corresponding fundamental restructuring of the federal government's relationship to Indians, and of its administration of Indian affairs. One 'theme' of this fundamental restructuring was the dismantling of the DIAND, which was seen to be part of the 'Indian problem' (not the solution) because it was encouraging Indian dependence by offering them expensive social programs. Another 'theme' of the restructuring was 'devolution' of responsibilities to bands/tribal councils – that is, the devolution of 'community management' responsibilities, but under capped block-funding arrangements. The remainder of the DIAND's functions would be transferred to other federal and provincial government departments and agencies. In particular, the task force's emphasis was on transferring as many as possible of Indian program and service responsibilities to the provinces, using the instrumentality of 'Memoranda of Agreements.' Federal government jurisdiction for Indians should accompany the transfer of fiscal responsibility to the provinces.

The Nielsen task force had taken precautions to minimize potential Indian opposition to its proposals by devising a careful strategy for communicating its recommendations to Indians and the Canadian public. But the premature public disclosures of the secret *Memorandum* blew this careful strategy out of the water. The report drew instant and vociferous criticism from all sides. The media denounced the drastic cuts in 'already underfunded' Indian and Native programs and services. Indian leaders condemned the recommendations as a betrayal by the federal government of its historical constitutional special relationship to Indians, and they drew parallels between it and the 'termination' policy embodied in the 1969 White Paper on Indian Policy.

In a concerted effort to staunch the political bleeding inflicted on his government by unrelenting attacks on the task force recommendations by Indians, the media, and concerned Canadians, Prime Minister Mulroney

and the minister of Indian affairs (Crombie) publicly disowned and dispar-
aged the deputy prime minister's recommendations. Crombie described the
report as 'the entrails of policies which have been found in the wastebas-
kets of the bureaucracy' (House of Commons, *Debates*, 10 May 1985,
4626). In a further measure to quell the storm of protest, the prime minister announced some vague 'principles of policy' designed to reassure Indians regarding the government's honourable intentions towards them. In
fact, none of the prime minister's principles contradicted the substance of
the Nielsen Report and, considering the federal government's actions since
the *Memorandum* was first leaked, there is much more evidence that the
recommendations it contains 'live on' than that they lie 'in the wastebas-
kets of the bureaucracy.'

Appendix 9

Statement of the Government of Canada on Indian Policy, 1969 ('The 1969 White Paper'): Excerpts

Foreword

The Government believes that its policies must lead to the full, free and non-discriminatory participation of the Indian people in Canadian society. Such a goal requires a break with the past. It requires that the Indian people's role of dependence be replaced by a role of equal status, opportunity and responsibility, a role they can share with all other Canadians.

This proposal is a recognition of the necessity made plain in a year's intensive discussions with Indian people throughout Canada. The Government believes that to continue its past course of action would not serve the interests of either the Indian people or their fellow Canadians.

The policies proposed recognize the simple reality that the separate legal status of Indians and the policies which have flowed from it have kept the Indian people apart from and behind other Canadians. The Indian people have not been full citizens of the communities and provinces in which they live and have not enjoyed the equality and benefits that such participation offers.

The treatment resulting from their different status has been often worse, sometimes equal and occasionally better than that accorded to their fellow citizens. What matters is that it has been different.

Many Indians, both in isolated communities and in cities, suffer from poverty. The discrimination which affects the poor, Indian and non-Indian alike, when compounded with a legal status that sets the Indian apart, provides dangerously fertile ground for social and cultural discrimination ...

Governments can set examples, but they cannot change the hearts of men. Canadians, Indians and non-Indians alike stand at the crossroads. For Canadian society the issue is whether a growing element of its population will become full participants contributing in a positive way to the general well-being or whether, conversely, the present social and economic gap will lead to their increasing frustration and isolation, a threat to the general well-being of society. For many Indian people, one road does exist, the only road that has existed since Confederation and before, the road of different status, a road which has led to a blind alley of deprivation and frustration. This road, because it is a separate road, cannot lead to full participation, to equality in practice as well as in theory. In the pages which follow, the Government has outlined a number of measures and a policy which it is convinced will offer another road for Indians, a road that would lead gradually away from different status to full social, economic and political participation in Canadian life. This is the choice.

Indian people must be persuaded, must persuade themselves, that this path will lead them to a fuller and richer life. Canadian society as a whole will have to recognize the need for changed attitudes and a truly open society. Canadians should recognize the dangers of failing to strike down the barriers which frustrate Indian people. If Indian people are to become full members of Canadian society they must be warmly welcomed by that society.

The Government commends this policy for the consideration of all Canadians. Indians and non-Indians, and all governments in Canada.

1 Background

The Government has reviewed its programs for Indians and has considered the effects of them on the present situation of the Indian people. The review has drawn on extensive consultations with the Indian people, and on the knowledge and experience of many people both in and out of government.

This review was a response to things said by the Indian people at the consultation meetings which began a year ago and culminated in a meeting in Ottawa in April.

This review has shown that this is the right time to change long-standing policies. The Indian people have shown their determination that present conditions shall not persist.

Opportunities are present today in Canadian society and new directions are open. The Government believes that Indian people must not be shut out of Canadian life and must share equally in these opportunities.

The Government could press on with the policy of fostering further education; could go ahead with physical improvement programs now operating in reserve communities; could press forward in the directions of recent years, and eventually many of the problems would be solved. But progress would be too slow. The change in Canadian society in recent years has been too great and continues too rapidly for this to be the answer. Something more is needed. We can no longer perpetuate the separation of Canadians. Now is the time to change.

This Government believes in equality. It believes that all men and women have equal rights. It is determined that all shall be treated fairly and that no one shall be shut out of Canadian life, and especially that no one shall be shut out because of his race.

This belief is the basis for the Government's determination to open the doors of opportunity to *all* Canadians, to remove the barriers which impede the development of people, of regions and of the country.

Only a policy based on this belief can enable the Indian people to realize their needs and aspirations.

The Indian people are entitled to such a policy. They are entitled to an equality which preserves and enriches Indian identity and distinction; an equality which stresses Indian participation in its creation and which manifests itself in all aspects of Indian life.

The goals of the Indian people cannot be set by others; they must spring from the Indian community itself–but government can create a framework within which all persons and groups can seek their own goals.

2 The New Policy

True equality presupposes that the Indian people have the right to full and equal participation in the cultural, social, economic and political life of Canada.

The government believes that the framework within which individual Indians and bands could achieve full participation requires:

1 that the legislative and constitutional bases of discrimination be removed;
2 that there be positive recognition by everyone of the unique contribution of Indian culture to Canadian life;
3 that services come through the same channels and from the same government agencies for all Canadians;
4 that those who are furthest behind be helped most;
5 that lawful obligations be recognized;
6 that control of Indian lands be transferred to the Indian people.

The Government would be prepared to take the following steps to create this framework:

1 Propose to Parliament that the Indian Act be repealed and take such legislative steps as may be necessary to enable Indians to control Indian lands and to acquire title to them.
2 Propose to the governments of the provinces that they take over the

same responsibility for Indians that they have for other citizens in their provinces. The take-over would be accompanied by the transfer to the provinces of federal funds normally provided for Indian programs, augmented as may be necessary.

3 Make substantial funds available for Indian economic development as an interim measure.

4 Wind up that part of the Department of Indian Affairs and Northern Development which deals with Indian Affairs. The residual responsibilities of the Federal Government for programs in the field of Indian affairs would be transferred to other appropriate federal departments.

In addition, the Government will appoint a Commissioner to consult with the Indians and to study and recommend acceptable procedures for the adjudication of claims.

The new policy looks to a better future for all Indian people wherever they may be. The measures for implementation are straightforward. They require discussion, consultation and negotiation with the Indian people – individuals, bands and associations – and with provincial governments.

Success will depend upon the co-operation and assistance of the Indians and the provinces. The Government seeks this cooperation and will respond when it is offered.

3 The Immediate Steps

Some changes could take place quickly. Others would take longer. It is expected that within five years the Department of Indian Affairs and Northern Development would cease to operate in the field of Indian affairs; the new laws would be in effect and existing programs would have been devolved. The Indian lands would require special attention for some time. The process of transferring control to the Indian people would be under continuous review.

Appendix 10

Aboriginal Rights and the Canadian Constitution: Summary and Excerpts

Canadian constitutional provisions relating to the aboriginal rights of Indians have a long history. As early as the Treaty of Utrecht (1713), under which France relinquished Acadia and Newfoundland to England, Indians were guaranteed the right to trade with French and British colonists 'without any molestation or hindrance.' Similarly, the Articles of Capitulation of Montreal (1760), the Royal Proclamation (1763), the Quebec Act (1774), the Constitution Act (1791), and the Royal Proclamation (1817) guaranteed the aboriginal right of Indians to live undisturbed in their lands.

The Constitution Act (1867), also known as the British North America (BNA) Act, which gave the Parliament of Canada jurisdiction over 'Indians, and lands reserved by Indians' (section 91[24]), and the Indian Act (1876) also acknowledge the aboriginal rights of Indians in Canada. The BNA and Indian acts were followed by a series of other legislative acts (the Manitoba Act [1870]; the Terms of Union of British Columbia [1871]; the Alberta and Saskatchewan Acts [1905]; the Quebec and Ontario Boundaries Extension Legislation [1912]; and the Natural Resources Transfer Agreement [1930]. All acknowledge the aboriginal rights of Indians. Similarly, the treaties (1764–1929) confirm the aboriginal rights of Indians. Moreover, the courts of Canada have consistently given judicial affirmation to the aboriginal rights of Indians.

Canadian recognition of Indian aboriginal rights was reaffirmed in the Constitution Act, 1982. Important in the process leading up to the entrenchment of aboriginal rights in the Constitution Act, 1982, is a 1978 White Paper on constitutional reform entitled 'A Time for Action.' In it the federal government set out aboriginal rights as one of the principles to guide the renewal of the Canadian federation. This had the effect of firmly entrenching aboriginal rights in the Canadian constitutional agenda. It also led to the idea of constitutional entrenchment of aboriginal rights becoming firmly embedded in the policy position of aboriginal people. Although the federal government (alternately responding to provincial opposition and to aboriginal and public pressure) flip-flopped several times between

1979 and 1982 on entrenchment of aboriginal rights it was unable to remove it from the constitutional table and, in the end, 'existing aboriginal and treaty rights' were entrenched in the Constitution Act, 1982. However, Indian leaders who had fought hard for entrenchment of aboriginal rights strongly opposed the ambiguous language of the act, with its potentially unknown consequences.

When the act came into force on 17 April 1982, it contained five provisions relating to aboriginal peoples:

- The Canadian Charter of Rights and Freedoms would not be interpreted so as to abrogate or derogate from aboriginal, treaty, or other rights or freedoms (section 25).
- Existing aboriginal and treaty rights were recognized and affirmed (subsection 35[1]).
- The definition of 'aboriginal peoples of Canada' included Indians, Inuit, and Metis (subsection 35[2]).
- A First Ministers' Conference (FMC) on aboriginal constitutional matters would be convened within one year (subsection 37[1]).
- The conference agenda of the FMC would include the definition and identification of aboriginal rights; representatives of aboriginal peoples would be invited as non-voting consultants to participate in discussions on agenda items affecting them (subsection 37[2]).

When the First Ministers met 15–16 March 1983, under the terms of section 37 of the Constitution Act, 1982, the federal government and nine provinces (Quebec was not officially present), with the concurrence of the four aboriginal associations (see Appendix 5) and the two territorial governments that took part in the talks, agreed on a constitutional accord as follows:

- Three further First Ministers' conferences would be convened before 17 April 1987. Their agenda would include constitutional matters directly affecting the aboriginal people of Canada. Aboriginal representatives would be invited to participate in the discussions on those matters.
- Elected representatives of the governments of the Northwest Territories and the Yukon would be invited to participate in these conferences.
- A commitment by the government of Canada and the provincial governments to the principle that, before any further amendment to constitutional provisions dealing with aboriginal peoples can be made, aboriginal leaders must be consulted in a conference with First Ministers.

- An equal guarantee in the constitution of 'existing aboriginal and treaty rights' to males and females.
- Recognition and affirmation as treaty rights of any and all rights or freedoms acquired through both existing and future land-claims settlements.

Following endorsement of the constitutional accord by the Senate, the House of Commons, and nine provincial legislatures, it was proclaimed part of the Constitution Act, and on 21 June 1984, as the Constitution Amendment Proclamation, 1983.

The sections pertaining to aboriginal peoples in the Constitution Act, 1982, as amended, stand as follows:

Part I. This part contains a specific section (25) designed to recognize and preserve Aboriginal rights from any challenge based on other provisions within the Charter itself, including the guarantee of equality in S. 15.

25. The guarantee in this Charter of certain rights and freedoms shall not be construed so as to abrogate or derogate from any aboriginal, treaty or other rights or freedoms that pertain to the Aboriginal peoples of Canada including (a) any rights or freedoms that have been recognized by the Royal Proclamation of October 7, 1763; and
(b) any rights or freedoms that now exist by way of land claims agreements or may be so acquired.

The current paragraph 25(b) was substituted for the repealed paragraph by the Constitution Amendment Proclamation, 1983.

Part II. 'Rights of the Aboriginal Peoples of Canada' (section 35) contains the substantive recognition of the unique position of the original inhabitants of Canada.

35(1) The existing aboriginal and treaty rights of the aboriginal peoples of Canada are hereby recognized and affirmed.
(2) In this Act, the 'aboriginal peoples of Canada' includes the Indian, Inuit and Metis peoples of Canada.
(3) For greater certainty, in subsection (1) 'treaty rights' includes rights that now exist by way of land claims agreements or may be so acquired.
(4) Notwithstanding any other provision of this Act, the aboriginal and treaty rights referred to in subsection (1) are guaranteed equally to male and female persons.

Subsections (3) and (4) of section 35 were added by the Constitution Amendment Proclamation, 1983.

Section 35.1 guarantees that Aboriginal peoples must be consulted on any future amendments to Ss. 91(24), 25, 35, and 35.1. However, it does not prevent amendments to these sections without Aboriginal consent.

35.1 The government of Canada and the provincial governments are committed to the principle that, before any amendment is made to Class 24 of section 91 of the 'Constitution Act, 1867,' to section 25 of this Act or to this Part,
(a) a constitutional conference that includes in its agenda an item relating to the proposed amendment, composed of the Prime Minister of Canada and the first ministers of the provinces, will be convened by the Prime Minister of Canada; and
(b) the Prime Minister of Canada will invite representatives of the aboriginal peoples of Canada to participate in the discussion on that item.

Section 35.1 was added by the Constitution Amendment Proclamation, 1983.

Part IV.1 Constitutional Conferences

37.1 (1) In addition to the conference convened in March 1983, at least two constitutional conferences composed of the Prime Minister of Canada and the first ministers of the provinces shall be convened by the Prime Minister of Canada, the first within three years after April 17, 1982 and the second within five years after that date.
(2) Each conference convened under subsection (1) shall have included in its agenda constitutional matters that directly affect the aboriginal peoples of Canada, and the Prime Minister of Canada shall invite representatives of those peoples to participate in the discussions on those matters.
(3) The Prime Minister of Canada shall invite elected representatives of the governments of the Yukon Territory and the Northwest Territories to participate in the discussions on any item on the agenda of a conference convened under subsection (1) that, in the opinion of the Prime Minister, directly affects the Yukon Territory and the Northwest Territories.
(4) Nothing in this section shall be construed so as to derogate from subsection 35(1).

Part IV.1, consisting of section 37.1, was added by the Constitutional Amendment Proclamation, 1983.

Appendix 11

Joint Proposal for Self-Government (Aboriginal Draft)*, 1987 First Ministers' Conference

(Presented by the Assembly of First Nations, the Native Council of Canada, the Metis National Council, and the Inuit Committee on National Issues, and tabled at the First Ministers' Conference on Aboriginal Constitutional Rights, 26–27 March 1987)

Statement of the Right of Self-Government

35(5)(a) For greater certainty, the inherent right of self-government and land of all the Indian, Inuit, and Metis peoples of Canada is recognized and affirmed in subsection (1).

The Commitment to Negotiate

35(5)(b)(i) Upon the request of an aboriginal people of a community or region, the government of Canada shall negotiate agreements relating to the matters referred to in (iii);

(ii) the government of a province shall participate in the negotiations, to the extent of its jurisdiction, if so requested by the aboriginal people concerned; and

(iii) the agreements referred to in this subsection shall be negotiated in good faith by all parties, and without limiting their scope, the negotiations shall include such matters as self-government, lands, resources, economic and fiscal arrangements, education, preservation and enhancement of language and culture and equity of access, as may be requested by the aboriginal people concerned.

(iv) For greater certainty, and without prejudice to the rights of any aboriginal peoples of a community or region, or its negotiation of agreements, all the aboriginal peoples of Canada are guaranteed equitable access to the processes and resources by which agreements will be negotiated pursuant to this section.

* Verbatim transcript (unrevised), doc. 800–23/030. Reproduced with the permission of the Canadian Intergovernmental Conference Secretariat

Negotiations Will Not Prejudice Other Programs

35(5)(c) No program, service, financial arrangement, claims or other process available to the aboriginal peoples of Canada shall be prejudiced by reason of the fact that negotiations have been entered into pursuant to this section.

Rights in Agreements Shall Be Treaty Rights

35(5)(d) For greater certainty, the rights of aboriginal people set forth in agreements reached pursuant to paragraph (b) shall be 'treaty rights' within the meaning of subsections (1) and (3).

Economic and Fiscal Arrangements

36(6)(a) Parliament and the government of Canada and, to the extent provided by agreements and other treaties referred to in this Part, the legislatures and the governments of the provinces, are committed to:

(i) ensuring that aboriginal governments have the legislative authority and other powers necessary to raise revenues and derive benefits by taxation and otherwise, within their territories or regions subject to their jurisdictions; and

(ii) providing aboriginal governments with sufficient fiscal resources in the form of direct payments and other fiscal arrangements to enable those governments to govern their affairs, to maintain and develop aboriginal cultures, to promote economic development and employment opportunities, and to provide services of reasonable quality and at levels reasonably comparable to those available to all Canadians.

36(6)(b) For the purposes referred to in this Part, Parliament and the Government of Canada have the primary financial responsibility concerning aboriginal peoples.

Commitment to the Principles of Promoting Self-Government and Self-Reliance

35(7) To the extent that each has jurisdiction, Parliament and the provincial legislatures, together with the Government of Canada and the provincial governments, are committed to the principle of promoting self-government and self-reliance among aboriginal peoples in communities or regions in Canada, in co-operation with them.

Treaty Process

35(8)(a) Parliament and the Government of Canada are committed to fulfilling the spirit and intent of each treaty made between an aboriginal people and the Crown.

35(8)(b) In order to fulfil the spirit and intent of treaties, the Government of Canada is committed to clarify, rectify, renovate or implement those treaties as may be requested by the aboriginal peoples concerned.

35(8)(c) The results of the negotiations contemplated in paragraph (b) shall be set out in

(i) an amendment to a treaty,

(ii) an adhesion to a treaty, or

(iii) a new treaty,

as determined by the aboriginal peoples concerned.

35(8)(d) At the request of the Indian, Inuit or Metis peoples concerned, the government of a province is committed to participate in the negotiations contemplated in paragraph (b) to the extent of its jurisdiction, in a manner that does not abrogate or derogate from the role and authority of the Government of Canada to conclude treaties with any of the aboriginal peoples of Canada.

35(8)(e) For the purposes of this subsection, references to 'treaties' include 'land claims agreements' subject to paragraph (f).

35(8)(f) Notwithstanding paragraph (d), a government of a province is committed to participate in negotiations contemplated in paragraph (b) for the purpose stated therein with respect to land claims agreements to which it is a party.

Interpretation

35(9)(a) The rights of the aboriginal peoples of Canada shall be interpreted in a broad and liberal manner, so as to promote the preservation and enhancement of the heritage and cultures of the aboriginal peoples.

35(9)(b) Without limiting the generality of subsection (a), treaty rights of the aboriginal peoples of Canada shall be interpreted in accordance with the spirit and intent of the specific treaties, including land claims agreements, concerned.

Non-derogation

35(10) Nothing in subsections (5) to (8) abrogates or derogates from any rights or freedoms of the aboriginal peoples of Canada.

Legislative Powers Not Extended

35(11) Nothing in this (sub)section extends the legislative powers of Parliament or a provincial legislature.

Appendix 12

Province of Quebec Statements on Indian Policy, 1983 and 1985

The Fifteen Principles of 1983 (Government of Quebec)

On 9 February 1983 the Quebec government adopted a list of fifteen principles governing its negotiations with Amerindians and Inuit:

1 Quebec recognizes that the aboriginal peoples of Quebec constitute distinct nations, entitled to their own culture, language, [and] traditional customs and the right to shape the development of their own identity.

2 It also recognizes the right of aboriginal nations, under Quebec legislation, to own and to control the lands that are attributed to them.

3 These rights are to be exercised by them as part of the population of Quebec and hence cannot imply sovereign rights that might jeopardize the territorial integrity of Quebec.

4 The aboriginal nations may exercise, on the lands agreed upon by them and the government, hunting, fishing, and trapping rights, the right to harvest fruit and game, and the right to barter between themselves. In so far as possible, their traditional occupations and needs are to be taken into account in designating these lands. The ways in which these rights may be exercised are to be defined in specific agreements concluded with each people.

5 The aboriginal nations have the right to take part in the economic development of Quebec. The government is also willing to recognize that they have the right to exploit to their own advantage, within the framework of existing legislation, the renewable and unrenewable resources of the lands allocated to them.

6 The aboriginal nations have the right, within the framework of existing legislation, to govern themselves on the lands allocated to them.

7 The aboriginal nations have the right to have and control, within the framework of agreements between them and the government, such institutions as may correspond to their needs in matters of culture, educa-

tion, language, health and social services as well as economic development.

8 The aboriginal nations are entitled to benefit, within the framework of laws of general application and of agreements between them and the government, from public funds to encourage the pursuit of objectives they deem to be fundamental.

9 The aboriginal rights recognized by Quebec apply to women and men alike.

10 From Quebec's point of view, the protection of existing rights includes the rights arising from agreements between aboriginal peoples and Quebec concluded within the framework of land claims settlement. Moreover, the James Bay and Northern Quebec Agreement and the Northeastern Quebec Agreement are not to be considered as treaties with full effect.

11 Quebec is willing to consider that existing rights arising out of the Royal Proclamation of 7 October 1763 concerning aboriginal nations be explicitly recognized within the framework of Quebec legislation.

12 Quebec is willing to consider, case by case, each issue raised in this proposal.

13 The aboriginal nations of Quebec, owing to circumstances peculiar to them, may enjoy tax exemptions in accordance with terms agreed upon between them and the government.

14 When the government legislates on matters related to the fundamental rights of the aboriginal nations as recognized by Quebec, it pledges to consult them through mechanisms to be determined by them and the government.

15 Once established, such mechanisms can be institutionalized so as to guarantee the participation of the aboriginal nations in discussions pertaining to their fundamental rights.

Resolution of 20 March 1985 (l'Assemblée Nationale du Québec)

On 20 March 1985, the Assemblée nationale du Québec adopted the following motion tabled by the premier of Québec René Lévesque:

THAT THIS ASSEMBLY

Recognize the existence of the Abenaki, Algonquin, Attikamek, Cree, Huron, Micmac, Mohawk, Montagnais, Naskapi, and Inuit nations in Quebec; recognize existing aboriginal rights and those set forth in the James Bay and Northern Quebec Agreement and the Northeastern Quebec Agreement;

consider these agreements and all future agreements and accords of the same nature to have the same values as treaties;

subscribe to the process whereby the government has committed itself with the aboriginal peoples to better identifying and defining their rights, a process which rests upon historical legitimacy and the importance for Quebec society to establish harmonious relations with the native peoples, based on mutual trust and a respect for rights;

urge the government to pursue negotiations with the aboriginal nations based on, but not limited to, the fifteen principles it approved on 9 February 1983, subsequent to proposals submitted to it on 30 November 1982, and to conclude with willing nations, or any of their constituent communities, agreements guaranteeing them the exercise of:

   a the right to self-government within Quebec;
   b the right to their own language, culture, and traditions;
   c the right to own and control land;
   d the right to hunt, fish, trap, harvest, and participate in wildlife management;
   e the right to participate in, and benefit from, the economic development of Quebec,

so as to enable them to develop as distinct nations having their own identity and exercising their rights within Quebec;

declare that the rights of aboriginal peoples apply equally to men and women;

affirm its will to protect, in its fundamental laws, the rights included in the agreements concluded with the aboriginal nations of Quebec; and

agree that a permanent parliamentary forum be established to enable the aboriginal peoples to express their rights, needs and aspirations.

Appendix 13

The Royal Commission on Aboriginal Peoples: Summary and Terms of Reference

On 29 April 1991, Prime Minister Brian Mulroney announced a royal commission on aboriginal people. The royal commission began its task on 27 August 1991, co-chaired by George Erasmus, former chief of the Assembly of First Nations, and Rene Dussault, Justice of the Quebec Court of Appeal. the other members of the commission were: the Honourable Allan Blakeney, former premier of Saskatchewan; Paul Chartrand, Department of Native Studies, University of Manitoba; Viola Robinson, president of the Native Council of Canada; Mary Sillett, president of the Inuit Women's Association of Canada; and the Honourable Bertha Wilson, retired Justice of the Supreme Court of Canada.

Established by order-in-council, under a broad mandate, the commission will examine the economic, social, and cultural situation of aboriginal peoples in Canada and will consider solutions conducive to a better relationship between aboriginal peoples (Indian, Inuit, and Metis) and the Canadian government and Canadian society as a whole. The commission will complement current efforts at constitutional reform. The royal commission was given terms of reference recommended by Chief Justice Brian Dickson, who served as the prime minister's special representative and consulted widely on the mandate and membership of the commission.

Terms of Reference

The Commission of Inquiry should investigate the evolution of the relationship among aboriginal peoples (Indian, Inuit, and Metis), the Canadian government, and Canadian society as a whole. It should propose specific solutions, rooted in domestic and international experience, to the problems which have plagued those relationships and which confront aboriginal peoples today. The Commission should examine all issues which it deems to be relevant to any or all of the aboriginal peoples of Canada, and in particular, should investigate and make concrete recommendations concerning:

1. The history of relations between aboriginal peoples, the Canadian government and Canadian society as a whole.

This investigation may include studies of historical patterns of aboriginal settlement and governance, the Royal Proclamation of 1763, the development and interpretation of pre- and post-confederation aboriginal treaties, the evolution of political arrangements in the North, and social tensions which have characterized the relationship between aboriginal and other Canadian communities. Building upon this historical analysis, the Commission may make recommendations promoting a reconciliation between aboriginal peoples and Canadian society as a whole, and may suggest means by which aboriginal spirituality, history and ceremony can be better integrated into the public and ceremonial life of the country.

2. The recognition and affirmation of aboriginal self-government; its origins, content and strategy for progressive implementation.

The Commission's investigation of self-government may focus upon the political relationship between aboriginal peoples and the Canadian state. Although self-government is a complex concept, with many variations, the essential task is to break the pattern of paternalism which has characterized the relationship between aboriginal peoples and the Canadian government. The Commission should review models of self-government which have been developed in Canada and around the world, and should make recommendations concerning fiscal arrangements and economic development initiatives necessary for successful transitions to self-government. The scope, effect and future elaboration of Ss 25 and 35 of the Constitution Act, 1982 may be evaluated.

3. The land base for aboriginal peoples, including the process for resolving comprehensive and specific claims, whether rooted in Canadian constitutional instruments, treaties or in aboriginal title.

The Commission may investigate and explain the deep spiritual and cultural ties which bind aboriginal peoples to the land, the relationship between an adequate land base and economic development, and the importance of environmental protection. It may also outline appropriate processes for the settlement of outstanding comprehensive and specific claims. The scope, effect and future elaboration of ss. 25 and 35 of the Constitution Act, 1982 may be evaluated in relation to the land base as well as to self-government.

4. The historical interpretation and application, and potential future scope, of s. 91(24) of the Constitutional Act, 1867 and the responsibilities of the Canadian Crown.

An investigation of s. 91(24) may include examination of the internal political organization of aboriginal communities, the obligations of the federal Crown towards aboriginal people, the representation of aboriginal people in Canadian political institutions, and the relationship and potential for conflict between s. 91(24) and aboriginal notions of law and the legal processes.

5. The legal status, implementation and future evolution of aboriginal treaties, including modern-day agreements.

An investigation of the historic practices of treaty-making may be undertaken by the Commission, as well as an analysis of treaty implementation and interpretation. The Commission may also want to consider mechanisms to ensure that all treaties are honoured in the future.

6. The constitutional and legal position of the Metis and off-reserve Indians.

The Commission may examine legislative jurisdiction concerning the Metis and Non-Status Indians, and investigate the economic base of, and the provision of government services to these people and to off-reserve and urban Indians.

7. The special difficulties of aboriginal people who live in the North.

The Commission may investigate the difficulties and cost of communications and transport, issues of environmental protection, sustainable economic and social development, access to natural resources, and any differential treatment of northern aboriginal people by the Canadian and Territorial Governments.

8. The Indian Act and the role, responsibilities and policies of the Department of Indian Affairs and Northern Development (DIAND).

The Commission may investigate in particular the legislative scheme of the Indian Act, the relationship between that scheme and the evolving policies of DIAND, the theory of aboriginal-government relations implicit in the Indian Act, and the future of the Act and of DIAND. All of these could be examined to determine whether existing federal legislation and administrative practices are consistent with evolving theories of Canadian law, including aboriginal and treaty rights.

9. Social issues of concern to aboriginal peoples.

In particular, the Commission may study and make concrete recommendations to improve the quality of life for aboriginal peoples living on reserve, in native settlements and communities, and in rural areas and cities. Issues of concern include, but are not limited to: poverty, unemployment and underemployment, access to health care and health concerns generally, alcohol and substance abuse, sub-standard housing, high suicide rates, child care, child welfare, and family violence.

10. Economic issues of concern to aboriginal peoples.

The Commission may investigate the problems of developing a viable economic base for aboriginal peoples, unemployment, access to labour markets, discrimination in employment, taxation and custom duties.

11. Cultural issues of concern to aboriginal peoples.

In particular, the Commission may investigate the protection and promotion of aboriginal languages, recognition by Canadian society and institutions of the intrinsic value of aboriginal spirituality, recognition by Canadian society and institutions of the intrinsic value of aboriginal family structures and child care patterns, and the protection of traditional hunting, fishing and trapping ways of life.

12. The position and role of aboriginal elders.

The Commission may examine the social and economic conditions of elders as a group, their traditional role in aboriginal societies and whether existing laws and governmental practices respect and accommodate that role, and the continuing role for elders in aboriginal societies.

13. The position and role of aboriginal women under existing social conditions and legal arrangements, and in the future.

The Commission may examine, in particular, issues related to financial and property provisions upon divorce, access to the labour market, definitions of membership in aboriginal groups and the role of native women in political institutions in their own communities and in non-native society.

14. The situation of aboriginal youth.

The Commission may investigate access to education, access to community leisure and sports facilities, alcohol and substance abuse, suicide amongst youth, and funding for youth programmes. The Commission may also focus upon means of enhancing and promoting a positive self-image in aboriginal youth, especially in the way they view the relationship between their historical and cultural roots and contemporary educational institutions.

15. Educational issues of concern to aboriginal peoples.

In particular, the Commission may investigate aboriginal control over primary and secondary education on reserves and in native communities (including issues of funding), the promotion and protection of aboriginal cultural identity in educational institutions (including institutions where aboriginal students are a minority group), the encouragement of aboriginal children to complete secondary education, and access to and funding for post-secondary education (including college, university and technical training).

16. Justice issues of concern to aboriginal peoples.

In particular, the Commission may investigate and make concrete recommendations concerning the relationships between aboriginal people and the police (with the policing function broadly conceived to include dispute resolution and community service), the promotion of respect for aboriginal people and culture within the justice system, techniques to aid aboriginal people in comprehending court processes especially through the provision of interpretation services, means to decrease the rate of incarceration of aboriginal offenders, methods to improve conditions of incarceration for aboriginal offenders, and the potential to elaborate aboriginal justice systems and to incorporate principles of aboriginal legal culture into the Canadian justice system.

Source: Press Release, Office of the Prime Minister, Ottawa, 27 August 1991

Appendix 14

The Aboriginal Constitutional Process: Summary and Recommendations

The Constitution Act, 1982, under section 35.1, requires the federal and provincial governments to consult with the aboriginal people prior to making any amendments that relate directly to them. When the Canadian government tabled its proposals for constitutional reform before the Special Joint Committee of the Senate and the House of Commons on a Renewed Canada, on 25 September 1991, some of the proposed amendments related directly to aboriginal people, making consultation with aboriginal people mandatory.

Aboriginal leaders were determined that the consultation process required under section 35.1 should meaningfully take into account the rights, interests, needs, and aspirations of their people. Accordingly, they demanded a mandate and adequate funds to engage their people in a process of consultation preliminary to putting forward their proposals for constitutional reform. The Canadian government acceded to these demands by mandating and funding selected national Indian, Inuit, and Metis organizations to consult their people and to bring forward their proposals resulting from these consultations to the special joint committee. This process has been titled by the government, 'The Aboriginal Constitutional Process' (also known as 'The Parallel Constitutional Process').

Under the Aboriginal Constitutional Process, the Assembly of First Nations (AFN) was mandated and funded to consult Indian peoples. The AFN carried out its mandate under the title 'The First Nations Circle on the Constitution (FNCC).' The FNCC consultation process was completed in March 1992. The consultations involved eighty hearings from coast to coast, and four constituent assemblies, comprised, respectively, of elders, youth, women, and off-reserve Indians. The consultation process was completed too late for presentation to the special joint committee, but the AFN pledged to its people that the recommendations resulting from the consultations would be emphasized in shaping the position presented to the Continuing Council of Ministers Responsible for Constitutional Development. The following 'recommendations' drawn from the report of the FNCC titled *To the Source* (13 April 1992) are divided into two parts: those originating from the 'hearings' and those generated by the 'Constituent Assemblies.'

Recommendations from hearings

That the Constitution recognize First Nations' inherent right to self-government.

That First Nations be recognized as separate and distinct societies

That First Nations self-government be implemented in a way and at a pace to be determined by each First Nation

That new fiscal relations between First Nations and the federal government will be necessary in order to answer the needs of First Nations governments, but that the fiduciary responsibility of the federal government must remain until such new arrangements have been satisfactorily completed

That these new fiscal arrangements should be built on the basis of resource sharing

That the Canada Clause acknowledge First Nations governments as being on equal terms with the federal and provincial governments

That the Canada Clause should refer to our ongoing contribution to this country and our presence in this land before either of the 'two founding peoples'

That past injustices to First Nations and their members be acknowledged and admitted

That First Nations languages be recognized as official languages of Canada, with the same status as French and English

That First Nations have exclusive jurisdiction for First Nations for taxation, including tax immunity

That First Nations justice systems be established to apply aboriginal principles and practices of justice to our own people, since the current application of Canadian justice to Aboriginal peoples has resulted in miscarriages of justice and the legal expression of racism

That federal and provincial governments take steps to appoint qualified First Nations lawyers to the Bench, up to and including the Supreme Court of Canada, in order to rectify bias against Native people in the courts of Canada

That First Nations language and culture be recognized, protected, and promoted throughout Canada

That the uniqueness of our cultures, traditions, and languages be specifically recognized in the Constitution and by the governments and people of Canada

That the Canadian Constitution be amended to reflect the original relationship of treaty federalism with First Nations

That the provinces recognize the territorial integrity of First Nations

That First Nations be compensated for the loss of rights such as hunting and fishing as a result of the establishment of parks, game preserves, wildlife areas, and private leases of Crown lands

That First Nations' relationship with federal and provincial governments be on a nation-to-nation basis, founded on equality and mutual respect

That treaties cease to be interpreted unilaterally, and that oral traditions be included as part of the treaties for purposes of interpretation

That the word 'existing' be removed from s. 35 of the Constitution Act, 1982, as the word is not in keeping with the partnership nature of treaties and does not address the absence of formal agreements when no treaties have been signed

That a moratorium be placed on laws, policies, and practices that have been detrimental to a good relationship between First Nations and the federal and provincial governments, including the Indian Act and all policies aimed at assimilation

That any future treaties be written in the pertinent Aboriginal language, to prevent misunderstandings arising from linguistic differences

That there be a moratorium on provincial laws of general application, with the inclusion of 'savings' clauses in order to prevent the development of legal vacuums

That First Nations, federal, provincial, territorial, and municipal jurisdictions be reexamined

That First Nations reclaim full jurisdiction over resources on reserves and shared jurisdiction on resources off reserves, not excluding the option for full jurisdiction over off-reserve resources, and that First Nations consent is required for any and all resource development

That an immediate moratoriam be placed on provincial laws and policies that violate or impede the full exercise of treaty rights

Recommendations from Constituent Assemblies

That Elders take a greater and increasing role in all major decisions involving First Nations

That First Nations governments and leaders carry out their duties honestly, fairly, and responsibly, keeping in mind the principles and values inherited from our ancestors

That Elders' wisdom and experience be fully applied, especially in environmental, educational, and healing activities

That First Nations governments ensure that their decisions follow the will of their people, in the spirit of equality and consensus

That affirmative action be taken to meet Elders' special needs

That Elders' knowledge be recorded, to preserve their wisdom for time to come

That women be equally represented in all decision-making processes

That a national day be established to honour the role and contribution of women in First Nations

That the Canadian Charter of Rights and Freedoms shall not override First Nations law, but that gender equality be formally established in formal Aboriginal Charters of Rights and Freedoms

That First Nations recognize their women's strength and spiritual beauty and that steps be taken to heal both men and women and to restore harmony and respect to the relationships between them

That First Nations governments recognize and rectify discrimination against women, both in decision-making and in day-to-day operations

That support services and affirmative action programs be put in place to counter such problems as physical and sexual abuse of women and children, lack of employment opportunities, and the problems of single parenthood

That social, medical, and educational programs delivered to First Nations communities be carried out in accordance with our traditions and culture

That treaty rights apply without regard to residence

That culturally appropriate services and programs for urban Natives be established, with adequate funding

That off- and on-reserve Aboriginal people receive the same services, without regard to residence

That better teacher education programs be instituted to prepare teachers for instruction in multicultural settings, and that school textbooks be rewritten to reflect the true role of First Nations and their full contribution to the development of Canada

That institutes of higher learning establish curricula in Aboriginal studies

That Aboriginal students have the right to be educated in their own language, and that schools with a sufficient number of Aboriginal students be required to provide education in the pertinent languages

Appendix 15

The Government of Canada's Policy on Indian Self-Government: Summary

In April 1986, the minister of Indian Affairs and Northern Development issued a policy statement on Indian self-government in Canada. Subsequently, this policy was elaborated and defined in operational form under the general title 'Indian Self-Government Community Negotiations' and the subsections 'Guidelines' (July 1988), 'Process' (May 1989), and 'Policy' (September 1989).

Policy statement: The minister's policy statement describes a legislative-administrative initiative (i.e., a non-constitutional initiative), that allows Indian bands/tribes to negotiate for expanded local administration within a framework of *delegated* federal and provincial authority. Although it is titled 'self-government,' this initiative is designed to provide a somewhat less restrictive alternative to the Indian Act in respect of band/tribal self-administration. The policy statement proposes a list of legislative and/ or administrative matters that the minister is prepared to negotiate with band/tribal councils. These include the institutions of self-government, fiscal arrangements, band/tribal membership criteria, land and resource management, and legal status and capacity. Other matters that may be negotiated are housing, education, health, child welfare, social services, environment, and the administration of justice.

The minister's policy statement sets out some basic legal and administrative parameters within which the 'community negotiations' must be conducted. Most consequential, the negotiations must be conducted within the framework of the Canadian constitution and existing federal-provincial jurisdictional mandates; that is, the negotiations must be compatible with the established jurisdictions, principles, and institutions of the Canadian federation. For example, they must conform with the Charter of Rights and Freedoms, with the Indian Act (some provisions of the act will be superseded by the negotiated agreement), and with federal and provincial laws of general application (some judicially defined exceptions will apply). The provincial government must be involved in the negotiations when dealing with subjects where provincial legislation, regulations, or standards currently apply.

The policy statement on Indian self-government sets out as a requirement that Indian communities develop a constitutional framework outlining what the structures and procedures of community self-government will be. But the Canadian government has stipulated rules, conditions, requirements, and constraints to which Indian communities must conform in developing their indigenous constitutions. These stipulations are analogous to those required of voluntary and charitable organizations when they develop their constitutions to qualify for legal incorporation. In other words, this is not a constitution for *nationhood*, that is, one that grows out of Indian cultures, interests, needs, wills and aspirations. Rather, this constitution is designed for continued government supervision over band/tribes as they assume the new administrative authority that is being delegated to them under this policy initiative.

Although the policy statement allows for some expansion of band/tribal authority over their financial affairs, no increase in current levels of program funding is permitted, and band/tribal financial authority will be limited to that which is delegated by the federal government. Ministerial responsibility for financial oversight will include authority to inspect the financial records of an Indian government, and authority to appoint an auditor and administrator if the minister deems the Indian government's financial affairs to be in disorder.

Process: The process of 'Indian self-government negotiations' is intended to be without prejudice to existing aboriginal and treaty rights and land claims or to the outcome of ongoing constitutional discussions on Indian self-government. Significantly, however, the federal government does consider this legislative initiative as being facilitative in defining the substance of an 'Indian self-government' constitutional amendment.

The process of 'Indian self-government negotiations' involves five sequential phases. The first phase begins upon application to the DIAND by a band/tribal council. A summary of the five phases follows:

Phase I ('The Development Phase') requires the band/tribe to undertake research and consultative work to develop a framework document that includes information on proposed changes to: existing structures and operations of band/tribal government, procedures and rules regarding membership, land-title, management of reserve lands and resources, financial arrangements and accountability, band/tribal legal status, political-administrative authority, provincial involvement, and community involvement.

Phase II ('The Framework Negotiation') involves a DIAND review of the band/tribe's Phase I framework document, and a preliminary DIAND response in the form of a discussion paper to clarify objectives. This DIAND discussion paper is reviewed with the band/tribe with the purpose of arriving at mutually acceptable 'terms of reference' (i.e., a 'framework agreement'). The 'terms of reference' must include an agenda for negotiations, a process and time frame for completing negotiations, and identification of negotiating parties. Following finalization of a 'framework agreement,' both parties (DIAND officials and Indian negotiators) must secure a mandate from their respective 'principals' to enter into the next phase.

Phase III ('The Substantial Negotiations') involves preparation of detailed proposals on each subject area accepted for negotiation in the Phase II 'framework agreement.' Areas of agreement and dispute are identified, and items of dispute are referred to appropriate 'principals' for negotiation. The final output of Phase III is a 'self-government agreement' that sets out, in appropriate detail, what has been agreed upon, including an implementation plan and a financial arrangement agreement.

Phase IV ('The Ratification') involves ratification of the 'self-government agreement' by both the Indian community and the federal Cabinet. A referendum as provided under the Indian Act, or some other mutually agreed-upon democratic and representative ratification process, is required of the band/tribe.

Phase V ('The Implementation') involves Parliament giving effect to the 'self-government agreement' through the normal legislative process. Implementation will be phased over whatever period of time has been agreed upon. The DIAND will ensure all aspects of the arrangement are implemented on time and in accordance with the agreement.

Appendix 16

A Declaration of the First Nations (1981)

We the Original Peoples of this Land know the Creator put us here.

The Creator gave us Laws that govern all our relationships to live in harmony with nature and mankind.

The Laws of the Creator defined our rights and responsibilities.

The Creator gave us our spiritual beliefs, our Language, our culture, and a place on Mother Earth which provided us with all our needs.

We have maintained our freedom, our Languages, and our traditions from time immemorial.

We continue to exercise the rights and fulfill the responsibilities and obligations given to us by the Creator for the Land upon which we were placed.

The Creator has given us the right to govern ourselves and the right to self-determination.

The rights and responsibilities given to us by the Creator cannot be altered or taken away by any other Nation.

TREATY AND ABORIGINAL RIGHTS PRINCIPLES

1 The aboriginal title, aboriginal rights and treaty rights of the aboriginal peoples of Canada, including:
   a all rights recognized by the Royal Proclamation of October 7th, 1763;
   b all rights recognized in treaties between the Crown and nations or tribes of Indians in Canada ensuring the Spiritual concept of Treaties;
   c all rights acquired by aboriginal peoples in settlements or agreements with the Crown on aboriginal rights and title;
   are hereby recognized, confirmed, ratified and sanctioned.

2 'Aboriginal people' means the First Nations or Tribes of Indians in Canada and each Nation having the right to define its own Citizenship.

3 Those parts of the Royal Proclamation of October 7th, 1763, providing for the rights of the Nations or tribes of Indians are legally and politically binding on the Canadian and British Parliaments.

4 No Law of Canada or of the Provinces, including the Charter of Rights and Freedoms in the Constitution of Canada, shall hereafter be construed or applied so as to abrogate, abridge or diminish the rights specified in Sections 1 and 3 of this Part.

5 a The Parliament and Government of Canada shall be committed to the negotiation of the full realization and implementation of the rights specified in Sections 1 and 3 of this Part.

  b Such negotiations shall be internationally supervised, if the aboriginal peoples parties to those negotiations so request.

  c Such negotiations, and any agreements concluded thereby, shall be with the full participation and the full consent of the aboriginal peoples affected.

6 Any amendments to the Constitution of Canada in relation to any constitutional matters which affect the aboriginal peoples, including the identification or definition of the rights of any of those peoples, shall be made only with the consent of the governing Council, Grand Council or Assembly of the aboriginal peoples affected by such amendment, identification or definition.

7 A Treaty and Aboriginal Rights Protection Office shall be established.

8 A declaration that Indian Governmental powers and responsibilities exist as a permanent, integral fact in the Canadian polity.

9 All pre-confederation, post-confederation treaties and treaties executed outside the present boundaries of Canada but which apply to the Indian Nations of Canada are international treaty agreements between sovereign nations. Any changes to the treaties requires the consent of the two parties to the treaties, who are the Indian Governments representing Indian Nations and the Crown represented by the British Government. The Canadian Government is only a third party and cannot initiate any changes.

JOINT COUNCIL OF THE NATIONAL INDIAN BROTHERHOOD
18 November 1981

Appendix 17

Selected Demographic Data on Indians in Canada

TABLE 2
Registered Indian population by region, 1989

Region	No.	%
Atlantic	18,433	4.0
Quebec	45,742	9.8
Ontario	107,862	23.1
Manitoba	67,092	14.4
Saskatchewan	72,111	15.5
Alberta	57,590	12.3
BC	80,742	17.3
Yukon	5,973	1.3
NWT	10,792	2.3
Canada	466,337	100

Source: Department of Indian Affairs and Northern
Development, *Basic Departmental Data, 1990* (Ottawa: Minister
of Indian Affairs and Northern Development 1990), 8

Figure 1
Registered Indian population growth on and off reserve

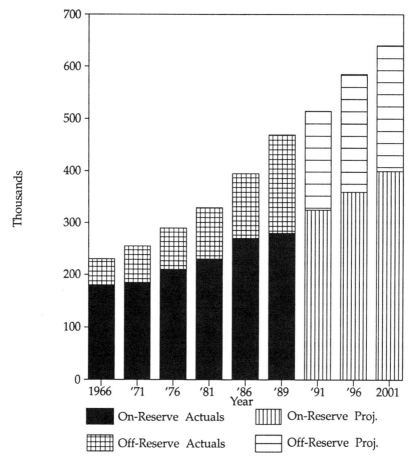

Highlights

The registered Indian population increased from 224,164 in 1966 to 466,337 in 1989, a twofold increase.

With the reinstatement of Indians through Bill C-31, this population is expected to reach approximately 623,000 at the turn of the century, a 34 per cent increase from 1989.

Eight out of ten registered Indians lived on reserve in 1966, but this proportion dropped to 60 per cent in 1989 and is expected to increase slightly by 2001.

The off-reserve population growth rate, which was quite significant between 1986 and 1989, is largely attributed to the reinstatement of Indians under Bill C-31.

Source: Department of Indian Affairs and Northern Development, *Basic Departmental Data, 1990* (Ottawa: Minister of Indian Affairs and Northern Development 1990), 4

Figure 2
Age structure of the populations: Canada and Indians, 1991

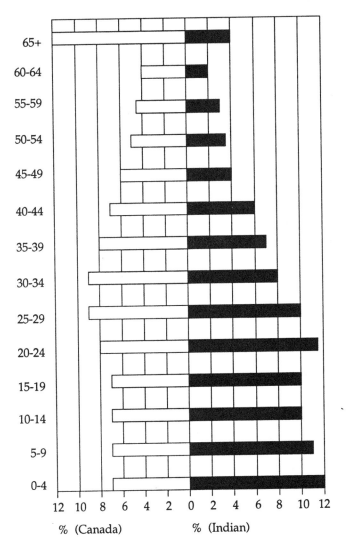

Median age: Canadian: 33, Status Indian: 23

Source: Department of Indian Affairs and Northern Development, *Highlights of Aboriginal Condition: 1981–2001 Part 1* (Ottawa: Minister of Indian Affairs and Northern Development 1989), 8

Appendix 18

Cultural and Linguistic Families: Summary, Maps, and Table

Cultural and linguistic classifications are based on particular assumptions – different assumptions yield different classifications. Cultural classifications generally rest on culture-trait commonalities, which in turn are related to ecological adaptations. Linguistic classifications rest on commonalities of vocabulary, meaning, and phonetic and grammatical features.

The maps in this appendix identify six cultural regions and eleven linguistic classifications, comprising 50–8 dialects. The eleven aboriginal linguistic families vary greatly in number of speakers, ranging from approximately 200 to 100,000. The number of speakers from the various dialects range from 5 to approximately 55,000.

Since cultural and linguistic classifications rest on different criteria, the identification of a linguistic family does not imply a corresponding cultural significance; that is, some culturally similar bands/tribes speak different languages, while some linguistically similar groups are culturally different from each other. However, the various linguistic families tend to have continuities with the seven cultural and ecological areas in which they are found.

Figure 3
Culture areas: Indians in Canada

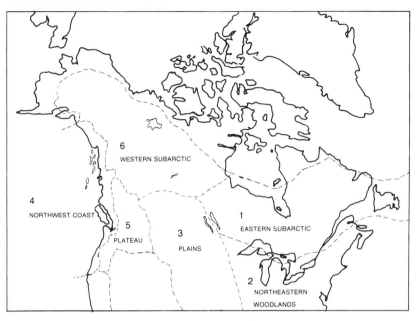

1 Migratory tribes of the Eastern Woodlands
2 Agricultural tribes of the Eastern Woodlands
3 Plains tribes
4 Tribes of the Pacific Coast
5 Tribes of the Cordillera
6 Tribes of the MacKenzie and Yukon River Basin

Sources: R. Bruce Morrison and C. Roderick Wilson, eds., *Native Peoples: The Canadian Experience* (Toronto: McClelland and Stewart 1986), front endpaper; Diamond Jenness, *Indians of Canada*, 7th ed. (Toronto: University of Toronto Press 1991)

Figure 4
Language families of Indians and Inuit

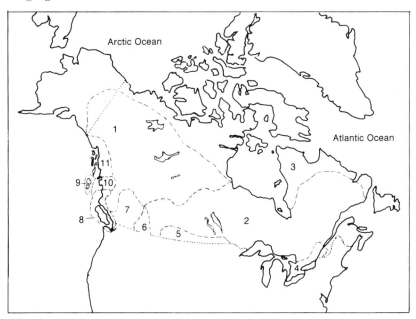

1 Athapaskan	5 Siouan	9 Haidan
2 Algonkian	6 Kootenayan	10 Tsimshian
3 Eskimo-Aleut	7 Salishan	11 Tlingit
4 Iroquoian	8 Wakashan	

Source: Hope McLean, *Indians, Inuit and Metis of Canada* (Toronto: Gage 1982), 10

TABLE 3
Languages and language families of Canada

		Number of speakers	
		In Canada	Outside Canada
Algonquian			
Eastern Branch	Abenaki	10	5
	Delaware	5–10	100
	Potawatomi	100	1,000
	Malecite	1,200	300
	Micmac	3–5,000	few
Cree	Cree	55,000	few
	Montagnais-Naskapi	5,000	none
Ojibwa	Ojibwa	30,000	10–20,000
	Odawa		
	Algonkin		
	Saulteaux		
Blackfoot	Blackfoot	4,000	1,000
Athabascan	Tagish	5	none
	Sarcee	10	none
	Han	few	few
	Sekani	1–500	none
	Kaska	2–500	none
	Beaver	300	none
	Hare	600	none
	Dogrib	800	none
	Chilcotin	1,000	none
	Tahltan	100–1,000	none
	Tutchone	1,000	none
	Slave	1–2,000	none
	Kutchin	500	700
	Carrier	5,000	none
	Chipewyan	5,000	none
	Yellowknife	4–600	none
Eskimo-Aleut	Inupik	16,000	47,000
Haida	Haida	225	100
Tlingit	Tlingit	500	1,500
Iroquoian	Onandaga	50–100	50
	Oneida	200	50
	Cayuga	360	10
	Seneca	25	400
	Mohawk	2,000	1,000
	Tuscarora	7	40

TABLE 3 (*continued*)

		Number of speakers	
		In Canada	Outside Canada
Kutenai	Kutenai	200	25
Salishan			
Interior	Lillooet	1,000	none
	Okanagan	1,000	none
	Thompson	1,000	none
	Shuswap	1–2,000	none
Coastal	Sechelt	10	none
	Squamish	12	none
	Straits	30	30
	Bella Coola	200	none
	Comox	400	none
	Halkomelem	500	none
	Songish	few	none
	Semiahmo	few	none
	Cowichan	500	none
	Pentlatch	?	none
Siouan	Dakota	5,000	15,000
	Assiniboine (Stoney)	1,000	–
Tsimshian	Southern Tsimshian	5	none
	Nass-Gitksan, Coastal Tsim.	3,500	200
Wakashan			
Northern Branch	Haisla	100–1,000	none
	Heiltsuk	300	none
	Kwakwala	1,000	none
Southern Branch	Nitinat	60	none
	Nootka	1–2,000	none

Source: Regna Darnell, 'Aboriginal Classification of Canada Native Peoples, and Theoretical Implications,' in *Native Peoples: The Canadian Experience*, R. Bruce Morrison and C. Roderick Wilson, eds. (Toronto: McClelland and Stewart 1986), 24–5

Appendix 19

Selected social-assistance data on Indians in Canada

TABLE 4
Average number of social-assistance recipients and dependants per month, registered Indian population, Canada, 1981/2–1990/1

Fiscal year	Average number of recipients per month[a]	Average number of dependants per month[b]
1981/2	39,146	88,079
1982/3	42,101	94,726
1983/4	43,750	98,438
1984/5	45,408	102,168
1985/6	48,494	109,112
1986/7	50,879	114,478
1987/8	54,170	121,882
1988/9	56,573	127,290
1989/90	59,680	134,280
1990/1	64,360	144,810

[a] Excludes Indians residing in NWT and Newfoundland

[b] The number of single recipients has been estimated by Social Development Branch to be 50 per cent of the average number of recipients per month. The average annual number of dependants living in a family has been calculated by multiplying the annual average number of recipients living in a family by the average size, which has been estimated to be 3.5. The total average number of dependants is the sum of the annual average number of single recipients and the average number of dependants living in a family. Excludes Indians residing in NWT and Newfoundland.

Source: Department of Indian Affairs and Northern Development, *Basic Departmental Data, 1990* (Ottawa: Minister of Indian Affairs and Northern Development 1990), 57

TABLE 5

Social assistance expenditures, registered Indian population, Canada, 1973/4–1990/1 (revised)

Fiscal year	Number of recipients[a]	Total expend- itures (current $)	Per recipi- ent (current $)	Total expendi- tures[b] (86 con- stant $)	Per recipient (86 constant $)
1973/4	n/a	53,319,000	n/a	148,108,333	n/a
1974/5	n/a	64,105,000	n/a	160,664,160	n/a
1975/6	n/a	73,023,000	n/a	165,210,407	n/a
1976/7	n/a	78,660,000	n/a	165,600,000	n/a
1977/8	n/a	85,753,000	n/a	167,159,844	n/a
1978/9	n/a	105,983,000	n/a	189,593,918	n/a
1979/80	n/a	122,004,400	n/a	200,007,213	n/a
1980/1	n/a	141,985,300	n/a	211,287,649	n/a
1981/2	39,146	165,030,100	4,216	218,582,914	5,584
1982/3	42,101	196,241,700	4,661	234,458,423	5,569
1983/4	43,750	216,157,600	4,941	244,245,876	5,583
1984/5	45,408	235,433,500	5,185	254,798,160	5,611
1985/6	48,494	255,288,200	5,264	265,925,208	5,484
1986/7	50,879	278,070,900	5,465	278,070,900	5,465
1987/8	54,170	314,446,000	5,805	301,193,487	5,560
1988/9	56,573	351,706,500	6,217	323,854,972	5,725
1989/90	59,680	392,498,900[c]	6,577[c]	344,297,281	5,769
1990/1	64,360	459,634,000	7,142	384,630,962	5,976

[a] Excludes Indians residing in NWT and Newfoundland.

[b] The expenditures in constant dollars have been calculated using the Consumer Price Index based on the year 1986 from Statistics Canada.

[c] Datum revised.

Source: Department of Indian Affairs and Northern Development, *Basic Departmental Data, 1990* (Ottawa: Minister of Indian Affairs and Northern Development 1990), 55

Notes

Chapter 1 Justice

1 Robert T. Ingram, *What's Wrong with Human Rights?* (Houston: St Thomas Press 1978)

2 *Lavell v The Attorney General of Canada* [1974] SCR 1349

3 Government of Nova Scotia, *Royal Commission of Inquiry into the Donald Marshall Jr. Prosecution* (Sydney and Halifax: Queen's Printer 1987–8)

4 Ontario: Government of Ontario, *Report of the Ontario Courts Inquiry,* The Honourable T.J. Zuker (Ottawa: Ministry of the Attorney General 1987). Manitoba: Government of Manitoba, *Report of the Aboriginal Justice Inquiry of Manitoba,* Public Inquiry into the Administration of Justice and Aboriginal People, Associate Chief Justices A.C. Hamilton and C.M. Sinclair, co-chairs (Winnipeg: Queen's Printer 1991). Alberta: Governments of Alberta and Canada, *Justice on Trial: Report of the Task Force on the Criminal Justice System and Its Impact on the Indian and Metis People,* Vol. 1: *Main Report* (Edmonton: Ministry of the Attorney General of Alberta March 1991)

5 Felix S. Cohen, 'The Erosion of Indian Rights,' *The Yale Law Journal* 62/3 (February 1953): 348

6 Government of Canada, 'Draft Cabinet Memorandum,' 12 April 1985 (also known as 'The Buffalo Jump of the 1980s' and as 'The Nielsen Report'). Derived from Ministerial Task Force on Program Review, *Improved Program Delivery: Indians and Natives* (Nielsen Report), vol. 12, the Honourable Erik Nielsen, Deputy Prime Minister, chair (Ottawa: Canadian Government Publishing Centre 1986), 51

7 *Globe and Mail,* 20 January 1989

8 L.F.S. Upton, 'The Origin of Canadian Indian Policy,' *Journal of Canadian Studies* 6/4 (November 1973): 54

9 Government of Canada, *A Future Together: The Task Force on Canadian Unity* (Ottawa: Supply and Services Canada 1979), 56–9, and *Report of the House of Commons Special Committee on Indian Self-Government* (The

Penner Report), Keith Penner, MP, chair (Ottawa: Queen's Printer 1983), 11–14

10 Pierre Elliott Trudeau, 'Transcript of the PM's Question-and-Answer Period,' University of Manitoba Students, Winnipeg, Manitoba, 13 December 1969

11 *Toronto Star*, 2 August 1969

12 From Prime Minister Trudeau's speech transcript, Parliament Hill, Ottawa, 4 June 1970

13 Union of British Columbia Indian Chiefs, *Treaty-Making and Title: A Non-Extinguishment Alternative for Settling the Land Question in British Columbia*. Discussion Paper no. 1, 21st Annual General Assembly 14–16 November 1989, Vancouver, BC

14 *The Queen* v *Sparrow* (1990) 70 DLR (4th) 385 (SCC). The Supreme Court's decision in *Sparrow* was to send the question back to trial to be answered according to the analysis set out in its reasons for judgment.

15 *Globe and Mail*, 1 June 1990

16 *Delgamuuleu* v *The Queen* (1991) 3 WWR 97

17 Hugh A. Dempsey, *Crowfoot, Chief of the Blackfoot* (Edmontohn: Hurtig 1972), 96

18 T. Buergenthal, 'International Human Rights Law and the Helskini Final Act,' in T. Buergenthal, ed., *Human Rights, International Law and the Helsinki Accord* (Montclair, NJ: Allenheld, Osmun and Co. 1977), 161–95

19 See U.N. Working Group on Indigenous Populations on Treatment of Indigenous Peoples, 1985; General Conference of UNESCO, Resolutions, 1966, 1972; U.N. Subcommittee on Prevention of Discrimination and Protection of Minorities, Resolutions; the International Convention of the Minority Rights Group, 1979; the International Covenant of the World Council of Indigenous Peoples, 1981; the Inter-American Commission on Human Rights.

20 Assembly of First Nations, *Memorandum Concerning the Rights of the First Nations of Canada and the Canadian Constitution* (Ottawa, 16 June 1982)

21 *Globe and Mail*, 6 August 1988

22 Supreme Court (1987) 1 SCR 1148, 40 DLR (4th) 18: 27, re: Bill 30 Amending the Ontario Education Act

23 *Globe and Mail*, 20 January 1989

Chapter 2 Policy

1 H.B. Hawthorn, ed., *A Survey of Contemporary Indians of Canada*, 2 vols.

(also known as 'The Hawthorn Report' (Ottawa: Department of Indian Affairs, 1966–7)

2 *Simon* v *The Queen* [1985] 2 SCR, 387 23 CCC (3d) 238

3 Leon Mitchell, 'Indian Treaty Land Entitlement in Manitoba,' in *Governments in Conflict: Provinces and Indian Nations in Canada*, J. Anthony Long and Menno Boldt, eds (Toronto: University of Toronto Press 1988), 134

4 *Sikyea* v *The Queen* 2 SCR 387, 23 CCC (3d) 238; *The Queen* v *George* 3 CCC 137; *Daniels* v *White and The Queen* 1968 SCR 517

5 Sally M. Weaver, 'The Joint Cabinet/National Indian Brotherhood Committee: A Unique Experience in Pressure Group Relations,' *Canadian Public Administration* 252 (Summer 1982), 211–39

6 *Globe and Mail*, 18 August 1984

7 Sally M. Weaver, 'Indian policy in the New Conservative Government, Part 2: The Nielsen Task Force in the Context of Recent Policy Initiative,' *Native Studies Review* 22 (1986), 32

8 The Honourable Bill McKnight, Minister of DIAND, 'Notes for Remarks to the 11th Northern Development Conference,' Edmonton, Alberta, 26 October 1988

9 *Globe and Mail*, 18 May 1990

10 Assembly of First Nations, Press Release, 18 April 1985

11 Government of Canada, 'Improved Program Delivery: Indians and Natives,' Vol. 12. Ministerial Task Force on Program Review, The Honourable Erik Nielsen, Deputy Prime Minister, chair (Ottawa: Supply and Service Canada 1985)

12 Hawthorn, ed., *A Survey of Contemporary Indians of Canada*, Vol. 1 (1966), 13; Indian Chiefs of Alberta, *Citizens Plus: A Presentation of the Indian Chiefs of Alberta to The Right Honourable P.E. Trudeau, Prime Minister of Canada and the Government of Canada* (Edmonton: Indian Association of Alberta 1969)

13 DIAND, *Indian Self-Government Community Negotiations* (Ottawa: Minister of Indian Affairs and Northern Development 1989)

14 DIAND, *Policy Statement on Indian Self-Government in Canada* (Ottawa: Minister of Indian Affairs, 1985)

15 Government of Canada, *Shaping Canada's Future Together: Proposals* (Ottawa: Minister of Supply and Services, Canada, 1991), 11

16 Government of Canada, *Aboriginal Peoples, Self-Government and Constitutional Reform* (Ottawa: Minister of Supply and Services, Canada, 1991), 19–22

17 Government of Canada, *Report of the Special Joint Committee on a Re-*

newed Canada, the Honourable Gerald A. Beaudoin, senator, and Dorothy Dobbie, MP, joint chair (Ottawa: Queens Printer, 28 February 1992, 27–34, 52

18 First Nations Circle on the Constitution, *To the Source* (Ottawa: Assembly of First Nations, 13 April 1992) (see Appendix 14)

19 Assembly of First Nations, *Special Chiefs' Assembly on the Constitution: Resolutions* (Ottawa, 23 April 1992)

20 'Scorecard,' *Globe and Mail*, 15 June 1992

21 Source: *Consensus Report on the Constitution* (Final text), Charlottetown, 28 August, 1992

22 House of Commons, *Debates*, 10 May 1985, 4626

Chapter 3 Leadership

1 *Globe and Mail*, 10 January 1992

2 Kurt Lewin, *Resolving Social Conflict* (New York: Harper and Row 1948)

3 Tom Holm, 'Indian Concepts of Authority and the Crisis of Tribal Government,' *The Social Science Journal* 193 (1982), 57–71

4 C. Wright Mills, *Power Elite* (New York: Oxford University Press 1959), 343

5 Westbank Indian Council, Kelowna, BC, Press Release, 22 April 1991

6 Section 21 of the Indian Act stipulates clearly that the DIAND shall keep a register 'in which shall be entered particulars relating to Certificates of Possession and Certificates of Occupation and other transactions respecting lands in a reserve.' However, despite repeated requests, I was unsuccessful in obtaining data on any transactions respecting lands in reserves. In consequence, I have relied on the assessments of knowledgeable informants as to the extent that privatization has occurred in reserves.

7 U.S. Senate Committee on the Judiciary, Subcommittee on Constitutional Rights, *Amendments to the Bill of Rights* (11 April 1969), 59–60

8 It should be noted that, as a 'shield' from the individualizing effects of the Charter of Rights and Freedoms, the 'notwithstanding' clause will assume much greater significance for Indians trying to preserve communal 'distinct societies' than for Québécois seeking to preserve their 'distinct society,' which is based on Western-liberal values.

9 DIAND, *Indian Self-Government Community Negotiations: Guidelines* (Ottawa: Minister of Indian Affairs and Northern Development, May 1989)

10 Wendell Bell and Ivar Oxaal, *Decisions of Nationhood: Political and Social Development in the British Caribbean* (Denver, COL: Social Science Foundation, University of Denver, 1964)

11 Anthony Long and Menno Boldt, 'Self-Determination and Extra-Legal Action: The Foundations of Native Indian Protests,' *Canadian Review of Studies in Nationalism* 15/1-2 (1988), 111–19

Chapter 4 Culture

1 Harold Cardinal, *The Unjust Society: The Tragedy of Canada's Indians* (Edmonton: Hurtig 1969), 51–62, 80–9
2 Oscar Lewis, 'The Culture of Poverty,' *Scientific American*, October 1966, 19–25
3 Province of Manitoba, *Report of the Aboriginal Justice Inquiry of Manitoba*, Public Inquiry into the Administration of Justice and Aboriginal People, Associate Chief Justices A.C. Hamilton and C.M. Sinclair, joint chair (Winnipeg: Queen's Printer 1991)
4 Jules Henry, *Culture Against Man* (New York: Random House 1956), 31
5 'Canada's Aboriginal Peoples: Who Are They?' Background Notes, First Ministers' Conference, Ottawa, 2–3 April 1985
6 D.G. Frantz, and N.J. Russell, *Blackfoot Dictionary of Stems, Roots and Affixes* (Toronto: University of Toronto Press 1989) and D.G. Frantz, *Blackfoot Grammar* (Toronto: University of Toronto Press 1991)
7 Vine Deloria, Jr, *God Is Red* (New York: Grossett and Dunlap 1973), 176
8 Regna Darnell, 'A Linguistic Classification of Canadian Native Peoples: Issues, Problems and Theoretical Implications,' in R.B. Morrison and C.R. Wilson, eds., *Native Peoples: The Canadian Experience* (Toronto: McClelland and Stewart 1986), 22–44 (see Appendix 19)
9 P.E. Trudeau, 'Canadian Culture: Announcement of Implementation of Policy of Multiculturalism Within Bilingual Framework,' Speech to House of Commons, 8 October 1971, Hansard, 8545–6
10 A.G. *Canada* v *Lavell* [1974] SCR 1349
11 Assembly of First Nations, 'Charter of Rights for First Nations: Equality,' statement to the First Ministers' Conference on Aboriginal Constitutional Matters, Ottawa, 15–16 March 1983
12 An exception to this generalization can be found in the deliberations of judges who have made a *negative* application of the cultural criterion by acknowledging Crown arguments that aboriginal claims are undermined when a band/tribe departs from traditional ways of living. See, for example, the comments of Justice Steele in the case of *The Attorney General of Ontario* v *Bear Island Foundation et al* (1984) 49 OR (2d), at 373, 387, 391, 392.
13 Union of British Columbia Indian Chiefs, *Treaty-Making and Title: A Non-Extinguishment Alternative for Settling the Land Question in British*

Columbia, Discussion Paper no. 1, 21st Annual General Assembly, 14–16 November 1989, Vancouver, BC

14 Ernest Benedict, *Sixth Sub-Committee Report: The Standing Committee on Indian Affairs*. Ottawa: Parliament of Canada 1982, 24–5

15 Chief Dan George, an address to the Southwestern Alberta Teachers' Association, Annual Convention, 24 February 1972

Chapter 5 Economy

1 Associated Press wire story, Geneva, 27 February 1988

2 Reported in *Transition* 23 (March 1989), 9

3 See *Norvegij* v *The Queen*, 1983, 144 DLR (3d) 193

4 This amount was computed by taking the Indian average annual income ($10, 694), calculating the average federal tax paid by Canadians in the $10,500–$11,000 income bracket ($486) minus federal sales and child tax credits ($144), and then multiplying this net figure ($342) by the number of Indian taxpayers (186,900). The result is $63,919,800. (Sources: Statistics Canada, 1986 census; Revenue Canada, *Taxation Statistics, 1990*, 89, Table 2)

5 This number was calculated by taking the average federal income tax paid by Canadian wage earners ($3,055) and multiplying this figure by the working-age segment (327,722) of the Indian population. The result is $1,001,190,700. (Sources: Revenue Canada, *Taxation Statistics, 1989*, 82, Table 2; Indian and Northern Affairs Canada, *Highlights of Aboriginal Canadians, 1981–2001: Part I, Demographic Trends* [Ottawa, October 1989] 25, Table 3B, 1991)

6 This figure was arrived at by calculating the ratio of social-assistance cases (1,048,900) to population (25,309,331) for all of Canada and then applying this ratio (0.0414432) to the total Indian population (490,178) in Canada. Based on this calculation there should be 20,315 Indian social-assistance cases instead of the current 64,360 cases. Computed on a pay-out of $7,142 per Indian recipient of social assistance, this yields a saving of $314,569,390. (Sources: National Council of Welfare, *Welfare in Canada: The Tangled Safety Net* [Ottawa: Minister of Supply and Services, November 1987], 8, Table 1; Indian and Northern Affairs Canada, *Basic Departmental Data: 1991* [Ottawa: Minister of Supplies and Services 1991], 5, 57)

7 J.D. La Cruz, P. Nash, S.S. Hayo, O. Lyons, and P.S. Deloria, 'What Indians Should Want: Advice to the President,' in Kenneth Philp, ed., *Indian Self-Rule* (Salt Lake City: Howe Brothers 1983), 311

This desk copy is sent to you with the compliments of

University of Toronto Press

Surviving as Indians: The Challenge of Self-Government

TITLE

Menno Boldt

AUTHOR

CLOTH:

PAPER:

If you choose to adopt this book as a course text, please contact your local University bookstore. If you have any questions regarding University of Toronto Press books, contact the marketing department at (416) 978-2239.

OUTSIDE OF CANADA DOLLAR PRICES ARE IN US DOLLARS

UNIVERSITY OF TORONTO PRESS - HEAD OFFICE:

10 St Mary Street, Suite 700, Toronto, ON, M4Y 2W8   Fax: (416) 978-4738

CANADIAN, US, AUSTRALIAN,
and R.O.W. (excluding Europe) ORDERS can be sent to:

University of Toronto Press, 5201 Dufferin Street, North York, ON, M3H 5T8
Tel: 800-565-9523 / (416) 667-7791 / Fax: 800-221-9985 / (416) 667-7832

US ORDERS can be sent to:

University of Toronto Press, 250 Sonwil Drive, Buffalo, NY, 14225-5516
Tel: (716) 638-4547 / Fax: (716) 685-6985

EUROPEAN ORDERS can be sent to:

Marston Book Services, PO Box 269, Abingdon, Oxon, OX14 4SD
Tel: (01235) 465500 / Fax: (01235) 465555

Selected References

Chapter 1 Justice

Relevant philosophical and theoretical discussions of the concept of justice, can be found in H.W. Bierhoff, R.L. Cohen, and J. Greenberg, eds, *Justice in Social Relations* (1986); R.L. Cohen, ed, *Justice: Views from the Social Sciences* (1986); John Rawls, *A Theory of Justice* (1971); and David Miller, *Social Justice* (1976).

The following provide diverse accounts of Canada's betrayal of promises made to aboriginal peoples: Harold Cardinal, *The Unjust Society: The Tragedy of Canada's Indians* (1969); David Raunet, *Without Surrender, Without Consent: A History of the Nishga Land Claims* (1984); Howard Adams, *Prison of Grass: Canada from a Native Point of View* (1989); R. Wilson, *Our Betrayed Wards: A Story of 'Chicanery, Infidelity and the Prostitution of Trust'* (1921, 1973); B. Ominayak and Joan Ryan, 'The Cultural Effects of Judicial Bias' (1987); John Goddard, *Last Stand of the Lubicon Cree* (1991); B.W. Hodgins and Jamie Benidickson, *The Temagami Experience* (1989); and A.J. Ray, 'Creating the Image of Savage in Defense of the Crown' (1990).

On deficiencies and defects in the Canadian criminal justice system's treatment of aboriginal people, see Government of Nova Scotia, *Royal Commission of Inquiry into the Donald Marshall Jr. Prosecution* (1987–8); Province of Manitoba, *Report of the Aboriginal Justice Inquiry of Manitoba*, Vol. 1: *The Justice System and Aboriginal People* (1991); and Governments of Alberta and Canada, *Report of the Task Force on the Criminal Justice System and Its Impact on Indian and Metis People* (1991).

For accounts on social pathologies in Native communities, see Geoffrey York, *The Dispossessed: Life and Death in Native Canada* (1989); Anastasia Skilnyk, *A Poison Stronger Than Love: The Destruction of an Ojibway Community* (1985); and J.K. Jarvis and Menno Boldt, 'Death Styles among Canada's Indians' (1982).

A broad understanding of the treaties can be gained from the following: from the perspective of a participant, see the Honorable Alexander Morris P.C., *The Treaties of Canada with the Indians*, 1880, 1971; from a Canadian government perspective, see Department of Indian Affairs and Northern Development, *Indian Treaties in Historical Perspective* (1977), and *Living Treaties: Lasting Agreements* (1985); from an Indian perspective, see Delia Opekokew, *The First Nations: Indian Government and the Canadian Confederation* (1980); and Chief John Snow, 'Identification and Definition of Our Treaty and Aboriginal Rights' (1985); and, from a legal and academic perspective, see B. Wildsmith, 'Pre-Confederation Treaties' (1985); Norman Zlotkin, 'Post-Confederation Treaties' (1985); and C.E. Cleland, 'Indian Treaties and American Myths: Roots of Social Conflict Over Treaty Rights' (1990).

On Indian title, see J.C. Smith, 'The Concept of Native Title' (1974); David Elliott 'Aboriginal Title' (1985); Bruce Clark, *Indian Title in Canada* (1987); Brian Slattery, *Ancestral Lands: Alien Laws, Judicial Perspectives on Aboriginal Title* (1983); and Department of Indian Affairs and Northern Development, *Indian Title to Land: An Historical Overview and Discussion of Some Current Issues* (1985).

For a range of different perspectives on aboriginal rights by Indian leaders, federal and provincial politicians and bureaucrats, and academics, see Menno Boldt and J.A. Long, eds, *The Quest for Justice: Aboriginal Peoples and Aboriginal Rights* (1985); see also Ira Barkin, 'Aboriginal Rights: A Shell without a Filling' (1990); Brian Slattery, 'Understanding Aboriginal Rights' (1987); and, D.B. Smith, 'Aboriginal Rights a Century Ago' (1987).

On the constitution and aboriginal rights, see Bryan Schwartz, *First Principles, Second Thoughts: Aboriginal Peoples, Constitutional Reform and Canadian Statecraft* (1986); H.W. Daniels, *Native People and the Constitution of Canada* (1981); Michael Asch, *Home and Native Land: Aboriginal Rights and the Constitution* (1984); and Noel Lyon, 'Constitutional Issues in Native Law' (1985).

For an analysis and discussion of collective rights, see Walker Connor, 'A Nation Is a Nation, Is a State, Is an Ethnic Group, Is a ...' (1978). See also Vernon Van Dyke, 'Human Rights and the Rights of Groups' (1974); 'Justice as Fairness: For Groups' (1975); 'The Individual, the State, and Ethnic Communities in Political Theory' (1977); and Frances Svensson, 'Liberal Democracy and Group Rights: The Legacy of Individualism and Its Impact on American Tribes' (1980).

On peoples' rights in the UN Charter of Rights, see Maureen Davies, 'Aspects of Aboriginal Rights in International Law' (1985).

Chapter 2 Policy

Information on Canadian government policy initiatives pertaining to Indian government can be found in the following: Government of Canada *The Report of the House of Commons Special Committee on Indian Self-Government* (The Penner Report) (1983) and the *Response of the Government to the Report of the Special Committee on Indian Self-Government* (Reply to the Penner Report) (1984). See also DIAND, *Policy Statement on Indian Self-Government in Canada* (1986); *Indian Self-Government Community Negotiations: Guidelines* (1988); *Indian Self-Government Community Negotiations: Process* (1989); *Concepts of Political and Financial Accountability and Decision-Making for Consideration in a Self-Government Setting* (1990); *Self-Government in Essential and Optional Subject Matters* (1990).

Insights into the dynamics of government policy development can be found in Walter Rudnicki, 'The Politics of Aggression' (1987); S.M. Weaver, *Making Indian Policy* (1981); 'Indian Policy in the New Conservative Government (Parts I and II), (1986); and F.L. Barron, 'A Summary of Federal Indian Policy in the Canadian West 1967–1984' (1984).

For an analysis relating to the Department of Indian and Northern Affairs, see Richard Paton, *New Policies and Old Organizations* (1982).

For a better understanding of the complexities and options subsumed under the concept of Indian government, see Menno Boldt and J.A. Long, 'Native Indian Self-Government' (1986); Frank Cassidy and R.L. Bish, *Indian Government* (1989); C.E. Etkin, 'The Sechelt Indian Band' (1988). See also the series of papers from the Institute of Intergovernmental Relations at Queen's University, including: Noel Lyon, *Aboriginal Self-Government* (1984); D.A. Boisvert, *Forms of Aboriginal Self-Government* (1985); Bradford Morse, *Aboriginal Self-Government in Australia and Canada* (1985); D.C. Hawkes, *Negotiating Aboriginal Self-Government* (1985); John Weinstein, *Aboriginal Self-Government Off a Land Base* (1986); Mac Malone, *Financing Aboriginal Self-Government in Canada* (1986); Richard Bartlett, *Subjugation, Self-Management and Self-Government of Aboriginal Lands and Resources* (1986); Evelyn Peters, *Aboriginal Self-Government in Canada: A Bibliography 1986* (1986), and *Aboriginal Self-Governments in Canada* (1987); David C. Hawkes and Evelyn Peters, eds, *Issues in Entrenching Aboriginal Self-Government* (1987); Ian Corvie, *Future Issues of Jurisdiction and Coordination Between Aboriginal and Non-Aboriginal Governments* (1987).

For a variety of perspectives on Indian-provincial government relationships, see J.A. Long and Menno Boldt, eds, *Governments in Conflict?* (1988).

Legal aspects of the concept of fiduciary obligation have been developed in R.H. Bartlett, 'You Can't Trust the Crown' (1984–5); L.C. Green, 'Trusteeship and Canada's Indians' (1976); P. Hogg, *Liability of the Crown* (1989); Darlene Johnston, 'A Theory of Crown Trust Towards Aboriginal People' (1986); W. McMurtry and A. Pratt, 'Indians and the Fiduciary Concept, Self-Government and Its Constitution' (1986); and J. Hurley, 'The Crown's Fiduciary Duty and Indian Title' (1985).

Chapter 3 Leaders

For an analysis of various issues concerning leadership and authority in Indian communities see Menno Boldt and J.A. Long, 'Tribal Traditions and European-Western Political Ideologies: The Dilemma of Canada's Native Indians' (1989); J.A. Long and Menno Boldt, 'Leadership in Canadian Indian Communities: Reforming the Present and Incorporating the Past' (1987); Tom Porter, 'Traditions of the Constitution of the Six Nations' (1984); Jessie Bernard, 'Political Leadership Among North American Indians' (1928); W.B. Miller, 'Two Concepts of Authority' (1955); L. Barsh, 'The Nature and Spirit of North American Political Systems' (1986); R.F. Berkhofer, 'Native Americans' (1978); and Walter Williams, ed, *Indian Leadership* (1984).

On incipient problems in Indian leadership, see Tom Holm, 'Indian Concepts of Authority and the Crisis of Tribal Government' (1982); Robert Brunette and John Koster, *The Road to Wounded Knee* (1974); John Tootosis, 'Senator John Tootosis Demands the Resignation of Chief Solomon Sanderson for Conflict of Interest' (1984).

A variety of perspectives on Indian government, many by Indian leaders, can be found in Leroy Little Bear, Menno Boldt, and J.A. Long, eds, *Pathways to Self-Determination: Canadian Indians and the Canadian State* (1984).

For a critique of band administrative systems and practices, see Howard Adams, 'Red Powerlessness: Bureaucratic Authoritariansim on Indian Reserves' (1984).

On land tenure in reserves, see DIAND, *Property Rules for Indian Lands Under Self-Government* (1990), and *Land Tenure in Indian Reserves* (1978).

A collection of papers on Indian sovereignty can be found in W.R. Swagerty, ed, *Indian Sovereignty: Proceedings of the Second Annual Conference on Problems and Issues Concerning American Indians Today* (1979); see also Assembly of First Nations, *Memorandum Concerning the Rights of the First Nations of Canada and the Canadian Constitution* (1982); and M. Mason, 'Canadian and United States Approaches to Indian Sovereignty' (1983).

For a discussion of human rights from a variety of ideological and theoretical perspectives, see Adamantia Pollis and Peter Schwab, eds, *Human Rights: Cultural and Ideological Perspectives* (1979); Jack Donnelley, 'Human Rights and Human Dignity: An Analytic Critique of Non-Western Conceptions of Human Rights' (1982); and Wendy Moss, 'Indigenous Self-Government and Sexual Equality Under the Indian Act: Resolving Conflicts Between Collective and Individual Rights' (1990).

The cultural and legal impact of the Charter of Rights and Freedoms on Indian government are explored in Menno Boldt and J.A. Long, 'Tribal Philosophies and the Canadian Charter of Rights and Freedoms' (1984); Kenneth Lysyk, 'The Rights and Freedoms of the Aboriginal Peoples of Canada ss 25, 35, 37' (1982); Mary Ellen Turpel, 'Aboriginal Peoples and the Canadian Charter: Interpretive Monopolies, Cultural Differences' (1991); L.C. Greene, 'Aboriginal Peoples, International Law, and the Canadian Charter of Rights and Freedoms' (1983); and P.W. Hogg 'Supremacy of the Canadian Charter of Rights and Freedoms' (1983).

Chapter 4 Culture

For insights into various aspects of traditional Indian cultures, see W.H. Capps, ed, *Seeing With a Native Eye: Essay on Native American Religion* (1976); Robert Vachon, 'Traditional Legal Ways of Native Peoples and the Struggle for Native Rights' (1975); Michael E. Melody, 'Lakota Myth and Government: The Cosmos and the State' (1980); A.D. McMillan, *Native Peoples and Cultures of Canada* (1988); DIAND and the Secretary of State, Canada, *The First National Indian Cultural Conference* (1970).

Analyses of government policies relating to Indian cultures can be found in Harold Cardinal, *The Unjust Society: The Tragedy of Canada's Indians* (1969); J. Tobias, 'Protection, Civilization, Assimilation: An Outline of Canada's Indian Policy' (1976); B. Dippie, 'Only One Truth: Assimilation and the American Indian' (1985); Jennie Joe, ed, *American Indian Policy and Cultural Values: Conflict and Accommodation* (1988).

For material relevant to the Indian cultural crises, see F. LaViolette, *The Struggle for Survival: Indian Culture and the Protestant Ethic in British Columbia* (1973); R.P. Bowles, J.L. Hanley, B.W. Hodgins, and G.H. Rawlyk, *The Indian: Assimilation, Integration or Separation* (1972); Province of Manitoba, *Report of the Aboriginal Justice Inquiry of Manitoba* (1991); J.H. Bodley, *Victims of Progress* (1975); Hugh Brody, *Maps and Dreams* (1981).

Scholarly discussions of the concept of culture are provided by J.Z. Namenwirth and R.P. Weber, *Dynamics of Culture* (1978); H.L. Shapiro, ed, *Man. Culture and Society* (1956); Robert Wuthnow, *Meaning and Moral Or-*

der: Explorations in Cultural Analysis (1987); Jules Henry, *Culture Against Man* (1965).

For various perspectives on indian cultural adaptation, see L. Gerber, 'The Development of Canadian Indian Communities: A Two-Dimensional Typology Reflecting Strategies of Adaptation to the Modern World' (1980); John Price, *Indians of Canada: Cultural Dynamics* (1979); F.L. Barron and J.B. Waldrom, eds, *Native Society in Transition* (1986); E. Friedl, *An Attempt at Directed Cultural Change: Leadership Among the Chippewa 1640–1948* (1950).

On Canadian government policies thwarting Indian cultural adaptation see Sarah Carter, *Lost Harvests: Prairie Indian Reserve Farmers and Government Policy* (1990); Noel Dyck, 'An Opportunity Lost: The Initiative of the Reserve Agricultural Program in the Prairie West' (1986); and R.W. Meyers, 'The Canadian Sioux: Refugees from Minnesota' (1981).

For sources of information on Indian linguistic and cultural classification, see Regna Darnell, 'A Linguistic Classification of Canadian Native Peoples: Issues, Problems and Theoretical Implications' (1986); Diamond Jenness, *Indians of Canada* (1991).

Data on the status of Indian languages in Canada can be found in G. Priest, *Aboriginal Languages in Canada* (1984); B. Burnaby and R. Beaujot, *The Use of Aboriginal Languages in Canada: An Analysis of 1981 Census Data* (1988); John Price, 'The Viability of Indian Languages in Canada' (1981).

On the ecological wisdom inherent in aboriginal cultures, see UN World Commission on Environment and Development, *Our Common Future* (1987), and Peter Knudston and David Suzuki, *Wisdom of the Elders* (1992).

Chapter 5 Economy

For materials on Indian poverty and dependence, see J.S. Frideres, 'Institutional Structures and Economic Deprivation: Native People in Canada' (1988); DIAND, *Indian Conditions: A Survey* (1980) and *Highlights of Aboriginal Conditions 1981–2001* (1989). For a U.S. perspective, see R.L. Bee, 'Tribal Leadership in the War on Poverty' (1969); Richard White, *The Roots of Dependency: Subsistence, Environment and Social Change Among the Choctawes, Pawnees, and Navajos* (1983); Martin Loney, 'The Construction of Dependency: The Case of the Grand Rapids Hydro Project' (1987).

Two American perspectives on the interaction between economic development and traditional Indian cultures are provided by Vine Deloria, Jr., and L. Ruffing, 'Navajo Economic Development Subject to Cultural Constraints' (1976), and D.L. Vinge, 'Cultural Values and Economic Development: U.S. Indian Reservations' (1982).

For a variety of perspectives on financing Indian government, see Thalassa Research Associates, *The Economic Foundation of Indian Self-Government* (1983); DIAND, *Indian Band Government Financial Implications: Annex III* (1981) and *Financial Considerations – The Funding System: Annex II* (1982); D.C. Hawkes and A.M. Maslowe, 'Fiscal Arrangements for Aboriginal Self-Government' (1989); Mac Malone, *Financing Aboriginal Self-Government in Canada* (1986); Sykes Powderface, 'Self-Government Means Biting the Hand That Feeds Us' (1984); Adrian Tanner, 'Introduction: Canadian Indians and the Politics of Dependency' (1983); Government of Canada, *Indian and Native Programs* (Nielsen Report) (1986). A U.S. perspective is provided by R. Erlich 'Sovereignty and the Tribal Economy' (1980); R. Ickes, 'Tribal Economic Independence: The Means to Achieve True Tribal Self-Determination' (1981).

R.H. Bartlett has provided two studies on taxation of Indians: *Indians and Taxation in Canada* (1987) and 'Taxation' (1985).

The following offer a variety of perspectives on Indian economic development and entrepreneurship: Harold Bherer, Sylvia Gagnon, and Jacinte Roberge, *Wampum and Letters Patent: Exploratory Study of Native Entrepreneurship* (1990); C. Mackie, 'Some Reflections on Indian Economic Development' (1986); National Indian Brotherhood, *A Strategy of the Socio-Economic Development of Indian People* (1977); F. Wien, *Rebuilding the Economic Base of Indian Communities: The Micmac in Nova Scotia* (1986); Government of Ontario, *Towards a Framework for Native Economic Development Policies and Programs in Ontario*, vol. 2 (1987); D.D. Stull, 'Reservation Economic Development in the Era of Self-Determination' (1990); R. Ortiz, ed, *Economic Development in American Indian Reservations* (1977).

A range of accounts on the Indian urban experience appear in Raymond Breton and Gail Grant, eds, *The Dynamics of Government Programs for Urban Indians in the Prairie Provinces* (1984); Raymond Breton and Gail Grant Akian, *Urban Institutions and People of Indian Ancestry* (1979); Hugh Brody, *Indians on Skid Road: The Role of Alcohol and Community in the Adaptive Process of Indian and Urban Migrants* (1971); Edgar Dosman, *Indians: The Urban Dilemma* (1972); Gail Grant, *The Concrete Reserve: Corporate Programs for Indians in the Urban Work Place* (1983); J.R. Miller, *Skyscrapers Hide the Heavens* (1991); William Reeves and J.S. Frideres, 'Government Policy and Indian Urbanization: The Alberta Case' (1975); S. Clatworthy and J. Gunn, *Economic Circumstances of Native People in Selected Metropolitan Centers in Western Canada* (1981); City of Edmonton, *Native Adjustment to the Urban Environment: A Report on the Problems Encountered by Newly Arrived Natives in Edmonton* (1976); Arthur Margon, 'Indians and Immigrants' (1977), Don McCaskill, 'The Urbanization of Indians in Winnipeg,

Toronto, Edmonton and Vancouver: A Comparative Analysis' (1981); Joan Ryan, *Wall of Words: The Betrayal of the Urban indian* (1978); and Lynda Shorten, *Without Reserve: Stories from Urban Natives* (1991).

For studies on prejudice towards Indians, see Marlene Mackie, 'Ethnic Stereotypes and Prejudice: Alberta Indians, Hutterites and Ukrainians' (1974); J.S. Frideres, 'Racism in Canada: Alive and Well' (1976); R. Gibbins and J.R. Ponting, 'Prairie Canadians' Orientation Towards Indians' (1984); and DIAND, *Images of Indians Held by Non-Indians: A Review of Current Canadian Research* (1984).

Bibliography

Adams, Howard. 'Red Powerlessness: Bureaucratic Authoritarianism on Indian Reserves.' *Cornell Journal of Social Relations* 18/1 (Fall 1984), 28–40
- *Prison of Grass: Canada from a Native Point of View.* Saskatoon: Fifth House 1989
Ahenakew, David. 'Aboriginal Title and Aboriginal Rights: The Impossible and Unnecessary Task of Identification and Definition.' In Menno Boldt and J.A. Long, eds, *The Quest for Justice: Aboriginal Peoples and Aboriginal Rights*, 24–30. Toronto: University of Toronto Press 1985
Alberta and Canada, Governments of. *Justice on Trial: Report of the Task Force on the Criminal Justice System and Its Impact on Indian and Metis People,* Vol. 1: *Main Report.* Edmonton: Attorney General of Alberta, March 1991
Asch, Michael. *Home and Native Land: Aboriginal Rights and the Constitution.* Toronto: Methuen 1984
- 'Penner and Self-Government: An Appraisal.' *Canadian Dimension* 19/5 (1985), 14–17
Assembly of First Nations. *Memorandum Concerning the Rights of the First Nations of Canada and the Canadian Constitution.* Ottawa, 16 June 1982
Barkin, Ira. 'Aboriginal Rights: A Shell Without a Filling.' *Queen's Law Journal* 15/2 (1990), 307–25
Barron, F.L. 'A Summary of Federal Indian Policy in the Canadian West 1967–1984.' *Native Studies Review* 1/1 (1984), 28–39
Barron, F.L., and J.B. Waldrom, eds. *Native Society in Transition.* Regina: Canadian Plains Research Centre, 1986
Barsh, R.L. 'Behind Land Claims: Rationalizing Dispossession in Anglo-American Law.' *Law and Anthropology* 1 (1986), 15–50
- 'The Nature and Spirit of North American Political Systems.' *American Indian Quarterly* 10/3 (1986), 181–98
Barsh, R.L., and J.Y. Henderson. *The Road: Indian Tribes and Political Liberty.* Berkeley: University of California Press 1980

- 'Aboriginal Rights, Treaty Rights and Human Rights: Tribes and Constitutional Renewal.' *Journal of Canadian Studies* 17/2 (1982), 55–81
Bartlett, R.H. 'You Can't Trust the Crown: The Fiduciary Obligation of the Crown to the Indians: Guerim v. The Queen.' *The Saskatchewan Law Review* 49 (1984–5), 367
- 'Taxation.' In Bradford Morse, ed, *Aboriginal Peoples and the Law,* 579–616. Ottawa: Carleton University Press 1985
- *Subjugation, Self-Management and Self-Government of Aboriginal Lands and Reserves in Canada.* Kingston: Institute of Intergovernmental Relations, Queen's University 1986
- *Indians and Taxation in Canada.* Saskatoon: Native Law Centre, University of Saskatchewan 1987
Bee, R.L. 'Tribal Leadership in the War on Poverty.' *Social Science Quarterly* 50/3 (1969), 676–86
Bell, Wendell, and J.A. Mau. 'Images of the Future: Theory and Research Strategies.' In Wendell Bell and J.A. Mau, eds, *The Sociology of the Future,* 6–44. New York: Russell Sage Foundation 1971
Bell, Wendell, and Ivar Oxaal. *Decisions of Nationhood: Political and Social Development in the British Caribbean.* Denver, Co: Social Science Foundation, University of Denver, 1964
Berger, T.R. *Fragile Freedoms: Human Rights and Dissent in Canada.* Toronto: Clarke, Irwin 1981
Berkhofer, R.F. 'Native Americans.' In John Higham, ed, *Ethnic Leadership in America,* 119–149. Baltimore: Johns Hopkins University Press 1978.
Bernard, Jessie. 'Political Leadership Among North American Indians.' *American Journal of Sociology* 34 (1928), 296–315
Bherer, Harold; Sylvia Gagnon; and Jacinte Roberge. *Wampum and Letters Patent: Exploratory Study of Native Entrepreneurship.* Halifax: Institute for Research on Public Policy 1990
Bienvenue, Rita, and A.H. Latif. 'Arrests, Dispositions and Recidivism: Comparison of Indians and Whites.' *Canadian Journal of Criminology and Corrections* 16 (1974), 105–16
Bierhoff, H.W.; R.L. Cohen; and J. Greenberg, eds. *Justice in Social Relations.* New York: Plenum Press 1986
Binney, W.I.C. 'The Sparrow Doctrine: Beginning of the End or End of the Beginning?' *Queen's Law Journal* 15/2 (Fall 1990), 217–53
Bodley, J.H. *Victims of Progress.* Don Mills, ON: Cummings Publishing 1975
Boisvert, D.A. *Forms of Aboriginal Government.* Kingston, ON: Institute of Intergovernmental Relations, Queen's University, 1985
Boldt, Menno. 'Indian Leaders in Canada: Attitudes Toward Equality, Iden-

tity, and Political Status.' Ph.D. dissertation, Yale University, New Haven, 1973
- 'Canadian Native Leadership: Context and Composition.' *Canadian Ethnic Studies* 12/1 (1980), 15–33
- 'Enlightenment Values, Romanticism and Attitudes Toward Political Status: A Study of Native Indian Leaders in Canada.' *Canadian Review of Sociology and Anthropology* 18/4 (1981) 545–65
- 'Philosophy, Politics, and Extralegal Action: Native Indian Leaders in Canada.' *Ethnic and Racial Studies* 4/2 (1981), 205–21
- 'Social Correlates of Nationalism: A Study of Native Indian Leaders in a Canadian Internal Colony.' *Comparative Political Studies* 14/2 (1981), 205–31
- 'Intellectual Orientations and Nationalism Among Leaders in an Internal Colony: A Theoretical and Comparative Perspective.' *British Journal of Sociology* 33/4 (1982), 484–510
Boldt, Menno, and J.A. Long. 'Tribal Philosophies and the Canadian Charter of Rights and Freedoms.' *Racial and Ethnic Studies* 4/4 (1984), 479–95
- 'Tribal Traditions and European-Western Political Ideologies: The Dilemma of Canada's Native Indians.' *Canadian Journal of Political Science* 17/2 (1984), 537–53
- 'Aboriginal Self-Government.' *Policy Options* 7/9 (1986), 33–6
- 'A Reply to Flanagan's Comment.' *Canadian Journal of Political Science* 19/1 (1986), 151–3
- 'Native Indian Self-Government: Instrument of Autonomy or Assimilation?' In J.A. Long and Menno Boldt, eds, with Leroy Little Bear, 38–56. Toronto: University of Toronto Press 1988.
Boldt, Menno, and J.A. Long, eds, with Leroy Little Bear. *The Quest for Justice: Aboriginal People and Aboriginal Rights.* Toronto: University of Toronto Press 1985
- *Indian-Provincial Government Relationships.* Alberta Law Foundation 1986
Bowles, R.P.; J.L. Hanley; B.W. Hodgins; and G.H. Rawlyk. *The Indian: Assimilation, Integration or Separation.* Scarborough, ON: Prentice-Hall Canada, 1972
Breton, Raymond, and Gail Grant, eds. *The Dynamics of Government Programs for Urban Indians in the Prairie Provinces.* Montreal: Institute for Research on Public Policy 1984
Breton, Raymond, and Gail Grant Akian. *Urban Institutions and People of Indian Ancestry.* Montreal: Institute for Research on Public Policy 1979

British Columbia Claims Task Force. *Report*. Vancouver, 28 June 1991

Brody, Hugh. *Indians on Skid Road: The Role of Alcohol and Community in the Adaptive Process of Indian and Urban Migrants*. Ottawa: Northern Science Research Group, Department of Indian Affairs and Northern Development, Information Canada, 1971

– *Maps and Dreams*. Markham, ON: Penguin 1981

Brown, Dee. *Bury My Heart at Wounded Knee*. New York: Holt, Rinehart and Winston 1971

Brunette, Robert, and John Koster. *The Road to Wounded Knee*. New York: Bantam Books 1974

Buergenthal, T. 'International Human Rights Law and the Helsinki Final Act.' In T. Buergenthal, ed, *Human Rights, International Law and the Helsinki Accord*, 161–95. Montclair, NJ: Allenheld, Osmun and Co. 1977

Burnaby, B., and R. Beaujot. *The Use of Aboriginal Languages in Canada: An Analysis of 1981 Census Data*. Ottawa: Minister of Supply and Services, Canada 1988

Calder, William. 'The Provinces and Indian Self-Government in the Constitutional Forum.' In J.A. Long and Menno Boldt, eds, with Leroy Little Bear, *Governments in Conflict?* 72–82. Toronto: University of Toronto Press 1988

Canada, Government of. *A Future Together: The Task Force on Canadian Unity*. Ottawa: Supply and Services Canada 1979

– *The Report of the House of Commons Special Committee on Indian Self-government* (The Penner Report). Keith Penner, MP, Chair. Ottawa: Queen's Printer 1983

– 'Draft Cabinet Memorandum.' Ottawa, 12 April 1985

– Improved Program Delivery: *Indians and Natives: A Study Team Report to the Ministerial Task Force on Program Review*. (The Nielsen Report), the Honourable Erik Nielsen, Deputy Prime Minister, Chair. Vol. 12. Ottawa: Canadian Government Publishing Centre 1986

– *Indian Act (Office Consolidation) 1989*. Ottawa: Minister of Supply and Services, Canada, 1989

– *The Fifth Report of the Standing Committee on Aboriginal Affairs: The Summer of 1990*. Ken Hughes, MP, Chair. Ottawa: House of Commons May 1991

Capps, W.H., ed. *Seeing with a Native Eye: Essay on Native American Religion*. New York: Harper and Row 1976

Cardinal, Harold. *The Unjust Society: The Tragedy of Canada's Indians*. Edmonton: Hurtig 1969

– *The Rebirth of Canada's Indians*. Edmonton: Hurtig 1977

– 'Indian Nations and Constitutional Change.' In J.A. Long and Menno

Boldt, eds, with Leroy Little Bear, *Governments in Conflict?* 83–9. Toronto: University of Toronto Press 1988

Carstens, Peter. 'Coercion and Change.' In Richard Ossenberg, ed, *Canadian Society*, 126–45. Scarborough, ON: Prentice-Hall Canada 1971

– *The Queen's People: A Study of Hegemony, Coercion, and Accommodation Among the Okanagan of Canada.* Toronto: University of Toronto Press 1991

Carter, Sarah. *Lost Harvests: Prairie Indian Reserve Farmers and Government Policy.* Montreal and Kingston: McGill-Queen's University Press 1990

Cassidy, Frank. 'The Government of Canadian Indians.' *Policy Options* 10/6 (1989), 25–9

– 'Aboriginal Governments in Canada: An Emerging Field of Study.' *Canadian Journal of Political Science* 23/1 (1990), 73–99

Cassidy, Frank, and R.L. Bish. *Indian Government: Its Meaning in Practice.* Halifax: Institute for Research on Public Policy 1989

Cassidy, Frank, and Norman Dale. *After Native Claims?* Halifax: Institute for Research on Public Policy 1989

Chartier, Clem. 'Aboriginal Rights and Land Issues: The Metis Perspective.' In Menno Boldt and J.A. Long, eds, with Leroy Little Bear, *The Quest for Justice*, 54–61. Toronto: University of Toronto Press 1985

Clark, Bruce, *Indian Title in Canada.* Toronto: Carswell 1987

– *Native Liberty, Crown Sovereignty: The Existing Aboriginal Rights to Self-Government in Canada.* Montreal and Kingston: McGill-Queen's University Press 1991

Clatworthy, S. *The Effects of Length of Urban Residency on Native Labour Market Behaviour.* Winnipeg: Institute of Urban Studies, University of Winnipeg, 1983

Clatworthy, S., and J. Gunn. *Economic Circumstances of Native People in Selected Metropolitan Centres in Western Canada.* Winnipeg: Institute of Urban Studies, University of Winnipeg, 1981

Cleland, C.E. 'Indian Treaties and American Myths: Roots of Social Conflict Over Treaty Rights.' *Native Studies Review* 6/2 (1990), 81–7

Clifton, J.A. 'Factional Conflict and the Indian Community: The Prairie Patawatami Case.' In Stuart Levine and N.O. Lurie, eds, *The American Indian Today*, 184–211. Baltimore: Penguin 1968

Clinebell, J., and J. Thomson. 'Sovereignty and Self-Determination: The Rights of Native Americans Under International Law.' *Buffalo Law Review* 27 (1978), 669–714

Cohen, Felix. 'The Erosion of Indian Rights,' *The Yale Law Journal* 62/3 (February 1953): 348–90

Cohen, R.L., ed. *Justice: Views from the Social Sciences*. New York: Plenum Press 1986

Collins, J.P. *Final Evaluation Report of the Lethbridge Alternate Disposition Project for Young Offenders, July 1980–June 1982*. Lethbridge, AL: Consultation Centre of the Solicitor General, Canada, Prairie Region, September 1983

Connor, Walker. 'A Nation Is a Nation, Is a State, Is an Ethnic Group, Is a ...' *Ethnic and Racial Studies* 1/4 (1978), 377–400

Corrigan, S. 'The Plains Indian Pow-wow: Cultural Integration in Manitoba and Saskatchewan.' *Anthropologia* 12/2 (1970), 253–71

Corvie, Ian. *Future Issues of Jurisdiction and Coordination Between Aboriginal and Non-Aboriginal Governments*. Kingston, ON: Institute of Integovernmental Relations, Queen's University, 1987

Cox, B.A. *Cultural Ecology: Readings on the Canadian Indian and Eskimo*. Toronto: McClelland and Stewart 1973

– ed. *Native People, Native Lands: Canadian Indians, Inuit and Metis*. Ottawa: Carleton University Press 1987

Cumming, P., and N. Mickenberg. *Native Rights in Canada*, 2d ed. Toronto: Indian-Eskimo Association of Canada 1972

Dacks, Gurston. 'The Politics of Native Claims in Northern Canada.' In Menno Boldt and J.A. Long, eds, with Leroy Little Bear, *The Quest for Justice*, 251–64. Toronto: University of Toronto Press 1985

– 'The Aboriginal Peoples and the Government of the Northwest Territories.' In J.A. Long and Menno Boldt, eds, with Leroy Little Bear, *Governments in Conflict?* 222–33. Toronto: University of Toronto Press 1988

Dalon, Richard. 'An Alberta Perspective on Aboriginal Peoples and the Constitution.' In Menno Boldt and J.A. Long, eds, with Leory Little Bear, *The Quest for Justice*, 222–33. Toronto: University of Toronto Press 1985

Daniels, H.W. *Native People and the Constitution of Canada*. Ottawa: Mutual Press 1981

Darnell, Regna. 'A Linguistic Classification of Canadian Native Peoples: Issues, Problems and Theoretical Implications.' In R.B. Morrison and C.R. Wilson, eds, *Native Peoples: The Canadian Experience*, 22–44. Toronto: McClelland and Stewart 1986

Davies, Maureen. 'Aspects of Aboriginal Rights in International Law.' In B. Morse, ed, *Aboriginal Peoples and the Law*, 16–47. Ottawa: Carleton University Press 1985

Davis, Arthur. 'Urban Indians in Western Canada: Implications for Social Theory and Social Policy.' *Transactions of the Royal Society of Canada* 614 (1968), 217–28

De La Cruz, Joe; Phileo Nash; S.S. Harjo; Oren Lyons; and P.S. Deloria. 'What Indians Should Want: Advice to the President.' In K.R. Philp, ed, *Indian Self-Rule*, 311–22. Salt Lake City: Harve Brothers 1986

Delisle, Andrew. 'How We Regained Control Over Our Lives and Territories: The Kahnawake Story.' In Leroy Little Bear, Menno Boldt, and J.A. Long, eds, *Pathways to Self-Determination*, 141–7. Toronto: University of Toronto Press 1984

Deloria, Jr, Vine. *God is Red.* New York: Grosett and Dunlap 1973

Deloria, Jr, Vine, and Clifford Lytle. *The Nations Within: The Past and Present of American Indian Sovereignty.* New York: Pantheon Books 1984

Deloria, Jr, Vine, and L. Ruffing. 'Navajo Economic Development Subject to Cultural Constraints.' *Economic Development and Cultural Change* 24 April 1976, 611–21

Dempsey, Hugh A. *Crowfoot, Chief of the Blackfoot.* Edmonton: Hurtig 1972

Denton, Timothy. 'Migration from a Canadian Indian Reserve.' *Journal of Canadian Studies* 7 (1972), 54–62

Diamond, Billy. 'Aboriginal Rights: The James Bay Experience.' In Menno Boldt and J.A. Long, eds, with Leroy Little Bear, *The Quest for Justice*, 265–85. Toronto: University of Toronto Press 1985

Dippie, B. ' "Only One Truth": Assimilation and the American Indian.' *The Canadian Review of American Studies* 16/1 (1985), 31–9.

Donelley, Jack. 'Human Rights and Human Dignity: An Analytic Critique of Non-Western Conceptions of Human Rights.' *American Political Science Review* 76/2 (1982), 303–16

Dosman, Edgar. *Indians: The Urban Dilemma.* Toronto: McClelland and Stewart 1972

Dyck, Noel. 'The Politics of Speical Status: Indian Associations and the Administration of Indian Affairs.' In J. Dahlie and T. Fernando, eds, *Ethnicity and Politics in Canada*, 279–89. Agincourt, ON: Methuen 1981

– 'An Opportunity Lost: The Initiative of the Reserve Agricultural Program in the Prairie West.' In F.L. Barron and J.B. Waldram eds, *1885 and After: Native Society in Transition*, 121–38. Regina: Canadian Plains Research Centre 1986

– ed. *Indigenous People and the Nation-State: Fourth World Politics in Canada, Australia and Norway.* St John's: Institute of Social and Economic Research, Memorial University of Newfoundland 1985

Ebona, Andrew. 'Federal Government Policies and Indian Goals of Self-Government.' In Leroy Little Bear, Menno Boldt, and J.A. Long, eds, *Pathways to Self-Determination*, 90–6. Toronto: University of Toronto Press 1984

Edmonton, City of. *Native Adjustment to the Urban Environment: A Report on the Problems Encountered by Newly Arrived Natives in Edmonton*. Edmonton: Social Services Department, Social Planning Division, 1976

Elias, P.D. 'Indian Politics in the Canadian Political System.' In Marc-Adelard Tremblay, ed., *The Patterns of 'Amerindian' Identity*, 35–64. Quebec: Les Presses de l'Université Laval 1976

– *The Dakota of the Canadian Northwest: Lessons for Survival*. Winnipeg: University of Manitoba Press 1988

Elliot, J.L. 'Native People, Power and Politics.' *Multiculturalism* 3/3 (1980), 10–74

Elliott, D. 'Aboriginal Title.' In B. Morse, ed, *Aboriginal Peoples and the Law*, 48–124. Ottawa: Carleton University Press 1985

Erlich, R. 'Sovereignty and the Tribal Economy.' *American Indian Journal* 6/11 (1980), 21

Etkin, C.E. 'The Sechelt Indian Band: An Analysis of a New Form of Native Self-Government.' *Canadian Journal of Native Studies* 8/1 (1988), 73–105

Exell, Robert. 'British Columbia and the Native Community.' In J.A. Long and Menno Boldt, eds, with Leroy Little Bear, *Governments in Conflict?* 93–101. Toronto: University of Toronto Press 1988

Federation of Saskatchewan Indians. *Indian Government: A Position Paper.* Prince Albert, SA, 1977

Fidler, Dick. *Red Power in Canada*. Toronto: Vanguard 1970

Fisher, A.D. 'White Rites versus Indian Rights.' *Transaction* 7 (November 1969), 29–33

Fisher, R. *Contact and Conflict: Indian-European Relations in British Columbia, 1774–1890*. Vancouver: University of British Columbia Press 1977

Fleras, Augie, and J.L. Elliot. *The Nations Within: Aboriginal-State Relations in Canada, the United States and New Zealand*. Toronto: Oxford University Press 1992

Fox, Chief Roy. 'Jurisdictional Conflicts and the Blood Indian Band.' In J.A. Long and Menno Boldt, eds, with Leroy Little Bear, *Governments in Conflict?* 188–91. Toronto: University of Toronto Press 1988

Franks, C.E.S. *Public Administration Questions Relating to Aboriginal Self-Government*. Kingston, ON: Institute of Intergovernmental Relations, Queen's University, 1987

Frantz, D.G. *Blackfoot Grammar*. Toronto: University of Toronto Press 1991

Frantz, D.G., and N.J. Russell. *Blackfoot Dictionary of Stems, Roots and Affixes*. Toronto: University of Toronto Press 1989

Friedl, E. 'An Attempt at Directed Cultural Change: Leadership Among the

Chippewa 1640–1948.' Ph.D. Dissertation, New York: Columbia University, 1950

Frideres, J.S. 'Indians and Education: A Canadian Failure.' *Manitoba Journal of Education* 7 (June 1972), 27–30

– *Canada's Indians: Contemporary Conflicts.* Scarborough, ON: Prentice-Hall Canada 1974

– 'Racism in Canada: Alive and Well.' *Western Canadian Journal of Anthropology* 6/4 (1976), 124–45

– 'Institutional Structures and Economic Deprivation: Native People in Canada.' In B. Singh Bolaria, ed, *Racial Oppression in Canada*, 2d ed., 71–100. Toronto: Garamond Press 1988

– *Native Peoples in Canada: Contemporary Conflicts*, 3d ed. Scarborough, ON: Prentice-Hall, Canada 1988

Friesen, J.W., ed. *The Cultural Maze: Complex Questions on Native Destiny in Western Canada.* Calgary, AL: Temeron 1991

Fuller, Lon. *The Morality of Law.* New York: Random House 1955

George, P.J., and R.J. Preston. 'Going In Between: The Impact of European Technology on the Work Patterns of the West Main Cree of Northern Ontario.' *Journal of Economic History* 48 (June 1987), 447–60

Gerber, L. 'The Development of Canadian Indian Communities: A Two-Dimensional Typology Reflecting Strategies of Adaptation to the Modern World.' *Canadian Review of Sociology and Anthropology* 16/4 (1980), 126–34

Getches, David. 'Resolving Tensions Between Tribal and State Governments: Learning from the American Experience.' In J.A. Long and Menno Boldt, eds, with Leroy Little Bear, *Governments in Conflict?* 195–208. Toronto: University of Toronto Press 1988

Getty, Ian, and A.S. Lussier, eds. *As Long as the Sun Shines and Water Flows.* Vancouver: University of British Columbia Press 1983

Gibbins, Roger. 'Canadian Indians and The Canadian Constitution: A Difficult Passage Toward an Uncertain Destination.' In J.R. Ponting, ed, *Arduous Journey*, 302–16. Toronto: McClelland and Stewart 1986

– 'Citizenship, Political and Intergovernmental Problems with Indian Self-Government.' In J.R. Ponting, ed, *Arduous Journey*, 369–77. Toronto: McClelland and Stewart 1986

Gibbins, R., and J.R. Ponting. 'Prairie Canadians' Orientations Towards Indians.' *Prairie Forum* 2/1 (1984), 57–81

– 'An Assessment of the Probable Impact of Aboriginal Self-Government in Canada.' In A. Cairns and C. Williams, eds, *Gender, Ethnicity and Language in Canada*, 171–241. Toronto: University of Toronto Press 1986

Goddard, John. *Last Stand of the Lubicon Cree.* Toronto: Douglas and Mc-Intyre 1991

Gormley, D.J. 'Aboriginal Rights as Natural Rights.' *Canadian Journal of Native Studies* 4/1 (1984), 29–49

Gourdeau, Eric. 'Quebec and Aboriginal Peoples.' In J.A. Long and Menno Boldt, eds, with Leroy Little Bear, *Governments in Conflict?* 109–25. Toronto: University of Toronto Press 1988

Grant, Gail. *The Concrete Reserve: Corporate Programs for Indians in the Urban Work Place.* Montreal: Institute for Research on Public Policy 1983

Green, Joyce. 'Sexual Equality and Indian Government: An Analysis of Bill C-31 Amendments to the Indian Act.' *Native Studies Review* 2 (1985), 81–96

Green, L.C. 'Trusteeship and Canada's Indians.' *Dalhousie Law Journal* 3/1 (May 1976), 104–35

– 'Aboriginal Peoples, International Law, and the Canadian Charter of Rights and Freedoms.' *Canadian Bar Review* 61 (1983), 339–76

Green, L.C., and O.P. Dickason. *The Law of Nations and the New World.* Edmonton: University of Alberta Press 1989

Grescher, Donna. 'Selected Documents from the Assembly of Manitoba Chiefs on the Meech Lake Accord.' *Native Studies Review* 6/1 (1990), 119–52

Guillemin, Jeanne. 'American Indian Resistance and Protest.' In J. Graham and T. Gurr, eds, *Violence in America*, 287–306. Beverly Hills: Sage Publications 1979

Haferkamp, Hans, ed. *Social Structure and Culture.* New York: de Gruyter 1989

Hall, A.J. 'Where Justice Lies: Aboriginal Rights and Wrongs in Temagami.' In Matt Bray and Ashley Thomson, eds, *Temagami: A Debate on Wilderness*, 223–53. Toronto: Dundurn Press 1990

– 'Aboriginal Issues and the New Political Map of Canada.' In J.L. Granatstein and Kenneth McNaught, eds, *English Canada Speaks Out*, 122–40. Toronto: Doubleday Canada 1991

– The St Catharine's Milling and Lumber Company versus The Queen: Indian Land Rights as a Factor in Federal-Provincial relations in Nineteenth Century Canada.' In Kerry Abel and Jean Friesen, eds, *Aboriginal Resource Use in Canada: Historical and Legal Aspects*, 267–86. Winnipeg: University of Manitoba Press 1991

Hawkes, D.C. *Aboriginal Self Government: What Does It Mean?* Kingston, ON: Institute of Intergovernmental Relations, Queen's University, 1985

– *Negotiating Aboriginal Self-Government: Developments Surrounding the First Ministers Conference.* Kingston, ON: Institute of Intergovernmental Relations, Queen's University, 1985

– *Aboriginal Peoples and Constitutional Reform: What Have We Learned?*
Kingston, ON: Institute of Intergovernmental Relations, Queen's University, 1989

– *Aboriginal Peoples and Government Responsibility.* Ottawa: Carleton University Press 1989

Hawkes, D.C., and A.M. Maslove. 'Fiscal Arrangements for Aboriginal Self-Government.' In D.C. Hawkes, ed, *Aboriginal Peoples and Government Responsibility*, 93–137. Ottawa: Carleton University Press 1989

Hawkes, D.C., and E.J. Peters. *Implementing Aboriginal Self-Government: Problems and Prospects.* Kingston, ON: Institute of Intergovernmental Relations, Queen's University, 1986

– eds. *Issues in Entrenching Aboriginal Self-Government.* Kingston, ON: Institute of Intergovernmental Relations, Queen's University, 1987

Hawthorn, H.B. *A Survey of the Contemporary Indians of Canada*, 2 vols. Ottawa: Indian Affairs Branch 1966–7

Haycock, R.G. *The Image of the Indian: The Canadian Indian as a Subject and a Concept in a Sampling of the Popular National Magazines Read in Canada 1900–1970*, Waterloo Lutheran University Mimeograph Series. Waterloo, ON, 1971

Health and Welfare Canada. *Health Status of Canadian Indians and Inuit: Update 1987.* Prepared by Bernice L. Muir. Ottawa: Minister of National Health and Welfare 1987

Henderson, J.Y. 'The Doctrine of Aboriginal Rights in Western Legal Tradition.' In Menno Boldt and J.A. Long, eds, with Leroy Little Bear, *The Quest for Justice*, 185–220. Toronto: University of Toronto Press 1985

Henry, Jules. *Culture Against Man.* New York: Random House 1965

Hertzberg, Hazel. *Search for an American Indian Identity: Modern Pan-Indian Movements.* Syracuse, NY: Syracuse University Press 1971

Hodgins, B.W., and Jamie Benidickson. *The Temagami Experience.* Toronto: University of Toronto Press 1989

Hoebal, E.A. 'Authority in Primitive Societies.' in C.J. Friedrich, ed., *Authority*, 222–34. Cambridge, MA: Harvard University Press 1958

Hogg, P.W. *Liability of the Crown.* Toronto: Carswell 1989

– 'Supremacy of the Canadian Charter of Rights and Freedoms,' *Canadian Bar Review* 1983: 69–80

Holm, Tom. 'Indian Concepts of Authority and the Crisis of Tribal Government.' *The Social Science Journal* 19/3 (1982), 59–71

Hurley, J. 'The Crown's Fiduciary Duty and Indian Title: *Guerin v The Queen.*' *McGill Law Journal* 30 (1985), 559–609

Ickes, R. 'Tribal Economic Independence: The Means to Achieve True Tribal Self-Determination.' *South Dakota Law Review* 26 (1981), 494–528

Indian Affairs and Northern Development, Department of [DIAND]. *Résumé*

of Reports of the Indian Act Consultation Meetings. Ottawa: Minister of Indian Affairs and Northern Development, 16 March 1969
- *Indian Treaties in Historical Perspective.* Prepared by G. Brown and R. Macguire. Ottawa: Minister of Indian Affairs and Northern Development 1977
- *Land Tenure in Indian Reserves.* Prepared by W.B. Henderson. Ottawa: Department of Indian Affairs and Northern Development 1978
- *Native Claims: Policy, Processes and Perspectives.* Ottawa: Queen's Printer 1978
- *Directional Plan for the 1980s.* Ottawa: Minister of Indian Affairs and Northern Development 25 July 1980
- *A History of Native Calims and Processes in Canada.* Prepared by R. Daniel. Ottawa: Minister of Indian Affairs and Northern Development 1980
- *Indian Government under Indian Act Legislation, 1868–1951.* Prepared by Wayne Daugherty and Dennis Magill. Ottawa: Minister of Indian Affairs and Northern Development 1980
- *Indian Conditions: A Survey.* Ottawa: Minister of Supply and Services, Canada 1980
- *In All Fairness: A Native Claims Policy.* Ottawa: Queen's Printer 1981
- *Indian Band Government Financial Implications: Annex III.* Ottawa: Minister of Supply and Services, Canada 1982
- *Financial Considerations – The Funding System: Annex II.* Ottawa: Minister of Supply and Services, Canada 1981
- *James Bay and Northern Quebec Agreement Implementation Review.* Ottawa: Minister of Supply and Services, Canada 1982
- *An Optional System of Indian Band Government.* Ottawa: Minister of Indian Affairs and Northern Development 1982
- *Outstanding Business: A Native Claims Policy.* Ottawa: Minister of Supply and Services, Canada 1982
- *Strengthening Indian Band Government in Canada.* Ottawa: Minister of Indian Affairs and Northern Development, November 1982
- *Evolution of the Indian Tribal Council Concept in Manitoba: Purpose and Progress 1966–1983.* Ottawa: Indian and Northern Affairs, Canada 1983
- *Images of Indians Held by Non-Indians: A Review of Current Canadian Research.* Prepared by Katie Cook. Ottawa: Indian and Northern Affairs, Canada 1984
- *Response of the Government to the Report of the Special Committee on Indian Self-Government* (Reply to the Penner Report). Ottawa: Minister of Indian Affairs and Northern Development 1984
- *Indian Title to Land: An Historical Overview and Discussion of Some Cur-*

rent Issues. Prepared by J. Ross. Ottawa: Indian and Northern Affairs, Canada 1985

– *Living Treaties: Lasting Agreements. Report of the Task Force to Review Comprehensive Claims Policy.* Murray Coolican, chair. Ottawa: Department of Indian Affairs and Northern Development, December 1985

– *Policy Statement on Indian Self-Government in Canada.* Ottawa: Minister of Indian Affairs and Northern Development 1986

– *Comprehensive Land Claims Policy.* Ottawa: Minister of Indian Affairs and Northern Development 1988

– *Indian Self-Government Community Negotiation: Guidelines.* Ottawa: Minister of Indian Affairs and Northern Development 1988

– *Lands, Revenues and Trusts Review: Phase I Report and Phase II Final Report.* Ottawa: Minister of Indian Affairs and Northern Development 1988, 1990

– *Highlights of Aboriginal Conditions 1981–2001.* Part I: Demographic Trends. Prepared by N. Janet Hagey, Gilles Larocque, and Catherine McBride. Ottawa: Minister of Indian Affairs and Northern Development, October 1989

– *Indian Self-Government Community Negotiations: Process.* Ottawa: Minister of Indian Affairs and Northern Development 1989

– *Annual Report, 1989–90.* Ottawa: Minister of Indian Affairs and Northern Development 1990

– *Basic Departmental Data 1990.* Ottawa: Minister of Indian Affairs and Northern Development 1990

– *Concepts of Political and Financial Accountability and Decision-Making for Consideration in a Self-Government Setting.* Ottawa: Minister of Indian Affairs and Northern Development 1990

– *Property Rules for Indian Lands Under Self-Government.* Ottawa: Indian and Northern Affairs, Canada 1990

– *Self-Government on Essential and Optional Subject Matters.* Ottawa: Minister of Indian Affairs and Northern Development 1990

– *University Education and Economic Well-Being: Indian Achievements and Prospects.* Prepared by Robin Armstrong, Jeff Kennedy, and P.R. Oberle. Ottawa: Minister of Indian Affairs and Northern Development 1990

Indian Association of Alberta. *The Native People*, Edmonton, 1971

Indian Chiefs of Alberta. *Citizens Plus: A Presentation of the Indian Chiefs of Alberta to Right Honourable P.E. Trudeau, Prime Minister, and the Government of Canada* (The Red Paper). Edmonton: Indian Association of Alberta 1970

Indian Claims Commission. *Indian Claims in Canada: An Essay and Bibliography.* Ottawa: Minister of Supply and Services, Canada 1975

Ingram, Robert T. *What's Wrong with Human Rights?* Houston: St Thomas Press 1978

Innis, H.A. *The Fur Trade in Canada.* Toronto: University of Toronto Press 1970

Jackson, M. 'The Articulation of Native Rights in Canadian Law.' *University of British Columbia Law Review* 18 (1984), 255–87

James, B.J. 'Social-Psychological Dimension of Ojibwa Acculturation.' *American Anthropologist* 63 (August) 1961, 721–45

Jarvis, G.K., and Menno Boldt. 'Death Styles Among Canada's Indians.' *Social Science and Medicine* 16/4 (1982), 1345–52

Jenness, Diamond. *Indians of Canada*, 7th ed. Toronto: University of Toronto Press 1991

Joe, Jennie, ed. *American Indian Policy and Cultural Values: Conflict and Accommodation.* Los Angeles: American Indian Studies Center, University of California, 1988

Johnson, B.H. *Indian School Days.* Toronto: Key Porter Books 1988

Johnston, Darlene. 'A Theory of Crown Trust Towards Aboriginal People.' *Ottawa Law Review* 18 (1986), 307–32

Josephy, Alvin M. *Red Power: The American Indian Fight for Freedom.* New York: American Heritage Press 1971

Kickingbird, Kirke. 'Indian Sovereignty: The American Experience.' In Leroy Little Bear, Menno Boldt, and J.A. Long, eds, *Pathways to Self-Determination* 46–53. Toronto: University of Toronto Press, 1984

Knudston, Peter, and David Suzuki. *Wisdom of the Elders.* Don Mills, ON: Stoddart 1992

Laslett, P. 'The Face-to-Face Society.' In P. Laslett, ed, *Philosophy, Politics and Society*, 155–76. Oxford: Basil Blackwell 1963

LaViolette, F. *The Struggle for Survival: Indian Culture and the Protestant Ethic in British Columbia.* Toronto: University of Toronto Press 1973

Levine, S. 'The Survival of Indian Identity.' In S. Levine and N.O. Lurie eds, *The American Indian Today*, 1–23. Deland, FL: Everett/Edwards 1968

Little Bear, Leroy. 'Aboriginal Rights and the Canadian "Grundnorm." ' In J. Rick Ponting, ed, *Arduous Journey*, 243–59. Toronto: McClelland and Stewart 1986

– 'Some Thoughts on the Canadian Constitution and Indian Government.' *Ontario Indian* 6, 22–3

– 'Section 88 of the Indian Act and the Application of Provincial Laws to Indians.' In J.A. Long and M. Boldt, eds, with Leroy Little Bear, *Governments in Conflict?* 175–87. Toronto: University of Toronto Press 1988

Little Bear, Leroy; Menno Boldt; and J.A. Long, eds. *Pathways to Self-Deter-*

mination: Canadian Indians and the Canadian State. Toronto: University of Toronto Press 1984

Loney, Martin. 'The Construction of Dependency: The Case of the Grand Rapids Hydro Project.' *Canadian Journal of Native Studies* 7/1 (1987), 57–78

Long, J.A. 'Political Revitalization in Canadian Native Indian Studies.' *Canadian Journal of Political Science* 23/4 (December 1990), 751–73

– 'Federalism and Ethnic Self-Determination: Native Indians in Canada.' *The Journal of Commonwealth and Comparative Politics* 29/2 (July 1991), 192-211

Long, J.A., and Menno Boldt. 'Political Attitudes of Members of an Internal Colony: A Study of Native Indian University Students in Canada.' *Plural Societies* 14/3-4 (1983), 85–98

– 'Concepts of Indian Government Among Prairie Native University Students.' *Journal of Canadian Studies* 19/1 (1984), 166–77

– 'Conformity Trap.' *Policy Options* 5/5 (1984), 5–8

– 'Leadership in Canadian Indian Communities: Reforming the Present and Incorporating the Past.' *Great Plains Quarterly* 7/2 (1987), 103–15

– 'Self-Determination and Extra-Legal Action: The Foundations of Native Indian Protests.' *Canadian Review in Nationalism* 25/1-2 (1989), 111–19

– eds, with Leroy Little Bear. *Governments in Conflict? Provinces and Indian Nations in Canada.* Toronto: University of Toronto Press 1988

Long, J.A.; Menno Boldt; and Leroy Little Bear. 'Federal Indian Policy and Indian Self-Government in Canada: An Analysis of a Current Proposal.' *Canadian Public Policy* 8/2 (1982), 189–99

Lower, A. *Colony to Nation: A History of Canada.* Toronto: Longman, Green 1957

Lyon, Noel. *Aboriginal Self-Government: Rights of Citizenship and Access to Governmental Services.* Kingston, ON: Institute of Intergovernmental Relations, Queen's University, 1984

– 'Constitutional Issues in Native Law.' In Bradford Morse, ed., *Aboriginal Peoples and the Law*, 408–51. Ottawa: Carleton University Press 1985

Lyons, Oren. 'Spirituality, Equality, and Natural Law.' In Leroy Little Bear, Menno Boldt, and J.A. Long, eds, *Pathways to Self-Determination*, 5–13. Toronto: University of Toronto Press 1984

– 'Traditional Native Philosophies Relating to Aboriginal Rights.' In Menno Boldt and J.A. Long, eds, with Leroy Little Bear, *The Quest for Justice*, 19–23. Toronto: University of Toronto Press 1985

Lysyk, K.M. 'Human Rights and the Native Peoples of Canada.' *Canadian Bar Review* 46/4 (1968), 695–705

– 'The Rights and Freedoms of the Aboriginal Peoples of Canada ss 25, 35, 37.' In W.S. Tarnopolsky and Gerald Beaudoin, eds, *The Canadian Charter of Rights and Freedoms: Commentary*, 467–88. Toronto: Carswell 1982

McCaskill, Don. 'The Urbanization of Indians in Winnipeg, Toronto, Edmonton and Vancouver: A Comparative Analysis.' *Culture* 1/1 (1981), 82–9

McDonald, M. 'Indian Status: Colonialism or Sexism.' *Canadian Community Law Journal* 9 (1986), 23–48

Mackie, C. 'Some Reflections on Indian Economic Development.' In J.R. Ponting, ed., *Arduous Journey*, 211–27. Toronto: McClelland and Stewart 1986

Mackie, Marlene. 'Ethnic Stereotypes and Prejudice: Alberta Indians, Hutterites, and Ukrainians.' *Canadian Ethnic Studies* 6/1-2 (1974), 39–53

McMillan, A.D. *Native Peoples and Cultures of Canada.* Toronto: Douglas and McIntyre 1988

McMurtry, W., and A. Pratt. 'Indians and the Fiduciary Concept, Self-Government and the Constitution: Guerin in Perspective.' *Canadian Native Law Reporter* 3 (1986), 19–46

Mah, A. 'Good Leadership Still Important.' *Native People* 10/4 (1977), 1–15

Malone, Mac. *Financing Aboriginal Self-Government in Canada.* Kingston, ON: Institute of Intergovernmental Relations, Queen's University, 1986

Manitoba, Province of. *Report of the Aboriginal Justice Inquiry of Manitoba, Vol. 1: The Justice System and Aboriginal People.* Public Inquiry into the Administration of Justice and Aboriginal People. Commissioners: Associate Chief Justices A.C. Hamilton and C.M. Sinclair. Winnipeg: Queen's Printer 1991

Manitoba Indian Brotherhood. *Wahbung: Our Tomorrows.* Winnipeg, October 1971

Manuel, George, and Michael Poslums. *The Fourth World: An Indian Reality.* Toronto: Collier-Macmillan Canada 1974

Margon, Arthur. 'Indians and Immigrants: Comparison of Groups New to the City.' *The Journal of Ethnic Studies* 4 (Winter 1977), 17–18

Marule, Marie Smallface. 'Traditional Indian Government: Of the People, by the People, for the People.' In Leroy Little Bear, Menno Boldt, and J.A. Long, eds, *Pathways to Self-Determination*, 36–45. Toronto: University of Toronto Press 1984

Mason, M. 'Canadian and United States Approaches to Indian Sovereignty.' *Osgoode Hall Law Journal* 21 (1983), 422–74

Melody, M.E. 'Lakota Myth and Government: The Cosmos and the State.' *American Indian Culture and Research Journal* 4/3 (1980), 1–19

Meyers, R.W. 'The Canadian Sioux: Refugees From Minnesota.' In R.L. Nichols, ed, *The American Indian: Past and Present*, 2d ed., 143–55. Toronto: John Wiley and Sons 1981

Miller, David. *Social Justice*. Oxford: Clarendon Press 1976

Miller, J.R. *Skyscrapers Hide the Heavens*. Toronto: University of Toronto Press 1991

Miller, W.B. 'Two Concepts of Authority.' *American Anthropologist* 57/2 (1955), 271–89

– ed. *Sweet Promises*. Toronto: University of Toronto Press 1991

Mitchell, Leon. 'Using Mediation to Resolve Disputes Over Aboriginal Rights: A Case Study.' In Menno Boldt and J.A. Long, eds, with Leroy Little Bear, *The Quest for Justice*, 286–91. Toronto: University of Toronto Press 1985

– 'Indian Treaty Land Entitlement in Manitoba.' In J.A. Long, Menno Boldt, and Leroy Little Bear, eds, *Governments in Conflict?* 129–38. Toronto: University of Toronto Press 1988

Morris, Alexander. *The Treaties of Canada with the Indians of Manitoba and the North West Territories*. Toronto: Belfords, Clarke & Co. 1880, reprt 1971

Morrison, R.B., and C.R. Wilson, eds. *Native People: The Canadian Experience*. Toronto: McClelland and Stewart 1986

Morse, Bradford. *Aboriginal Self-Government in Australia and Canada*. Kingston, ON: Institute of Intergovernmental Relations, Queen's University, 1985

– 'Aboriginal-Government Relations in Australia and the Implications for Canada.' In J.A. Long and Menno Boldt, eds, with Leroy Little Bear, *Governments in Conflict?* 209–21. Toronto: University of Toronto Press 1988

– , ed. *Aboriginal Peoples and the Law: Indian, Metis and Inuit Rights in Canada*. Ottawa: Carleton University Press 1985

Moss, Wendy. 'Indigenous Self-Government and Sexual Equality Under the Indian Act: Resolving Conflicts Between Collective and Individual Rights.' *Queen's Law Journal* 15/2 (Fall 1990), 279–305

Mulroney, The Right Honourable Brian. 'Notes from an Opening Statement to the Conference of First Ministers on the Rights of Aboriginal Peoples.' In Menno Boldt and J.A. Long, eds, with Leroy Little Bear, *The Quest for Justice*, 157–64. Toronto: University of Toronto Press 1985

Nagler, Mark. *Indians in the City*. Ottawa: Canadian Research Centre for Anthropology, St Paul University, 1971

Namenwirth, J.Z., and R.P. Weber. *Dynamics of Culture*. Winchester, MA: Unwin Hyman 1987

National Indian Brotherhood. *A Strategy for the Socio-Economic Development of Indian People*. Ottawa, 17 October 1977

Nichols, R.L. ed., *The American Indian: Past and Present*, 2d ed. Toronto: John Wiley and Sons 1981

Nicholson, David. 'Indian Government in Federal Policy: An Insider's Views.' In Leroy Little Bear, Menno Boldt, and J.A. Long, eds, *Pathways to Self-Determination*, 59–64. Toronto: University of Toronto Press 1984

Nock, D.A. *A Victorian Missionary and Canadian Indian Policy*. Waterloo, ON: Wilfrid Laurier Press 1988

Nova Scotia, Government of. *Royal Commission of Inquiry into the Donald Marshall Jr. Prosecution*. Sydney and Halifax, Queen's Printer: 1987–8

Old Person, Chief Earl. 'Problems, Prospects, and Aspirations of the "Real People" in America.' In Leroy Little Bear, Menno Boldt, and J.A. Long, eds, *Pathways to Self-Determination*, 148–51. Toronto: University of Toronto Press 1984

Ominayak, Bernard, and Joan Ryan. 'The Cultural Effects of Judicial Bias.' In S. Martin and K. Mahoney, eds, *Equality and Judicial Neutrality*, 346–57. Scarborough, ON: Carswell 1987

Ontario, Government of. *Report of the Ontario Courts Inquiry*. Toronto: Ministry of Attorney General 1987

– *Towards a Framework for Native Economic Development and Policies in Intario*, Vol. 2. Toronto: Native Affairs Directorate 1987

Opekokew, Delia. *The First Nations: Indian Government and the Canadian Confederation*. Saskatoon: Federation of Saskatchewan Indians 1980

– *The Political and Legal Inequities Among Aboriginal Peoples in Canada*. Kingston, ON: Institute of Intergovernmental Relations, Queen's University, 1987

O'Reilly, James. 'Indian Land Cliams in Quebec and Alberta.' In J.A. Long and Menno Boldt, eds, with Leroy Little Bear, *Governments in Conflict?* 139–47. Toronto: University of Toronto Press 1988

Ortiz, R., ed. *Economic Development in American Indian Reservations*. Albuquerque: Native American Studies, University of New Mexico, 1979

Parkinson, J.M. 'Sources of Capital for Native Businesses: Problems and Prospects.' *Canadian Journal of Native Studies* 8/1 (1988), 27–58

Paton, Richard. *New Policies and Old Organizations: Can Indian Affairs Change?* Ottawa: School of Public Administration, Carleton University, 1982

Patterson II, E.P. *The Canadian Indians: A History Since 1500*. Toronto: Collier-Macmillan Canada 1972

Penner, Keith. 'Their Own Place: The Case for a Distinct Order of Indian First Nation Government in Canada.' In J.A. Long and Menno Boldt, eds, with Leroy Little Bear, *Governments in Conflict?* 31–7. Toronto: University of Toronto Press 1988

Peters, E.J. *Aboriginal Self-Government in Canada: A Bibliography 1986.* Kingston, ON: Institute of Intergovernmental Relations, Queen's University, 1986

– *Aboriginal Self-Government Arrangements in Canada: An Overview.* Kingston, ON: Institute of Intergovernmental Relations, Queen's University, 1987

– 'Federal and Provincial Responsibilities for the Cree, Naskapi and Inuit Under the James Bay and Northern Quebec and Northeastern Quebec Agreements.' In D.C. Hawkes, ed, *Aboriginal Peoples and Government Responsibility*, 173–242. Ottawa: Carleton University Press 1989

Plain, Fred. 'A Treatise on the Rights of the Aboriginal Peoples of the Continent of North America.' In Menno Boldt and J.A. Long, eds., with Leroy Little Bear, *The Quest for Justice*, 31–40. Toronto: University of Toronto Press 1985

Pollis, Adamantia, and Peter Schwab. 'Human Rights: A Western Construct with Limited Applicability.' In Adamantia Pollis and Peter Schwab, eds, *Human Rights: Cultural and Ideological Perspectives*, 1–18. New York: Praeger 1979

Ponting, J.R., ed. *Arduous Journey: Canadian Indians and Decolonization.* Toronto: McClelland and Stewart 1986

– *Profiles of Public Opinion on Canadian Natives and Native Issues: Special Status and Self Government.* Calgary: Research Unit for Public Policy Studies, University of Calgary 1987

Ponting, J.R., and Roger Gibbins. *Out of Irrelevance: A Socio-political Introduction to Indian Affairs of Canada.* Toronto: Butterworth & Co. (Canada) 1980

– 'Thorns in a Bed of Roses: A Socio-political View of the Problems of Indian Government.' In Leroy Little Bear, Menno Boldt, and J.A. Long, eds, 122–35. Toronto: University of Toronto Press 1984

Porter, Tom. 'Traditions of the Constitution of the Six Nations.' In Leroy Little Bear, Menno Boldt, and J.A. Long, eds, *Pathways to Self-Determination*, 14–21. Toronto: University of Toronto Press 1984

Powderface, Sykes. 'Self-Government Means Biting the Hand That Feeds Us.' Leroy Little Bear, Menno Boldt, and J.A. Long, eds, *Pathways to Self-Determination*, 164–7. Toronto: University of Toronto Press, 1984

Prairie Treaty Nations Alliance. *Canada-Indian Natives Relationships.* Regina: Federation of Saskatchewan Indian Nations 1985

Price, John. *Indians of Canada: Cultural Dynamics.* Scarborough, ON: Prentice-Hall Canada 1979
- 'The Viability of Indian Languages in Canada.' *Canadian Journal of Native Studies* 1/2 (1981), 346–9
Price, Richard, ed. *The Spirit of the Alberta Indian Treaties.* Montreal: Institute for Research on Public Policy 1979
Priest, G. *Aboriginal Languages in Canada.* Ottawa: Minister of Supply and Services, Canada 1984
Prime Minister's Office. 'Statement of Prime Minister Regarding Development of Aboriginal Policy,' Press Release. Ottawa, 18 April 1985
Purich, D. *Our Land: Native Rights in Canada.* Toronto: Lorimer 1986
Raunet, Daniel, *Without Surrender, Without Consent: A History of the Nishga Land Claims.* Vancouver: Douglas and McIntyre 1984
Rawls, John. *A Theory of Justice.* Cambridge, MA: Harvard University Press 1971
Rawson, Bruce. 'Federal Perspectives on Indian-Provincial Relations.' In J.A. Long and Menno Boldt, eds, with Leroy Little Bear, *Governments in Conflict?* 23–30. Toronto: University of Toronto Press, 1988
Ray, A.J. 'Creating the Image of the Savage in Defence of the Crown: The Ethnohistorian in Court.' *Native Studies Review* 6/2 (1990), 13–29
Reeves, William, and J.S. Frideres. 'Government Policy and Indian Urbanization: The Alberta Case.' *Canadian Public Policy* 7/4 (Autumn 1981), 584–95
Richardson, Boyce, ed. *Drumbeat.* Toronto: Summerhill Press 1989
Riley, Del. 'What Canada's Indians Want and the Difficulties of Getting It.' In Leroy Little Bear, Menno Boldt, and J.A. Long, eds, *Pathway to Self-Determination,* 159–63. Toronto: University of Toronto Press 1984
Robinson, Eric, and H.B. Quinney. *The Infested Blanket: Canada's Constitution: Genocide of Indian Nations.* Winnipeg: Queenston House 1985
Romanow, Roy. 'Aboriginal Rights in the Constitutional Process.' In Menno Boldt and J.A. Long, eds, with Leroy Little Bear, *The Quest for Justice,* 73–82. Toronto: University of Toronto Press, 1985
Rudnicki, Walter. 'The Politics of Aggression: Indian Termination in the 1980s.' *Native Studies Review* 3/1 (1987), 81–93
Ryan, Joan. *Wall of Words: The Betrayal of the Urban Indian.* Toronto: Peter Martin Associates 1978
Ryser, Rudolph. Nation-States, Indigenous Nations, and the Great Lie.' In Leroy Little Bear, Menno Boldt, and J.A. Long, eds, *Pathways to Self-Determination,* 27–35. Toronto: University of Toronto Press 1984
- 'Fourth World Wars: Indigenous Nationalism and the Emerging New International Political Order.' In Menno Boldt and J.A. Long, eds, with

Leroy Little Bear, *The Quest for Justice*, 304–15. Toronto: University of Toronto Press 1985

Sanders, Douglas. 'The Rights of the Aboriginal Peoples of Canada.' *Canadian Bar Review* 61 (1983), 314–38

– 'Some Current Issues Affecting Indian Government.' In Leroy Little Bear, Menno Boldt, and J.A. Long, eds, *Pathways to Self-Determination*, 113–21. Toronto: University of Toronto Press 1984

– 'Aboriginal Rights: The Search for Recognition in International Law.' In Menno Boldt and J.A. Long, eds, with Leroy Little Bear, *The Quest for Justice*, 292–303. Toronto: University of Toronto Press 1985

– 'Aboriginal Rights in Canada: An Overview.' *Law and Anthropology* 2 (1987), 177–93

– 'The Constitution, the Provinces, and Aboriginal Peoples.' In J.A. Long and Menno Boldt, eds, with Leroy Little Bear, *Governments in Conflict?* 15–74. Toronto: University of Toronto Press 1988

Sanderson, Sol. 'Preparations for Indian Government in Saskatchewan.' In Leroy Little Bear, Menno Boldt, and J.A. Long, eds, *Pathways to Self-Determination*, 152–8. Toronto: University of Toronto Press 1984

Schwartz, Bryan. *First Principles, Second Thoughts: Aboriginal Peoples, Constitutional Reform and Canadian Statecraft.* Montreal: Institute for Research on Public Policy 1986

Scott, I.G., and J.T.S. McCabe. 'The Role of the Provinces in the Elucidation of Aboriginal Rights in Canada.' In J.A. Long, Menno Boldt, and Leroy Little Bear, eds, *Governments in Conflict?* 59–71. Toronto: University of Toronto Press 1988

Shapiro, H.L., ed. *Man, Culture and Society.* New York: Oxford University Press 1956

Shorten, Lynda. *Without Reserve: Stories From Urban Natives.* Edmonton: NeWest Press 1991

Siggner, A. 'The Socio-demographic Conditions of Registered Indians.' *Canadian Social Trends*, Winter 1986, 2–9

Silman, Janet (as told to). *Enough Is Enough: Aboriginal Women Speak Out.* Toronto: Women's Press 1987

Skilnyk, Anastasia. *A Poison Stronger than Love: The Destruction of an Ojibway Community.* New Haven, CT: Yale University Press 1985

Slattery, Brian. 'Ancestral Lands: Alien Laws, Judicial Perspectives on Aboriginal Land Title.' Regina: Native Law Centre, University of Saskatchewan, 1983

– 'The Hidden Constitution: Aboriginal Rights in Canada.' In Menno Boldt and J.A. Long, eds, with Leroy Little Bear, *The Quest for Justice*, 114–38. Toronto: University of Toronto Press 1985

– 'Understanding Aboriginal Rights.' *Canadian Bar Review* 1987, 727–82

Smith, D.B. 'Aboriginal Rights a Century Ago.' *The Beaver* 67/1 (1987), 4–15

Smith, J.C. 'The Concept of Native Title,' *University of Toronto Law Journal* 24 (1974): 1–16

Snow, Chief John. 'Identification and Definition of Our Treaty and Aboriginal Rights.' In Menno Boldt and J.A. Long, eds, with Leroy Little Bear, *The Quest for Justice*, 41–6. Toronto: University of Toronto Press 1985

Soop, Everett. *I See My Tribe Is Still Behind Me?* Calgary: Glenbow-Alberta Institute 1990

Spiegel, Shelley. 'Ontario Provincial Native Policy and Directions.' In J.A. Long and Menno Boldt, eds, with Leroy Little Bear, *Governments in Conflict?* 102–8. Toronto: University of Toronto Press 1988

Stanbury, W.T., and J. Siegal. *Success and Failure: Indians in Urban Society.* Vancouver: University of British Columbia Press 1975

Stull, D.D. 'Reservation Economic Development in the Era of Self-Determination.' *American Anthropologist* 92 (1990), 206–10

Svensson, Frances. 'Liberal Democracy and Group Rights: The Legacy of Individualism and Its Impact on American Tribes.' *Political Studies* 27 (1980), 421–39

Swagerty, W.R., ed. *Indian Sovereignty: Proceedings of the Second Annual Conference on Problems and Issues Concerning American Indians Today.* Chicago: Newbury Library 1979

Tanner, Adrian. 'Introduction: Canadian Indians and the Politics of Dependency.' In Adrian Tanner, ed, *The Politics of Indianness in Canadian Society*, 1–35. St John's Institute of Social and Economic Research, Memorial University of Newfoundland, 1983

– , ed. *The Politics of Indianness.* St Johns: Institute of Social and Economic Research, Memorial University of Newfoundland, 1983

Taylor, J.P., and Gary Paget. 'Federal/Provincial Responsibility and the Sechelt.' In D.C. Hawkes, ed, *Aboriginal Peoples and Government Responsibility*, 297–348. Ottawa: Carleton University Press 1989

Tennant, Paul. 'Native Indian Political Activity in British Columbia 1969–1983.' *B.C. Studies* 57 (1983), 112–36

– 'Aboriginal Rights and the Penner Report on Indian Self-Government.' In Menno Boldt and J.A. Long, eds, with Leroy Little Bear, *The Quest for Justice*, 321–32. Toronto: University of Toronto Press 1985

Thalassa Research Associates. *The Economic Foundation of Indian Self-Government.* A report prepared for the House of Commons Special Committee on Indian Self-Government, Victora, BC, 31 May 1983

Thiessen, H.W. 'Indian Self-Government: A Provincial Perspective.' In
Leroy Little Bear, Menno Boldt, and J.A. Long, eds, *Pathways to Self-Determination*, 85–9. Toronto: University of Toronto Press 1984

Titley, E.B. *A Narrow Vision: Duncan Campbell Scott and the Administration
of Indian Affairs in Canada*. Vancouver: University of British Columbia
Press 1986

Tobias, J. 'Protection, Civilization, Assimilation: An Outline of Canada's
Indian Policy.' *Western Canadian Journal of Anthropology* 6/2 (1976),
13–30

Tootosis, John. 'Senator John Tootosis Demands the Resignation of Chief
Solomon Sanderson for Conflict of Interest,' Speech to the Chiefs Legis-
lative Assembly of the Federation of Saskatchewan Indian Nations, 7–12
May 1984

Trigger, B. *Natives and Newcomers*. Montreal and Kingston: McGill-Queen's
University Press 1985

Trudeau, Pierre Elliott. 'Transcript of PM's Question-and-Answer Period.'
Winnipeg: University of Manitoba Students, 13 December 1969

– *Toronto Star*, 2 August 1969

– 'Transcript of Speech.' Ottawa, Parliament Hill, 4 June 1970

– 'Statement by the Prime Minister of Canada to the Conference of First
Ministers on Aboriginal Constitutional Matters.' In Menno Boldt and J.A.
Long, eds, with Leroy Little Bear, *The Quest for Justice*, 148–56. Toronto:
University of Toronto Press 1985

Turpel, Mary Ellen. 'Aboriginal Peoples and the Canadian Charter: Interpretive Monopolies, Cultural Differences.' In Richard F. Devlin, ed,
Canadian Perspectives on Legal Theory, 505–38. Toronto: Emond Montgo-
mery Publications 1991

U.N. World Commission on Environment and Development. *Our Common
Future*. Geo. Harlem Brundtland, chairman. Oxford: Oxford University
Press 1987

Union of British Columbia Indian Chiefs. 'Treaty-Making and Title: A
Non-Extinguishment Alternative for Settling the Land Question in British Columbia,' Discussion Paper no. 1, 21st Annual General Assembly,
14–16 November, 1989, Vancouver, BC

United States, Government of. *A Report of the Special Committee on Investi-
gations of the Select Committee on Indian Affairs, United States Senate*.
Washington, DC: US Government Printing Office 1989

Upton, L.F.S. 'The Origin of Canadian Policy.' *Journal of Canadian Studies*
6/4 (November 1973): 51–61

Vachon, Robert. 'Traditional Legal Ways of Native Peoples and the Struggle for Native Rights.' *Inter-Culture* 15/2-3 (1975–6), 1–18

Van Dyke, Vernon. 'Human Rights and the Rights of Groups.' *American Journal of Political Science* 18/4 (1974), 725–42
– 'Justice as Fairness: For Groups.' *American Political Science Review* 69/2 (1975), 607–14
– 'The Individual, the State, and Ethnic Communities in Political Theory.' *World Politics* 29/3 (1977), 343–69
Verdun-Jones, S., and G. Muirhead. 'Natives in the Criminal Justice System: An Overview.' *Crime and Justice* 7–8/1 (1979–80), 3–21
Vinge, D.L. 'Cultural Values and Economic Development: U.S. Indian Reservations.' *The Social Science Journal* 19/3 (1982), 87–100
Waddell, J.O. *The Sun Dance Religion: Power for the Powerless.* Chicago: University of Chicago Press 1972
Waubageshig. *The Only Good Indian: Essays by Canadian Indians.* Toronto: New Press 1970
Weaver, S.M. *Making Canadian Indian Policy: The Hidden Agenda.* Toronto: University of Toronto Press 1981
– 'The Joint Cabinet/National Indian Brotherhood Committee: A Unique Experiment in Pressure Group Relations.' *Canadian Public Administration* 25 (1982), 211–39
– 'Indian Government: A Concept in Need of a Definition.' In Leroy Little Bear, Menno Boldt, and J.A. Long, eds, *Pathways to Self-Determination*, 65–8. Toronto: University of Toronto Press 1984
– 'Federal Difficulties with Aboriginal Rights Demands.' In Menno Boldt and J.A. Long, eds, with Leroy Little Bear, *The Quest for Justice*, 139–47. Toronto: University of Toronto Press 1985
– 'Indian Policy in the New Conservative Government' (Parts 1 and 2). *Native Studies Review* 2/1 (1986), 1–43 and 2/22, 1–45
Weinstein, John. *Aboriginal Self-Determination Off a Land Base.* Kingston, ON: Institute of Intergovernmental Relations, Queen's University, 1986
Werhan, K. 'The Sovereignty of Indian Tribes: A Reaffirmation and Strengthening in the 1970's.' *Notre Dame Lawyer* 54 (1978), 20–36
White, Richard. *The Roots of Dependency: Subsistence, Environment and Social Change Among the Choctawes, Pawnees, and Navajos.* Lincoln: University of Nebraska Press 1983
Whyte, J.D. 'Indian Self-Government: A Legal Analysis.' In Leroy Little Bear, Menno Boldt, and J.A. Long, eds, *Pathways to Self-Determination*, 101–12. Toronto: University of Toronto Press 1984
Wien, F. *Rebuilding the Economic Base of Indian Communities: The Micmac in Nova Scotia.* Montreal: Institute for Research on Public Policy 1986
Wildsmith, B. 'Pre-Confederation Treaties.' In Bradford Morse, ed, *Aborigi-*

nal *Peoples and the Law*, 122–271. Ottawa: Carleton University Press 1985

Williams, Walter, ed. *Indian Leadership*. Manhatten, KA: Sunflower University Press 1984

Wilson, Bill. 'Aboriginal Rights: The Non-status Indian Perspective.' In Menno Boldt and J.A. Long, eds, with Leroy Little Bear, *The Quest for Justice*, 62–8. Toronto: University of Toronto Press 1985

Wilson, R. *Our Betrayed Wards: A Story of 'Chicanery, Infidelity, and the Prostitution of Trust.'* Montreal: Oseris Publications 1973

Woodward, Jack. *Native Law*. Toronto: Carswell 1990

Wuthnow, Robert. *Meaning and Moral Order: Explorations in Cultural Analysis*. Berkeley: University of California Press 1987

Wuttunee. W. *Ruffled Feathers*. Calgary: Bell Books 1972

York, Geoffrey. *The Dispossessed: Life and Death in Native Canada*. Toronto: Lester and Orpen Dennys 1989

York, Geoffrey, and Loreen Pindera. *People of the Rivers: The Warriors and the Legacy of Oka*. Toronto: Little, Brown 1991

Zentner, Henry. *The Indian Identity Crisis*. Calgary: Strayer Publications 1973

Zlotkin, Norman. 'Post-Confederation Treaties.' In B. Morse, ed, *Aboriginal Peoples and the Law*, 272–407. Ottawa: Carleton University Press 1985

Index